PENGUIN BUSINESS

QUEST FOR RESTORING FINANCIAL STABILITY IN INDIA

Viral V. Acharya is the C.V. Starr Professor of Economics in the Department of Finance at New York University Stern School of Business (NYU Stern). He was the deputy governor of the Reserve Bank of India (RBI) from 23 January 2017 to 23 July 2019. During his tenure, he was in charge of monetary policy, financial markets, financial stability and research.

Celebrating 35 Years of
Penguin Random House India

ADVANCE PRAISE FOR THE BOOK

'Viral Acharya took over as the deputy governor of India's Reserve Bank in 2017, at a tumultuous time for monetary and fiscal policies. India's non-performing loans to assets ratio was reaching for the skies, and there was the risk of financial and fiscal instability, and growth slowdown. The book is a masterly record of his two years at the helm of India's monetary policy. What makes it special is Acharya's eye for theoretical insights into the hurly-burly of India's monetary and fiscal world.

'The Reserve Bank of India has, in practice, been a remarkably autonomous body, even though the formal statutes do not give it that much autonomy. This means reliance on the government's capacity for good judgement and abstinence from interference. This also means that monetary policy in India has to navigate a difficult terrain between politics and economics.

'Monetary economics fascinates me because it is such a mixture of science and intuition. If you ignore either, you can mess up the policy with devastating consequences for the people. Viral Acharya's book, and especially the new edition with the new introduction [using bicycling in New York as an analogy of policymaking, can be an excellent primer for students wanting to learn macroeconomics and policymaking [not to mention bicycling in crowded cities]'—Kaushik Basu, professor of economics and Carl Marks Professor of International Studies, Cornell University, Ithaca and New York

'The India story has legs, but its weakest links are in infrastructure, both physical and financial. Viral's knowledge of the Indian financial infrastructure, acquired from the inside, and mastery of first principles and theory in finance make him uniquely qualified to create a template for a growing and financially healthy India. I hope that this book gets widely read, and even more, that its prescriptions find their way into policy'— Aswath Damodaran, professor of finance, Stern School of Business, New York University

'Quotes for personal testimonies of central bankers written in real time are few and far between, especially for large emerging economies. Viral Acharya's account of his efforts as deputy governor of the Reserve Bank of India to resist the "fiscal dominance", undermining the pursuit of financial stability, is both compelling and often moving. We can all learn from his experience, not least because fiscal dominance is growing around the world'—Mervyn King, British economist and former governor of the Bank of England (2003–13)

'The art of central banking is essentially about balancing conflicting objectives, given the available degrees of freedom in the political economy context. The author, bringing an insider's perspective to some of the most hotly contested policy issues of the recent past, presents a comprehensive analysis of the various manifestations of this constant struggle and underscores the need for a wider public debate in the quest for financial stability. The speeches included in the collection are all works of considerable rigour and traverse a broad range of issues, which are very useful for practitioners and academics alike and a must-read for anyone interested in the culture and practice of policymaking in India'—Shyamala Gopinath, chairperson, HDFC Bank and former deputy governor, Reserve Bank of India (2004–11)

'Dr Viral Acharya, one of the foremost financial economists in the world, served as the deputy governor of the Reserve Bank of India during a tumultuous period. His insightful speeches on the challenges faced by the Indian financial and monetary systems always cut to the core of the issues, in simple, direct and extremely readable language. In this book, he brings together the edited speeches along with connecting commentary to explain what the Reserve Bank was trying to do. It is an important and timely contribution to our understanding of the Indian economy and deserves to be read carefully by anyone interested in understanding where India is going'—Raghuram Rajan, Katherine Dusak Miller Distinguished Service Professor of Finance at the University of Chicago Booth School of Business and former governor, Reserve Bank of India (2013–16)

'Viral Acharya has produced a comprehensive and valuable guide to understanding the multiple issues associated with financial stability and monetary-policy independence—a scholarly presentation linking theory with the issues of the day. Fiscal dominance and its impact on financial markets, monetary policy and regulation constitute the core of the book. Policymakers need to ponder over the concerns raised in the book'—C. Rangarajan, chairman of the Madras School of Economics, former chairman of the Economic Advisory Council to the Prime Minister (2009–14) and former governor of the Reserve Bank of India (1992–97)

'India's economic reforms since the early 1990s lifted many millions out of poverty. Yet the stubborn persistence of a distorted state-dominated banking sector increasingly threatens the country's financial stability and growth. Already one of the world's leading scholars on the causes and treatment of financial crises, Viral Acharya joined the Reserve Bank of India in January 2017, intent on advocating for badly needed reforms. This book, which collects important speeches from his eventful tenure, will be required reading for anyone seeking to understand the political obstacles that can impede principled and effective central bank policy.

A new preface linking India's longstanding monetary and regulatory challenges to public-sector fiscal dominance is a tour de force of broad applicability'—Maurice Obstfeld, professor of economics at the University of California, Berkeley and former chief economist at the International Monetary Fund (2015–18)

'This thought-provoking and lucid collection vividly portrays a key policymaker's frontline battles to influence major policy debates in India. Dr Acharya's intellectual rigour and honesty, along with his humility and grasp of practical realities, shine through in these speeches. It is fascinating to read his carefully considered views on how best to design and implement much-needed reforms to India's financial system'—Eswar Prasad, Tolani Senior Professor of Trade Policy at Cornell University and former Chief of the Financial Studies Division at the International Monetary Fund's Research Department

'Speeches by Reserve Bank deputy governors are generally used as the vehicle for public expression of the bank's thinking on issues. Dr Acharya's speeches are different. They reveal his deep concern on several matters connected with the financial system and often his impatience with the pace of change. This is what makes them interesting and provocative'—Yezdi Malegam, chartered accountant and former board member of the Reserve Bank of India

'Viral Acharya was deputy governor of the Reserve Bank of India during a very interesting period when debates were raging about the autonomy of the central bank and the stability of the financial system was under severe threat due to the proliferation of non-performing assets. With regard to these and other issues, Viral Acharya's speeches in various forums were very frank, thought-provoking and received critical acclaim from the discerning public. I am happy that his speeches are now being compiled in the form of a book and I have no doubt that this will be an important contribution to the history of our times'—Narayanan Vaghul, Padma Bhushan and former chairman of ICICI Bank Limited

'Viral Acharya's latest book represents distilled wisdom on how fiscal dominance can threaten financial stability. Combining passion and rigour, it's built on his prodigious academic knowledge, research and global experience in interacting with regulators and central bankers after the global financial crises as well as his practical experience as a deputy governor of the Reserve Bank of India. The book also contains a constructive prescription for reform and is a must-read for all concerned with the dynamics of policymaking, especially central bankers'—Usha Thorat, member of the task force on the offshore rupee market constituted by the RBI and former deputy governor of the Reserve Bank of India (2005–10)

'The precipitous erosion of public sector bank balance sheets and consequent fall in bank lending growth in India in recent years are arguably the key causes of the country's very concerning economic slowdown. This collection of erudite speeches delivered by Viral Acharya in his all-too-short tenure at the Reserve Bank of India is a very timely, important, closely argued and passionate plea for all the measures that need to be taken to restore financial sector health, stability and growth in India. The essays are, at once, analytical, scholarly, deeply researched with solid empirics, and yet down to earth and written in a style that makes them very accessible to the concerned layman. Informed by extensive knowledge of international practice and experience in the resolution of similar financial crises, he provides eminently doable practical solutions to the vexed problems at hand. What is unusual and touching is the connection he eloquently makes between the malfunctioning Indian financial sector and the travails faced by the everyday Indian. Every page of this book exhibits Viral's deep-felt engagement and concern for India's current predicaments; it deserves to be read'—Rakesh Mohan, professor in the practice of international economics of finance, Yale School of Management and former deputy governor, Reserve Bank of India (2005–09) and former executive director of the International Monetary Fund (2012–15)

Quest for Restoring Financial Stability in India

Viral V. Acharya

VINTAGE

An imprint of Penguin Random House

PENGUIN BUSINESS

USA | Canada | UK | Ireland | Australia
New Zealand | India | South Africa | China | Singapore

Penguin Business is part of the Penguin Random House group of companies
whose addresses can be found at global.penguinrandomhouse.com

Published by Penguin Random House India Pvt. Ltd
4th Floor, Capital Tower 1, MG Road,
Gurugram 122 002, Haryana, India

First published by Sage Publications India Pvt. Ltd 2020
Published in Penguin Business by Penguin Random House India in 2023

Copyright © Viral Acharya 2023

ISBN 9780143461456

Typeset in Minion Pro

www.penguin.co.in

Dedicated to

Manjiree and Siddhant

and

Shailesh Shah Sir
(13 July 1949 to 5 January 2019)
Fellowship School, Mumbai,
for setting my mind on fire.

'ભલે મારું જીવન હતું એક માત્ર નાની દીવાસળી,
પ્રગટાવ્યા સર્વ કોડિયાં ને નામ દીધું દીપાવલી'

In Gujarati:
Bhale maroon jeevan hatoon ek matra nani divasali,
Pragtavya sarva kodiyaan ne naam didhoon Deepavali . . .

Translation:
Though my life was just a small matchstick,
I lit all the lamps and they called it Deepavali . . .

CONTENTS

List of Figures   xv

List of Tables   xix

Acknowledgements   xxi

Foreword by Dr Y. V. Reddy, Former Governor,
Reserve Bank of India   xiii

Prelude to the New Edition   xxix

Preface: Fiscal Dominance—A Theory of Everything in India   li

PART 1

**Resolving Non-Performing Assets (NPAs) and
Recapitalizing Banks**   1

  1 Some Ways to Decisively Resolve Bank Stressed Assets   3

  2 A Bank Should Be Something One Can 'Bank' Upon   15

  3 The Unfinished Agenda: Restoring Public Sector Bank
Health in India   27

  4 Prompt Corrective Action: An Essential Element of
Financial Stability Framework   43

PART 2

Creating a Public Credit Registry   79

  5 A Case for Public Credit Registry (PCR) in India   81

  6 Public Credit Registry and Goods and Services
Tax Network (GSTN): Giant Strides to Democratize and
Formalize Credit in India   91

7 Some Reflections on Microcredit and How a Public
   Credit Registry Can Strengthen It   103

8 What Can India's Banking System Learn from
   Shampoo Sachet Revolution?   115

PART 3

**Incorporating the Financial Cycle in the Monetary
Policy Framework**   **119**

9   Monetary Policy under a Changing Financial and
    Macroeconomic Environment   121

10 Managing the Financial Cycles in EMEs: A Central
    Banker's Perspective   153

PART 4

Improving Monetary Policy Transmission   **159**

11 Monetary Transmission in India: Why Is It Important
    and Why Hasn't It Worked Well?   161

12 Improving Monetary Transmission through the
    Banking Channel: The Case for External Benchmarks
    in Bank Loans   177

PART 5

**Developing Viable Capital Markets and Ensuring External
Sector Resilience**   **195**

13 Understanding and Managing Interest Rate Risk at Banks   197

14 Global Spillovers: Managing Capital Flows and
    Forex Reserves   217

15 Development of Viable Capital Markets: The Indian
    Experience   255

PART 6

Striking the Right Balance: 275
Enhancing the Autonomy of the Central Bank,
the Markets and the Real Economy

16   On the Importance of Independent Regulatory
     Institutions: The Case of the Central Bank   277

17   Why Less Can Be More: On the Crowding Out Effects
     of Government Financing   299

Epilogue   327

LIST OF FIGURES

Figure 3.1a.   Stressed Assets Ratio (%) for Indian Banks   28
Figure 3.1b.   Gross Non-Performing Assets (NPAs) Ratio (%)
               for Indian Banks   29
Figure 3.1c.   Provisional Coverage Ratio (%) for Indian Banks   29
Figure 3.1d.   Growth in Advances (%YoY) for Indian Banks   30
Figure 3.2.   Nominal Residential Land Prices and the
               Consumer Price Index (CPI) in Japan   31
Figure 3.3.   Prevalence of Firms Receiving Subsidized
               Loans in Japan   33
Figure 3.4.   Volume of New Loans to Non-Financial
               Corporations up to 1 Million Euro, 12-Month
               Cumulative Flows   34
Figure 3.5.   Spread between German and Spanish/Italian
               10-year Sovereign Bond Yields   35

Figure 4.1.   Capital to Risk-Weighted Assets Ratio (CRAR)   55
Figure 4.2.   Tier 1 Capital Ratio   55
Figure 4.3.   Gross Non-performing Assets Ratio
               (GNPA) (%)   56
Figure 4.4.   Net Non-performing Assets Ratio
               (NNPA) (%)   56
Figure 4.5.   Stressed Assets Ratio   57
Figure 4.6.   Capital Infusion by the Government of
               India in Public Sector Banks (PSBs)   58
Figure 4.7.   Yearly Growth in Advances (%)   58
Figure 4.8.   Provision Coverage Ratio (%)   59
Figure 4.9.   Credit Growth in Scheduled Commercial
               Banks (SCBs) (year on year %)   60

Figure 6.1.   Credit-to-GDP Ratio of Select Countries
               (Q4: 2017)   92
Figure 6.2.   Proposed Public Credit Registry (PCR)
               Information Architecture   97
Figure 6.3.   Goods and Services Tax (GST) Ecosystem   100

Figure 11.1.   Transmission from Policy Rate to Bank
               Lending Rates: Some Issues   171

Figure 12.1.   Lending Rates of Scheduled Commercial
               Banks (SCBs)   183
Figure 12.2.   Saving Deposits Rate and Policy Repo Rate   184
Figure 12.3.   Cost of Deposits/Funds and Policy Repo Rate   188

Figure 13.1.   Holding of Sovereign Bonds by Resident
               Banks and Non-residents for GIIPS and
               Germany   201
Figure 13.2.   Statutory Liquidity Ratio   203
Figure 13.3a. Investment in Central Government
               Securities as Percentage of Total Investment 204
Figure 13.3b. Investment in Central Government
               Securities as Percentage of Total Assets   205
Figure 13.4.   Weighted Average Maturity/Yield of Central
               G-Secs   206
Figure 13.5.   Public Sector Banks' (PSBs) Income on
               Investment as a Percentage of Total Income
               versus Generic Yield Movement   207
Figure 13.6.   10-Year Generic G-Sec Yield and Daily
               Change in Yield   208

Figure 14.1.   Volatility of Foreign Portfolio Investment (FPI)
               and Foreign Direct Investment (FDI) Flows   218
Figure 14.2.   Exchange Rate and 2013 Taper Tantrum   219
Figure 14.3.   Aggregate Foreign Reserves and External
               Short-Term Debt for Emerging Markets   222
Figure 14.4.   Foreign Exchange Reserves for India
               (USD Billion)   223
Figure 14.5.   (A) India Total External Debt (B) Short-
               Term External Debt   224
Figure 14.6.   Country Liquidity   225

Figure 14.7.   Sovereign Bond Yield, Stock Market Return
                and Currency Appreciation for Emerging
                Markets versus Liquidity   227
Figure 14.8.   Debt Stock and Flows   244
Figure 14.9.   All-in-Cost for External Commercial
                Borrowings (ECBs) with 5-Year Minimum
                Maturity   250

Figure 15.1.   Growth in Outstanding Stock of the Indian
                Capital Markets   257
Figure 15.2.   Secondary Market Liquidity in Terms of
                Average Daily Volume   260
Figure 15.3.   Average Bid-Ask Spread for Liquid
                Government Securities   260
Figure 15.4.   Ten-Year Benchmark G-Sec Liquidity in
                Different Countries   261
Figure 15.5.   Corporate Bond Market Size and Recovery Rate   262
Figure 15.6.   Holding Pattern for G-Secs (% Held by Each
                Investor Group)   264
Figure 15.7.   Average Daily Volume in G-Sec and Corporate
                Bond Repo   265
Figure 15.8.   Trends in GDP Growth in India   265
Figure 15.9.   Trends in Inflation in India   266
Figure 15.10.   Reduction in the Statutory Liquidity Ratio
                (SLR) for Banks   268
Figure 15.11.   Foreign Portfolio Investment (FPI) Investment
                in G-Secs vis-à-vis Limit   268
Figure 15.12.   Foreign Portfolio Investment (FPI) Investment
                in Corporate Debt vis-à-vis Limit   269

Figure 17.1a.   Fiscal Deficit of G20 Countries in 2018   301
Figure 17.1b.   Government Debt to GDP and Corporate
                Leverage: USA and Japan   303
Figure 17.2.   Sectoral Resource Gaps (Net Financial
                Saving-Investment Balance) for India   305
Figure 17.3.   General Government Gross Debt (Percent
                of GDP) for Select EMEs   307
Figure 17.4.   Central and State Government Borrowing
                (India)   307

Figure 17.5.   Government Borrowing and Total Corporate
               Debt (India)   311
Figure 17.6.   Government Debt Bank Credit and Corporate
               Bond Debt (India)   312
Figure 17.7.   Government Debt and Bank Holdings of
               Government Debt (India)   313
Figure 17.8.   Bank Holdings of Government Debt and Bank
               Loan Advances (India)   313
Figure 17.9.   Government Debt and Corporate Borrowing
               for Firms with Access to the Bond Markets
               (India)   315
Figure 17.10. Corporate and Sovereign Spreads and
               Government Debt to GDP (India): Impact
               of Government Borrowing (2006–2016) on
               (a) AAA Corporate Yields (b) the Spread
               of Corporate AA Bonds over AAA Bonds   317
Figure 17.11. Government Debt and the Share of Long-
               Term Borrowing by Corporates (India)   319
Figure 17.12. Monetary Policy Transmission during
               Period of High and Low Government
               Borrowing (India)   321

LIST OF TABLES

Table 3.1.   Capital Injection Programmes in Japan
              (in Trillions of Yen)   32

Table 4.1.   Capital Adequacy Ratio: Select Countries   46

Table 6.1.   Number of Countries with Public Credit
              Registries (PCRs) and/or Private Credit
              Bureaus (PCBs)   95

Table 11.1.   Transmission from the Policy Repo Rate to
              Banks' Deposit and Lending Rates   169
Table 11.2.   Maturity Profile of Term Deposits of Scheduled
              Commercial Banks (SCBs)   172

Table 12.1.   Transmission from the Policy Repo Rate to
              Banks' Deposit and Lending Rates   182
Table 12.2.   Proportion of Loans Linked to Internal and
              External Benchmarks: A Cross-Country
              Comparison   185
Table 12.3.   Distribution of Outstanding Interest
              Rate Swap Products across Tenors
              (End-November 2018)   189
Table 12.4.   Category-Wise Participation in Mumbai
              Inter-Bank Offer Rate (MIBOR) Overnight
              Indexed Swaps (End-November 2018)   190

Table 14.1.   Liquidity and Shocks to Global Factor   228
Table 14.2.   Currency Composition of External Debt (%),
              End-of-March   245

Table 14.3.   Foreign Portfolio Investment (FPI) Limits
               (USD Billion)   246
Table 14.4.   Debt Investment Restrictions   248
Table 14.5.   Evolution of All-in-Cost (AIC) Spread (in bps)
               over Libor-6 Month/Swap   249

Table 15.1.   Characteristics of Central G-Secs   259
Table 15.2.   Issuance Profile of Government Borrowings
               (in US $ Billion)   259

ACKNOWLEDGEMENTS

Public memory can be short. In recognition of this sobering truth of life, I decided to bind together the speeches and monetary policy committee minutes that I had delivered while serving as a deputy governor of the Reserve Bank of India (RBI) from 23 January 2017 to 23 July 2019. These speeches and minutes were truly my voice, my lifeblood, my raison d'être. They were the result of toiling tirelessly throughout many a night, distilling and pouring every drop, I could find inside me, of economic reasoning and persuasion. While already out there in cyberspace, I am hopeful that there will be something useful for each one of you in revisiting them, rearranged in the book around specific themes, and with potentially a new insight or two into the preface titled 'Fiscal Dominance—a Theory of Everything in India'.

First, let me convey my sincere thanks to many who made it all possible.

For the opportunity to serve the people of India within the confines of the legal mandate of the RBI, I remain grateful to the Government of India, Governor Urjit R. Patel under whom I joined as a deputy governor, Governor Shaktikanta Das under whom I also served, fellow deputy governors I had the pleasure of working with— especially N. S. Vishwanathan with whom I collaborated most closely (and with whom, Governor Patel and I formed a formidable team in my view for tackling many financial stability issues), and several former governors and deputy governors who have all not only been my supporters and well-wishers through thick and thin but also are a constant source of inspiration to me.

I am also deeply indebted to the staff of the RBI that worked selflessly on many endeavours with me, including on some of the content of this book. I wish to particularly thank Vineet Srivastava, my executive assistant; Vaibhav Chaturvedi, my first executive assistant; Lathika Pillai, Hardik Savla and Narendra Keni, my personal assistants; and the other office staff, drivers and protocol officers, who collectively amplified my productivity.

I would like to make a special mention of the Bombay Gymkhana Tennis Club, its Chairman Dr Bhandari, the markers (Naresh, Vishwas, Ganesh, Lavesh and Gaurav), Mukadam and the ballboys fellow tennis players and other staff, who helped my mind stay fresh while attempting to ace the working day even as I mostly failed to serve an ace on its either side!

As I left home each day from Vile Parle (West) in the Mumbai suburbs for the RBI and returned in the night, I felt unmistakably the steady courage and endurance of my mother, the ambition and perseverance of my father, and the unconditional support of my brother and his family, giving my sorties into central banking several knots of tailwind—thank you!

Putting the book together would not have been as satisfying without Dr Y.V. Reddy agreeing to write the foreword, and Mrs Shyamala Gopinath, Dr Mervyn King, Mr Y.H. Malegam, Dr Rakesh Mohan, Dr Maurice Obstfeld, Dr Eswar Prasad, Dr Raghuram G. Rajan, Dr C. Rangarajan, Mrs Usha Thorat and Mr N. Vaghul endorsing it wholeheartedly.

Finally, thank you also to several others whose company and friendship were priceless to me, including the birds of India and friends who introduced me to them, but who have not been individually mentioned here.

FOREWORD

Dr B.R. Ambedkar, an eminent economist who specialized in public finance and monetary economics, is acknowledged as the principal architect of the Constitution of India. In the Constituent Assembly Debates in 1949, he said:

This Article specifically says that the borrowing power of the executive shall be subject to such limitations as Parliament may by law prescribe. If Parliament does not make a law, it is certainly the fault of Parliament and I should have thought it very difficult to imagine any future Parliament which will not pay sufficient or serious attention to this matter and enact a law.[1]

No such legislation has been passed till today.

However, in 2003, the Parliament enacted the Fiscal Responsibility and Budget Management (FRBM) Act, which covers a similar ground. This Act has, however, been repeatedly diluted over time. An amendment in 2018 introduced the 'escape clause', which allowed the Government of India to breach its fiscal deficit target by 0.5 per cent of gross domestic product (GDP) in an extraordinary economic situation. This amendment also allowed the government to approach the RBI to subscribe to the primary issues of central government securities to deal with such an extraordinary economic situation.

The report of the Comptroller and Auditor General assessing compliance with the FRBM Act for the year 2018 observed that the

---

[1] https://www.rbi.org.in/scripts/BS_SpeechesView.aspx?Id=45 (accessed on 25 April 2020).

Central government has increasingly resorted to off-budget financing for revenue as well as capital spending and that such off-budget financing is not part of calculation of the fiscal indicators despite obvious fiscal implications. Consequently, a distinction is now being made between the 'official deficit' and the 'real deficit'. The Central government, which has adequate powers to enforce fiscal discipline over the states, has, by tradition, not exactly been a good example of such discipline.

The 14th Finance Commission in its report observed that:

There is increasing recognition globally that the conduct of sustainable fiscal policy by governments and imparting greater realism to the forecasts (including testing their consistency with the fiscal rules) calls for the establishment of an independent fiscal institution which could undertake ex-ante assessment of the impact of fiscal policy and the fiscal implications of budget proposals.

It also recommended the establishment of an Independent Fiscal Council (IFC). IFC was not established even after the FRBM Review Committee recommended to establish and report to the Finance Ministry, and thus IFC was not exactly independent.

Even the recourse to funding by the International Monetary Fund (IMF) or the World Bank, over the years, and the balance of payments crisis in 1991 have not altered India's basic approach to fiscal laxity. This is the fiscal dominance that Dr Acharya so eloquently describes in this book.

The banking sector, particularly public sector banking, has played a hugely supporting role in this reality of fiscal laxity. Public sector banks do demand fiscal support through recapitalization (recap), but the benefits they provide in terms of direct support to fiscal (despite regulatory prescription to avoid the conflict of interest) and indirect resources available to the government outside fiscal (such as the ability to affect bank lending outcomes) are both significant to the government of the day. That has been the political economy of banking of India since Independence.

The banking system currently has two distinct important segments, namely public sector banks and private sector banks. The origin of public sector banks lies in the nationalization of the Imperial

Bank of India in 1955 and, more importantly, the nationalization of banks in 1970.

The nationalization of banks in 1970 changed the balance in a fundamental manner. First, large financial resources, namely bank deposits, became available for the government, which could be used without parliamentary oversight. The banking system in India, thus, became a useful means to launch countrywide programmes of many prime ministers. Second, the private sector had to depend on banks owned by the Central government for funding their activities since financial intermediation in the formal sector was mostly confined to banks. Third, the Reserve Bank of India's command over monetary policy, especially transmission and regulation of banks, was diluted as most of the Indian banking system comprised public sector banks. Fourth, the Central government had no official functionaries in the states for initiating or implementing its programmes, but now the government has acquired a countrywide presence of its functionaries, albeit indirect.

By nationalizing larger banks in 1980, private sector banks were told that 'if you grow, you are dead'. This stifled the growth of private sector banks for about three decades.

The government, the public sector banks and the RBI became part of a big joint family (Hindu undivided family!) where no one kept proper accounts of what they were doing with each other and with the rest of the economy. The common belief was that they were all serving people.

Even after diluting its share in public sector banks, the government gave limited autonomy to the boards of public sector banks and the Department of Banking (now, the Department of Financial Services) continued to exercise control over the operations of banks.

The Narasimham Committee recommended the dilution of government shareholding to 30 per cent, abolition of dual control by the RBI and the Ministry of Finance, and the synergy-driven merger of banks among the public sector banks. None of these recommendations were implemented even though they were accepted in principle.

There were two phases of significant recap: in the early 1990s and after 2010. In the early 1990s, the government was the only shareholder and recap was needed mostly on account of years of social banking (1970–90). In the second phase of recap, it was mostly needed owing to the negative impact of non-performing assets (NPAs) on banking sectors because of large exposures—that too at a time when there were also private shareholders. Recap was neither incentive-driven nor selective (i.e., not based on performance). More recently, mergers have been undertaken but not of the kind envisaged by the Narasimham Committee. Further, there is no move to abolish dual control. Despite the RBI repeatedly protesting about farm loan waivers, both the Centre and states have recourse to such waivers periodically.

This is the political economy of banking and the financial repression that Dr Acharya laments about.

Historically, the borrowing requirements of the Central government led to rising fiscal deficits plan after plan. Despite the significant monetization of fiscal deficits, banks were forced to buy government bonds at pre-fixed interest rates, and such coercive subscription to government bonds became easier after nationalization and continued till the early 1990s when the Central government bonds started getting auctioned. High statutory liquidity ratio (SLR) and behest subscription for state government bonds continued in the banking sector. The private placement of fresh issues with the RBI was phased out with the enactment of the FRBM Act in 2003. For state government borrowings, phone calls from the RBI to bank chairmen were not unusual. Once private placement with the RBI was banned, managing the smooth completion of the borrowing programme had to be facilitated through liquidity operations consistent with monetary policy compulsions.

Large market borrowing by the governments (both Central and state) meant that the private corporate bond market got crowded out. Despite this, the corporate bond market grew mainly because of the issuance of bonds by public financial institutions, public infra institutions and financial institutions. A major part of bonds thus has implicit sovereign guarantee. Efforts to broad-base the corporate bond markets have been made, but the bond market in India remains overwhelmed by the public sector borrowing requirement (PSBR). The development of mature bond markets in India has thus been cramped by the requirements of the fiscal as rightly diagnosed by Dr Acharya.

The RBI has always been among the least independent central banks in the world as per the relevant statute but had till recently the reputation of being more independent in practice. The RBI's policy was in line with planned priorities from 1950 to 1970. This period was characterized by a system of automatic monetization with which the RBI connived. Further, the RBI protested the nationalization of banks but it was of no avail. The central bank's subservience to the Central government during this period was not unique to India. Pooling of central funds, state funds, the RBI's refinancing and credit from banks with active involvement from the RBI and centralized allocation of these funds were adopted as a national policy. The 1980s was also characterized by a large increase in budget deficits. At this stage, the RBI started warning the Central government of serious consequences of fiscal mismanagement. From 1990, the stress on balance of payments was evident, and the political instability made effective governmental actions difficult. The RBI played an active part in managing the ensuing crisis in 1991. This was followed by the close involvement of the central bankers in the evolution of the reform package in the initial years. The committees on reform of the financial sector, banking sector, external sector, capital account and insurance sector were all headed by former or serving central bankers.

Dr C. Rangarajan was, perhaps, the first deputy governor to deliver well-prepared speeches containing elements and communications that we normally attribute to central bankers. The speeches seldom referred to matters on which there was a difference of opinion between the government and the RBI. He used various platforms to create public opinion in the relevant circles in favour of what the central bank should do and occasionally hinted at what the government should be doing. These speeches were more in the nature of educating our own financial markets, which were at very initial stages. His speeches were brought out in a series of books from time to time. Among the speeches that influenced the course of events, the most noteworthy is the Kutty Memorial Lecture, which set out the case for ending the system of automatic monetization. It had such a profound influence that it was possible to have a memorandum of agreement between the government and the RBI before it was incorporated into a law.

Mr S.S. Tarapore, who succeeded Dr Rangarajan, followed his example. He continued articulating his opinions essentially on matters relating to money, banking and financing, even after retirement. His speeches also were brought out as a book.

The tradition was continued by most succeeding governors and deputy governors. Viral V. Acharya was a deputy governor for most of Dr Urjit Patel's time as Governor and they dealt with the issues of NPAs, bank recap, dual control over public sector banks and profit transfer from the RBI, each of which became controversial.

Although most of the speeches of Governors and deputy governors are well researched and messages delivered effectively, Dr Viral V. Acharya's style was truly unique. He had the courage of conviction. He was comprehensive; he laid bare the theoretical basis, reviewed the empirical research, linked the practical global experience on the subject and drew lessons for India's needs—all this done in a language that was passionate, hard-hitting and occasionally, even deliberately, provocative.

Dr Viral V. Acharya is a very congenial and charming person. His passion for making a difference in the monetary and regulatory history of the RBI comes across through the pages of the book.

I had the privilege and pleasure of interacting with Dr Viral V. Acharya during his tenure in the RBI. Dr Acharya lost no time in winning the loyalty and admiration of professionals while retaining the trust of the Governor. I have also been closely watching his devotion, his frustration, his leadership qualities and the joy he derived in applying his knowledge to the complex task of policies in a responsible position at a very young age. More importantly, I have been reading his speeches regularly. I encouraged him to bring them out as a book with an introduction that would capture the soul of his experience. He has done it. He has produced a unique book that is informative, analytical, contextual and, without doubt, a lasting contribution.

2 March 2020,   —Y.V. REDDY
Hyderabad   Former Governor, Reserve Bank of India

PRELUDE TO THE NEW EDITION

With the Benefit of (Some) Hindsight[1]

'... I keep them [my fishing lines] with precision. Only I have no luck anymore. But who knows? Maybe today. Every day is a new day. It is better to be lucky. But I would rather be exact. Then when luck comes you are ready.'
—Santiago, in Ernest Hemingway's *The Old Man and the Sea*

Central banks and the fiscal authorities responded strongly to the Covid-19 shock. Inflation reacted strongly too. As interest rates are being hiked sharply now, easy monetary conditions have tightened and financial stability concerns are appearing on the horizon. This book, my journey as a deputy governor of the Reserve Bank of India during 2017–19, is about navigating such concerns amid much uncertainty.

After this book's first print was released in July 2020, I delivered several online presentations to enthusiastic college audiences throughout India. The engagement and the interest of students kept me going for a while. Then, international interest in the book grew, especially over the past year, given its relevance not just for central banking in India but also in other emerging market economies and advanced market economies.

My understanding of economics is deeply rooted in my education at the Fellowship School in Mumbai, where our teacher, Shailesh

---

[1] I am grateful to Tamal Bandyopadhyay, Rahul Singh Chauhan, Vivek Kaul, Shruti Rajagopalan and Dr Y.V. Reddy for helpful feedback and insightful comments.

Shah sir, taught us the age-old Gujarati proverb, *'Jyaan raja vyapari, tyaan praja bhikhari* [Where the king is a trader, citizens are beggars]'. At some point in life, after many reflections on this proverb, a Eureka moment occurred to me! It became clear that this was a grain of wisdom powerful enough as an economic telescope to look back and make sense of long stretches of underperformance by several countries in different parts of the world. The rest of economics is detail, I have realized over time, even if it is important to get the details right.

I was struck by a similar—however, much more modest—eureka! moment when I was thinking about a preface to the book's reprint edition. I was on my way to work on a Citi Bike,[2] as it dawned upon me that my efforts as a central banker were not unlike my efforts at navigating New York on a bike.

Citi Biking

I ride the Citi Bike from my home to New York University each morning. Several secrets of life get revealed along the way.

It is important to stick to the lane and obey the traffic lights.

Hazards abound. Drivers of cars, cabs, buses and trucks mostly do not care about small travellers, like bikers. The pedestrians, too, believe that occupying bike lanes is their birthright.

Look! A delivery guy is coming at you speeding in the wrong direction. He has no plans to brake. From his standpoint, perhaps you are the one who is in the wrong way.

And wait, don't get distracted by music or podcasts. You need all your senses to perceive hazards in advance—to avoid a nasty accident.

A regular bike is safer even if slower. If you start late for the destination, consider opting for the electric bike. E-bike journeys can be quick but stressful. If it all works out, one feels triumphant, 'I can think on my feet and problem-solve.' When it fails, a question lingers, 'Was it worth the risk?'

The morning that I am talking about was rough. I could not start my journey on time. There were no bikes at the closest docking station. And just as I thought I was close, I could not end the trip. All docks were filled up on the other end.

---

[2] A public bicycle sharing system serving New York City.

I need to avoid these late starts and failing-to-exit traps. Where can I locate early-warning indicators? The Citi Bike app shows the availability of bikes and docks in real time. I must track the app to plan better.

Above all, no matter how long or short the ride, on a regular bike, and especially on an e-bike, a helmet is a must. Safety comes first!

From Citi Biking to Central Banking

Riding a public bike in a city feels like a simple activity but is actually rather unpredictable. There are new settings, new companions and new hazards each day. Pretty much anyone can do it, but it requires some thought, application and, indeed, some courage. To be safe and keep others safe, there are mostly no shortcuts. One rarely finishes a ride concluding 'Aaj, tukka lag gaya [Today, a random guess worked]!' Instead, one reminds oneself to be disciplined daily; in fact, before each ride. Then you are the master of your fate and the captain of your soul, no matter how crowded the lane or how many impediments lie on the road.

Central banking appears to me not too different from this. At the end of the day, it is about taking the economy safely from the source to a desired destination.

Each day is a new challenge, with new developments globally, new risks locally. Central banking is neither a perfect science nor a formless art. It is certainly complex. So, it requires checklists to avoid hazards. Relying on 'tukkas' usually leads to bigger problems down the lane. In contrast, some guiding principles help:

Banks must be kept well-capitalized at all times to absorb cyclical shocks.

Underwriting standards can't be let loose to satisfy short-term political growth objectives lest they manifest as intractable non-performing assets and choke long-term growth.

Volatility in the currency must be managed by deploying the stock of dollar or safe-asset reserves built in good times—a saving-for-the-rainy-day strategy.

To ensure that capital outflows can be managed with reserves, capital inflows must be controlled to manageable levels ahead of time.

Most of all, inflation is a tax on the poor. It erodes their meagre savings and disproportionately hurts their consumption. Particularly, emerging market economies must keep inflation at bay.

Taming inflation requires raising interest rates and giving up on some short-term growth spurts. It preserves the consumption capacity of the economy and ensures that savings are parked in safe assets rather than chasing speculative bubbles. This keeps long-term borrowing costs low, which in turn favours long-term investment and growth.

Raising rates can tame inflation but with a lag, so a stitch in time can save nine. When inflation rises persistently, household and investor expectations become unanchored and do not budge easily. So, the central bank can get trapped between requiring excessive and fast raising of rates and keeping rates low to avoid financial accidents. All this can be avoided by tracking the 'core' inflation measure[3] and keeping it around the headline inflation target. Headline veers towards the core and eventually around it.

And, of course, there is little point in turning the dial of interest rates up and down in central bank offices if there is no pass-through to the borrowers in the real economy.

Bank lending should therefore be linked to benchmarks that fluctuate reasonably with the policy rate set by the central bank. Banks must learn to manage any interest rate risk resulted by letting others in markets take it on if they are better at it.

The central bank may be asked—and find it tempting—to join forces with a deficit-oriented finance ministry that is riding too fast and hoping for a 'tukka lag gaya' finish, 'tukka' being an expedient policy shortcut or a knee-jerk reaction to an unexpected, often self-triggered, crisis. Is this partnership similar to a tandem bike with both riders on equal footing? Or is the front rider in a tow truck? Towing the bike and allowing the tandem no control? Or is it a bulldozer? Worse, all of the above but each at a different time?

It's never clear. In the end, the central bank must find a way to ride its bike safely.

A Paean to the Reserve Bank of India

I contend that the Reserve Bank of India and its governors, top management and hard-working staff have, over the past three decades

---

[3] Put simply, the 'core' inflation measure strips out the inflation due to food and fuel prices, which tend to be both volatile and driven more by supply-side frictions than by consumer demand, the latter being more sensitive to the central bank's monetary policy (which includes foremost the setting of interest rates in the economy).

and slightly more, strived to follow such a checklist to keep the economy safe and its long-run prospects stable.

Inevitably, different governors and their teams have differed in their pursuits to an extent, and they have had somewhat different weights on items on the checklist, given that they were fending off different economic challenges, with some in fact battling full-blown crises—abroad and/or domestic; some were under more pressure from Indian governments' deficit-oriented policies, and others, even when not under pressure, chose to retain greater flexibility in their target-setting and attainment of preset targets.

Given the varied approaches, success has not always been uniform or durable. Nevertheless, the Reserve Bank has played a consequential role in helping push India in the right direction from a centralized, socialist, bank- and government-dominated economy to one that is more decentralized, capitalist and market-oriented. It would be a mistake to not observe that some of these gains have unfortunately reversed since the global financial crisis and remain at risk of further attrition.

And yet, taking a longer, three-decade-plus view, it is hard not to sing a paean to the Reserve Bank as an institution that has served the country admirably well. Reading and learning from the memoirs of past governors offer perhaps the best way to join in the singing of such a paean, with the most recent being C. Rangarajan's *Forks in the Road: My Days at RBI and Beyond* (Penguin Random House India, 2022).

For a while, after I started out at the Reserve Bank in January 2017, I considered being a deputy governor the best job there. Rakesh Mohan, former deputy governor of the Reserve Bank, had told me this as well when I had sought his guidance before starting my term. Early on, I had reasonable powers to execute changes or at least be an agent of change. I enjoyed formal as well as real authority on matters in my portfolio. At times, I was able to venture even beyond. I could speak my mind through speeches and on the monetary policy minutes with little, if any, intervention. This helped catalyse actions on outstanding problems like bank non-performing assets and the need to resolve underlying distressed companies. I ended up being the public face when it helped the Reserve Bank's purpose but was often shielded from having to face the brickbats, as Dr Mohan had rightly predicted.

I hope that this book, which is a summary of my stint as a deputy governor of the Reserve Bank, structured around my speeches then and reflections since, serves a useful purpose, and that this reprint helps some of the new readers get a sense of what was attempted during my term, which objectives have been achieved since then and what remains an unfinished agenda.

Taking Stock of My Term as a Deputy Governor

So, how do the policies of 2017–19, specifically during my term from 23 January 2017 to 23 July 2019, fare when viewed today with the benefit of some hindsight?

While I fully acknowledge my self-congratulatory bias in what follows, I'd like to point out that many policies implemented or proposed then collectively fit into the theme of 'quest for restoring financial stability in India', which is also the title of this book. It is organized into six parts and led by an introductory chapter, 'Fiscal Dominance—A Theory of Everything in India'. The sections cover:[4]

1. Resolving non-performing assets (NPAs) and recapitalizing banks
2. Creating a public credit registry
3. Incorporating the financial cycle into the monetary policy framework
4. Improving monetary policy transmission
5. Developing viable capital markets and ensuring external sector resilience
6. Striking the right balance: enhancing the autonomy of the central bank, the markets and the real economy

Each one of these represents a 'line' that the Reserve Bank in those years laid down with a fair degree of precision. Part of the work of laying the lines was still underway when I left to reunite with my family in New York. There wasn't always an immediate success from laying down the lines. In some cases, the eventual success has been greater than I had imagined. Some have taken the institutional quality of the financial sector a definitive notch up and are bearing fruits even now. Others, though, are yet to pay off fully.

---

[4] The book's truly masterful foreword by Dr Y.V. Reddy, former governor, Reserve Bank of India, remains its best and most-cited part since the first print run in July 2020.

Let me elaborate on a couple of the primary lines.

1. Clean-up of banks

On the overdue clean-up of bank balance sheets and their much-needed recapitalization, especially of public-sector banks by the national exchequer, the benefits of our reforms are the most visible and long-lasting. The underlying issues were conveyed as ones of pressing urgency in my early speeches, notably in 'Some Ways to Decisively Resolve Bank Stressed Assets', delivered at the Indian Banks' Association on 21 February 2017.

The quest for pushing this agenda forward had an emphatic response all around. Hobbling along the way, the government eventually came on board too.

When a banking sector holds over 10 per cent non-performing assets relative to advances (over Rs 10 lakh crore or a trillion rupees, or over $150 billion at the then exchange rate, in absolute terms), with public-sector banks closer to a ratio of 15 per cent and comprising over 85 per cent of the overall non-performing assets,[5] and all of these statistics are likely to be substantially higher in reality than implied by the accounting numbers due to a lack of timely recognition of losses . . . well, the clean-up takes time. To ensure the process didn't end up like *Birbal ki khichdi*,[6] issues had to be dealt with decisively and pursued with obstinacy.

The Reserve Bank has stuck to the task relentlessly ever since. The bulk of the work in recognizing and acknowledging the full stock of the banking sector's non-performing assets—Asset Quality Review— was completed by early 2017. In the second half of the year, an initial round of large non-performing assets was directed successfully to the Insolvency and Bankruptcy Code. Thereafter came the 12 February 2018 circular which sought to adopt a principle-based approach to directing pending and future such cases. The circular was ill-fated legally, but the seeds of a good idea never disappoint. Its spirit has now been reflected in alternate, even if diluted, circulars.

The banking sector now looks in substantially better shape in terms of capitalization relative to potential losses; it is in a position to

---

[5] See https://www.rbi.org.in/scripts/PublicationsView.aspx?id=19791
[6] An assignment that knows no completion or an undertaking that drifts on and on.

support credit growth if there is healthy demand and is no longer as vulnerable as it was in the past decade.

In fact, we may have underestimated the beneficial *deterrence* effect of the clean-up. Promoters and companies that have not yet defaulted pay up and manage their leverage and businesses better now in order to avoid a bankruptcy filing that can cause a loss of control over the assets. Eighteenth-century English writer Samuel Johnson put it just right: 'Depend upon it, sir, when a man knows he is to be hanged in a fortnight, it concentrates his mind wonderfully.'[7]

As a financial stability warrior, nothing has been more satisfying than to see progress on this front.[8] Not many get an opportunity even in a lifetime to write something that can contribute to making such a meaningful difference.

For this, I am grateful to the encouragement and leadership of Governor Urjit R. Patel, and to the generosity fellow deputy governors, S.S. Mundra and N.S. Vishwanathan (who headed supervision and regulation, respectively, at that point in time) gracefully granted me in letting me speak on an issue outside my portfolio and more squarely in theirs.

The then Board for Financial Supervision of the Reserve Bank played a key role too in making all this happen. When external board members are not just acting as spokespersons of the government, they too can help champion the Reserve Bank's mandates and move forward meaningful reforms for the economy.

2. *Improving the transmission of monetary policy*

As another example of a difficult but successful reform, consider the *external benchmarking* of bank loan rates.

The issue was simple. When interest rates change, loan rates should change. 'By how much?' is determined by how much benchmark rates—to which loan rates are tethered—move when (say) the central bank policy rate shifts.

---

[7] Samuel Johnson's comment made on 19 September 1777, about the execution of Dr William Dodd, as recounted in *The Life of Samuel Johnson*, by James Boswell, Penguin Classics, 2008.

[8] One lament is that of late, case resolution through the Insolvency and Bankruptcy Code seems to be taking far longer than originally envisaged and this is resulting in lower recoveries for creditors.

When benchmarks are 'internal', that is, set by an individual bank or substantially controlled by a bank, they end up being manipulated and interest rate changes are not passed through adequately to the borrowers. For instance, if rates are cut, banks can keep rates artificially high for their captive borrowers. This prevents easy monetary policy from stimulating the economy as desired.

'External' benchmarks are outside the control of individual banks as they are market- or directly central-bank-determined. Such benchmarks affect all banks in an identical or at least a similar way. Crucially, when rates are cut, loan rates move in lockstep with lowered benchmark rates. This ensures a better pass-through of monetary policy to the borrowers.

At the inaugural Aveek Guha Memorial Lecture, 'Monetary Transmission in India: Why Is It Important and Why Hasn't It Worked Well?', on 16 November 2017, I explained the problems with the internal benchmarking of bank loans and made, what I believe, was a compelling case for developing and adopting external benchmarks in bank loans.

Banks lobbied hard against the external benchmarking of loan rates as they do against pretty much any reform that requires generating margins by better underwriting and provision of credit. In this case, it would mean banks having to compete more aggressively for deposits and loans to garner a larger share of the market than to sit cozy with little pass-through of beneficial rate cuts to borrowers in the economy. While the lobbying efforts delayed the rollout to 2018 and into 2019, the implementation appears to have gone through smoothly.

When interest rates were cut sharply in 2020 following the Covid-19 outbreak, the reform enabled an immediate benefit to borrowers with externally benchmarked loans easing their interest-rate burden and preventing the collapse of aggregate demand.

Conversely, in the rate hike cycle by the Reserve Bank since May 2022, banks have in fact been the biggest beneficiaries of the reform. They have not yet fully passed on rate hikes to deposit savers, but their loan books have adjusted automatically to higher rates. Bank lending profits have improved, protecting them against treasury losses from rate hikes. In turn, their capitalization has remained intact or improved in some cases, and they seem to be in good shape to provide credit if agents in the economy have reasons to borrow. While the pass-through to loan rates has not been one-for-one, it has been faster than it was in the past cycles.

This evidence of a faster pass-through augurs well for the Reserve Bank as it seeks to tame inflation by raising policy rates and, in turn, the cost of borrowing, with the intent of slowing down aggregate demand.

The Reserve Bank staff in the Monetary Policy Department persevered with top management in seeing this important reform through and deserve much of the credit.

Both lines—the clean-up of banks and the external benchmarking of bank loan rates—illustrate the virtue of adopting financial sector reforms that make good economic sense despite initial resistance by incumbents, that address the friction at play in a targeted or even surgical manner, but that also require patience after the structural reforms have been put in place. Sound logic, data-based evidence from other parts of the world where similar policies were adopted and focus on long-term economic outcomes won the day.

Public Assessment and Some Disagreements

The actions of public servants are always up for criticism, debate and scrutiny, as they should be. Mine have been too. I welcome that, but I also wish to highlight here a few significant points of disagreement with some of the public assessments.

1. Was the bank clean-up too swift?

Some view that the clean-up of bank non-performing assets, which started with an Asset Quality Review during Governor Raghuram G. Rajan's term and was then dealt with head-on during Governor Patel's term, was too swift for the system to stomach. They argue that it should have been slower.

I could not disagree more. The scale of the problem was gargantuan, Indian banks' non-performing assets ratio was among the worst in the entire world, the Reserve Bank was seen as among the weakest banking regulators in emerging markets, and the wounds had festered for so long that there was economic sclerosis.

There was no other way to tackle the beast other than to take it by its horns. Swift corporate change of ownership and resolution of assets under bankruptcy was the necessary medicine. Of course, those losing control did not particularly fancy that outcome. They complained to the government, the process got somewhat stalled, and there were legal obstacles, but in the end, the overall thrust of the Reserve Bank's approach seems to have prevailed.

2. *Was liquidity provision during the IL&FS and housing-finance debacle inadequate?*

When the problems of IL&FS (Infrastructure Leasing and Financial Services) and some housing finance companies came to the fore in August 2018, the Reserve Bank was seen as not flooding the market with abundant liquidity.

The Reserve Bank did expand aggregate liquidity. It did so by acting as a lender-of-last-resort to banks which could on-lend to non-banks. The central bank did not wish to—and I believe, should not—be in the business of taking on the credit risk of questionable non-bank balance sheets. I say 'questionable' as we had legitimate concerns and specific intelligence on their health. First, many non-bank financial companies had dramatically shortened their debt maturity structure in the easy-money environment post demonetization. Secondly, and more worryingly, they had created liens against real-estate assets that in many cases simply did not exist and were actually shell companies, likely to siphon off the funds being lent.

In essence, what was on the surface a liquidity or rollover risk problem in the face of rising oil prices, inflation and interest rates of August 2018, was likely also a solvency problem. Several non-bank financial firms had too much leverage and too little prospective cash flow.

Upon the arrival of an unpleasant shock, such as the IL&FS and housing-finance stress, it is not entirely unsurprising for the private sector, non-banks and government to collectively lean on the central bank to ease monetary policy. If the central bank takes on credit risk that ex post smells foul, it will, after all, be the central bank's reputational problem.

I remain convinced that the Reserve Bank struck an appropriate compromise. The lender-of-last-resort to non-banks was through banks, wherein banks were entrusted with the task of credit assessment of non-banks. In support of our concerns, banks and markets were indeed discriminating between healthier and weaker non-bank borrowers.

One possibility is that an Asset Quality Review of non-banks could have been undertaken by the Reserve Bank, creating the possibility of direct lender-of-last-resort support for the healthier ones. However, this is not something that would have been possible to undertake in the short time horizon over which all constituencies wanted to be flooded with liquidity. Since then, the regulation of non-bank financial institutions has been tightened and this part of the financial sector too seems perched at overall a safer place.

3. *Should the Reserve Bank have asserted its independence and operational autonomy?*

Let us turn now to my A.D. Shroff Memorial Lecture, 'On the Importance of Independent Regulatory Institutions—The Case of the Central Bank', delivered on 26 October 2018. The lecture brought matters of debate within the Reserve Bank Board and between the top management and the government out in the open. Providing such transparency to the public at large was the entire purpose of the lecture.[9]

This shocked many critics. Some found it feisty and called it even anti-national. The reactions reminded me of Kabir's retort: 'Saadho, dekho jag baurana. Saanchi kaho toh maaran dhaave. Jhoonthe jag patiyana [Saints, see this world is going insane. If I tell the truth, they rush to beat me. If I lie, they trust me].'

The context in 2018 was that regardless of measured statistics, growth had been uneven for different parts of the economy in the two years since demonetization. The well-intended but somewhat botched, hurriedly delivered rollout of the Goods and Services Tax had added to the stress in the informal sector of the economy. Core inflation had risen. The Federal Reserve was raising rates and withdrawing dollar liquidity. The United States was considering sanctions on Iran, and oil prices were simmering to a full boil. The inflation-targeting Reserve Bank had to raise rates to keep the extent of price rise in check. The INR was depreciating steadily but in an orderly manner. The Reserve Bank spent several tens of billions of dollars to manage the INR volatility.

---

[9] Incidentally, the first draft of the speech was written in a single sitting on a non-stop flight from New York to Mumbai. My 'pen' has never felt as much in complete unison with or absolute immersion into a capsule of time as it did then. I consider it the most important piece I have written to date.

These conditions were undoubtedly challenging but not extreme, neither like the global financial crisis of 2008–9 nor like the 'taper tantrum' of May–September 2013.

The real catch was that a national election was due from April to May 2019. Some creative minds in the bureaucracy and the government conjured up an idea for generating INR 2–3 lakh crore (trillion), or equivalently $30–40 billion at the then exchange rate, for populist spending. Demonetization was of course another such idea. In this case, however, the magic wand would be waved on the Reserve Bank balance sheet rather than on currency notes.

The Reserve Bank generates revenues primarily via *seigniorage*. It prints money and distributes it through banks, or credits banks with electronic reserves, to help settle transactions in the economy. Typically, it does not pay interest on the currency or reserve liabilities. At times, it also makes money by buying dollars when INR is strong and selling them when INR is weak. It incurs costs too, an important one being that of printing and replacing currency notes.

Each year, the Reserve Bank Board sets aside some provisions out of the profits so generated rather than distributing them all to the central government. The Bank owns a healthy mix of dollar and rupee assets, typically various government bonds. The provisions, which can be considered a loss-absorption buffer, and the stock of safe assets, are meant for the rainy day. For example, when the Reserve Bank needs to act as a counterparty in foreign exchange transactions (as after the 'taper tantrum' of 2013), they ensure that it is perceived to be of the highest credit quality, that is, AAA credit rating, even though India's sovereign credit rating is much lower.[10]

In short, the Reserve Bank saves from its profits, maintains provisions and holds safe assets for financial stability purposes. This grants the bank operational autonomy at the time of undertaking foreign exchange interventions, lender-of-last-resort operations and even monetary tightening, which results in mark-to-market losses on its assets.

---

[10] The situation is different in emerging markets and advanced market economies on this front. For instance, the Federal Reserve pays *all* of its profits each week to the treasury of the United States government. Key distinctions to note, relative to India and other emerging markets, are that (presently) the US government has among the highest credit ratings, and by the virtue of the US dollar being the world's reserve currency, the US economy does not face a 'sudden stop' risk of capital outflows.

The 'idea' conjured up was to transfer a significant portion of these provisions from the central bank balance sheet to the account of the present-day government—provisions accumulated over several terms of prior governments and needed to smoothen financial fragility during several terms of future governments. The fact that the transfer to the government was low during the demonetization year, given the heightened cost of currency printing, intensified this demand, even though the central government had received record transfers out of the Reserve Bank profits in the three years preceding demonetization.

The government had also failed to raise much through divestment revenues. The divestment goals set in each Budget are mostly just a terminal 'adjustment' entry to deliver the desired fiscal deficit number after the rest has been accounted for. It is an annual ritual now that the realized divestment shortfall is sought to be met via transfers from the Reserve Bank (and tunnelling of dividends from the public-sector units that starve them of investment capital). Effectively, this is a back-door monetization of the fiscal deficit by the central bank.

In addition, the government had to recapitalize public-sector banks which was now critical for their health and lending. Why cut populist expenditures in an election year to meet such long-term needs of the economy when the central bank balance sheet can be raided and surging fiscal deficits essentially monetized?

As is now publicly known, the Reserve Bank did not play along with the idea. In response, a proposal started floating around in the government that it should invoke Section 7 of the Reserve Bank of India Act to give 'directions to the Bank as it may, after consultation with the Governor of the Bank, [consider] necessary in the public interest' (Section 7 in the Reserve Bank of India Act, 1934).

No democratic emerging market government with reasonable institutions is likely to get its way without meeting formidable resistance when it repeatedly proposes plans to raid its central bank's balance sheet for short-term populist expenditures. Doing so in the run-up to a national election in somewhat stressed but not exactly calamitous times simply made no long-term economic sense. Worse, it risked being seen by the choppy INR market of 2018 as the adoption of a fiscal policy that was openly populist, likely wasteful and certainly inflationary.

At a minimum, this matter of 'public interest' needed to be debated publicly rather than in closed-door meetings. Any purported benefit needed to be established in a public report of an expert committee as being worth more than the likely significant erosion in the perception of central bank independence and restrictions on its future activity.

The Reserve Bank going public in the form of my A.D. Shroff Memorial Lecture guaranteed eventually that even if some in the government were unhappy about it, wise counsel prevailed. A committee was set up under the chairmanship of Dr Bimal Jalan, former governor of the Reserve Bank, and vice-chairmanship of Dr Rakesh Mohan. A reasonable framework is laid out for future transfers from the Reserve Bank balance sheet to the government. To its credit, the government sidelined most of the original architects of the 'idea'. And indeed, a rather large transfer, which unlike in 2018 could be well justified during the pandemic in 2020, was delivered to the government by the then Reserve Bank Board.

In summary, while there are a few outcomes that could have been better and a few decisions that could have been paced differently, it is unclear if, given the information we had in real time, I would rewind the clock and do anything differently. We did all we could, given where we were, using all the tools we had at hand.

I always debated hard on these issues with the Reserve Bank staff, including the governors I reported to and worked with, and, when there was a possibility, with the government that had appointed me. It is in part because of this approach, which has been generally allowed to flourish at the Reserve Bank, that I believe the lines for financial stability laid down over decades are playing out today to the economy's, and each government's, advantage. As is typical with financial stability reforms, the full scale and scope of results materialize only with a substantial—in fact, several years of—lag.

A Wish List

India lives as much inside me as outside, be it through my middle-class upbringing of optimizing around scarce resources, playing cricket on the streets and grounds in South Mumbai, toiling ceaselessly to crack the SSC and HSC board exams and then the Indian Institute of Technology Joint Entrance Exam, working with the executive team of Pratham India Education Initiative that runs *baalwadis* and catalytic literacy programmes, raising funds wherever I have been to support the tireless efforts of Pratham's staff to prepare our children and skill our youths for the future, doing up and down from Vile Parle

West to Fort each day and then back each evening during my central bank stint, and most recently, battling like so many other Indians for weeks during the worst of the Delta Covid wave to help a family member survive in the intensive care unit and hospital ward.

My heart still skips a beat when India is about to win a cricket match and sinks when it loses. I watch again and again the movies that most Indians cherish—from *Pather Panchali* to *Sholay*. Play *Antakshari* or a Bollywood trivia quiz, and I am almost surely a contender. And like all fellow Indians and Lord Ganesh, I consider loving, worshipping and taking care of one's parents as the greatest religion to practise.

I have always felt one with—and like one of—India's common men. That is my only identity. And this identity drove my checklists as a central banker at the Reserve Bank—to protect the interests of the ordinary Indian.

And last but not least, it is neither necessarily a guaranteed virtue nor a distinct disadvantage to have been an academic before one has become a central banker.

Central banking is ultimately a day-to-day job that one must do well and with care. The job does require some clarity of thought, a healthy respect for data, loads of humility to be able to learn something new each day and a willingness to take help when needed. I hasten to add that the job also requires an unwavering focus on the economy's long-term health, financial stability, financial inclusion and meeting the targets legislatively mandated by the central bank.

It is meeting the last of these requirements, that is, not giving in to short-term political pressures, that I found is most commonly associated in India with being impractical and professorial. However, when the half-science, half-art nature of central banking simply creates discretion for seeking growth at all costs and pushing aside the structural soundness of the financial system in favour of quick fixes, is it really about being more practical and less academic? Or is it about being a politician in the guise of an unelected central banker?[11]

---

[11] Paul Tucker, the former deputy governor of the Bank of England, has laid out the challenges of expanding the central banking mandate in such discretionary manner in his book *Unelected Power: The Quest for Legitimacy in Central Banking and the Regulatory State*, Princeton University Press, 2019.

Let me then turn to my wish list for India and the Reserve Bank. The list has three items:

Undertake more fiscal consolidation, keep headline inflation on target and reach the last mile.

1. Undertake more fiscal consolidation

The government has made some progress in the last four years in doing away with accounting tricks to 'manage' the fiscal deficit and focused instead on rationalization from revenue to capital expenditures. It has had to absorb the unprecedented Covid shock.

Nonetheless, the overall level of fiscal deficit, public-sector borrowing requirement and the centre-plus-state debt-to-GDP, all remain uncomfortably high. I say 'uncomfortably high' as relatively moderate shocks still have the potential to leave the economy precarious to short-term policymaking—including central banking compromises—that will start managing the fiscal arithmetic rather than enabling the private engines of stable long-term growth.

In the introductory chapter, 'Fiscal Dominance—A Theory of Everything in India', I lay out why during my term general fiscal deficit was a persistent concern and kept raising its ugly head in dominating virtually everything about India's central banking. With a part of fiscal consolidation at the centre occurring at the expense of states, inflation remaining stubbornly high, job creation lagging the pace at which youths are entering the labour force and a national election coming up soon, the level of the general fiscal deficit remains a relevant concern. I propose in the chapter ways to improve our institutions, e.g., setting up an independent fiscal council to restore prudence.

Presently, macroeconomic shocks are arriving as per their timetable and without notice, converting what are meant to be one-off temporary deviations from fiscal targets into repetitions and an entrenched characteristic of the economy.

Therefore, as former Reserve Bank governors keep reminding us, further course correction and fiscal institutional reforms are indeed necessary to achieve targets set by the Fiscal Responsibility and Budget Management (FRBM) Act, lest they be undertaken only upon an adverse shock.

Simply kicking the can down the road, while celebrating and enjoying fiscal flexibility each year, is unlikely to suffice if we are to attain the long-run growth potential of an increasingly private-sector Indian economy.

2. Keep headline inflation on target

The Reserve Bank had sound reasons, such as the Covid-19 outbreak and lockdowns in 2020, to adopt expansive monetary stimulus and help arrest any further collapse of growth.

In parallel, however, inflation outcomes keep slipping away from the consumer price inflation target of 4 per cent. Supply shocks to food and fuel enter inflation expectations of households, professional forecasters and even corporations. These expectations all shape realized inflation by affecting wage expectations, among other effects.

The Russian invasion of Ukraine and the imminent Federal Reserve tightening in March–April 2022 appear to have restored the Reserve Bank's focus on target inflation and led to a Fed-coincident phase of monetary tightening. However, most other emerging market central banks used their inflation-targeting mandates to rein in inflation *ahead* of the Fed tightening and even before the invasion. Inflation forecasts from the Reserve Bank immediately before the Fed tightening seemed to most to be too rosy to be backed by the adequate weight of data. The forecasts appeared to have emerged instead from a mindset that was predetermined to undertake sustained monetary easing.

Therein lies the real danger of a central bank getting distracted from inflation-targeting to swinging for the fences on growth. Public commentary, analyst sighs of relief or cries of concern, and bond market expectations, are now all centred around 6 per cent, the upper limit of the band around the consumer price inflation target for the Reserve Bank, rather than at the target of 4 per cent.[12] This suggests that inflation expectations risk becoming unanchored.

The bottom line is that neither the size of the economy is at the pre-pandemic trend nor is headline inflation close to the target.

Even central banks such as the Fed, which have a much longer track record and therefore greater inflation-targeting credibility, have not been left unpunished by the stickiness of revisions in

---

[12] The +/- 2 per cent band around the target headline inflation rate of 4 per cent was meant to account for inevitable measurement noise in inflation rather than to allow the Monetary Policy Committee, and its Reserve Bank members, to shift around the focal point of monetary marksmanship.

inflation expectations. The Reserve Bank is relatively a new kid on the block and needs to build greater inflation credibility first. That may require some growth sacrifice, but, I stress, only in the short term.

It would be good for India, its common man, and its domestic and external financial stability, if the Reserve Bank were to revert credibly and soon, to delivering *realized* inflation prints that average around the mandated target on a durable basis, that is, for several years. The gains from adopting inflation targeting as a central bank, such as a permanent lowering of inflation expectations and long-term borrowing costs, will not fully materialize otherwise.

3.   Reach the last mile

In addition to avoiding these late starts and failing-to-exit traps of fiscal and monetary policy, my third wish is that the central bank reaches the 'last mile'.

As elucidated in speeches in Section II of the book, 'Improving Information Infrastructure—Public Credit Registry', micro, small and medium-sized enterprises (MSMEs) often cannot borrow as their cash-flow patterns are not recorded and hence lenders find it difficult to fine-tune lending terms for them. Public credit registries, which help track the entire history of a borrower's credit flows, in conjunction with other public data records, have been shown globally to improve the MSME access to credit, lead to micro entrepreneurship and unleash growth precisely in those pockets of the economy where low wealth constrains consumption the most. Such registries are typically housed inside and managed by central banks. Hence, at the initiative of some Reserve Bank staff, we made steady institutional progress during 2018–19 towards the setting up of a public credit registry for India.

Private credit bureaus, some with significant foreign investments, had gone against such a move as it threatened their legally enshrined oligopoly. Their data coverage for MSMEs was, however, found in our analysis to be neither comprehensive nor adequate for algorithmic credit scoring that can assist cash-flow-based lending. Worse, private credit bureaus have a stronger incentive to gather data where there is current business than to make exploratory public-good investments in data of borrowers for whom the business will open up in the future.

Right now, with India's uniquely placed digital plumbing built around Aadhaar, Unified Payments Interface (UPI), 'India Stack', Account Aggregators and Open Credit Enablement Network (OCEN), combined with the explosion in e-commerce and Goods and Services Tax Network (GSTN) footprints, the potential to expand credit to starved MSMEs is immense.

To the best of my knowledge, it has not been made transparent anywhere why the public credit registry efforts initiated at the Reserve Bank stalled. Perhaps the Reserve Bank and/or the government have good reasons for this lack of progress. In that case, it would be good to demonstrate that a convincing alternative is—or is being put—in place.

The Budget speech for 2023–24 offers a ray of hope: 'A national financial information registry [NFIR] will be set up to serve as the central repository of financial and ancillary information. This will facilitate the efficient flow of credit, promote financial inclusion, and foster financial stability.'

Such a repository should be kept at arm's length from the government, given it owns and manages several lenders and borrowers in the economy. The standard practice would be to house it inside the Reserve Bank. Another option could be to house it outside—like the Central Clearing Corporation of India (CCIL) and National Payments Corporation of India (NPIC)—but still entrust the central bank with its timely phased rollouts, its evolution into a comprehensive registry and maintaining the integrity of its records.

Better technology is certainly not a substitute for better risk management. Hence, the Reserve Bank is right to be designing with alacrity safeguards for the financial system against risks of new technologies in lending, even as the registry simultaneously enables the onboarding of excluded MSME borrowers into the formal credit system.

Let us hope this time around, efforts to set up the registry are not just a false start.

Beyond these three wishes, most of all, I truly hope India can deliver on its promise in the coming decade. As I stress in my Brookings piece, forthcoming in March 2023, India @75 is 'replete with contradictions, brimming with opportunities, saddled with challenges'.

It might help to meet these challenges with the mindset of riding a Citi Bike: Always plan for safety!

'*Alvida* [Goodbye].'

For now, I must revert to the company of my most enduring friend, Kishore Kumar, who is changing my mood and shifting my gear by asking musically—in lyrics by Sahir Ludhianvi set to a haunting melody by Rahul Dev Burman—'*Kiska rasta dekhe, ae dil ae saudai* [For whom are you awaiting, oh heart, oh lunatic]?'

As I sign off on that contemplative note, let me not waste a single moment in expressing deep gratitude to all critics, friends and well-wishers who still remain in touch.

14 February 2023   **Viral Acharya**

PREFACE

Fiscal Dominance—A Theory of Everything in India[*]

I left New York for Mumbai on the evening of 21 January 2017. As I sat at Newark Airport awaiting to board a United Airlines flight, I couldn't help reflect on the fact that the Indian banking sector was sitting on one of the highest non-performing loans to assets ratio among the G20 countries and even among the group of emerging markets—a marked departure since its standing in 2009. The poor capitalization of Indian banks from an economic standpoint had been evident in the stock market data at least since 2013. Indian public sector banks stood out as having particularly weak balance sheets in terms of their ability to withstand further stress, as captured by the New York University Stern School of Business Systemic Risk (SRISK) rankings (available at vlab.stern.nyu.edu/welcome/risk). It was thus obvious to most that financial stability of the banking sector and economic growth in India were at risk. Ambiguity about the exact impact that demonetization undertaken in November 2016 would have on the real economy and the financial sector had only aggravated these concerns.

Banking sector stress in India tends to play out somewhat silently, just as in China where state-owned banks hold the majority of deposits and loans. This is because government ownership rules out that depositors en masse 'run' on public sector banks even if bank borrowers default en masse, which some consider a positive backdrop for financial stability, unless and until the sovereign balance sheet solvency is itself considered to be on the brink. Nevertheless,

[*] I am grateful to Dr Rakesh Mohan, Ananth Narayan, Dr Y. V. Reddy and participants at the New York University Stern School of Business Luncheon Seminar (28 January 2020) for their valuable inputs.

undercapitalization of public sector banks combined with the lack of significant market discipline and possible behest lending leads to a serious misallocation of credit, most commonly in the form of ever-greening or zombie lending. Effectively, there is 'extend and pretend' of severely distressed or even defaulted borrower loans in an effort to not recognize the erosion of bank capital, a phenomenon that is usually supported by explicit or implicit regulatory forbearance (i.e., the banking regulator turns a blind eye). Undercapitalized public sector banks are thus a significant cost to the healthier parts of the real economy even if these banks never witness bank runs.

Such a 'silent crisis' had been playing out in the Indian banking sector since at least five years given the boom and bust of credit-driven fiscal stimulus post the global financial crisis of 2008.

Could a push be made to address this unfortunate state of affairs in a decisive manner?

I felt energized that if there were to be a meeting of minds on this issue with the RBI (which turned out to be the case), then I could help hit the ground running as soon as I reached Mint Street. I promptly sat down to make a checklist manifesto, titled 'Restoring Financial Stability in India', of the critical steps we must undertake so that economic growth in India could in future be smooth sailing rather than a bumpy ride. The list was short, comprising two bullet points as follows:

- Fix the health of the banking sector, especially that of public-sector banks, with reforms such as consideration for a change of ownership, recapitalization, prompt corrective action (PCA) for undercapitalized banks with repeated track record of poor underwriting standards, timely recognition of losses and decisive resolution of stressed assets.
- Develop financial markets to improve the efficiency of capital allocation, reducing the dependence of the system on bank credit and allowing for market-based mechanisms to reward and punish the borrowers and the financial sector for their outcomes.

At the risk of judging too soon, I provide an assessment of our (as in RBI's) performance on both fronts.

- We achieved moderate success in terms of fixing the health of the banking sector. In fact, within a year since I had joined, considerable progress had been made in restoring financial stability in India: the asset quality review initiated in 2014–2015 under Governor Rajan's term had reached its conclusion, marking bank assets more accurately for the losses incurred; the Government of India had announced a significant recapitalization package for public sector banks with a plan to reward healthier banks with 'growth' capital; weaker public sector banks were put under the PCA framework which was tightened to get closer to the framework in the United States; and, most significantly, the resolution of large non-performing bank assets was put on a fast track on the back of the Insolvency and Bankruptcy Code. At times, it seemed—even if only as wishful thinking for a moment—that (re)privatization of a few public sector banks might also be on the table.

Everything was on track with markets, rating agencies and multi-lateral institutions recognizing the potential of these structural financial stability reforms for India's long-term growth and sovereign credit rating. Yet in about 10 months to follow, not only did progress stall but also several policies regressed. Capital was injected in weaker rather than healthier public sector banks; not much market capital was raised by any of these banks as originally envisaged; capital standards and PCA framework were diluted; forbearance in loss recognition crept in again for some asset classes; and the resolution of several non-performing borrowers under the Insolvency and Bankruptcy Code was stayed. The central bank came under intense pressure to open up liquidity and credit taps to prop up the economy—pressures that had to be, and were, resisted and reasoned against.

In the end, even as some compromises were reluctantly struck, the ambition and institutional anchoring of our early steps in 2017 to restore financial stability helped save the day. There was no doubt a marked attrition in outcomes relative to our original objectives, but a complete degeneration into excessive monetary and credit stimulus that had caused the Indian financial sector to lose its stability in just the previous decade had been rendered difficult. Nevertheless, attempts to alter the governance structure of the RBI to institutionalize such outcomes in future would have meant crossing the Rubicon and had to be foiled. As a result, the RBI lost its governor on the altar of financial stability.

- On the second issue of developing and unleashing the allocative power of financial markets, we were more successful in the sense that a series of reforms, all the way until the end of my term and thankfully beyond, have made the regulation of fixed-income and currency markets (cash markets and, especially, the derivatives segments) more principle based. This builds on the continuous efforts since the 1990s to develop these markets and will allow over time for freer entry of financial products, market participants and foreign capital.

My one lament here is that the play in the Indian government bond markets—and the media and analyst chorus that goes with it—is gradually evolving into bets on the extent of the central bank's market interventions, creating a vicious trap of meeting ever-rising expectations that the RBI hasn't been unshackled from and a crutch that bond markets haven't learned to walk without. The result is that the RBI's liquidity management policy affects in a significant measure, and is affected by, prices in the government bond market and, in turn, the cost of financing government borrowing.

These two points—the regression of efforts on the financial stability front and the continuing presence of the RBI in setting government bond prices—are interlinked and provide a natural segue into the main point I wish to make in these introductory remarks.[1]

---

[1] I also had the privilege of contributing to other areas and teams at the RBI: Consolidating and strengthening research and data-based analytics, especially, but not exclusively, for the flexible inflation-targeting monetary policy framework; providing a conceptual framework for operationalizing currency market interventions and macroprudential capital flow measures; deepening the financial stability analysis with a greater use of market data; and making the human resource management incentive-, specialization- and performance based around a medium-term strategy for the central bank as a whole. Some of these areas are touched upon in the speeches in the book. I hope others will be taken by the RBI staff to their natural completion in due course.

Let me start by raising some questions that kept me up at nights during my term:

- Why are efforts at restoring financial stability seen as contradictory to pursuing growth even though all evidence points to financial stability being a necessary condition for long-term growth?
- Why does the central bank, when it seeks to implement financial stability reforms fully and sustainably, always face an uphill battle with the entire system?
- Is there a common undercurrent of resistance which makes it hard to achieve consensus on long-term structural reforms to the financial sector even if they make much economic sense?
- Does the pursuit of growth in India focus mostly on credit-based stimulus in the short run and is this what causes efforts to restore financial stability to routinely stall?
- What prevents the central bank from letting it go as far as price-setting in government bond markets is concerned?

I explain below that although there may be specific triggers for each example and setting that can explain the resistance to a particular financial stability reform, the uniform answer to all these questions lies in *fiscal dominance*, which I will position as *a theory of everything in India*.

Fiscal Dominance in India

In economics, 'fiscal dominance' is traditionally defined as a state of the country in which large government debt and deficit (spending over and above revenues) prevent the monetary policy authority such as a central bank from meeting its mandated economic targets such as inflation, growth and employment. Instead, the central bank is kept primarily focused on ensuring that the government can roll over its debt and deficit and, in particular, that the government does not default on its liabilities. For instance, the central bank becomes willing to accept excessively low levels of interest rate and high levels of monetization by participating in primary and/or secondary market for government debt—put simply, printing a lot of money and handing it out cheap—even if inflation is, or risks being pushed, beyond reasonable thresholds; the central bank does so as it is focused not on inflation but on aiding the government's borrowing programmes.

Such a state is by and large considered undesirable for the country as large-sized government debt and deficit tend to be driven by short-term populist pressures, whereas the central bank is mandated to achieve long-term stable objectives for the economy and the financial sector. Fiscal dominance of the central bank can thus be adverse on at least two counts: first, it prevents the central bank and thereby the economy from achieving its long-run stability goals; and second, instead of the central bank being an independent regulatory institution that can serve a useful 'checks and balances' role for the government's excessive borrowing and spending programmes, the latter are facilitated even more as the monetary policy decisions get fiscally dominated.

Although this traditional notion of fiscal dominance is centred around *monetary policy*, I will generalize its application to potentially *all* financial sector policies and regulations. It has been my experience that fiscal dominance can induce the central bank (and even other regulators such as the securities exchange board) into adopting a range of suboptimal regulations for the financial sector that compromise stability and macroprudential considerations.

At the outset, it should be clear that India is a likely candidate for the prevalence of fiscal dominance. However, to ensure we are on the same page, I will make the case, explaining along the way its relevance for external sector stability.

1. The Indian government's fiscal deficit has always been rather large, at the time of writing among the top two in the G20 nations, and by some consolidated measures, the highest. Much of the spending is incurred due to revenue expenditures (e.g., subsidies) and only a tiny share is attributable to capital expenditures (e.g., infrastructure development). The deficit composition is thus titled towards short-term economic support rather than towards expanding the economy's pie in the long term; therefore, the size of the fiscal deficit has

the potential to accelerate swiftly while serving short-sighted objectives of the government when political compulsions arise. The deficit also depends heavily on tax revenues, thereby on economic growth and notably on oil excise taxes. The latter become harder for the government to pass onto consumers when oil prices rise, a significant vulnerability in the fiscal deficit of the Indian government.[2]

2. In addition to the large fiscal deficit, India runs a current account deficit (imports exceed exports), which is also heavily dependent on the oil import bill. As a result, a part of India's consumption is regularly financed by the outside world. A coincident balance-of-payments outcome is the following. Among the three sectors of the economy—government, corporate and household—only the household sector in India is a saving net of consumption and investment. The net household savings have been steadily declining over the past several years, an important yet often ignored macroeconomic development. As a result, the dissaving by the Indian government—what it raises from others to meet its fiscal deficit—which has been rising, is now above the level of household savings.[3] Thus, the government is reliant at the margin on financing its deficit from the rest of the world. In turn, the corporate sector in India—which also dissaves— is also increasingly reliant on external financing.

3. These 'twin deficits'—fiscal deficit and current account deficit—make India vulnerable to a 'sudden stop' in which a deterioration in the quality of government or corporate balance sheets, rising inflation (either due to domestic stimulus or oil price shock), Federal Reserve rate hikes and dollar absorption or a surge in global risk aversion, can trigger a

---

[2] The problem had been recognized by successive governments and the FRBM Act of 2003. However, the inability to enforce compliance to the Act's fiscal deficit targets within the stipulated time frame reflects the strength of myopic preference of governments to spend relative to their long-term commitment to building fiscal credibility.

[3] Estimates of consolidated government borrowing—the so-called Public Sector Borrowing Requirement (PSBR)—are in the range of 9–10 per cent of GDP. Net household savings are estimated to be around 7 per cent of GDP.

withdrawal by foreign investors who have financed the external funding of the government and the corporate sector. The resulting fallout in the form of a sharply depreciating Indian rupee, a rise in oil import bill and inflation, further widening of the twin deficits, and the 'death spiral' or loss of investor confidence that ensues present a substantial risk to India's financial stability. Such risk has materialized unexpectedly at least once a decade over the past 30 years with several minor hiccups in between. History tells us that we ignore this risk at our own peril.

4. One way that the government can try to address problems of large debt and deficit is not to undertake the tough structural adjustments in their level and composition, but instead do what is more expedient, which is to economically and financially repress the economy to fund its borrowings. The reason that such fiscal dominance has the potential to affect virtually *all* financial sector policies and regulations in India is that there are other important conflating factors. What is key to understanding in the present Indian context is that there are strong remnants even today of the pre-1990 era of centralized economic structure and control, including over-regulatory institutions like the central bank. The implications are as follows:

   - On the one hand, the overarching presence of public sector banks, other large state-owned financial institutions (e.g., the Life Insurance Corporation of India) and state-owned enterprises creates the incentive that the government dominates the central bank and its financial sector policies to affect outcomes for the entities it owns and for its borrowing programmes. This skews the market terms against the private sector and distracts the central bank from its long-term policy goals.

   - On the other hand, recognition that the government has incentives to influence policies as such and that it is not at arm's length from the regulators drives the private sector into hyperactive lobbying (read an overdose of 'consultations' with the government and regulators); this, in turn, induces an overall culture in the system of putting in place business-friendly policies that are pro-incumbents, at the cost of market-friendly policies that encourage creative destruction, asset reallocation, ease of doing business and new entry.

Of course, fiscal dominance in India is neither new nor unique to the period I served at the RBI.

Prior to the 2000s, the RBI used to participate in 'automatic monetization' of the Indian government's deficits as it purchased directly the ad hoc treasury bills (T-bills). This form of fiscal dominance of the central bank's monetary policy was institutionally ruled out by the FRBM Act of 2003 that prevented the central bank from participating in the primary market for government securities.

Similarly, the RBI had in the 1990s imposed statutory liquidity ratio (SLR) requirement on banks of levels as high as 40 per cent and the cash reserve ratio requirements as high as 25 per cent, effectively making the government the preferred, if not the only, borrower of bank credit in the economy. Significant progress has been made in minimizing such repression of the economy by substantially lowering these requirements since the 2000s.

These progressive steps limiting fiscal dominance were undertaken in an economic environment of consolidating government debt and fiscal deficit trajectories, high economic growth, and rise in household financial savings. However, fiscal dominance has once again taken hold of the Indian economy as these conducive factors have gradually reversed. The most striking example is that a recent amendment of the RBI Act allows the central bank to re-enter the primary market for government debt under certain conditions, annulling the reform of 2003 and recreating investor expectations of deficit monetization.

As I share my experience of fiscal dominance, I stress that its ramifications do reflect a legacy of the past, but importantly convey its potential to compromise financial stability in future.

In What Ways Does Fiscal Dominance Affect India's Financial Stability?

I will lay out several channels through which I observed fiscal dominance affecting India's financial stability. The list is by no means exhaustive and not all channels may be active at all times.

1. *Bank recapitalization and regulation.* Since the timely recognition of losses leads to an additional capital requirement for public sector banks which is typically met out of the government budget, the central bank finds itself pulled into regular negotiations with the government regarding regulatory forbearance.[4] Such forbearance takes the form of relaxed standards for loan-loss recognition, protracted schedules for provisioning against realized losses, postponement in switching to modern accounting standards that recognize losses in anticipation rather than only after defaults have materialized, etc.[5] In the case of some asset classes such as loans to micro, small- and medium-sized enterprises, the forbearance is not just a temporary reprieve of a few months, which could be justified if the underlying issues were cyclical, but is also a steadily evolving near-permanent feature of bank regulation, preventing the recognition that underlying stress of this asset class is, in fact, structural in nature.

   Given the repeating regulatory forbearances, most public sector banks remain short of true economic capital adequacy, even as their regulatory capital keeps being 'managed' to look just about right. Rating agencies view such forbearances as 'credit negative' for banks, highlighting that forbearances do not serve the purpose of ensuring financial stability. Even worse, the compromised standards also apply to private sector banks, thereby weakening their prudential regulation in the process and resulting in a race to the bottom. Overall, this is a

---

[4] It needs to be acknowledged here that the government practice of recapitalizing banks with 'recapitalization bonds' rather than outright capital injection implies that as per extant fiscal accounting norms, only the interest expense on these bonds adds to the immediate fiscal deficit. However, regardless of the fiscal norms, there is an increase in the government's debt as a result of the recapitalization. More subtly, if banks are to create credit upon recapitalization, they would need to generate liquidity against some of their other government bond holdings by selling them in secondary markets, a move that is akin to the government directly raising the liquidity by issuing new bonds and transferring it as capital injection to public sector banks.

[5] There may also be other political considerations in government preference for regulatory forbearance such as favouring incumbent defaulted borrowers, who by virtue of not being classified as non-performing, enjoy continued asset control and 'extend and pretend' loans from banks.

rather unfortunate compromise of accounting integrity and capital adequacy of banking balance sheets, a form of window dressing to keep government's fiscal deficit available for alternate expenditures.

2. *Default disclosure norms.* It would seem that the government's fiscal deficit should not have much to do with the disclosure of defaults by companies to their investors. Yet, in India it does! Most stock exchanges of the world or the securities regulations that govern them require that any materially relevant information must be disclosed by a firm with immediacy to investors who purchase the firm's publicly-traded securities such as shares or bonds. From an investor's standpoint, a firm's default on a bank loan, in fact default on a promise to any counterparty, would constitute one of the most important materially relevant pieces of information. Its timely disclosure would improve market discipline, aid efficient allocation of capital in favour of better performing firms, protect minority investors from being front-run by those privy to information about defaults, and help rating agencies provide more accurate credit assessments (or at the least, reduce their scope for engaging in rating inflation).

In spite of a clear recommendation by an independent committee and earnest efforts of the securities market regulator, India avoided providing timely default information to markets. The rationale is rather convoluted. If defaults are disclosed, then rating agencies would correct the ratings of defaulted entities. Downward rating migrations would increase the capital that banks have to put up against such borrowers as they would need to be recognized as being truly of worse credit quality. This would increase the capital requirement of public sector banks and thus the required budgetary allocation from the government. To rule out the latter, default disclosure to market investors was not required in spite of the regulatory push for the same.

This is an extraordinary chain of calculations whereby the disclosure policy of stock exchanges around firm defaults was determined by fiscal dominance. The lack of timely default disclosure implies that even some of India's top-rated firms do not always make payments when due to their lending banks; similarly, many state-owned enterprises which are publicly listed and borrow in bond markets default regularly on required payments to their counterparties and yet are rated higher than safer private firms.

It should not then come as a surprise that the aggregate loan-loss ratio of credit intermediaries in India has been one of the highest in the world and loan recovery one of the lowest. Fiscal dominance of disclosure norms ensured that relevant parts of the financial system simply did not possess the knowledge as to when the process of accelerating and collecting payments from a borrower should start. It is of some relief that the securities regulator has pushed through the requirement of immediate (within 24 hours) disclosure by a listed borrower, failing to repay securities such as bonds; in the case of loans from banks or other financial institutions, disclosure is required for delays in payment of more than 30 days. Although this bodes well all around for the efficiency of the credit ecosystem in India, a single-day (rather than only 30-day) default disclosure norm—in line with global standards—would be the natural next step for loan repayments.

3. *Monetary policy.* A convenient way to recapitalize public sector banks is by showering them with treasury gains which arise on banking books when interest rates are cut or expectations of future rate cuts bring down the yield curve and cause bond prices to rally. Given the desire to keep the budgetary allocation for public sector banks' capital needs low, there is implicit asymmetric pressure on the monetary policy authority's interest rate decisions: rate cuts are preferred and inflation forecasting errors on the downside are okay (even welcome!), whereas rate hikes are particularly disliked along with inflation forecasting errors on the upside. Such asymmetric pressure can potentially induce deviations in the monetary policy authority's objective and prevent it from attaining its mandated target of stable inflation. Of course, there is nothing wrong with rate cuts leading to treasury gains on bank books; that this channel creates asymmetric pressure on the monetary authority to cut rates is what is rooted in fiscal dominance.

A corollary to the fiscal dominance of interest-rate policy is the asymmetric use of liquidity tools by the central bank. Liquidity injections that transfer a stock of government bonds to the central bank balance sheet are seen more favourably than liquidity absorptions in which the central bank supplies government bonds to the market. When undertaken in large quantities, liquidity injections improve bond prices and transfer treasury gains to banks, helping recapitalize public sector banks while simultaneously lowering the cost of rolling over government debt. This creates an incentive to get the liquidity policy to be fiscally dominated rather than keeping it unconstrained to achieve the objective of ensuring that short-term money market rates tug closely the policy repo rate set by the monetary policy authority. In fact, once sufficiently fiscally dominated, the liquidity policy can control most of the government bond yield curve and prices, rendering the rate-setting process of monetary policy authority effectively irrelevant. For example, one arm of the central bank can keep the policy rate unchanged due to inflation concerns, whereas its other arm can act fiscally dominated in moving all other rates.

Similarly, fiscal dominance can imply that bank cash reserve requirement can become a tool to look to relax for backdoor heaping of profits onto banks for their recapitalization. As such, the primary purpose of this requirement is prudential and developmental in nature: first, cash is the most robust defence against liquidity needs; and second, a cash requirement facilitates arbitrage as well as price discovery in overnight interbank markets as banks are induced to actively manage their liquidity to meet the requirement.

4. *Market regulations.* In the eventuality that the monetary policy authority does manage to raise interest rates and if expectations of future rate hikes build up too (e.g., because inflation prints and measures of sustained 'core' inflation are incontrovertibly hardening), then banks make losses on their treasury positions, reversing the gains from rate cuts. Again, to reduce the budgetary allocation of capital to public sector banks, the mark-to-market accounting treatment of government bonds by the central bank is nudged for being set as

asymmetric: treasury gains are transferred for the most part as soon as bond prices rally; in striking contrast, treasury losses are allowed to be recognized over several quarters. The end result is another form of deep interference of fiscal deficit pressures on the accounting treatment of banking balance sheets. Indeed, the central bank is often working the hardest to ensure that public sector banks can show profits and adequate capital to markets at quarter ends (rather than the bankers and the owners of banks bending over backwards to manage the interest rate risk they willingly took on).

More perversely, government bond yields could be hardening also due to the risk of fiscal slippage. This too leads to losses on bank treasury positions. Therefore, regulatory forbearance in the form of asymmetric mark-to-market treatment of such losses weakens an important form of market discipline on fiscal slippage.

Furthermore, it can be difficult to generate interest in government bond auctions when investors face risks of rising deficits and borrowings by the government. In such a scenario, public sector banks and other government-owned entities in the financial sector can be, and are, required—through moral suasion—to buy up entire issue amounts in individual auctions at above-market prices. A natural financial regulation to respect the integrity of market auctions (prices and quantities) would impose concentration limits whereby no individual buyer can participate in an auction for greater than some threshold share. Such regulation, commonplace in treasury auctions around the world, is not in place in India as it would be heavily contested by the government, creating another channel through which fiscal dominance affects bond market regulations. I must add that RBI's continuing role as the debt manager for the Government of India only accentuates this channel.

5. *Capital flow measures.* As I explained earlier, government dissaving in India has in recent years exceeded the net savings of the rest of the economy and, hence, the government is increasingly reliant on external finance. By implication, capital management on the external sector front, which determines the extent of foreign debt flows that can enter the Indian

economy and limits the short-term nature of such flows, becomes a regular bone of contention between the central bank and the government. Although getting the central bank to monetize deficits and support bond markets remains the first line of fiscal dominance by the government, relaxing capital flow measures also represents an important line of such dominance.

As such, capital flow measures are macroprudential in nature, that is, aimed primarily at financial stability rather than at relaxing government's financing constraints. Hence, these measures must be calibrated as a long-run strategy that is fine-tuned in relation to the stock of foreign exchange reserves that the central bank has—and is likely to be able to maintain—on its balance sheet to defend the currency against sudden outflows. The calibration should also meet the 'stress test' at least as severe as the past experience of such outflows witnessed during sudden-stop episodes such as the global financial crisis during September–December 2008 and the 'taper tantrum' of May–August 2013.

In contrast, a short-term government focus on tiding over its next borrowing or budget hurdle can lead to preference for measures that make the external sector vulnerable. For instance, foreign-currency-denominated sovereign bonds can be tempting to issue when global interest rates are low but would exacerbate the death spiral during a suddenstop episode. Similarly, unless structural reforms are undertaken and fiscal consolidation credibly committed to, short-duration bonds may be the only feasible external source of funds during stress and therefore be preferred by the government, but such flows can promptly reverse should the stress worsen, aggravating the downward currency spiral.

If a central bank concedes to such myopic preferences arising out of government borrowing constraints, it ends up setting macroprudential capital flow measures that are fiscally dominated rather than aimed at ensuring external sector resilience.

6. *Central bank balance sheet.* Finally, given India's external sector vulnerabilities, it is paramount that the central bank balance sheet be perched on the highest hill (think of

Chhatrapati Shivaji Maharaj's choice for locating his fortresses): it should remain untouched and unperturbed in the midst of almost any macroeconomic storm. The RBI has undertaken in the past—and in future too may have to undertake—massive foreign currency operations. The RBI has also been a counterparty for providing insurance against currency risk while raising emergency external funds from otherwise unwilling financiers. For performing this critical function seamlessly, the central bank must be regarded as being a counterparty of the highest credit quality, the equivalent of an AAA+ rating and perhaps even better.[6] This necessitates that the central bank takes a long-term view of its balance sheet resilience and saves from its annual earnings on a regular basis for the rainy day.

However, such preservation of central bank 'capital' via transfer of its profits to future contingencies has seemed overly conservative to governments that have at times narrowly focused on filling up their bottomless pit of deficits year after year. There have also been successful demands in recent years for an 'interim dividend' from the central bank, bypassing other arrangements such as ways and means of advances which limit the extent of interim monetization of government deficits by the central bank. The result has been an erosion of central bank balance sheet strength and an increasing compromise of the severity of stress scenarios it can withstand in future. Such fiscal dominance of the central bank balance sheet could perhaps be justified if the credit rating of the sovereign is of the highest quality and government bond markets benefit from foreign investors' flight to safety when the global scenario turns adverse. Neither of these conditions is met by the Indian economy at

---

[6] Note that central banks are typically not rated by credit rating agencies. However, subjecting the central bank balance sheet to stress scenarios and examining its equity capital in such scenarios relative to its liabilities can provide a simulated likelihood of default, and, in turn, an effective credit rating, for the central bank. Counterparties often 'cap' their internal central bank rating to that of the sovereign; this practice only reinforces my point that central bank balance sheet must be managed independently from that of the government so that the effective central bank rating can pierce through the sovereign rating, which would be desirable in times of external sector stress.

present. As a result, the erosion of the central bank capital to pay dividends to the government is tantamount to a coercive monetization of fiscal deficits.[7]

Indeed, many observers see the erosion of the central bank balance sheet strength as only an extension of the fiscal dominance of state-owned enterprises, whose cash flows appear to be heavily tunnelled to meet government deficits and whose balance sheets are providing leverage-financed dividends via on-paper divestments of one state-owned unit to another. In the long run, it would be better if these state-owned enterprises deployed their cash flows to engage in capital expenditures, but this conflicts with the government's short-term objective of maintaining high fiscal deficit to finance its populist revenue expenditures.

Given such pervasive influence that fiscal dominance in India has on financial sector regulation and policies, it is a natural corollary that it poses significant risks to the country's long-term financial stability and growth.

Other Side Effects of Fiscal Dominance

Factors underlying fiscal dominance have several other pernicious side effects as follows:

- *Crowding out of the corporate sector*, not only of micro-, small- and medium-sized enterprises as banks stuff their balance sheets with government bonds rather than lend to these enterprises, but also of highly rated firms as investor appetite for safe bonds is more than met by government bonds, thereby widening the gap between bond yields of highly rated firms and the government. Such crowding out results in financial constraints and lower growth for the private sector.

---

[7] One exception to this is if the government uses the dividend to extinguish the central bank holdings of government bonds, whereby it reduces its future debt payments. This, however, has not been the manner in which the dividend from the central bank has been deployed by the government.

- *External sector fragility* of corporate sector financing and investments, as lack of domestic savings beyond government dissaving, induces corporates to borrow abroad in substantial amounts, exposing them to the risk of sudden-stop withdrawals by foreign bond 'tourists', in turn exposing the rest of the economy too to currency depreciations.

- *Financial fragility* of firms reliant on market financing, as over-supply of government paper at typically longer durations of borrowing induces the private sector to borrow at shorter tenors, leading to rollover risk. This can have adverse financial stability implications, especially if non-bank financial companies first increase reliance on short-term debt in search of lower yields to pay and then are unable to roll it over.

- *Poor transmission of monetary policy* to the real economy, given that the government and corporate bond market yield curve as well as bank deposit rates are determined under fiscal dominance, not just by inflationary expectations and central bank policy rate decisions, but also by (a) quantity constraints imposed by the large supply of government paper, and (b) administered interest rates on extra-budgetary resource mobilization by the government (e.g., above-market rates offered by the Indian government on its borrowings through National Small Savings Funds). A central bank attempting to improve the transmission of its policy rate decisions by altering the quantity constraints, for example, by buying up or lending long-term against government paper, is effectively fiscally dominated and only ends up subsidizing further fiscal slippage.

From Fiscal Dominance to Crises and Low Productivity Traps

Factors that make fiscal dominance a theory of everything in India imply that financial sector risk-absorption capacity and regulations that try to maintain it at a minimum prudential level are always stretched thin to meet the requirements of over-stretched government finances. They are like rubber bands being pulled so hard that they can snap unexpectedly!

These same factors drive the external sector towards fragility as the levels of government and corporate financing by foreign investors far exceed what would be necessary, absent the domestic savings being drained out by government borrowing.

With such vulnerabilities, accidents can occur swiftly. For instance, if an external sector shock in the form of a significant oil price rise coincides with the approaching of an election—when rise in government spending and increase in cash circulation create short-term stimulus and inflationary spike, then all hell can break loose for the macroeconomy.

My assessment is that such a scenario materialized in the Summer of 2018 and the months to follow, one that the RBI sought to navigate without compromising its focus on restoring the foundations of financial stability. The navigation required putting up stiff resistances against headwinds from fiscal dominance that could have derailed these foundations in the midst of a macroeconomic storm. Specifically, these headwinds aimed to (a) relax financial sector regulation as well as macroprudential capital flow measures and (b) erode the balance sheet strength of the central bank.

Midway through this storm, there emerged additional headwinds relating to defaults and rollover risks of some large non-bank and housing finance companies. This was a complex problem with multiple causes. Demonetization flooded banks with deposits as almost all money circulating as black had found its way into the formal system. Large recipients of these deposits were public sector banks whose undercapitalization meant that these deposits were hardly a boon; they were mostly a cost as banks lacked capital to expand their credit books. Bank deposit rates fell and savers searched for yield through liquid-debt mutual funds; these funds, in turn, sought a higher yield in the short-term commercial paper of non-bank and housing finance companies.

Some non-bank and housing finance companies—affected by demonetization, real-estate sector regulations and excess housing inventory in traditionally 'hot' markets—found issuing short-term paper a convenient way to keep rolling over their troubled assets at low costs; even some of the healthier ones switched funding dramatically to short-term commercial paper. The switch was partly driven by the rising cost of issuing long-term bonds that were competing with the increased supply of the government paper given the widening fiscal deficit of the government. External sector shock in the form of a significant surge in oil prices and the resulting withdrawal by foreign portfolio investors only amplified this switch to short-term paper.

Let me reiterate two points: first, the demand for high-yielding paper was linked to the inability of the undercapitalized banking sector to deploy the glut of post-demonetization deposits for creating credit; and second, this demand was met by the supply of the short-term paper of non-bank and housing finance companies so that they could avoid paying higher rates at longer maturities that were being crowded out by the government paper. In this sense, both the lack of financial stability in the banking sector and the fiscal dominance of the bond markets contributed to the build-up of the non-bank and housing companies' boom and bust cycle.

Early conversations with short sellers suggested that besides poor underwriting, there had been diversion of funds to shell companies during the boom. Consistent with the saying 'the shadow always touches the feet', ever-greening of poor loans by a part of India's shadow banking lay at the doorsteps of India's banking, notably of one private bank. RBI's internal analysis showed that the mutual fund investors had finally begun to separate between healthier and weaker non-bank and housing finance companies; rating agencies also followed suit. This was desirable in the sense that market discipline was for once at work in the financial sector in India. Furthermore, these companies had enjoyed several exemptions from banking regulations such as not having to maintain cash reserve requirements precisely with the expectation that their funding stress should be privately resolved by wholesale financiers. Although the RBI improved aggregate liquidity supply, it avoided being a 'lender of first resort' to the stressed companies while committing to be a 'lender of last resort' if necessary; it also focused on long-term structural adjustment to ensure that these companies held adequate high-quality liquid assets in relation to their short-term liabilities, akin to the liquidity coverage ratio for banks.

RBI's decision not to offer substantial regulatory forbearance and emergency funding to non-bank and housing finance companies had support from some parts of the government but not others. It is notable that, in this case, the decision did not have direct fiscal implications for the government unlike the decision to forbear on banks.[8]

The other pressures on the RBI, however, remained unabated and even intensified as the year 2018 progressed.

When pressures to alter banking regulation and external sector policies were applied on us as being in public interest, but we remained unconvinced about their desirability for the economy and the financial sector in the long run, we stood up for the independence of regulatory institutions, in general, and for the RBI's operational autonomy, in particular. We transparently informed the public of the underlying issues. We considered this the most measured option available to safeguard financial stability. I believe, as a result, the worst outcomes that could have transpired in the short run were avoided; the macroeconomic storm eventually passed due to the easing of oil prices; however, the government debt and deficit situation has significantly worsened since and financial sector policies continue to remain at the risk of being fiscally dominated.

Even outside such episodes, fiscally dominated economies feature poor efficiency of capital allocation by the undercapitalized financial sector and favouring of incumbents over new entrants. In my view, these channels have slowed down India's transition from a rent-seeking economy to a value-creating one and translated into an overall loss of productivity and growth. If fiscal dominance remains unchecked in the wake of slowing growth, the outcome can, in fact, end up being a low-productivity trap for the economy.

---

[8] It is my view that after the initial stress had calmed down, a comprehensive asset quality review of non-bank and housing finance companies would have helped various regulators ensure that (a) the better-quality companies enjoyed reasonable funding costs; (b) the worst ones were resolved (in absence of the Financial Resolution and Deposit Insurance Bill, with a suitable amendment to the Insolvency and Bankruptcy Code which has since been made); and (c) the ones in between could have been required to recapitalize or be subjected to a PCA along the lines of the banking sector. Such an asset quality review has not been undertaken for public disclosure of the results; instead, the period of regulatory forbearance to the financial sector for delayed recognition of stressed assets in the housing sector has been further extended.

How Can We Protect the Economy from Fiscal Dominance and Attendant Side Effects?

It goes without saying that ideally, fiscal dominance must be addressed at its roots. Therefore, the heavy lifting for protecting the economy from fiscal dominance must come from those individuals within the government who value the quality of long-term outcomes for the economy. Such individuals, for example, bureaucrats with careers spanning government terms and economic advisors who are typically technocrats, can strive for:

- A fiscal consolidation path to reasonable targets with prudent undertaking and management of spending programmes.
- Reorientation of expenditure towards items that have economically meaningful long-term multiplier effects such as education and infrastructure.
- Objective monitoring of consolidated debt and deficit numbers by helping set up an independent, ideally bi-partisan, fiscal council (as already recommended by the FRBM Review Committee of 2016).
- Improved disclosure standards for government expenditure and deficit that preclude the obfuscation of numbers by accounting *jugaad* (tricks), such as moving expenditures from before to immediately after the accounting date and from 'above the line' (on-balance sheet) to 'below the line' (off-balance sheet or extra-budgetary); such improvement would pave the way for a focus away from accounting sleight of hand towards fiscal management and disinvestments in a true economic sense.

The emergence of bureaucrats and technocrats in the government who take and stick to the far-sighted view rather than seek to dominate financial sector policies is the need of the hour.

Given my experience at the RBI, I will highlight in greater detail the steps that a central bank can undertake to limit being fiscally dominated.

1. *Firm commitment to long-term financial stability.* First and foremost, the central bank must take the overall stance that financial stability must be persevered for in its every

decision and even in the face of imminent government pressures. The central bank objectives are inherently long term in nature:

- As a banking regulator, the central bank is in charge of preserving the value of deposits from bank insolvency.
- As a monetary authority, the central bank is in charge of ensuring that inflation does not erode economy's savings, facilitating the financial inclusion of households over their holding primarily real assets such as gold and housing.
- As the economy's primary defence against external sector stress, the central bank is also in charge of managing the currency's excessive volatility and limiting imported inflation.

These objectives can and must be interpreted to have a truly long-term dimension. In turn, such interpretation must be used over and over to resist and defend pressures to compromise financial stability for short-term benefits of the government and other influential constituencies. Unfortunately, there are no shortcuts to grow well sustainably. Restoring and maintaining financial stability must come first for the central bank.

2. *Independence and autonomy over regulatory decisions.* The central bank must be granted true independence in the letter of the law (de jure), and by implication, effective autonomy over its operations and regulatory decisions. Where the law itself renders the central bank independence weak, the central bank has a handicap to start with and is effectively (de facto) always under duress from the government.

- To this end, appointments of top management and others governing the central bank must be undertaken in a timely manner and subject to an accountable process that limits the scope for opportunistic placements.
- Top management appointments must be for a term length that is at least as long as that of the government, ideally spanning government terms, and subject to termination only with cause and after a due process.

- Regulation should be ownership-neutral in that the central bank must be allowed by law to exercise the same powers over all regulated entities, whether they are state-owned or private.

  Given the substantial presence of public sector banks and government-owned entities in the financial sector, ownership-neutrality of regulation is an essential structural reform to move India towards establishing and maintaining financial stability on a durable basis.

3. *Adoption of policy rules over discretion.* The central bank should 'tie itself to the mast' by adopting rule-based policy-making, that is, deploying specific tools for specific well-articulated objectives, so as to avoid the temptation to respond to the 'calls of sirens'. Without such discipline, there can be a mission creep into objectives, loss of focus in strategy to meet the objectives and sidelining of long-term stability goals. In particular,

   - Basel capital and liquidity norms should be upheld in their true and full spirit, rather than softened through regular forbearances for the financial sector; forbearances must be exceptional and subject to a 'sunset clause' of no longer than six months and not become permanent dilutions of the norms.
   - Prompt Corrective Action (PCA) framework for banks must be adhered to, and even strengthened, in terms of ownership-neutral actions over all regulated entities, including public sector banks and other government-owned finance companies.
   - Default disclosure with immediacy for even one-day delay in meeting loan repayments needs to be mandated not only for publicly listed firms but also to a Public Credit Registry for all borrowers (public or private, in a phased manner by size). This would improve creditor discipline and quality of lending allocations.
   - Asset quality reviews and macroprudential stress tests need to be conducted on an annual basis for the entire financial sector (banks as well as non-banking financial companies), preparing for their eventual role as the

standard for capital requirements. It is not good enough that the financial sector survives stress; it must continue to function and intermediate well, for which it must maintain extra capital buffers in good times. Specialized supervisory cadre at the central bank could just be the medicine that doctors prescribe for such treatment.

- Flexible inflation targeting framework adopted in 2016 has been recognized by rating agencies and multilateral institutions as a critical structural reform of the Indian financial sector. It is meant to build inflation credibility with external investors and to dampen the impact of sudden stops which risk external sector stability. It is a folly, therefore, to think that the framework does not factor in financial stability. The framework needs to be persisted with so that inflation and inflation expectations are more durably anchored; savers can't be short-changed in favour of borrowers by switching the target index from consumer price inflation to wholesale price inflation, the moment rate cuts can no longer be justified.

- Cash reserve ratio requirement for banks must be maintained for prudential purposes rather than be tinkered with as a way of undertaking sectoral credit allocation, the latter being a feature of the pre-1990s centralized economy that the RBI has long moved away from. The cash reserve ratio requirement in India is already at its historical low level; hence, the Chinese model of using it as a sectoral credit allocation tool is best not emulated in India, especially given the Chinese requirement is 4–5 times higher than that in India.

- Macroprudential capital management needs to be kept on a well-telegraphed path, calibrated in relation to the central bank's stock of foreign exchange reserves that is likely to survive external sector stress. The long-standing wisdom at the RBI, articulated by its top management in the 1990s and 2000s, of allowing foreign capital in a pecking order—from direct equity investment (the most preferred) to foreign-currency sovereign bond (the least preferred)—is well founded given the fragility of various kinds of flows and financing instruments under a sudden-stop scenario.[9]

- Central bank balance sheet strength must be maintained at pristine quality at all times by adopting the minimum standard of an effective AAA+ rating as the basis for any distribution to the government. A complete distribution of central bank profits to the government must be eschewed as under fiscal dominance, this sets a precedent which catalyzes the setting up of committees to rewrite existing rules as soon as the distribution is partial and requires some provisioning of profits by the central bank for the rainy day.

4. *Leaning against the wind and playing the game of chicken.* Under extreme fiscal dominance, whichever point of accommodation the central bank agrees to today becomes the starting point for further compromise tomorrow. Hence,

- The central bank must recognize this possibility in its policymaking by maintaining even higher standards of financial stability. This requires 'leaning against the wind' in good times, for instance, by building buffers into the level of real interest rates, financial sector's capital and liquidity, and its own balance sheet strength. Emerging risks at vulnerable banks and financial firms also need to be proactively managed rather than at the edge of the precipice.

- The central bank must also defer pressures born out of government myopia by 'playing the game of chicken'.[10]

---

[9] The complete pecking order can be stated as: (a) direct equity investment (the most preferred), (b) portfolio equity flows, (c) portfolio flows in domestic-currency long-term corporate and government bonds, (d) long-term external commercial borrowings of corporates which are foreign-currency denominated, (e) portfolio flows in domestic-currency short-term corporate and government bonds, (f) short-term external commercial borrowings, and, finally, (vii) foreign-currency sovereign bond (the least preferred).

[10] In a strategic (game-theoretic) sense, fiscal dominance implies that the government moves first, making a take-it-or-leave-it offer to the regulators, essentially tying them down to its preferred sequential choices. In reality, the outcomes are better described as an alternating bargaining game between the government and the regulators.

The more readily the central bank is willing to compromise, the weaker is its bargaining and persuasive power with the government. The central bank must therefore learn to draw a line sometimes and say 'No'. Such obduracy can help shift the government focus to more serious ways of dealing with its debt and deficit problems, such as expenditure prioritization, disinvestments and fixing governance at public sector banks.[11]

5. *Democratic accountability*. The central bank's adherence to rules must be demonstrated to the public at large to the extent possible and at least with some reasonable lag. Although the preparation and dissemination of statutory reports go a long way in achieving this, even extraordinary measures—rather than just being a fiat privilege of the top management—must be supported with well-articulated reports on their desired outcomes and possible unintended consequences. This way, the case for sunset clauses on extraordinary measures can be laid out upfront and escalating expectations for their extension be managed in advance.

Such accountability requirement in itself would limit the scope of fiscal dominance over central bank policies: explicitly spelling out the underlying rationales for compromises would be difficult in many cases and simply hiding the truth under the rug would risk public embarrassment and possibly even opprobrium. Overall, transparency of actions and intent as well as an open acknowledgment of the limitations of the central bank and its tools in addressing issues beyond its scope and remit can lead to a more professional way of dealing with outside pressures instead of the present policy of striking backdoor, and therefore, opaque compromises. I stress that the central bank must do this in

---

[11] Such obduracy was one of the many hallmarks of the late Federal Reserve Governor Paul Volcker (1927–2019), in arresting double-digit inflation in the United States, and once arrested, in keeping inflation at bay by refusing to compromise monetary policy for cheaper funding of President Ronald Reagan's expansionary manifesto. In the end, Paul Volcker's stance prevented the United States government from undertaking massive tax cuts and incurring significant fiscal slippage, and thereby stabilized the government's long-term bond yields.

public interest to remain democratically accountable and, by so doing, reduce the risk of its fiscal dominance along the way.

6. *Providing and encouraging reason and voice.* The central bank has a unique position from where it can provide both a 35,000 feet view of the macroeconomy and a microscopic documentary on whether and how the plumbing of the financial sector is functioning or impaired. Indeed, it usually relies on extensive research and data to inform its policy-making. Such research should be freely and widely publicized, explaining on the one hand the reasons for adopting specific policies and, on the other, encouraging its downstream researchers to conduct incisive analysis and unearth new facts that can provide early warning signals of instability. The quality of such research inquiries can reach the highest standards only when it is subject to careful scrutiny of outside experts and is required to clear a minimum hurdle for public dissemination.

Last but not least, the central bank must use its voice and speak truth to the power by putting public interest before its personnel's career growth and promotions. Most take the factors driving fiscal dominance—a large-sized government debt and deficit—as given and operate without attempting to influence them; however, the central bank can and should use its role as the economy's institutional safeguard of financial stability to highlight the risks that fiscal dominance entails.

Dissent and diversity of thinking, while seemingly confrontational, help lift the quality of debate and discussion for a better aggregation of views and eventually superior decision-making. Conversely, discouraging dissent and diversity risks errors from system-wide group-think and cognitive capture; the central bank becomes a flock of birds with a feather; and, public discussion gravitates towards its predictable choices, as after all, most analysts, commentators and media get rewarded if they correctly forecast what the central bank will do rather than agonize painstakingly over what the central bank should do!

Let me conclude.

The Right Stance: Financial Stability Comes First

The long, punctuated history of financial crises and growth slow-downs across the world illustrates beyond reasonable doubt that lack of financial stability impairs long-term growth and external sector resilience of economies. It has also been documented that the lack of financial stability is, by and large, not a matter of misfortune; it ends up being engineered as the long-term side-effect of short-term policies such as providing sustained debt-fuelled stimulus to the economy, repeatedly monetizing in one guise or the other fiscal deficits of an extravagant sovereign and perennially hiding the true losses on financial sector balance sheets.

Given the vantage point of having been exposed to this economic history, I started at the RBI with a clear conviction: as the non-performing loans to assets ratio of the banking sector was close to double digits and at the top of the G20 countries, India needed to focus first on restoring financial stability, thereby positioning itself in a sound structural position for sustainable economic growth. The former Federal Reserve Governor, Janet Yellen, famously noted in January 2009, while pressing for comprehensive reforms in the aftermath of the global financial crisis: 'A clear lesson of history is that a "sine qua non" for sustained economic recovery following a financial crisis is a thoroughgoing repair of the financial system.' There is an important message therein for India. The historical strategy of levering up yet another asset class to grow when prior leverage boom has gone bust and its mess not yet cleaned up has repeatedly failed; this strategy has derailed the Indian economy's long-term growth plans; unsurprisingly, there is no asset class left to lever up and structural reforms are now critical. Unfortunately, pandemic stress in the form of COVID-19 outbreak has struck just as financial instability clouds over parts of India's financial sector have gathered again. It should be clear that to restore financial stability comprehensively, we can no longer keep kicking the can down the road. The right time to save for the rainy day is right now.

Let me provide an analogy from cricket to explain how a central bank can guard against such risks to financial stability. A central bank can take the same stance as that of Rahul Dravid—first and foremost, protect the wicket, know where the off-stump is, leave the tempting balls outside the wicket, wait for the rank-bad ball to hit a cover drive or a pull rather than swing for fences on the first ball, especially on tricky wickets or in difficult weather conditions, and overall play the game of endurance, not of excitement—try to win the test match, not just a T20!

It was my constant endeavour during the term as a deputy governor of the RBI to take and persist with a similar stance— supporting growth without ever compromising financial stability—to the best of my ability and against all odds, whether I was receiving adulation for it as during the early phase of my term or was in the line of fire as towards the end of my term.

I hope to have convinced you that this stance I took with some others at the RBI was the right one, especially in the face of rising fiscal dominance of financial sector policies.

It is moot point whether fiscal dominance in India at present is more or less than in the past.

When India was a less open economy and the private sector was smaller than it is today, the central bank could uphold financial stability even in the face of fiscal dominance by engaging in high levels of financial repression—effectively directing savings from the financial sector to fund fiscal deficits. This is simply not an option any more to build a fast-growing economy.

Monetization of fiscal deficits by the central bank participating directly in the primary market for government debt or indirectly in the secondary market through its liquidity management operations would mean regressing to errors of the 1970s and the 1980s. Adopting this approach is also deeply flawed as it risks run-away inflation and external sector stress.

Hence, a system-wide correction is what is called for, both in terms of fiscal restraint by the government and resistance of fiscal dominance by the central bank. The constant refrain that given the lack of fiscal space, the central bank must accommodate that growth is a slippery slope.

If our quest for restoring financial stability leads to a more open and objective public discussion—by the government, the central bank, other financial sector regulators, corporates, investors, analysts and media—of fiscal dominance and ways in which we can pre- commit to avoiding its perilous consequences, then I would consider the quest to have been even more worthwhile:

WHERE the mind is without fear and the head is held high;
Where knowledge is free;
Where the world has not been broken up into fragments
by narrow domestic walls;
Where words come out from the depth of truth;
Where tireless striving stretches its arms towards perfection;
Where the clear stream of reason has not lost its way into
the dreary desert sand of dead habit;
Where the mind is led forward by thee into ever-widening
thought and action—
Into that heaven of freedom, my Father, let my country awake.

—Rabindranath Tagore (*Chitto Jetha Bhayshunyo*, 1910)

PART 1

Resolving Non-Performing Assets (NPAs) and Recapitalizing Banks

CHAPTER 1

SOME WAYS TO DECISIVELY RESOLVE BANK STRESSED ASSETS*

Technology, 'Fintech' as you say, is taking banking and intermediation into unchartered territories. I have yet to fathom the full import of these sweeping changes. In the meantime, my subject matter today will be more prosaic and somewhat sobering. I reflect with a certain sense of urgency the need and possible ways to decisively resolve Indian banks' stressed assets.

Since the Reserve Bank of India (RBI) initiated the asset quality review of banks in the second half of 2015, it appears that possibly up to a sixth of public sector banks' (PSBs) gross advances are stressed (non-performing, restructured or written off), and a significant majority of these are, in fact, non-performing assets (NPAs). For banks in the worst shape, the share of assets under stress has approached or exceeded 20 per cent. This estimate of stressed assets has doubled from 2013 in terms of what had been recognized by banks. The doubling of stressed assets is the case also for private sector banks (PvtSBs), but their ratio of stressed assets to gross advances is far lower and their capitalization levels far greater. There have been several hints—in the declining price-to-book ratios of bank equity, as

---

* Speech delivered at the Indian Banks' Association Banking Technology Conference, Hotel Trident, Nariman Point, Mumbai, on 21 February 2017; also see Das et al. (2017).

Thanks to the organizers of the Indian Banks' Association for inviting me. To all the Award winners, congratulations on your stellar achievements and the innovative spirit you have shown to be today's worthy recipients. I am grateful to my colleagues and teams at the Reserve Bank of India for many stimulating discussions and insights, to many banking-sector stalwarts of today and the past and to several practitioners and policymakers in sectors and institutions related to the resolution of bank stressed assets. All errors remain my own.

I had observed in an op-ed page of the *Mint* in September 2013 and in the incisive research reports of banking sector analysts—that many assets 'parked' by banks under the Corporate Debt Restructuring cell were severely stressed. These assets were deserving of advance capital provisioning against future recognition as NPAs.

The asset quality review has taken a massive stride forward in bringing the scale of this problem out in the open and stirring a public debate over it. However, relatively little has been achieved in resolving the underlying assets to which banks had lent. Several resolution mechanisms and frameworks have been offered by the RBI to banks to get this going, but the progress has been painfully slow. Most of the assets remain laden with such high levels of bank debt that their interest coverage ratio is lower than one; they have little or no capacity to raise funds for working capital and capital expenditures or to attract private investors to turn them around. Original promoters—who rarely put in any financing and primarily provide sweat equity—have had somewhat of a field day, facing limited dilution, if any, of their initial stakes without much of a threat of outright replacement.

There is a connection between these two outcomes—the lack of a comprehensive recognition of stressed assets by banks and the absence of any resolution. Both stem from the structure of incentives at our banks and the fact that stressed assets have been an outcome of excessive bank lending, en masse, in a relatively short period from 2009 to 2012, and to a concentrated set of large firms in a number of sectors such as infrastructure, power, telecom, metals (iron and steel, in particular), engineering-procurement-construction (EPC) and textiles.

Let me first discuss the bank incentives. Only a bank that fears losing its deposit base or incurring the wrath of its shareholders is likely to recognize losses in a timely manner. In many of our banks, such market discipline is simply not present at the moment. In others, even if some such discipline is at work, banker horizon is excessively short until the end of the CEO's term. Banks lobby for regulatory forbearance; perhaps some loan prospects have turned sour due to bad luck, but beyond a point, concessions in recognizing losses just ends up being a strategy of kicking the can down the road and leaving them as legacy assets for the next management team to deal with.

The sectoral concentration of losses substantially amplifies this problem. Given the scale of assets that needs restructuring, it is natural that the turnaround capital at asset-restructuring companies (ARCs) has been limited in comparison. Some capital is simply sitting on the fence until serious asset restructuring picks up speed. In the meantime, any assets put up for sale can raise financing only at steep discounts, implying significant haircuts for bank debt. The loss of capital that would result in bank books and the fear of vigilance actions that such haircuts might trigger have made it almost impossible to get banks to embrace restructuring.

Effectively, there is no right price at which the market for stressed assets clears if left alone to private forces. Even with an orderly resolution mechanism such as the Insolvency and Bankruptcy Code (IBC) in place, why would banks rush to file cases? In the unlikely scenario that assets are in fact being sold by banks to investors at steep discounts, ARCs may just asset-strip rather than do the economic turnaround. After all, these investors have waited far too long and now wish to generate quick returns to meet the expectations of their own investors.

All this is playing out to near perfection in our setting. Its consequences are pernicious.

At one end, PSBs are running balance sheets that seem to be in a perennial need of recapitalization from its principal owner, that is, the government, and shying away from lending to potentially healthier industrial credits. Bank credit growth has been steadily declining at the stressed banks. Some PvtSBs face such headwinds too.

At the other end, sectors with the most stressed assets have excess capacity relative to current or near-term utilization and no sight of immediate pickup in economic prospects. Promoters have continued to operate, staying afloat with rollovers from banks which only increase indebtedness, partly disengaged, partly disgorging cash from the few assets that are running.

The end result has been a silent atrophy of the true potential of these assets.

This situation should be a cause for concern to all of us. It is reminiscent of weak banks and stagnating growth witnessed by Japan in the 1990s, with repercussions to date, and by Italy since 2010. Japan has experienced, and Italy is in my opinion experiencing, a lost decade.

I believe we are at crossroads and have an important choice to make.

We can choose status quo, but this would be insanity, 'doing the same thing over and over again and expecting different results,' as Albert Einstein put it. It would risk a Japanese- or an Italian-style outcome.

Or we can choose to call a spade a spade as Scandinavia did to resolve its banking problems in the early 1990s and the United States did from October 2008 to June 2009, even if only after letting a significant bank fail. Ireland and Spain, where the recoveries since the global financial crisis have not been as salubrious as in the United States, have nevertheless fared better than Italy; they too first adopted measures to pretend and extend troubled bank assets, but eventually recognized the scale of the problem and dealt with them in a decisive manner.

With our healthy current level of growth and future potential, with our hard-fought macroeconomic stability, with our youth climbing echelons of entrepreneurial success day after day, with our vast expanses of rural India that need infrastructure and modernization and with our levels of poverty that have steadily declined but still need substantial reduction, we simply do not as a society have any excuse or moral liberty to let the banking sector wounds fester and result in amputation of healthier parts of the economy.

How do we embark on a better path? I have been thinking hard of ways to swiftly resolve bank stressed assets. I have tried to draw on the analysis and documentation of similar episodes in economic history that I just alluded to, which in some cases I have had the good fortune to contribute to and learn from.

Let me mention the key principles to successful restructuring that I have managed to glean.

First, there has to be an incentive provided to banks to get on with it and restructure the stressed assets at a price that clears the market for these assets. If they don't do it in a timely manner, then the alternative should be costlier in terms of the price they receive.

Second, the ultimate focus of restructuring and of assessment as to whether the restructuring package being offered to the bank is at the 'right' price must be the efficiency and viability of the restructured asset. Generating the best price for the bank at all costs may only result in cosmetic changes and risk serial non-performance of the assets.

Third, not all of the resulting bank losses should simply be footed by the government. As a majority shareholder of PSBs, the government runs the risk of paying for it all at the end. It should manage the process at the outset to avoid that outcome. Wherever possible, private shareholders of banks should also be asked to chip in. Some surgical restructuring should be undertaken to consolidate and strengthen bank balance sheets so that private capital will come in at better valuations. It might have to accept that it is best to let some banks shrink over time. Divestments should also be on the table. Historically, significant restructuring of stressed assets has almost always involved significant bank restructuring.

Let me now elaborate 'a' plan that employs two different models for stressed assets resolution and recognizes the concomitant need for bank resolution. I will provide the plan in detail to make the point that it can be done. What I enunciate should be viewed as an attempt to address all dimensions of the problem. Its individual parts are, however, not meant to be cherry-picked by or for the constituency favoured by it. That would not work well.

So here it is.

1. Model I: Private Asset Management Company (PAMC). This plan would be suitable for sectors where the stress is such that the assets are likely to have economic value in the short run, with moderate levels of debt forgiveness. I conjecture based on anecdotal observations that sectors such as metals, engineering, procurement and construction (EPC), telecom and textiles, qualify for this.

a.   In terms of timeline, the banking sector will be asked to resolve and restructure say its 50 largest stressed exposures in these sectors by 31 December 2017. The rest can follow a similar plan in six months thereafter.

b.   For each asset, turnaround specialists and private investors— other than affiliates of banks exposed to the asset—will be called upon to propose several resolution plans. Each resolution plan will lay out sustainable debt and debt-for-equity conversions for banks to facilitate the issuance of new equity and possibly some new debt to fund the investment needs. We may have to consider that the sustainable portion of bank debt does not have to be greater than some minimum amount, so as to allow for a large haircut if necessary for economic recovery of the asset. Each plan would lay out cash flow prospects, whether the promoter stays or not, and if yes, with what stake.

c. Each resolution plan would then get vetted and rated by at least two credit rating agencies to assess the financial health (interest coverage ratio, leverage, etc.), economic health (sector, margins, etc.) and management quality (promoter or the new team). The rating would be for the asset and not just for bank debt in case additional debt is issued under the plan.

d. Feasible plans would be those that improve the rating of the asset (presently likely to be 'C' or 'D') such that *minimum* of the two credit ratings is at or above a threshold level, for example, at least just below the investment-grade level. The intention is that the asset should not have a high likelihood of ending up in stress soon after restructuring. Therefore, bank's debt forgiveness may have to be high enough and its converted equity stake low enough so that new investors can come in with a controlling stake and have incentives to turn the asset around.

e. Banks can then choose among the feasible plans. Coordination problems can be reduced by employing RBI's Central Repository for Information on Large Credits (CRLIC) and requiring that all plans with two-third approval by outstanding bank credit can proceed. The selected plan would simply be crammed down on any dissenting creditors.

f. Haircuts taken by banks under a feasible plan would be required by government ruling as being acceptable by the vigilance authorities. Sustainable debt would be upgraded to standard status for all involved banks. The promoters, however, would have no choice as to what restructuring plan is accepted, and may potentially get replaced and/or diluted, as per the preference of and depending on the price at which the new managing investors come in.

g. At expiration of the timeline, each exposure that is not resolved will be subject to a steep sector-based haircut for the bank consortium, possibly close to 100 per cent. The promoter will automatically have to leave. These assets would be put into our new IBC regime. Alternately, they could be put up for sale to ARCs and private equity investors who can turn around the assets, levering them up with fresh finance, if necessary. If designed right, only the worst assets should end up in this scenario. However, the possibility of ending up here would serve as a credible off-equilibrium threat so that banks, even the most exposed ones, cannot hold up the restructuring.

There are ways to arrange and concentrate the management of these assets into a single or few PAMCs, at the outset or right after restructuring plans are approved. These companies would resemble a large private-equity fund run by a team of professional asset managers. Besides bringing in their own capital, they could raise financing from investors against equity stakes in individual assets or in the fund as a whole, that is, in the portfolio of assets. The portfolio approach might help investors diversify risks on individual assets, improve valuations and attract greater capital. Bank creditors can set up an oversight committee to ensure cash flows are flowing in and out of the asset restructuring company as per the security rights agreed in the restructuring plans.

Let me emphasize that under this model, the asset management company would be entirely private, like the 'Phoenix' structure set up in Spain after 2012 to deal with bank NPAs in machinery, steel and winery.

Let me now turn to:

2. Model II: The National Asset Management Company (NAMC).
This plan would be necessary for sectors where the problem is not just one of excess capacity but possibly also of economically unviable assets in the short–medium term. Take, for example, the power sector, where projects have been created to deliver aggregate capacity that is beyond the estimated peak utilization anytime soon. Many of these are stalled as they have no fuel inputs and little or no income realization due to lack of credible purchase agreements. Their scrap value is likely to be small, and the only efficient use is as an ongoing concern. If input and output requirements are sorted out, and as power consumption needs rise, these projects could eventually provide value. For a country with per-capita consumption of electricity that is only one-third of the world average, it is reasonable to expect that a well-run power asset won't end up being a white elephant.

Unlike the first model (PAMC) where asset recovery is likely to be relatively quick, these assets may require a long time to start generating cash flows. In addition, the government should have incentives to clear approvals and purchase agreements to make them viable. For both these reasons, such assets would be best quarantined into a NAMC. The NAMC would perform several functions to get the ball rolling: raise debt, say government-guaranteed in part, for its financing needs; possibly raise some more to pay off banks at a haircut, likely steep but softened by payment in the form of security receipts against the asset's cash flows; keep a minority equity stake for the government and bring in asset managers such as ARCs and private equity to manage and turn around the assets, individually or as a portfolio. Infrastructure assets that are also long lived and create externalities (development of townships, improvements in overall productivity, etc.) could be resolved in similar way.

These two models of asset restructuring—one private and the other quasi government—share many common features with approaches that have been adopted for resolution of stressed assets in history: Sweden ('Securum' and 'Retriva') in the early 1990s, United States in dealing with the savings and loans (S&L) crisis ('Resolution Trust Corporation'), Japan (post-1998 via its Deposit Insurance Corporation); Indonesia ('IBRA'), Malaysia ('Danaharta') and South Korea ('KAMCO') to deal with the Southeast Asian crisis; and in the recent times, Ireland ('NAMA'), Spain ('Sareb') and again the United States ('TARP' along with Fannie Mae, Freddie Mac and Federal Housing Administration). In fact, the European Banking Authority has proposed a similar structure to deal with the NPAs of European banks.

Before discussing what all this would imply for bank balance sheets, let me pose and answer the question: are these supposed to be 'bad banks'? The answer is 'no'. While I have previously used the phrase 'bad bank' for such ideas, over the time I have come to dislike the title. A 'bad bank' conveys the impression that this entity is to operate as a bank but has bad assets to start with. In fact, the idea is not to operate these entities as banks at all. Resolution agencies set up as banks that originate or guarantee lending have ended up being future reckless lenders, notably in the case of Germany which has often aggregated stressed assets of its Landesbanken into bad banks. I would argue this has also been the story of Fannie Mae and Freddie Mac with respect to housing booms and busts in the United States.

It would be better to limit the objective of these asset management companies to orderly resolution of stressed assets with graceful exit thereafter; in other words, no mission creep over time to do anything else such as raise deposits, start a new lending portfolio or help deliver social programs. It is essential to keep the business model of these entities simple to make them attractive for private investors with expertise for the main task on hand—asset restructuring.

A moment of reflection clarifies that under both models I proposed, bank balance sheets would be freed up from the overhang of stressed assets and allowed to focus on their healthier activities. The catch is that given the haircuts involved, there will also be a need for a decisive action.

3. Bank resolution. We keep hearing clarion calls for more and more government funding for recapitalization of our PSBs. Clearly, more recapitalization with government funds is essential. But few have suggested that the government should adopt measures to econ-omize its total cost. It should ask in return from banks whether to recapitalize significant corrective actions, or wherever possible, inject private capital for loss-sharing with the taxpayers. The expec-tation of government dole outs might have been set by the past practice of throwing more money after the bad. Take for instance, our bank recapitalization plan of 2008–2009 after the global financial crisis: banks that experienced the worst outcomes received the most capital in a relative sense to get back to the regulatory capital norms. We must not allocate capital so poorly, recreate 'heads I win, tails the taxpayer loses' incentives and sow the seeds of another lending excess.

There are better ways to do it building upon some performance targets already set under the ongoing recapitalization plan. Let me propose five options:

a. **Private capital raising:** The healthier PSBs could have raised private capital by issuing deep discount rights in 2013, and some can still do so now. They must be required to do this to share the government's burden of recapitalizing banks. It might be a good way to restore some market discipline and get their shareholders to more seriously care about bank board and management decisions.

b. **Asset sales:** Some banks will have assets or loan portfolios that are in good enough shape to be sold in the market. Assets could be collected across banks and securitized into tranches that are credit rated, potentially creating some investor demand for buying it at different levels of risk profiles. Such asset sales can generate some of the needed recapitalization.

c. **Mergers:** As many have pointed out, it is not clear we need so many PSBs. The system will be better off if they are consolidated into fewer but healthier banks. After all, we do have cooperative banks and microfinance institutions to provide community-level banking. So some banks can be merged, as a quid pro quo for timely government capital injection into the combined entity. It would offer the opportunity to rejig management responsibility away from those who have under-performed or dragged their feet the most. Synergies in lending activity and branch locations could be identified to economize on intermediation costs, allowing sales of real estate where branches are redundant. Voluntary retirement schemes (VRS) can be offered to manage headcount and usher in a younger, digitally savvy talent pool into these banks.

d. **Tough PCA:** Undercapitalized banks could be shown some tough love and be subjected to corrective action. Such action should entail no further growth in deposit base and lending. This will also restore some market discipline in deposit migration, away from the weakest PSBs that have price to book equity (P/B) ratios of around 0.5 or lower, to healthier PSBs (P/B ratios around 1) and PvtSBs (P/B ratios of 1.5–4.5). The market has given its verdict as to where the growth potential in our banking sector lies and deposit growth should be allowed to reflect that.

e. **Divestments:** Undertaking these measures would improve overall banking sector health and market-to-book valuations, creating an opportune time for the government to divest some of its ownership of the restructured banks. This would also reduce the overall amount the government needs to inject.

There are many details to work out. But I hope this provides a start. It is going to require being balanced and creative, holistic and uncompromising, in achieving the end goal. Piece-by-piece approach with all discretion given to banks simply hasn't worked. Time is of the essence if we are to restore corporate investment and job creation.

Sustainable progress in an economy cannot occur when a set of players is allowed to hold up the efficient allocation of capital. Their owning a smaller share of assets can help unlock economic value; their hogging of these assets will only lead to further value-erosion.

I hope we can work together and collectively make the right choice.

Reference

Das, A., S. Mohapatra, S. Gokarn, F. G. Sander, D. Subbarao, S. Z. Chinoy, A. S. Gupta, S. Bhattacharya, and V. V. Acharya. 2017. 'India's International Integration and Challenges to Sustaining Growth.' *Vikalpa* 42, no. 3 (September): 168–205.

CHAPTER 2

A BANK SHOULD BE SOMETHING ONE CAN 'BANK' UPON*

In this chapter, I hope I can explain the important role that banks play in an economy so that I can make a small contribution, offering if not a flower at least a petal, to help the financial planning undertaken by women workers, educators and entrepreneurs.

I wish to try and simplify the mechanics of how a bank works, why we put our savings into banks, what does a bank do with our savings, when should we question which bank we are banking with and why, when such questions are asked 'en masse', is there a banking crisis and economic growth comes to a screeching halt. I will then draw implications for the current condition of the Indian banking sector and suggest some ways to restore it to healthier levels.

The gist of what I want to say can be summarized in a one-line message: 'A bank should be something one can "bank" upon', inspired by the real meaning behind 'banking upon something', a statement of credibility, of confidence, of trust—something that ideally a bank must earn over time by making prudent choices.

To understand this, we need to first grasp three simple concepts: 'what are bank deposits, what are bank loans, and that bank deposits can be demanded immediately by depositors, but bank borrowers may not repay their loans exactly at that time'.

So let us work step by step.

___

*Speech delivered on 28 April 2017 at the FICCI FLO Mumbai Chapter. I am grateful to the Federation of Indian Chambers of Commerce and Industry—FICCI Ladies Organisation, Mumbai Chapter, for inviting me to speak. I salute FLO's mission and wish the very best to the incoming office bearers on their efforts to empower and educate women, unlocking a potential workforce for the Indian economy that can both balance gender distribution of jobs and identify new sources of enterprise and entrepreneurship.

What Are Bank Deposits?

In its simplest form, my bank deposit is an amount of savings I have deposited into an account at a bank on my street corner. Once I have created the deposit account and put my savings into it, I can withdraw up to that amount at will. A deposit is something that the bank owes me; in other words, it is the bank's 'liability'.

Crucially, the deposit can be redeemed with immediacy. I can show up at the bank ATM or at the bank teller, demanding that my money be paid back to me—show me the money! Why might I need to do this? A bank deposit is the place where I save for the rainy day—my health expenses, my tuition fees, my everyday expenses. Some of these needs are predictable, some random; each time I withdraw at the ATM or the teller or write a cheque or do a wire transfer, I am demanding my money from the bank. Each instance I do not demand my money back, I am rolling over the deposit to the next instance.

Bank deposits are thus savings that I have kept with a bank. I trust them to be safe and to be demandable at will. I am happy to earn a low interest rate on them as they provide me valuable liquidity services, allowing me to meet my day-to-day and the occasional lumpy payment needs.

What Are Bank Loans?

There are many depositors like me parking their savings in the bank. Viewed this way, the bank is a safety vault or a storage technology. However, most of the times, the deposits are not being withdrawn and are simply being rolled over. Even when withdrawn, the deposits are not being redeemed at the same time. For instance, my health expenses are not coincident with those of my neighbour. In other words, there is much savings in the bank that is lying idle.

Let us now bring into picture others in the economy who are potential borrowers. A bright young woman down the street has been a successful consultant but wants to have a shot at building a new enterprise. She needs financing beyond her savings to put her bright ideas to test. There is a new construction just completed and several young couples, first-time home buyers, are looking to purchase houses there. They have some capacity to make down payments for the properties but must avail of extra monies that they can repay over the course of their lives. An old family needs money for medical expenses to treat a long-term illness. They cannot afford to spend out of their savings, but they do own a property against which they would like to borrow.

These potential borrowers can visit the bank branch to meet such financing needs. The bank makes loans to these individuals and families, assessing their ability to repay the loans, signing appropriate agreements to claim repayments in due course, and attaching the property and other assets as collateral that it can have access to in case the repayments fall through for some reason.

Such loans are bank's 'assets'. They typically earn a higher rate of interest than bank deposits and make banking activity an attractive proposition.

Demand Deposits Are Short-Term; Bank Loans Are Long-Term

This way, a bank takes shape. It has liabilities, the right-hand side of its balance sheet, in the form of deposits that must be repaid when depositors so demand; it has assets, the left-hand side of its balance-sheet, in the form of bank loans that have some fixed points of time at which the bank can command repayments.

By being so organized, the bank is performing the economic function of 'maturity transformation'. A deposit, which is potentially demandable at any instance, has effectively been lent out through financial intermediation in the form of a longer-term bank loan that is not making repayments at each instance.

And yet... the beauty of the arrangement is that most of the time, this works out. The day my health expenses arise and I take out money from the bank, my neighbour and others have likely received monthly paycheques, a part of which remain deposited in the bank, or that same day, some loan repayments have been made, extending the savings pool of the bank and allowing it to meet my deposit withdrawals.

In the background, financing has been made available to new entrepreneurs, first-time home buyers and ageing parents. Their undertakings are creating a whole second-round of economic activity, in the form of job creation at new enterprises, construction and cement industry and medical services and hospitals. Those involved in these activities have their own savings and borrowings needs and will in turn deal with their banks.

'Banking, in this manner is the lifeblood of an economy'; it channels savings in the form of demand deposits into borrowings in the form of bank loans or bank credit; it fuels and lubricates growth and improves everyone's welfare.

All of our lives would be easy, including those of central bankers, if banking worked as serenely as I have described so far. But, of course, that would be too good to be true. There are risks, there are tools to deal with these risks and, yet occasionally, there are banking crises. So let me turn to these next.

'What are the risks from maturity transformation and how can a bank manage them?'

What if by coincidence, the bank receives a series of withdrawal requests at once. There could be an epidemic in the area of its operations; may be the bank serves a community that is buying a lot of gold for *Akshaya Tritiya*; or there is a wealth shock to the farming community it serves due to poor monsoon and new deposits do not come in at the expected rate.

In such a scenario, when many depositors need to withdraw their monies at once, the bank faces 'risk' from maturity transformation. Given the coincident money demand, it is no longer sufficient to simply manage deposit withdrawals with new deposits and repayments on existing loans. What options does the bank have to manage these risks to ensure that it will show the money to its depositors when they need it and thus retain their trust?

To this end, let me briefly introduce three concepts: 'bank liquidity', 'bank capital' and 'interbank markets'.

Bank Liquidity

One simple idea is that a bank need not deploy all of its deposits for extending bank loans. It can save some purely as a reserve or a buffer to meet the unexpected coincidence in deposit withdrawals. The benefit of such bank 'liquidity' is that it is an impeccable defence as long as withdrawals are smaller than the size of the reserve. The cost is that by not being able to extend bank loans on part of its deposits, economic activity is compromised.

Bank Capital

Another idea is that a bank need not fund its extension of bank loans only with deposits in its liability structure. It can also raise some other forms of non-demandable liabilities. For example, the banker can put their own capital, beyond the savings needs, into the bank. A large bank can also raise public equity by being listed on a stock exchange. This way, the impact of the bank's unexpected deposit withdrawals can be made smaller relative to the overall size of the bank and the loan repayments it receives.

Such bank 'capital' would be supported through profits that a bank makes, by charging loan rates that exceed deposit rates and net of the costs of its operations. Bank capital would then be the first line of defence in case the bank faces unexpected withdrawals: bankers can take less bonus out of the bank; dividends being paid out to bank equity could be temporarily suspended; and in fact, bankers and equity owners can inject new finance to meet the temporary needs anticipating that future profits will nevertheless render such capital injection profitable for them.

Interbank Markets

An even more involved idea is for the bank to try and raise liquidity on the fly, from other banks (more generally, other financial intermediaries). Not all banks may be, in the region, hit by the epidemic or natural disaster. As long as these banks trust that the bank in need of liquidity only has a temporary need but has a high quality of long-term assets otherwise, they can lend their liquidity surplus to the bank in need. This would be an 'interbank deposit'. At other times, the surplus bank may be unprepared to deposit its money but instead may simply buy some of the needy bank's assets, creating an 'interbank market for asset sales'. In 'extremis', the surplus bank can simply assume all liabilities of the needy bank and, in return, take over the entire bank itself, creating a market for 'interbank mergers'.

It should be clear then that a bank has many tools to manage the risk of maturity transformation, the risk that deposits are demanded with immediacy while its assets are yet to make full repayments. The worse the quality of its assets, the less a bank can rely on cash flows from assets to meet unexpected withdrawals, and the more it must pre-arrange in the form of liquidity and capital. The tools—liquidity, capital and interbank markets—are not mutually exclusive though they clearly affect each other and are more attractive than others at times.

'With such tools to manage its risks, can we not always bank upon our bank?'

One possibility is that the bank has raised little equity capital and also held little liquidity of its own. Once depositors know this, they realize that the only way they can be redeemed against their withdrawals is if the bank can use interbank markets to raise liquidity. As I explained, this would be possible only if the bank's assets are deemed good enough to repay the interbank transaction in future. But then the following question arises: What if the asset quality of the bank is suspect as it has betted the bank's money on the upside leaving depositors at risk of losing their savings if the bets don't pay off? And, even if the asset quality is not entirely suspected, what if the interbank markets dry up themselves, which could happen if there is in fact no healthy bank, or only a few healthy banks around as most banks betted the economy's savings imprudently?

Systemic Shock, Bank Runs, Financial Disintermediation

In essence, if an economic tsunami—like massive house price crash or global economic collapse or underperformance in many industrial sectors—comes and hits the banking system, and it had chosen to remain heavily exposed to it by being on the shores, so that a large portion of its assets is deemed to be risky at once, then an unexpected large deposit withdrawal could be rather hard to meet for *any* bank. Worse, when this happens, if some depositors start being repaid by the bank, other depositors fear that bank liquidity is getting depleted and their savings might be at risk given the underlying assets are either not safe or not liquid enough in interbank markets. Now, these depositors may start demanding their deposits too. And a bank 'run' starts. Fearing the asset-quality signal revealed by such a run at one bank, depositors could start running on other banks too, especially ones with similar assets; and a full-fledged banking panic takes hold.

When this happens, the entire banking system is at the risk of being disintermediated; payments and settlements of financial transactions can come to a standstill; banks have no capacity on balance sheets to make new loans to new entrepreneurs, first-time home buyers and/or old families; the economic activity can come to a grinding halt. There are banks around, but no banking—the lifeblood of the economy—to channelize savings for productive use and job creation.[1]

The Present Indian Context

Let me now turn to what all this means for the present Indian context. To put things in perspective, let me mention that the recently released Global Financial Stability Report by the International Monetary Fund (IMF) brings out the following salient facts:

1. The Indian industrial sector is now among the most heavily indebted in the world in terms of the ability of its cash flows to meet its bank loan repayments[2],

   and

2. The Indian banking sector comes out as worse-off compared to other emerging economies in terms of how little bank capital it has set aside to provision for losses on its assets, that is, on its non-performing loans, made primarily to the industrial sector.[3]

What does it mean to have little bank capital as provision for losses? I like the following analogy. A bank not keeping adequate capital buffer to absorb losses on its loans that are more or less known to be arriving soon is akin to not preparing to rescue, in an emergency, a person who has slipped off the terrace of a skyscraper, and instead, in the midst of his almost surely fatal descent, hoping that the laws of gravity would somehow freeze and work differently this time. While such an under-provisioning problem extends to some of the private banks too, the scale of the problem is three to four times magnified in case of PSBs.

---

[1] Interestingly, the word 'bankruptcy'—a term used to describe the situation when a borrower defaults on repayments to be made—derives from the Italian term *banca rotta* or 'broken bank', describing the depositors of a bank breaking the bench or the counter of the teller in the Republic of Genoa when the banker was unable to meet their demands on deposit withdrawals.
[2] Figure 1.15, Global Financial Stability Report, April 2017.
[3] Table 1.2, Global Financial Stability Report, April 2017.

By and large, this scenario meets the adverse conditions of the narrative I provided about banking and banking panics. But in our context, several questions immediately come to mind: Why should I worry about whether I can bank upon my bank when my deposit is insured by the government? More so, if my deposits are with a state-owned bank, why should I bother about my bank's asset quality?

The Double-Edged Sword of Deposit Insurance and State Ownership of Banks

Answering these questions is crucial to understanding how problems of our banking sector are likely to play out. A moment of reflection reveals that as long as I trust the deposit insurance and the guarantee of the state behind the PSBs, I have no good reason to run and pull my deposit out of an insured deposit or a state-owned bank. The catch is this. When banks are in poor health, it does affect the potential borrowers. Once a bank's asset quality is adequately impaired, the bank does not grow its lending book much with fresh loans. Bank management of a thinly capitalized bank is interested in primarily making two kinds of loans. First, evergreening of an existing bad debt—throwing more money after the bad so as to help the borrower repay past loan, not acknowledge its true quality and simply kick the can down the road. Second, risky loans that repay high returns to the bank so that it can make a last-ditch effort to rebuild capital quickly—doubling up bets in a casino when the first round of gambling has all gone sour. Faced with such borrowing prospects, healthy borrowers who have access to alternate forms of finance may switch out of bank borrowing. Financial intermediation, however, is likely to grow at an anaemic pace and many deserving borrowers, such as the ones I have alluded to, are likely to remain starved of credit.

Ironically, the presence of a large safety net of deposit insurance and state ownership, which ensure that there are likely to be no bank runs, end up eroding any disciplining force that gets the bank health restored to a state where the economy can bank upon its banks to perform the economic functions of fuelling and lubricating growth. Deposit insurance and state ownership help the sick patient survive but on their own and do not guarantee good health; they may prevent financial instability but do not restore credit growth to levels that a vibrant economy needs.

And, indeed, recent global experiences have shown that governments need to be watchful as to how large the safety net adds up to relative to its own capacity to provide for it. Countries such as Ireland and Spain as a response to their banking sector woes in 2008 got engaged with massive guaranteeing of bank deposits and other liabilities. This, however, ended up being a Pyrrhic victory as they emerged with troubled balance sheets themselves, raising their debt to gross domestic product (GDP) ratios from healthy to questionable levels and triggering sovereign debt crises.

Bank Resolution Options

It is with the objective of avoiding such a contingency under any circumstance that I wish to propose that we deal with the ailing PSBs in creative ways instead of just propping them up with state aid.[4]

Let me elaborate. We keep hearing clarion calls for more and more government funding for recapitalization of our PSBs. Clearly, more recapitalization with government funds is essential. However, as a majority shareholder of PSBs, the government runs the risk of ending up paying for it all. The expectations for government dole outs might have been set by the past practice of throwing more money after the bad. Take, for instance, our bank recapitalization plan of 2008–2009 after the global financial crisis: Banks that experienced the worst outcomes received the most capital in a relative sense. Most of these banks need capital again.

We must not allocate capital so poorly, recreate 'Heads I Win, Tails the Taxpayer Loses' incentives and sow the seeds of another lending excess. There are better ways to do it. Let me offer five options:

1. **Private capital raising:** The healthier PSBs could have raised private capital by issuing deep discount rights in 2013, and some can still do so now. They must be required to do this to share the government's burden of recapitalizing the banks.

---

[4] The part of the speech that follows, builds and expands upon the section on Bank Resolution in my speech 'Some Ways to Decisively Resolve Bank Stressed Assets', 21 February 2017, delivered at the Indian Banks' Association Banking Technology Conference, Hotel Trident, Nariman Point, Mumbai. Available at https://rbi.org.in/Scripts/BS_SpeechesView.aspx?Id=1035

It might be a good way to restore some discipline and get the shareholders, boards and management of the banks to care more seriously about the quality of lending decisions.

2. **Asset sales:** Some banks will have assets or loan portfolios that are in good enough shape to be sold in the market. Modern banks no longer just make bank loans but also hold non-core assets such as insurance subsidiaries, market-making divisions, foreign branches, etc. Such non-core assets can be readily sold. Other assets could be collected across banks and organized into different risk profiles, so as to build transparency and trust with healthier banks and other intermediaries with an interest in purchasing them. Such asset sales can generate some of the needed recapitalization.

3. **Mergers:** As many have pointed out, it is not clear if we need so many PSBs. The system will be better off if they are consolidated into fewer but healthier banks. After all, we do have cooperative banks and micro-finance institutions to provide community-level banking. So, some banks can be merged, as a 'quid pro quo' for timely government capital injection into the combined entity. It would offer the opportunity to rejig management responsibilities, away from those who have under-performed or dragged their feet the most. Synergies in lending activity and branch locations could be identified to economize on intermediation costs, allowing sales of real estate where branches are redundant. Voluntary retirement schemes (VRS) can be offered to manage headcount and usher in a younger, tech-savvy talent pool into these banks. Historically, bank stress of the order we face has almost always involved significant bank restructuring.

4. **Tough prompt corrective action (PCA):** Undercapitalized banks could be shown some tough love and be subjected to corrective actions like the revised PCA guidelines recently released by the RBI. Such actions should entail no further growth in deposit base and lending for the worst-capitalized banks. This will ensure a gradual 'run-off' of such banks and encourage deposit migration away from the weakest PSBs to healthier public and PvtSBs. It is not rocket science to figure out where the growth potential in our banking sector lies and deposit growth should be allowed to reflect that.

5. **Divestments:** Undertaking these measures would improve the overall health of the banking sector, creating an opportune time for the government to divest some of its ownership of the restructured banks, as it has done over time in many other sectors of the economy. Perhaps the time has come for re-privatizing some of the nationalized banks. All this would reduce the overall amount the government needs to inject as bank capital and help preserve its hard-earned fiscal discipline, which along with stable inflation outlook and the diverse nature of our growth engine, appears to have made India the darling of foreign investors at present. We should grapple this macroeconomic stability to our shores with hoops of steel.

Let Me Conclude

I wish to encourage you to reflect on all this, read about the current state of Indian banking sector in newspapers and economic writings, try to make sense of it from first principles and ask the question if we really have a banking sector that our economy can bank upon.

At any rate, I hope that I have provided enough food for thought for the weekend, so when you do a financial transaction next week—with a bank, a mutual fund, a stock broker or an insurance company—you will be tempted to follow the river along which the money flows in that transaction from its source to its destination, invariably finding a few banks along the way!

And if you find the rafting exciting enough, do apply to the RBI where we are looking to rebalance our gender distribution of personnel that has gone a bit askew. We are ready to have dedicated women in our workforce such as all of you.

CHAPTER 3

THE UNFINISHED AGENDA: RESTORING PUBLIC SECTOR BANK HEALTH IN INDIA*

Every institution must remember, venerate and celebrate the immense contributions of those who helped lay down and solidify its character for future generations to build upon. Principles, careers and lives such as those of Mr R. K. Talwar, State Bank of India (SBI)'s greatest Chairman, inspire us, as in Henry Wadsworth Longfellow's *The Psalm of Life*:

> *Lives of great men all remind us*
> *We can make our lives sublime,*
> *And, departing, leave behind us*
> *Footprints on the sands of time;*
> *Footprints, that perhaps another,*
> *Sailing o'er life's solemn main,*
> *A forlorn and shipwrecked brother,*
> *Seeing, shall take heart again.*

I hope that I can do some justice to the rich legacy left behind by Mr Talwar, considered as the 'father of small-scale industries' in India, a banker ahead of his times who put tremendous emphasis on a comprehensive credit appraisal culture at SBI, and someone who had the courage to stand up against political pressure on his bank to

*Speech delivered at the 8th R. K. Talwar Memorial Lecture organized by the Indian Institute of Banking and Finance on 7 September 2017 at Hotel Trident, Mumbai. I am grateful to the Indian Institute of Banking and Finance (IIBF) for inviting me to deliver the 8th R. K. Talwar Memorial Lecture. I would like to thank Vaibhav Chaturvedi, B. Nethaji and Vineet Srivastava for valuable inputs, as well as my co-authors, Tim Eisert, Christian Eufinger and Christian Hirsch (parts of the Japanese and the European stories are based on joint work with them). All errors remain my own. Views expressed do not necessarily reflect those of the RBI.

undertake targeted lending to undeserving borrowers (an episode recollected in a booklet by another stalwart of Indian banking, Mr Narayanan Vaghul).

I have since had a change of heart. The RBI's internal committee on improving monetary policy transmission will be finishing its report by the last week of September 2017.[1] I should neither pre-judge nor pre-announce its findings. Therefore, and at the cost of belabouring some of my remarks earlier in the year, I will focus on what remains, to my mind, the most important unfinished agenda in the journey we have embarked upon to resolve our stressed assets problem, namely that of restoring PSBs' health in India. I will indirectly end up conveying why bank credit growth and transmission are weak at present.

I would like to contend that a primary cause for the recent slowdown in our growth is the stress on the banking sector's balance sheets, especially of PSBs. As Figures 3.1a and 3.1b show using RBI's data, the stress in bank assets has been mounting since 2011 and has now materially crystallized in the form of NPAs. Some banks are under the RBI's PCA having failed to meet the asset-quality, capitalization and/or profitability thresholds; others meet these thresholds for now but are precariously placed in case the provisioning cover for loan losses against their gross NPAs (Figure 3.1c) is raised to

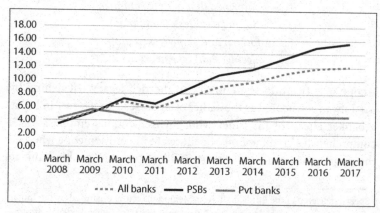

Figure 3.1a. Stressed Assets Ratio (%) for Indian Banks
Source: RBI.

[1] https://rbidocs.rbi.org.in/rdocs/PublicationReport/Pdfs/MCLRCFF20B31A4A24D0487D8659079CF392B.PDF

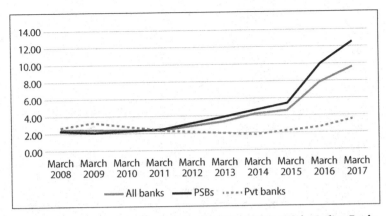

Figure 3.1b. Gross Non-Performing Assets (NPAs) Ratio (%) for Indian Banks
Source: RBI.

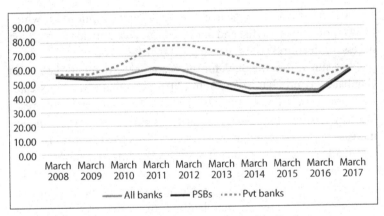

Figure 3.1c. Provisional Coverage Ratio (%) for Indian Banks
Source: RBI.

international standards and made commensurate with the low loan recoveries in India.

When bank balance sheets are so weak, they cannot support healthy credit growth. Put simply, under-capitalized banks have capital only to survive, not to grow; those banks barely meeting the capital requirements will want to generate capital quickly, focusing on high interest margins at the cost of high loan volumes. The resulting weak loan supply (see in Figure 3.1d, the steady decline in loan advances growth since 2011 for PSBs), and the low efficiency of financial intermediation have created significant headwinds for economic activity.

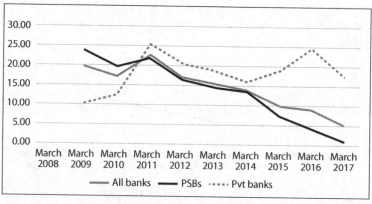

Figure 3.1d. Growth in Advances (%YoY) for Indian Banks
Source: RBI.

A decisive and adequate bank recapitalization, options for which I will lay out (again) at the end of my remarks, is a critical intervention necessary to address this balance sheet malaise.

In a study from the Bank for International Settlements, Leonardo Gambacorta and Hyun-Song Shin (2016) document that bank capitalization has a strong effect on bank loan supply: a 1 per cent increase in a bank's equity-to-total assets ratio is associated with a 0.6 per cent increase in its yearly loan growth. In fact, if a banking system remains systematically undercapitalized and new lending is not kept under a tight supervisory watch, then the economy can suffer significantly from a credit misallocation problem, now commonly known as 'loan evergreening' or 'zombie lending'. In particular, undercapitalized banks have an incentive to roll over loans from financially struggling existing borrowers so as to avoid having to declare these outstanding loans as non-performing. With these zombie loans, the impaired borrowers acquire enough liquidity to be able to meet their payments on outstanding loans. Banks thus avoid the short-run outcome that these borrowers might default on their loan payments, which would lower their net operating income, force them to raise provisioning levels and increase the likelihood of them violating the minimum regulatory capital requirements. By evergreening these loans, banks effectively delay taking a balance sheet hit, while taking on significant risk that their borrowers might not regain solvency and remain unable to repay, now even larger loan payments. While unproductive firms receive subsidized credit to be just kept alive, loan supply is shifted away from more creditworthy firms.

Thus, adequate bank capitalization, more generally, financial intermediary, is a pre-requisite for efficient supply and allocation of credit. Its central role in supporting economic growth is consistent with what other economies and regulators have experienced in the past episodes of banking sector stress. I will briefly cover the Japanese crisis in the 1990s and early 2000s, and the European crisis since 2009. Professor Ed Kane (1989), Boston College, had reached similar conclusions for the United States based on the savings and loans crisis of the 1980s.

The Japanese Story

In the early 1990s, a massive real estate bubble collapsed in Japan (see Figure 3.2). This caused problems for Japanese banks in two ways: First, real estate assets were often used as collateral; second, banks held the affected assets directly, so that the decline in asset prices had an immediate impact on their balance sheets. These problems in the banking system quickly translated into negative real effects for borrowing firms along the lines I laid out above.

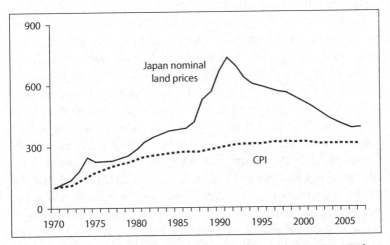

Figure 3.2. Nominal Residential Land Prices and the Consumer Price Index (CPI) in Japan

Source: Bank of Japan, Government of Japan (taken from Wilcox, 2008).

Table 3.1. Capital Injection Programmes in Japan (in Trillions of Yen)

Legislation	Date of Injection	Amount Injected
Financial Function Stabilization Act	March 1998	1.816
Prompt Recapitalization Act	March 1999–March 2002	8.605
Financial Reorganization Promotion Act	September 2003	0.006
Deposit Insurance Act	June 2003	1.960
Act for Strengthening Financial Functions	November 2006–March 2009	0.162

Source: Hoshi and Kashyap (2010).

Subsequently, the Japanese government introduced several measures to stabilize the banking sector and spur economic growth. Among these measures were a series of direct public capital injections into impaired banks, mostly in the form of preferred equity or subordinated debt. However, as conclusively shown by Table 3.1 from Takeo Hoshi and Anil Kashyap (2010), bulk of the injections came after 1999, close to a decade after the collapse; the economic scale of earlier recapitalizations was small relative to that of the banking sector's real estate exposure so that these half-hearted measures failed to adequately recapitalize the Japanese banking sector.

Joe Peek and Eric Rosengren (2005) were among the first to provide evidence that this inadequate recapitalization of the Japanese banking sector had major consequences for the allocation of credit to the real economy. Specifically, they showed that firms were more likely to receive additional loans if they were, in fact, in poor financial condition. They interpreted this finding as being consistent with the 'zombie lending' incentives of undercapitalized banks. Figure 3.3 shows that the percentage of zombie firms increased from roughly 5 per cent in 1991 to roughly 30 per cent in 1996. In related work, Mariassunta Giannetti and Andrei Simonov (2013) found that the banks that remained weakly capitalized after the introduction of the recapitalization programmes provided loans to impaired borrowers, while well-capitalized banks increased credit to healthy firms. The authors estimated that the credit supply to the healthy firms could have been 2.5 times higher in 1998 if the banks had been recapitalized sufficiently.

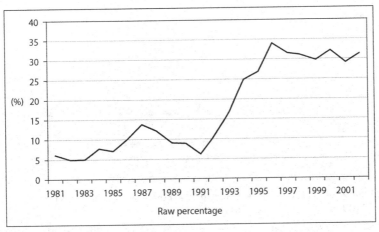

Figure 3.3. Prevalence of Firms Receiving Subsidized Loans in Japan
Source: Caballero et al. (2008).

In turn, this misallocation of loans translated into significant negative effects for the real economy. Because 'zombie lending' kept distressed borrowers alive artificially, the respective labour and supply markets remained congested; for example, product market prices were depressed and market wages remained high. Sectoral capacity utilization also remained low, which destroyed the pricing power and attractiveness of investments for healthy firms competing in the same sectors. Ricardo Caballero, Takeo Hoshi and Anil Kashyap (2008) showed that, as a result of these spillover effects, healthy firms that were operating in industries with a high prevalence of zombie firms had lower employment and investment growth than healthy firms in those industries that did not suffer from distortions of zombie firms. They estimated that due to the rise in the number of zombie firms, a typical non-zombie firm in the real estate industry experienced a 9.5 per cent loss in employment and a whopping 28.4 per cent loss in investment during the Japanese crisis period.

The European Story

In recent years, the Eurozone has been following a similar path to that of the Japanese economy in the 1990s and early 2000s. Starting in 2009, countries on the periphery of the Eurozone drifted into a severe sovereign debt crisis. At the peak of the European debt crisis, in 2012,

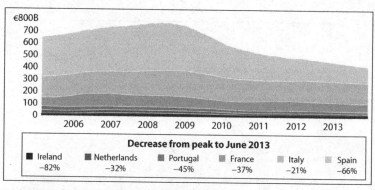

Figure 3.4. Volume of New Loans to Non-Financial Corporations up to 1 Million Euro, 12-Month Cumulative Flows

Source: Restoring Financing and Growth to Europe's SMEs, IIF/Bain report, 2013.

anxiety over excessive levels of national debt led to interest rates on government bonds issued by the countries which were considered unsustainable in the European periphery. For instance, from mid-2011 to mid-2012, the spreads of Italian and Spanish 10-year government bonds increased by 200 and 250 basis points, respectively, relative to German government bonds. Since this deterioration in the sovereigns' creditworthiness fed back into the financial sector (Acharya et al. 2015), lending to the private sector contracted substantially in Greece, Ireland, Italy, Portugal and Spain (the 'GIIPS' countries), as shown in Figure 3.4. In Ireland, Spain and Portugal, for example, the volume of newly issued loans fell by 82 per cent, 66 per cent and 45 per cent respectively, over the period between 2008 and 2013.

However, the impact of the European debt crisis on bank lending is more complex than in the case of the Japanese banking crisis, which was mainly caused by the bursting of an asset price bubble and the resulting impairment of the banks' financial health. The European debt crisis also caused a hit on banks' balance sheets due to the substantial losses on their sovereign bond-holdings; in addition, it created gambling-for-resurrection incentives for weakly capitalized banks from countries in the European periphery. These banks sought to increase their risky domestic sovereign bond-holdings even further as they were an attractive bet to rebuild capital quickly given zero risk-weights. This incentive led to a crowding-out of lending to the real economy, thereby intensifying the credit crunch (Acharya and Steffen 2014).

This vicious cycle of poor bank health and sovereign indebtedness became a matter of great concern for the European Central Bank (ECB), as this cycle endangered the monetary union as a whole. As a result, the ECB began to introduce unconventional monetary policy measures to stabilize the Eurozone and to restore trust in the periphery of Europe. Especially important in restoring trust in the viability of the Eurozone was the ECB's Outright Monetary Transactions (OMT) programme, which ECB President Mario Draghi announced in his famous speech in July 2012 saying that 'the ECB is ready to do whatever it takes to preserve the euro. And believe me, it will be enough'.

There is now ample empirical evidence that the announcement of the OMT programme significantly lowered sovereign bond spreads, as shown by Figure 3.5. By substantially reducing sovereign yields, the OMT programme improved the asset side, the capitalization and the access to financing of banks with large GIIPS sovereign debt holdings.

Due to its positive effect on banks' capital, it was expected that the OMT announcement would lead to an increase in bank loan

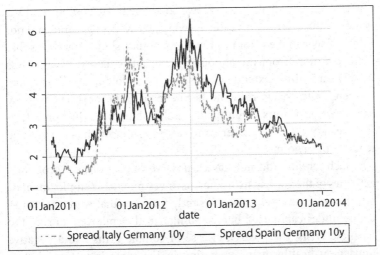

Figure 3.5. Spread between German and Spanish/Italian 10-year Sovereign Bond Yields

Source: Thomsan Datastream.

supply, thus benefiting the real economy. However, when Mario Draghi reflected on the impact of the OMT programme on the real economy during a speech in November 2014, he noted that:

> (T)hese positive developments in the financial sphere have not transferred fully into the economic sphere. The economic situation in the euro area remains difficult. The euro area exited recession in the second quarter of 2013, but underlying growth momentum remains weak. Unemployment is only falling very slowly. And confidence in the overall economic prospects is fragile and easily disrupted, feeding into low investment.

An important reason why the positive financial developments did not fully transfer into economic growth is as follows: An indirect recapitalization measure like the OMT programme produced treasury gains for banks (much like our policy-rate cuts do); such a measure allows the central bank to benefit banks that hold troublesome assets, but it does not tailor the recapitalization to the banks' specific needs. As a result, some European banks remained significantly undercapitalized from an economic standpoint even post-OMT.

In joint work with Tim Eisert, Christian Eufinger and Christian Hirsch (Acharya et al. 2016), I have confirmed that 'zombie lending' is indeed the likely explanation for why the OMT programme did not fully translate into economic growth. Our study shows that banks that benefited more from the announcement but remained nevertheless weakly capitalized, extended loans to existing low-quality borrowers at interest rates that were below the rates paid by the most creditworthy European borrowers (high-quality public borrowers in non-GIIPS European countries, e.g., Germany), a strong indication of the 'zombie lending' behaviour.

Such lending did not have a positive impact on real economic activities of the zombie firms: neither investment, nor employment or return on assets changed significantly for firms that were connected to the under-capitalized banks. Similar to the spillovers during the Japanese crisis, the post-OMT rise in zombie firms had a negative impact on healthy firms operating in the same industries due to the misallocation of loans and distorted market competition. In particular, healthy firms in industries with an average increase in the proportion of zombie firms invested up to 13 per cent less capital and experienced about 4 per cent lower employment growth rates compared to a scenario in which the proportion of zombies stayed at its pre-OMT level. In extremis, for an industry in the 95th percentile increase in zombie firms, healthy firms invested up to 40 per cent less capital and experienced up to 15 per cent lower employment growth rates.

The Indian Story: Can We End It Differently?

In many ways, the problems experienced in Japan and Europe have been rather similar. Both regions went through a period of severe banking sector stress (although triggered by different causes) and failed to adequately recapitalize their struggling banking sectors. Bank and other stressed balance sheet problems were neither fully recognized nor addressed expediently.

In Japan, a likely explanation for the cautious introduction of recapitalization measures is that the authorities were afraid of strong public resistance while announcing large-scale recapitalization, as initial smaller support measures had already caused public outrage. In addition, Japanese officials generally feared sparking a panic in financial markets when disclosing more transparent information about the health of banks.

In Europe, introducing proper recapitalization measures has been challenging due to political circumstances and constraints of the Eurozone. In contrast to a single country like Japan, 19 member states have to come together in the Eurozone and decide on a particular policy measure. In addition, even if a particular policy is helping the Eurozone as a whole, it might not be optimal for each individual country experiencing divergent economic outcomes.

While our initial conditions look ominously similar to these episodes and there are many parallels with how things have played out at our end, we may be fortunate in not having many of these constraints. Hence, I believe we can, we should and in fact, we must do better. We are at a substantially lower per-capita GDP than these countries and a sustained growth slowdown has the potential to really hurt economic prospects of the common man.

With this overall objective, let me first turn to what I consider the positives of the balance sheet resolution agenda that the RBI and the GoI have embarked upon. I will then highlight the unfinished part of this agenda—its Achilles' heel—the lack of a clear and concrete plan for restoring PSBs health.

Resolution of Stressed Assets

To address cross-bank information asymmetry and inconsistencies in asset classification, the RBI created the Central Repository of Information on Large Credits (CRILC) in early 2014. To end the asset classification forbearance for restructured accounts, the RBI announced the AQR from 1 April 2015. The objective was to get the banks to recognize the hitherto masked stress in their balance sheets. The AQR is now complete. The RBI is neither denying the scale of the NPAs nor trying to forbear on them. Instead, it is fully focused on resolving the assets recognized as NPAs.

In the absence of an effective, time-bound statutory resolution framework, various schemes were introduced by the RBI to facilitate viable resolution of stressed assets. While the schemes were designed, and later modified, to address some of the specific issues flagged by various stakeholders in individual deals, the final outcomes have not been too satisfactory. The schemes were cherry-picked by banks to keep loan-loss provisions low rather than to resolve stressed assets. It is in this context that enactment of the IBC in December 2016 can be considered to have significantly changed the rules of the game. It is still early days but the number of bankruptcy cases which have been filed by operational as well as financial creditors is encouraging. Many cases have been admitted and the 180-day clock (extendable by further 90 days) for the resolution of these cases has already started.

The promulgation of the Banking Regulation (Amendment) Ordinance 2017 (since notified as an Act) and the subsequent actions taken thereunder, have made the IBC a lynchpin of the new resolution framework. There were legitimate concerns that if the RBI directs banks to file accounts under the IBC, it would enter the tricky domain of commercial judgments on specific cases. However, the approach recommended by the Internal Advisory Committee (IAC) constituted by the RBI for this purpose has been objective and has allayed these misgivings. The IAC recommended that the RBI should initially focus on stressed assets which are large, material and aged, in that they have eluded a viable resolution plan despite being classified as NPAs for a significant amount of time. Accordingly, the RBI directed banks to file insolvency applications against 12 large accounts comprising about 25 per cent of the total NPAs. The RBI has now advised banks to resolve some of the other accounts by December 2017; if banks fail to put in place a viable resolution plan within the timelines, these cases also will be referred to for resolution under the IBC.

The RBI has also advised banks to make higher provisions for these accounts to be referred under the IBC. This is intended to improve bank provision coverage ratios (see Figure 3.1c) and to ensure that banks are fully protected against likely losses in the resolution process. The higher regulatory minimum provisions should enable banks to focus on what the borrowing company requires to turn-around rather than on narrowly minimizing their own balance sheet impacts. This should also help transition to higher, and more countercyclical, provisioning norms in due course.

Going forward, the RBI hopes that the banks utilize the IBC extensively and file for the insolvency proceedings on their own without waiting for regulatory directions. Ideally, in line with international best practice, out-of-court restructuring may be the right medicine at 'pre-default' stage, as soon as the first signs of incipient stress are evident or when covenants in bank loans are tripped by the borrowers. Once a default happens, the IBC allows for filing for insolvency proceedings, time-bound restructuring and failing that, liquidation. This would provide the sanctity that the payment 'due date' deserves and improve credit discipline all around, from bank supply as well as borrower demand standpoints, as borrowers might lose control in IBC to competing bidders.

Whither Are We Headed on Restoring PSBs Health?

So far so good. Oft, when I lie on my couch in a vacant or in a pensive mood, the realization that we have put in place a process that not just addresses the current NPA issues, but is also likely to serve as a blueprint for future resolutions, becomes the bliss of my solitude! A whole ecosystem is evolving around the IBC and the RBI's steps have contributed to this structural reform. I smile and rest peacefully at night with this thought.... But every few days, I wake up with a sense of restlessness that time is running out; we have created a due process for stressed assets to resolve but there is no concrete plan in place for PSBs' balance sheets; how will they withstand the losses during resolution and yet have enough capital buffers to intermediate well to the huge proportion of economy's savings that they receive as deposits; can we end the Indian story differently from that of Japan and Europe?

The GoI has been infusing capital on a regular basis into the PSBs, to enable them to meet regulatory capital requirements and maintain the government stake in the PSBs at a benchmark level (set at 58 per cent in December 2010, but subsequently lowered to 52 per cent in December 2014). In 2015, the Government announced the 'Indradhanush' plan to revamp the PSBs. As part of that plan, a programme of capitalization to ensure the PSBs remain BASEL III compliant was also announced. However, given the correctly recognized scale of NPAs in the books of PSBs and the lower internal capital augmentation given their tepid, now almost moribund, credit growth, substantial additional capital infusion is almost surely required. This is necessary even after tapping into other avenues, including the sale of non-core assets, raising of public equity and divestments by the government.

The Cabinet Committee on Economic Affairs has recently authorised an alternative mechanism to take a decision on the divestment in respect of PSBs through exchange-traded funds or other methods subject to the government retaining 52 per cent stake. Synergistic mergers may also be part of the broader scheme of things. The Union Cabinet has also authorized an alternative mechanism for approving amalgamation of PSBs. The framework envisages initiation of merger proposals by the bank boards based on commercial considerations, which will be considered for in-principle approval by the alternative mechanism. This could provide an opportunity to strengthen the balance sheets, management and boards of banks and enable capital raising by the amalgamated entity from the market at better valuations in case synergies eventually materialize.

All of this is good in principle. There are several options on the table and they would have to work together to address various constraints. What worries me however is the glacial pace at which all this is happening.

Having embarked on the NPA resolution process, indeed having catalyzed the likely haircuts on banks, can we delay the bank resolution process any further?

Can we articulate a feasible plan to address the massive recapitalization need of banks and publicly announce this plan to provide clarity to investors and restore confidence in the markets about our banking system?

Why aren't the bank board approvals of public capital raising leading to immediate equity issuances at a time when liquidity chasing stock markets is plentiful? What are the banks' chairmen waiting for, the elusive improvement in market-to-book which will happen only with a better capital structure and could get impaired by further growth shocks to the economy in the meantime?

Can the government divest its stakes in PSBs right away, to 52 per cent? And, for banks whose losses are so large that divestment to 52 per cent won't suffice, how do we tackle the issue?

Can the valuable and sizable deposit franchises be sold off to private capital providers so that they can operate as healthy entities rather than be in the intensive care unit under the RBI's PCA? Can we start with the relatively smaller banks under PCA as test cases for a decisive overhaul?

These questions keep me awake at nights. I fear time is running out. I worry for the small-scale industries that Mr Talwar cared the most about, which are reliant on relationship-based bank credit. The Indradhanush was a good plan, but to end the Indian story differently, we need soon a much more powerful plan—a *sudarshan chakra*—aimed at swiftly, within months if not weeks, for restoring PSB health, in the current ownership structure or otherwise.

References

Acharya, V. V., T. Eisert, C. Eufinger, and C. W. Hirsch. 2015. 'Real Effects of the Sovereign Debt Crisis in Europe: Evidence from Syndicated Loans'. *CEPR Discussion Paper* No DP10108. Available at: https://ssrn.com/abstract=2501580 (accessed on 25 April 2020).

Acharya, V. V., T. Eisert, C. Eufinger, and C. W. Hirsch. 2016. 'Whatever it Takes: The Real Effects of Unconventional Monetary Policy'. Working Paper. New York, NY: New York University Stern School of Business.

Acharya, V. V., and S. Steffen. 2014. 'The Greatest Carry Trade Ever? Understanding Eurozone Bank Risks'. *Journal of Financial Economics* 115: 215–236.

Caballero, R. J., T. Hoshi, and A. K. Kashyap. 2008. 'Zombie Lending and Depressed Restructuring in Japan'. *The American Economic Review* 98, no. 5: 1943–1977.

Gambacorta, L., and H. S. Shin. 2016. 'Why Bank Capital Matters for Monetary Policy'. BIS Working Papers No 558. Available at: https://www.bis.org/publ/work558.pdf (accessed on 16 June 20).

Giannetti, M., and A. Simonov. 2013. 'On the Real Effects of Bank Bailouts: Micro Evidence from Japan'. *American Economic Journal: Macroeconomics* 5, no. 1: 135–167.

Hoshi, T., and A. K. Kashyap. 2010. 'Will the U. S. Bank Recapitalization Succeed? Eight Lessons from Japan'. *Journal of Financial Economics* 97: 398–417.

Kane, E. J. 1989. *The S & L Insurance Mess: How Did it Happen?* Washington, DC: Urban Institute.

Peek, J., and E. S. Rosengren. 2005. 'Unnatural Selection: Perverse Incentives and the Misallocation of Credit in Japan'. *American Economic Review* 95: 1144–1166.

Wilcox, J. A. 2008. 'Why the US Won't Have a "Lost Decade"'. Working Paper. Haas School of Business, U C Berkeley, Berkeley, CA.

CHAPTER 4

PROMPT CORRECTIVE ACTION: AN ESSENTIAL ELEMENT OF FINANCIAL STABILITY FRAMEWORK*

This chapter explains why the PCA framework of the RBI is an essential element of its financial stability framework. It lays out the case for structured early intervention and resolution by regulators for banks that become undercapitalized due to poor asset quality or vulnerable due to loss of profitability. Detailing the mandatory and discretionary actions under the RBI's revised PCA framework, it compares and contrasts these with the PCA framework operating in the USA. Finally, it documents empirically how Indian banks under the PCA framework are being restored back to health through better capitalization, preservation of capital and provisioning for losses.

It is always an occasion of great pride and immense satisfaction for me to go to the Indian Institute of Technology (IIT) Mumbai's Powai campus and be reminded of what I learnt there—the importance of identifying big problems to solve, approaching them with an analytical mindset, scything through seemingly attractive but incomplete fixes and in the process, discovering durable solutions that address the root causes underlying the problems.[1]

* Speech delivered at the Indian Institute of Technology, Bombay on 12 October 2018. I am grateful to Governor Dr Urjit R. Patel and Deputy Governor N. S. Vishwanathan for their constant encouragement, feedback and guidance. I also thank Vaibhav Chaturvedi for his excellent support throughout the preparation of this speech; R Gurumurthy, Jagan Mohan, B Nethaji, Sooraj Menon and Vineet Srivastava of the RBI; and, my co-authors, Sascha Steffen of Frankfurt School of Management and Finance and Lea Steinruecke of University of Mannheim.
[1] I would like to thank the IIT, Bombay, in particular, Professor Pushpa Trivedi, who inspired me to pursue Economics and Finance, for inviting me back to IIT, my undergraduate alma mater.

On 7 September 2017, I spoke at the eighth R. K. Talwar Memorial Lecture about 'The Unfinished Agenda: Restoring Public Sector Bank Health in India' (Acharya 2017), wherein, I touched upon three themes:

1. How undercapitalized banking systems engage in evergreening of the distressed borrowers ('zombie lending'), as witnessed in the USA during the S&L crisis of the 1980s, Japan in the 1990s and the Eurozone following the global financial crisis.
2. What steps the RBI had undertaken to address the stressed assets problem of Indian banks, namely the creation of CRILC in early 2014, the AQR in 2015 and reference of the largest, aged NPAs to the IBC under the powers bestowed upon the bank by promulgation of the Banking Regulation (BR; Amendment) Ordinance 2017 (since notified as an Act); and, finally,
3. The need for the Government of India (GoI) to meet the recapitalization needs of PSBs in their current ownership structure or otherwise.

Since then, the GoI has announced a recapitalization package for PSBs in October 2017 of ₹2.11 trillion, comprising ₹1.53 trillion of government capital infusion and balance to be raised from market funding by March 2019. Equally importantly, the RBI issued a circular on 12 February 2018 for the resolution of stressed assets, which employs the IBC reference as its lynchpin for resolution and is aimed at improving the credit culture in both borrowers and lenders.

Another significant step has been taken by the RBI in parallel, which has been somewhat underappreciated, namely the imposition of PCA on a number of banks whose capital, asset quality and/or profitability do not meet pre-specified thresholds. I wish to explain why PCA is an essential element of the RBI's (and more generally, of a banking supervisor's) financial stability framework.

Loss-Absorption Role of Bank Capital

Before I discuss the PCA approach, it would be useful to briefly talk about the critical role of bank capital in relation to the process of resolution of stressed banks.

In its simplest form, a bank balance sheet has assets on the left-hand side of the balance sheet, and liabilities on the right-hand side in the form of equity capital and deposits (and other forms of debt liabilities such as unsecured bonds and wholesale finance such as inter-bank liabilities or short-term commercial paper).

Equity capital is the primary loss-absorption buffer—means of protection—against the asset losses of a bank. It is meant to be at levels high enough to absorb unanticipated losses with enough margin so as to inspire confidence and enable the bank to continue as a going concern, in particular, without passing on losses to bank creditors. Once the capital level is fully consumed by the deteriorating financials, it exposes the unsecured creditors, including depositors, to bear the losses. While the deposits typically are insured up to a certain level, economic history shows that more often than not the ultimate costs of paying off all deposits fall on the sovereign, especially in the case of large, complex and interconnected banks.

Capital constraints at a wider and systemic level also impact the resolution of weak banks. The US experience, empirically documented by Granja, Matvos and Seru (2017), shows that an optimal bidding strategy of a healthier bank—a potential acquirer, which may value the weaker bank for its franchise value from deposits, gets adversely impacted if it is itself poorly capitalized. In such a scenario, the overall value realization for the weak bank goes down. The poor capitalization of potential acquirers can also drive a wedge between their willingness and ability to pay for a failed bank. In this manner, bank capital being at healthy levels also has a system-wide loss-absorption role by helping sell weak banks to healthy ones in an efficient manner.

Given this criticality of bank capital in absorbing losses, it is natural why minimum bank capital requirements are in place globally and why capital becomes one of the most important factors for supervisors to monitor. In the aftermath of the global financial crisis, there has been a complete overhaul of the international regime for minimum regulatory capital requirements of banks, as enshrined in the revised Basel norms, namely Basel III.

The goal of Basel III is to raise the quality, consistency and transparency of the capital base of banks to withstand unanticipated losses and to strengthen the overall risk coverage of the capital framework. In addition to revising the minimum capital ratio requirements for credit risk, Basel III also introduced a capital conservation buffer (CCB) and a countercyclical capital buffer. CCB is designed to ensure that banks build up a capital buffer outside periods of financial stress that can be drawn down when banks face financial (systemic or idiosyncratic) stress. Banks which draw down their capital conservation buffer during a stressed period are required to have a definite plan to replenish the buffer and face capital distribution constraints. The objective of the countercyclical capital buffer is to use capital as a macroprudential instrument aimed at protecting the banking sector from periods of excess aggregate credit growth, that have often been associated with the build-up of system-wide risk.

In this regard, it is instructive to note that the minimum bank capital ratio (to suitably risk-weighted assets) required to be held under the Basel norms is only a floor. Since the global financial crisis, many countries require their banks to hold capital at higher levels (Table 4.1). Further, in other major jurisdictions such as the USA and the United Kingdom, effective capital requirements tend to be

Table 4.1. Capital Adequacy Ratio: Select Countries

Jurisdictions	Minimum Common Equity Ratio	Minimum Tier-1 Capital Ratio	Minimum Total Capital Ratio
Basel III prescriptions	4.5	6.0	8.0
Brazil			11 from 2013, gradually aligning to Basel III by 2019—subsequently as per Basel
China	5.0	6.0	8.0
India	5.5	7.0	9.0
Mexico (CCB is integrated into minimum requirements)	7.0	8.5	10.5
Singapore	6.5	8.0	10.0
South Africa	5.0	6.75	9.0
Switzerland	4.5–10.0	6.0–13.0	8.0–19.0
Turkey	4.5	6.0	12.0

Source: Regulatory Consistency Assessment Programme (RCAP) reports of the Bank for International Settlements (BIS).

even higher on account of several add-ons; for instance, in the USA, higher leverage ratio (put simply, bank capital to unweighted assets ratio) and the stress tests—annual Comprehensive Capital Analysis and Review (CCAR)—also push up the effective capital requirements beyond Basel requirements for systemically important and/or large banks.

While this view of bank capital focuses on its benefits in the form of loss-absorption adequacy at individual bank and systemic levels, there is an equally important incentive role played by bank capital that is worthy of discussion.

Incentive Role of Bank Capital

Let me now explain why it becomes imperative for bank supervisors to intervene in a weak bank much 'before' the capital is completely eroded. Conceptually, there are at least two reasons why, the world over, banks that make losses to the point of being undercapitalized do not recapitalize, or are not recapitalized, promptly.

First, while private banks typically hold greater capital than required by regulatory requirements, shareholders are reluctant to inject capital once the capital is eroded by losses as it gets primarily deployed in stabilizing bank liabilities. To compensate for this wealth transfer for injecting capital, shareholders require a much higher rate of return than when banks are better capitalized, but such highly-required returns may render banking activity unprofitable to pursue. This is the well-known 'debt overhang' problem studied extensively in financial economics (Myers, 1977).

Secondly, when banks become undercapitalized en masse or are government-owned to start with, it is often thought that recapitalization should occur swiftly given the attendant real and systemic risk costs of not recapitalizing banks—costs that a government should internalize. In practice, however, banking sectors are sometimes 'too big to save' relative to the size of government balance sheets. Even when that is not so, governments may themselves be financially constrained; bank recapitalizations must earn effective returns that exceed the costs of raising additional finance (usually additional borrowings) or from cutting back on other fiscal expenditures? Hence, it is quite common, even for government-owned undercapitalized banks to take a while to get adequately recapitalized, if at all.

Regardless of the reason for the undercapitalization of banks to persist, what is observed is that creditors of undercapitalized banks are not only offered off-balance sheet government guarantees, notably deposit insurance, but also implicit guarantees to uninsured creditors. This is done in the interest of financial stability and safeguarding of payment and settlement systems but carries the downside that under-capitalized banks often continue to access credit markets at artificially low costs of borrowing. Consequently, without appropriate supervisory constraints in place, such banks are in a position to delay the recognition of losses and engage in evergreening or zombie lending, which is essentially the rolling over of debts of unviable borrowers that would have otherwise defaulted.

In fact, this was precisely what happened in Japan at the turn of the last century when the problem of non-performing loans and bank capital shortage persisted for over a decade. Hoshi and Kashyap (2010) attribute this to two factors: first, banks not recognizing the true losses on NPAs, thereby overstating the quality of their loans; second, prevalence of zombie lending by undercapitalized banks. It was only after the implementation of the of Financial Revival Program (Takenaka Plan) started in 2003, involving more rigorous evaluation of bank assets, increasing of bank capital and strengthening of governance for recapitalized banks, that the Japanese banks finally stopped the process of evergreening non-performing loans and started to accumulate capital through retained earnings over the next five years.

In addition to the above evidence on Japan, which I covered in some detail in the eighth R. K. Talwar Memorial Lecture, my recent joint work with Sascha Steffen and Lea Steinruecke titled 'Kicking the Can Down the Road: Government Interventions in the European Banking Sector,' (Acharya, Steffen and Steinruecke 2018) examined all government interventions in the Eurozone banking sector during the 2007–2009 financial crisis. In particular, we analyzed the implications of these interventions in the European banking sector for the subsequent sovereign debt crisis and found that:

1. Governments with weaker public finances were more reluctant to recapitalize distressed banks during the financial crisis.
2. The resulting insufficient recapitalization of distressed banks had significant negative consequences for the efficiency of real sector lending. In particular, weak banks remained

vulnerable to future shocks and increased their risk taking. Furthermore, these banks did not write down defaulted loans but instead evergreened loans to zombie borrowers, crowding out in the process credit extension to healthier borrowers.

The Case for Regulatory PCA

How should undercapitalized banks, and more generally, banks whose asset quality and profitability make them vulnerable to further stress, be dealt with, taking cognizance of the reality that the strength of market discipline by bank creditors is blunted by the presence of explicit and implicit government guarantees?

This question received significant academic and policymaker attention in the USA following the S&L crisis, in which by the mid-1980s, so many thrifts had to be resolved at such low levels of capitalization that in the end, a significant government bailout in the form of blanket deposit insurance had to be engineered. Effectively, it had been left until too late to exercise regulatory discipline that could have substituted for the lack of adequate market discipline; as a result, the authorities had to engage in excessive forbearance and full-scale bailout.

The key insight that emerged from the debate around the S&L crisis was that the banking regulator needed to adopt a 'structured early intervention and resolution' (SEIR) approach (see, for instance, Benston and Kaufman 1990; White 1991). This insight, in turn, led to the passage of the Federal Deposit Insurance Corporation (FDIC) Improvement Act (FDICIA) 1991, and thus was born the PCA framework of the FDIC as modern banking has witnessed. (Another twin born then was risk-based deposit insurance premium!)

PCA frameworks adopt the core principles of structured early intervention and resolution in the following manner:

1. Thresholds of performance (in case of FDIC, bank capitalization) are identified to classify banks that breach the thresholds into categories, for instance, in the case of FDIC into 'undercapitalized', 'significantly undercapitalized' and 'critically undercapitalized'. The first thresholds are set at levels that are well above what would allow for an effective resolution or revival of banks.

2. Banks that do not meet the thresholds are subjected to a layered, progressively stringent 'program', consisting of mandatory and discretionary regulatory actions, which aim to prevent further haemorrhaging, effectively quarantining the banks in breach until they are resolved. Another important rationale is to help supervisors enforce corrective measures in a rule-based manner and this way reduce the risk of forbearance.

Put simply, this is what PCA is intended to achieve, to intervene early and take corrective measures in a timely manner, so as to restore the financial health of banks that are at risk by limiting deterioration in their health and preserving their capital levels. By construction then, PCA involves some restrictions on bank scope and expansion as not doing so would lead to excessive risks on the balance sheets of these banks. Similarly, putting up PCA banks for sale in the market and/or replacing bank management become potential mechanisms for prompt resolution. It follows as a corollary that the strength of the PCA framework depends crucially on the extent of regulatory powers that can be exercised by the banking regulator.

While the intent of PCA is primarily remedial, it can also act as a deterrence and incentivize bank management and shareholders to contain risks so they do not end up in PCA in the first place. And, by the virtue of being reasonably rule based, PCA reduces the scope for discretion; like Odysseus, bank regulators tie themselves to the mast to evade the voices of the forbearance sirens.

RBI's PCA Framework

The RBI's PCA framework was introduced in December 2002 as a structured early intervention mechanism along the lines of the FDIC's PCA framework. Subsequently, the framework was reviewed by the Reserve Bank keeping in view the international best practices and recommendations of the working group of the Financial Stability and Development Council (FSDC) on resolution regimes for financial institutions in India (January 2014) and the Financial Sector Legislative Reforms Commission (FSLRC, March 2013). The revised PCA framework was issued by the RBI on 13 April 2017 and implemented with respect to the bank financials as on 31 March 2017.

Annex 4A.1 provides the thresholds deployed under the revised framework, publicly available at rbi.org.in, linked to capital (regulatory capital to risk-weighted assets ratio [CRAR]—and leverage ratio), asset quality (net NPA [NNPA] to advances ratio) and profitability (return on assets [ROA]). Under each measure, once the initial threshold is crossed, successive thresholds are employed to categorize banks into those violating Threshold 1 only, Threshold 1 and Threshold 2 only, or even Threshold 3.

The revised PCA framework strengthened the earlier one along several dimensions, the salient changes being as follows:

1. While capital, asset quality and profitability continue to be the key areas for monitoring under the revised framework, common equity Tier-1 (common equity Tier-1 CRAR) ratio has also been included to constitute an additional trigger along with monitoring of leverage. This change acknowledges that it is common equity capital of a bank that has the highest loss-absorption capacity and is the least like debt. Overall, risk thresholds under the revised framework have been made more granular.

2. Some of the corrective actions which were earlier a part of 'structured (mandatory) actions' to be taken by the supervisor have been moved to a more comprehensive menu of 'discretionary actions' under the revised framework (detailed comparison is in Annex 4A.2). Thus, the scope of mandatory actions across all risk thresholds has been restricted essentially to:

   a. Restriction on dividend distribution/remittance of profits
   b. Requirement on promoters/owners/parents to bring in more capital
   c. Restrictions on branch expansion
   d. Higher provisioning requirement
   e. Restrictions on management compensation.

3. While no restriction has been imposed on the retail deposit-taking activity of any bank till date, banks can be advised under the revised framework as a cost reduction measure to reduce or avoid altogether the high-cost bulk deposits and

instead improve their current account and savings account (CASA) deposit levels.

It is useful to compare this revised PCA framework of the RBI to the PCA framework of the FDIC as an international benchmark.

Comparison with the FDIC's PCA Framework

Details of various thresholds as well as the mandatory and discretionary actions under the PCA framework of the FDIC are given in Annex 4B.1. In terms of the conceptual design, both frameworks mirror the core principles of structured early intervention and resolution. However, there are at least three significant differences:

1. While FDIC triggers the PCA based only on bank capital thresholds, the RBI's PCA thresholds also include asset quality and profitability. The rationale for this difference is as follows. When provision coverage ratio (PCR; provisions to gross NPAs ratio) of banks is at international standards as in the USA, most anticipated losses are already built into the bank capital. In other words, NPAs net of provisions (NNPA ratio) is low. However, the PCR of Indian banks has historically been much lower as we will see below (Figure 4.8), in part due to their maintaining only the minimum-required provisions. As a result, the present level of bank capital masks the expected capital write-offs that will occur in future; this risk of future undercapitalization is captured by looking for below-threshold asset quality (if NNPA ratio is high) and profitability (if return on assets or ROA is low so that capital accretion in future will be weak).

2. The mandatory actions are much stricter and triggered earlier in terms of capitalization levels in case of the FDIC. For instance, restrictions on asset growth and prior approval of certain expansion proposals kick in right at the breach of Threshold-1 ('undercapitalized' category of FDIC's PCA bank classification).

3. Beyond Threshold-2 ('significantly undercapitalized'), the mandatory actions by FDIC may include recapitalization, change in management or even divestiture. Indeed, most

banks under FDIC's PCA are resolved through auctions where typical outcome is a purchase by another bank with an assumption of the PCA bank's liabilities. Powers to undertake such actions in case of India's PSBs lie with the GoI. As enunciated in Governor Patel's speech in March 2018, 'Banking Regulatory Powers Should Be Ownership Neutral' (Patel 2018), the RBI lacks legislative powers to enforce divestiture or change in management at PSBs.

On balance, therefore, it can be concluded that the RBI's PCA framework is less onerous as compared to the FDIC's PCA framework.

Let me elaborate on point 2 above. 'Purchase and Assumption' (P&A) is the most commonly used resolution method by the FDIC, as part of which a healthy institution purchases some or all of the assets of a failed bank and assumes some or all of the liabilities. When deciding which of these techniques to employ, the FDIC is guided legislatively by the 'least cost to the taxpayers' requirement. The FDIC seeks bids from qualified bidders for the failed bank's assets and the assumption of certain liabilities, including deposits, and accepts the bid that is judged least costly.

If no viable P&A buyer can be found, then the FDIC typically deploys a deposit payoff. A deposit payoff involves repaying insured depositors, liquidating assets of the bank and dividing the proceeds from asset liquidation between itself and uninsured bank creditors. The FDIC might also use a Deposit Insurance National Bank (DINB) or bridge banks to resolve a failed bank, which entail establishing a new national bank with a short-period charter from the Office of the Comptroller of the Currency (OCC). The FDIC retains the majority of the assets in its corporate capacity as the receiver and eventually sells them.

In India, merger of weak banks with stronger ones has been the primary mode of resolution of weak banks in the past. Section 45 of BR Act 1949 empowers the RBI to make a scheme of amalgamation of a bank with another bank if it is in the depositors' interest or in the interest of the overall banking system. The operation of the weak bank may be kept under moratorium for a certain period of time to ensure smooth implementation of the scheme. Many PvtSBs have been merged with other PvtSBs or the PSBs under this mechanism. Since the onset of reforms in 1991, there have been 22 mergers in the

Indian banking space, 11 of which were compulsory mergers under Section 45 of the BR Act 1949 (Bishnoi and Devi 2015). However, one of the critical preconditions for this approach to succeed is that a substantial part of the banking sector be well capitalized. If the potential acquirers are poorly capitalized, it may result in inefficiencies in prices as well as timing in resolution of weak banks, besides increasing the risk of weakening the acquirers themselves through such acquisitions.

Performance of the PCA Banks in India

Let me now turn to some data. The goal of the exercise will be to help understand the 10-year performance (wherever data is available) of banks on which the RBI has imposed the PCA. The reason for examining the performance of these banks over a long time period is to appreciate the fact that the progress of banks under PCA cannot be judged over a relatively short time scale. The longer the undercapitalization and asset quality problems have festered, the more patient one has to be during the rehabilitation process. There is no quick fix or overnight silver bullet here; the reforms have to be implemented and allowed to run their course; they can't be chopped or diluted midstream; the focus has to be on stability that is durable.

As I explain below, there are emerging signs that the performance of banks under PCA is slowly but steadily being restored.

Presently, there are 12 banks, 11 in the public sector and 1 in the private sector, under the RBI's revised PCA framework, with PCA having been imposed on them between February 2014 and January 2018. I will focus below only on the 11 PSBs under the PCA. The share of these PCA banks in advances and deposits as on 31 March 2018 was 18.5 per cent and 20.8 per cent, respectively.

The following trends emerge as one can track the performance of these banks in terms of capitalization and asset quality:

1. **Capitalization** (Figures 4.1 and 4.2): The declining trend of CRAR and Tier-1 capital ratio for PCA banks that started in 2011 has been arrested and the ratio has been maintained steady since 2014 at or above internationally prescribed levels. It may, however, be noted that the PCA banks have had lower CRAR and Tier-1 capital ratio as compared to

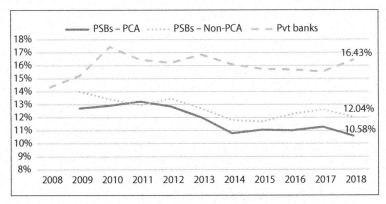

Figure 4.1. Capital to Risk-Weighted Assets Ratio (CRAR)

Source: RBI.
Note: Total capital/risk-weighted assets.

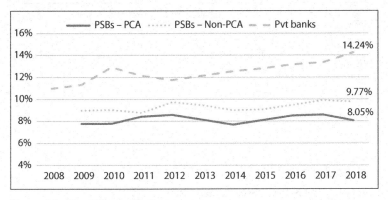

Figure 4.2. Tier 1 Capital Ratio

Source: RBI.
Note: Tier-1 CRAR.

the non-PCA banks, and especially private banks, right since 2009.

2. **Asset quality** (Figures 4.3–4.5): Both the gross and NNPAs ratios of PCA banks mirrored those of non-PCA banks up until about 2014. However, post the AQR exercise, the NPA recognition at PCA banks has led to a sharper rise in both gross and net NPAs, relative to non-PCA banks and, especially, relative to private banks. This does not mean that

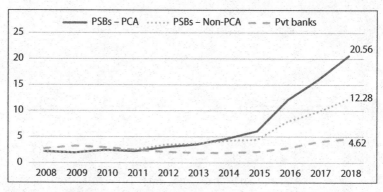

Figure 4.3. Gross Non-performing Assets Ratio (GNPA) (%)
Source: RBI.
Note: Gross NPAs/gross advances.

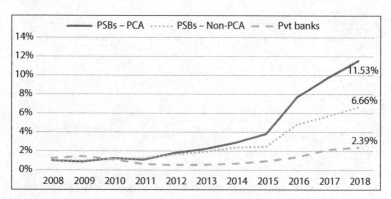

Figure 4.4. Net Non-performing Assets Ratio (NNPA) (%)
Source: RBI.
Note: (Gross NPAs–NPA provisions)/(Gross advances–NPA provisions).

AQR caused the NPAs; it simply induced the long-overdue recognition of NPAs. Notably, the stressed assets ratio, which besides NPAs includes the restructured standard assets (that enjoyed the regulatory forbearance under the earlier guidelines), reveals that the underlying asset quality at PCA banks was deteriorating at a sharper pace compared to non-PCA banks right since 2011, which is now accepted as the time by which the lending boom of 2009–2010 began to unravel.

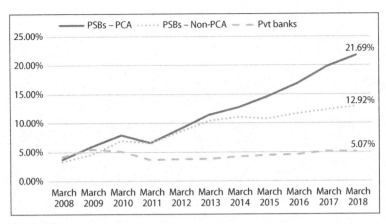

Figure 4.5. Stressed Assets Ratio

Source: RBI.
Note: (Gross NPAs + restructured standard advances)/Gross advances.

The Tide Is Turning for the PCA Banks

As I have tried to explain, an important objective of the PCA is to first and foremost limit further losses and prevent erosion of bank capital, creating a platform of stability for the bank and, in turn, set the stage for structural interventions to be implemented and pushed through.

In assessing whether this objective is being attained, three observations are in order:

1. **Recapitalization** (Figure 4.6): The GoI has infused more than ₹2,300 billion in PSBs since 2005, more than half of which has gone into banks currently under PCA. Within PCA banks, almost half of the total infusion (i.e., ₹635 billion) has occurred between FY2018 and FY2019, after the banks were classified under PCA. This recapitalization has been an important contributor to financial stability of these banks and of the rest of the banking system they deal with.

2. **Preventing further deterioration** (Figure 4.7): In spite of their worse capitalization and stressed assets ratio compared to other banks, PCA banks had credit growth that was as strong as that of other banks up until 2014. However, since the AQR exercise and the imposition of PCA, the year on year growth in advances for PCA banks has declined from over 10 per cent in 2014 to below zero (contraction) by 2016

Prompt Corrective Action | 57

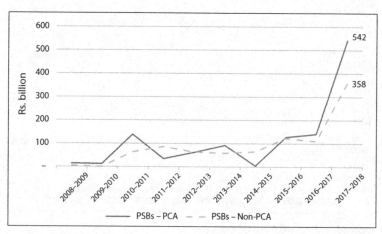

Figure 4.6. Capital Infusion by the Government of India in Public Sector Banks (PSBs)

Source: RBI.

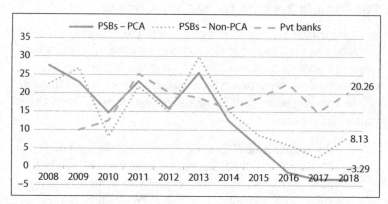

Figure 4.7. Yearly Growth in Advances (%)

Source: RBI.

and remained in the contraction zone since. Given the evidence presented above on PCA bank's sustained problem of asset quality (Figures 4.3–4.5), this is indeed the required medicine to prevent further haemorrhaging of their balance sheets.

3. **Improvement in provision coverage ratio** (Figure 4.8): Given the recapitalization and prevention of further haemorrhaging, the PCR of PCA banks which had fallen off relative

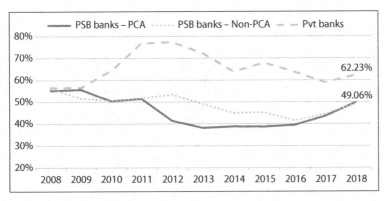

Figure 4.8. Provision Coverage Ratio (%)
Source: RBI.
Note: Total NPA Provisions /Gross NPAs.

to that of other banks starting 2011 and reached below 40 per cent during 2012–2016, has now recovered to that of non-PCA PSBs. The recovered level of PCR remains at present at around 50 per cent, which is 10 per cent below that of private banks, and away from the desirable 70 per cent. These numbers suggest that the loss-absorption capacity of PCA banks is on the mend, but that there is some distance to go in their catch-up with healthy levels.

There is an assertion being made in some circles that imposition of the PCA has starved the Indian economy of credit. There is little factual basis for this assertion, either for the overall economy or at the sectoral level. While it is true as shown above that PCA banks are experiencing lending contraction on average (in terms of their year on year growth in overall advances), the nominal non-food credit growth of scheduled commercial banks has been close to or above double-digit levels, for the past several quarters, and with a robust distribution across the sectors of the real economy (Figure 4.9). This is because the reduction in lending at PCA banks is being more than offset by credit growth at healthier banks. This is indeed what one wants—efficient reallocation of credit for the real economy with a financially stable distribution of risks across bank balance sheets. Indeed, the funding for the economy as a whole has become diversified over this period, also due to the growth of capital markets.

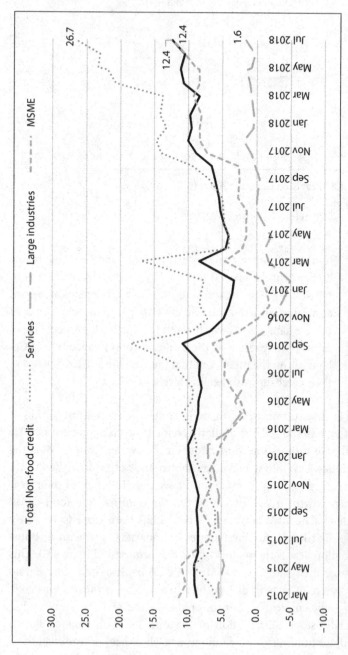

Figure 4.9. Credit Growth in Scheduled Commercial Banks (year on year %)

Source: RBI.

There is also a call for more lending by PCA banks to large industries where the overall credit growth remains muted. Note that many of these industries are heavily indebted to start with and are going through a deleveraging process under the IBC (so that at present, their sectoral capacity is still somewhat in excess and credit demand itself weak). The key point is that PCA banks are undergoing a de-risking the asset side of their balance sheets by moving away from riskier sector loans to less riskier ones and government securities; the first and foremost priority is to limit (effectively, taxpayer) losses at PCA banks and prevent further erosion of their capital.

Conclusion

Let me conclude.

I have tried to explain why adequate bank capital is critical to fortify bank balance sheets and a key indicator for the bank supervisors to closely monitor; and how the PCA framework is employed internationally by bank supervisors and regulators as an accepted form of structured early intervention and resolution, designed to help banks regain health by preserving capital.

I, then, briefly explained the primary features of the RBI's PCA framework, which is an essential element of its apparatus for safeguarding overall financial stability.

The evidence I presented suggests that without the PCA imposition, some banks would have incurred even higher losses and required even more of taxpayer money for recapitalization. Imposition of PCA can, thus, be seen as first, stabilizing the banks at risk and then, undertaking the deeper bank reforms needed for long-term viability of the business model of these banks.

It is important, therefore, that the PCA framework to deal with financially weak banks is persisted with. Any slackening of the approach in the midst of required course action is an all too familiar and ultimately harmful habit that we must eschew.

Well begun is only half done, as they say!

References

Acharya, Viral V. 2017. 'The Unfinished Agenda: Restoring Public Sector Bank Health in India.' R. K. Talwar Memorial Lecture, Indian Institute of Banking and Finance, Mumbai.

Acharya, Viral V., Sascha Steffen and Lea Steinruecke. 2018. 'Kicking the Can Down the Road: Government Interventions in the European Banking Sector.' Working Paper, Frankfurt School of Management and Finance, Frankfurt, Germany.

Benston, George, and George Kaufman. 1990. 'Understanding the Savings and Loan Debacle.' *The Public Interest* 99, (Spring): 79–95.

Bishnoi, T.R., and Sofia Devi. 2015. 'Mergers and Acquisitions of Banks in Post-Reform India.' *Economic & Political Weekly* 50, no. 37 (September): 50–58.

Granja, Joao, Gregor Matvos and Amit Seru. 2017. 'Selling Failed Banks.' *Journal of Finance*, 72, no. 4 (April): 1723–1784.

Hoshi, T., and A. K. Kashyap. 2010. 'Will the U.S. Bank Recapitalization Succeed? Eight Lessons from Japan.' *Journal of Financial Economics* 97, no. 3 (September): 398–417.

Myers, Stewart. 1977. 'Determinants of Corporate Borrowing.' *Journal of Financial Economics*, 5, no. 2 (November): 147–175.

Patel, Urjit R. 2018. 'Banking Regulatory Powers Should be Ownership Neutral.' Inaugural Lecture—Center for Law & Economics; Center for Banking & Financial Laws, Gujarat National Law University.

White, Lawrence J. 1991. *The S&L Debacle: Public Policy Lessons for Bank and Thrift Regulation.* Oxford: Oxford University Press.

Annex 4A.1. RBI's Revised PCA Matrix (April 2017): Indicators and Risk Thresholds

Revised PCA Framework				
	Indicator	Risk Threshold 1	Risk Threshold 2	Risk Threshold 3
Capital **(Breach of either CRAR or CET 1 ratio to trigger PCA)**	CRAR: Minimum regulatory prescription for capital to risk assets ratio + applicable CCB	Up to 250 bps below indicator	More than 250 bps but not exceeding 400 bps below indicator	–
	Current minimum RBI prescription of 10.875% (9% minimum total capital plus 1.875%* of CCB as on March 31, 2018)	<10.875% but >=8.375%	<8.375% but >=6.875%	–
	And/or			
	Regulatory pre-specified trigger of common equity tier 1 (CET 1$_{min}$) + applicable CCB	Up to 162.50 bps below indicator	More than 162.50 bps below but not exceeding 312.50 bps below indicator	In excess of 312.50 bps below indicator
	current minimum RBI prescription of 7.375% (5.5% plus 1.875%* of CCB as on March 31, 2018)			
	Breach of either CRAR or CET 1 ratio to trigger PCA	< 7.375% but >= 5.75%	< 5.75% but >=4.25%	< 4.25%
Asset quality	NNPA ratio	>=6.0% but <9.0%	>=9.0% but < 12.0%	>=12.0%

(continued)

(continued)

	Indicator	Risk Threshold 1	Risk Threshold 2	Risk Threshold 3
Revised PCA Framework				
Profitability	ROA	Negative ROA for two consecutive years	Negative ROA for three consecutive years	Negative ROA for four consecutive years
Leverage	Tier-1 leverage ratio	<= 4.0% but > = 3.5% (leverage is over 25 times the tier-1 capital)	< 3.5% (leverage is over 28.6 times the tier-1 capital)	

Annex 4A.2. Mandatory and Discretionary Corrective Actions under RBI's Old (2002) and Revised (2017) PCA Frameworks

Specifications	Mandatory/Structured Actions		Discretionary Actions	
	Old PCA Framework (Structured Actions)	Revised PCA Framework (Mandatory Actions)	Old PCA Framework	Revised PCA Framework
Capital risk threshold 1	• Submission and implementation of capital restoration plan by the bank • Bank will restrict expansion of its risk-weighted assets • Bank will not enter into new lines of business • Bank will not access/renew costly deposits and CDs • Bank will reduce/skip dividend payments	Restriction on dividend distribution/ remittance of profits to the parent in the case of foreign banks Promoters/owners/ parent in the case of foreign banks to bring in capital	• RBI will order recapitalization • Bank will not increase its stake in subsidiaries • Bank will reduce its exposure to sensitive sectors such as capital market, real estate or investment in non-SLR securities • RBI will impose restrictions on the bank on borrowings from inter-bank market • Bank will revise its credit / investment strategy and controls	Common menu Special supervisory interactions: • Special supervisory monitoring meetings (SSMMs) at quarterly or other identified frequency • Special inspections/targeted scrutiny of the bank • Special audit of the bank Strategy related: RBI to advise the bank's board to: • Activate the recovery plan that has been duly approved by the supervisor • Undertake a detailed review of business model in terms of sustainability of the business model, profitability of business lines and activities, medium- and long-term viability, balance sheet projections, etc.
NPA risk threshold 1	• Bank to undertake special drive to reduce the stock of NPAs and contain generation of fresh NPAs • Bank will review its loan policy		• Bank will not enter into new lines of business • Bank will reduce /skip dividend payments • Bank will not increase its stake in subsidiaries	• Review short-term strategy focusing on addressing immediate concerns • Review medium term business plans, identify achievable targets and set concrete milestones for progress and achievement

(continued)

(continued)

Specifications	Mandatory/Structured Actions		Discretionary Actions	
	Old PCA Framework (Structured Actions)	Revised PCA Framework (Mandatory Actions)	Old PCA Framework	Revised PCA Framework
	• Bank will take steps to upgrade credit appraisal skills and systems • Bank will strengthen follow-up of advances including loan review mechanism for large loans • Bank will follow-up suit filed/decreed debts effectively • Bank will put in place proper credit-risk management polices/process/procedures/prudential limits • Bank will reduce loan concentration–individual, group, sector, industry, etc.			• Review all business lines to identify scope for enhancement/ contraction • Undertake business process reengineering as appropriate • Undertake restructuring of operations as appropriate **Governance related** • RBI to actively engage with the bank's board on various aspects as considered appropriate • RBI to recommend to owners (government/ promoters/parent of foreign bank branch) to bring in new management/board • RBI to remove managerial persons under Section 36AA of the BR Act 1949 as applicable • RBI to supersede the Board under Section 36ACA of the BR Act 1949/ recommend supersession of the board as applicable • RBI to require bank to invoke claw back and malus clauses and other actions as available in regulatory guidelines, and impose other restrictions or conditions permissible under the BR Act, 1949 • Impose restrictions on directors' or management compensation as applicable.

ROA risk threshold 1	• Bank will not access/ renew costly deposits and CDs • Bank will take steps to increase fee-based income • Bank will take steps to contain administrative expenses • Bank will launch special drive to reduce the stock of NPAs and contain generation of fresh NPAs • Bank will not enter into new lines of business • Bank will reduce/skip dividend payments • RBI will impose restrictions on the bank on borrowings from interbank market	• Bank will not incur any capital expenditure other than for technological upgradation and for such emergent replacements within board approved limits • Bank will not expand its staff/fill up vacancies	**Capital related** • Detailed board-level review of capital planning • Submission of plans and proposals for raising additional capital • Requiring the bank to bolster reserves through retained profits • Restriction on investment in subsidiaries/ associates • Restriction in expansion of high risk-weighted assets to conserve capital • Reduction in exposure to high risk sectors to conserve capital • Restrictions on increasing stake in subsidiaries and other group companies **Credit risk related** • Preparation of time bound plan and commitment for reduction of stock of NPAs • Preparation of and commitment to plan for containing generation of fresh NPAs • Strengthening of loan review mechanism • Restrictions on/ reduction in credit expansion for borrowers below certain rating grades

(continued)

(continued)

Specifications	Mandatory/Structured Actions		Discretionary Actions	
	Old PCA Framework (Structured Actions)	Revised PCA Framework (Mandatory Actions)	Old PCA Framework	Revised PCA Framework
Capital risk threshold 2	• All structured actions as in earlier zone • Discussion by RBI with the bank's board on corrective plan of action • RBI will order recapitalization • Bank will not increase its stake in subsidiaries • Bank will revise its credit/ investment strategy and controls	In addition to mandatory actions of threshold 1, Restriction on branch expansion; domestic and/or overseas Higher provisions as part of the coverage regime	• Bank/Government to take steps to bring in new management/ board • Bank will appoint consultants for business/organizational restructuring • Bank/government to take steps to change promoters/to change ownership • RBI/Government will take steps to merge the bank if it fails to submit/implement recapitalization plan or fails to recapitalize pursuant to an order, within such period as RBI may stipulate	• Reduction in risk assets • Restrictions on/reduction in credit expansion to unrated borrowers • Reduction in unsecured exposures • Reduction in loan concentrations; in identified sectors, industries or borrowers • Sale of assets • Action plan for recovery of assets through identification of areas (geography wise, industry segment wise, borrower wise, etc.) and setting up of dedicated recovery task forces, *adalats*, etc. **Market risk related** • Restrictions on/reduction in borrowings from the interbank market • Restrictions on accessing/renewing wholesale deposits/costly deposits/ certificates of deposits • Restrictions on derivative activities, derivatives that permit collateral substitution • Restriction on excess maintenance of collateral held that could contractually be called any time by the counterparty

HR related
- Restriction on staff expansion
- Review of specialized training needs of existing staff

Profitability related
- Restrictions on capital expenditure, other than for technological upgradation within board approved limits
- Restrictions on dividend payments
- Restriction on staff expansion

Operations related
- Restrictions on branch expansion plans; domestic or overseas
- Reduction in business at overseas branches/ subsidiaries/in other entities
- Restrictions on entering into new lines of business
- Reduction in leverage through reduction in non-fund based business
- Reduction in risky assets
- Restrictions on non-credit asset creation
- Restrictions in undertaking businesses as specified.

(continued)

(continued)

Specifications	Mandatory/Structured Actions		Discretionary Actions	
	Old PCA Framework (Structured Actions)	Revised PCA Framework (Mandatory Actions)	Old PCA Framework	Revised PCA Framework
NPA risk threshold 2	• All structured actions as in earlier zone • Discussion by RBI with the bank's Board on corrective plan of action • Bank will not enter into new lines of business • Bank will reduce/skip dividend payments • Bank will not increase its stake in subsidiaries			Any other
Capital risk threshold 3	• All structured actions as in earlier zone • RBI will observe the functioning of the bank more closely • RBI/government will take steps to merge/amalgamate liquidate the bank or impose moratorium on the bank if its CRAR does not improve beyond 3% within one year or within such extended period as agreed to.	In addition to mandatory actions of threshold 1, Restriction on branch expansion; domestic and/or overseas Restriction on management compensation and directors' fees, as applicable	–	

Annex 4B.1. FDIC PCA Matrix

Thresholds	Well Capitalized (All Thresholds to Be Met)	Adequately Capitalized (All Thresholds to Be Met)	Undercapitalized (Any One or More Thresholds in Breach)	Significantly Undercapitalized (Any One or More Thresholds in Breach)	Critically Undercapitalized
					Tangible equity/Total Assets ≤ 2%
Total risk-based capital ratio	> 10%	> 8%	< 8%	< 6%	
Tier-1 risk-based capital ratio	> 8%	> 6%	< 6%	< 4%	
Common equity tier-1 ratio	> 6.5%	> 4.5%	< 4.5%	< 3%	
Leverage ratio	>5%	>4%	< 4%	< 3%	
Capital directive/ other	Not subject to a capital directive to meet a specific level for any capital measure	Does not meet the definition of well capitalized			

(continued)

(continued)

Provisions	Well Capitalized (All Thresholds to Be Met)	Adequately Capitalized (All Thresholds to Be Met)	Undercapitalized (Any One or More Thresholds in Breach)	Significantly Undercapitalized (Any One or More Thresholds in Breach)	Critically Undercapitalized

Mandatory actions		No brokered deposits except with FDIC approval	1. Restricting payment of capital distributions and management fees
			2. Requiring that the FDIC monitor the condition of the FDIC-supervised institution
			3. Requiring submission of a capital restoration plan within the established schedule
			4. Restricting the growth of the assets
			5. Requiring prior approval of certain expansion proposals
				In addition to threshold 1
				
				Restrict compensation paid to senior executive officers of the institution
				
				Any 1 or more of the following:
				1. Requiring recapitalization
				2. Restricting transactions with affiliates
				3. Restricting interest rates paid.
				4. Restricting asset growth.
				5. (v) Restricting activities
				6. (vi) Improving management
				   a. new election of directors.
				   b. dismissing directors or senior executive officers
					In addition to threshold 1
					
					Restrict compensation paid to senior executive officers of the institution
					
					Prohibited on making any principal or interest payment on subordinated debt beginning 60 days after becoming critically undercapitalized.
					
					Prohibited from doing any of the following without the FDIC's prior written approval:
					1. Entering into any material transaction other than in the usual course of business, including any investment, expansion, acquisition, sale of assets, or other similar action with respect to which the depository institution is required to provide notice to the appropriate Federal banking agency.

c. employing qualified senior executive officers 7. Prohibiting deposits from correspondent banks 8. Requiring prior approval for capital distributions by bank holding company. 9. Requiring divestiture 10. Any other action	2. Extending credit for any highly leveraged transaction. 3. Amending the institution's charter or bylaws, except to the extent necessary to carry out any other requirement of any law, regulation, or order. 4. Making any material change in accounting methods. 5. Engaging in any covered transaction 6. Paying excessive compensation or bonuses. 7. Paying interest on new or renewed liabilities at a rate that would increase the institution's weighted average cost of funds to a level significantly exceeding the prevailing rates of interest on insured deposits in the institution's normal market areas.		

(continued)

(continued)

	Well Capitalized (All Thresholds to Be Met)	Adequately Capitalized (All Thresholds to Be Met)	Undercapitalized (Any One or More Thresholds in Breach)	Significantly Undercapitalized (Any One or More Thresholds in Breach)	Critically Undercapitalized
					The appropriate Federal banking agency shall, not later than 90 days after an insured depository institution becomes critically undercapitalized: (i) appoint a receiver (or, with the concurrence of the Corporation, a conservator) for the institution; or (ii) take such other action as the agency determines, with the concurrence of the Corporation, would better achieve the purpose of this section, after documenting why the action would better achieve that purpose.

Discretionary actions	(i) Requiring recapitalization (ii) Restricting transactions with affiliates (iii) Restricting interest rates paid. (iv) Restricting asset growth. (v) Restricting activities (vi) Improving management (a) new election of directors. (b) dismissing directors or senior executive officers (c) employing qualified senior executive officers	(i) Restrict the activities, and (ii) at a minimum, prohibit any such institution from doing any of the following without the Corporation's prior written approval: (a) Entering into any material transaction other than in the usual course of business, including any investment, expansion, acquisition, sale of assets, or other similar action with respect to which the depository institution is required to provide notice to the appropriate Federal banking agency.	

(continued)

(continued)

Well Capitalized (All Thresholds to Be Met)	Adequately Capitalized (All Thresholds to Be Met)	Undercapitalized (Any One or More Thresholds in Breach)	Significantly Undercapitalized (Any One or More Thresholds in Breach)	Critically Undercapitalized
		(vii) Prohibiting deposits from correspondent banks (viii) Requiring prior approval for capital distributions by bank holding company. (ix) Requiring divestiture Any other action	(b) Extending credit for any highly leveraged transaction. (c) Amending the institution's charter or bylaws, except to the extent necessary to carry out any other requirement of any law, regulation, or order. (d) Making any material change in accounting methods.	

(e) Engaging in any covered transaction

(f) Paying excessive compensation or bonuses.

(g) Paying interest on new or renewed liabilities at a rate that would increase the institution's weighted average cost of funds to a level significantly exceeding the prevailing rates of interest on insured deposits in the institution's normal market areas.

PART 2

Creating a Public Credit Registry

CHAPTER 5

A CASE FOR PUBLIC CREDIT REGISTRY IN INDIA*

Statistics Day in India is celebrated on the birth anniversary of Late Professor P. C. Mahalanobis, who graduated with honours in Physics in 1912 and was subsequently attracted to the realm of statistics. In modern management parlance, Professor Mahalanobis was an 'out of the box' thinker. All his contributions emanated while studying statistical problems of immediate importance. Professor Mahalanobis set up the Indian Statistical Institute (ISI) and the survey lab there subsequently blossomed into the present National Sample Survey Office (NSSO).[1] The RBI has benefitted immensely over the years from its collaboration with the ISI on statistical issues and the NSSO on measurement issues.

Let me now dwell on 'the new frontiers on statistical methods and information base for central banks'. Statistical techniques are an integral part of economic analysis. An interesting acknowledgement

* Speech delivered by Dr Viral V. Acharya, Deputy Governor, RBI at the 11th Statistics Day Conference held at RBI, Central Office, Mumbai on 4 July 2017. Valuable insights provided by Dr O. P. Mall and Shri Anujit Mitra are gratefully acknowledged.
[1] This conference of the RBI is eleventh in the series but, for me, it was my first Statistics Day Conference. In the conference, we were privileged to have with us several distinguished guests. Dr Martine Durand, our keynote speaker and also Chief Statistician and Director, OECD Statistics Directorate and a leading voice on global statistical issues; Professor Chetan Ghate of the ISI-Delhi and member of the Monetary Policy Committee (MPC) and a regular teacher at the RBI Academy, as well as Professor N. Balakrishna of the Cochin University of Science and Technology; We also welcomed Dilip Nachane, Professor Emeritus, IGIDR-Mumbai and former member of the RBI's Technical Advisory Committee on Monetary Policy (TAC-MP) and the Prime Minister's Economic Advisory Council (PMEAC); Dr D. K. Joshi of CRISIL, Ms Pranjul Bhandari of HSBC and Dr Samiran Chakraborty of Citibank, who were the other distinguished panel members.

of this is the good share of 'method awards' in award of the Nobel Prize for Economic Sciences. The first Nobel in Economics in 1969 went to Ragnar Frisch and Jan Tinbergen for their pioneering work on econometric model building, that is, for their integration of economic theory and statistical methods. Over the years, Nobel 'method awards' have also been awarded for input-output method, national accounts, micro-econometrics, co-integration and ARCH (to Rob Engle, colleague, co-author and dear friend when I was at NYU Stern).

The central role of statistical methods in economic analysis is also reflected in their constantly growing share in the curriculum for students in economics and finance. The global financial crisis and its aftermath has been a big structural break to explain which new approaches and methods are gaining ground. Macroeconomic forecasters have faced interesting questions during this last decade, as the outbreak of banking and sovereign crises has led to the most basic assumptions behind forecasts being violated. This has also necessitated further efforts towards methodological refinements, not just in economic theory but also in statistical methods to test the theory. In many ways, this is an exciting time in my view to be studying economics.

The meeting of the G20 Finance Ministers and Central Bank Governors in 2009 endorsed the G20 Data Gap Initiatives (DGI), which focuses on (a) build-up of risk in the financial sector; (b) cross-border financial linkages; (c) vulnerability of domestic economies to the shocks and (d) improving communication of official statistics. After the first phase of DGI was largely implemented, the second phase commenced in 2015 with the objective to strengthen the global statistical systems so as to aid deeper economic analysis. India's progress in this regard has been good so far and we are taking further strides, recognizing that such initiatives help individual countries and also the global economic system.

The Case for a Public Credit Registry (PCR) in India

I will focus in the rest of this chapter on a topic which I feel is vital for Indian economy at this juncture and where I expect the RBI and, more specifically, the Statistics Department, to play a rather important role. It concerns the setting up of a PCR, an extensive database of credit information for India that is accessible to all stakeholders. Generally, a PCR is managed by a public authority like a central bank or a banking supervisor and reporting of loan details to the PCR by the lenders and/or the borrowers is mandated by law. The contractual terms and outcomes covered and the threshold above which the contracts are to be reported vary in different jurisdictions, but the idea is to capture all relevant information of the borrower in one large database, in particular, the borrower's entire set of borrowing contracts and outcomes.

A PCR, if put in place for India, will help in (a) credit assessment and pricing by banks; (b) risk-based, dynamic and countercyclical provisioning at banks; (c) supervision and early intervention by regulators; (d) understanding if transmission of monetary policy is working, and if not, where are the bottlenecks and (e) to find out how to restructure stressed bank credits effectively. The extensive and incisive work of Professor José-Luis Peydró of Universitat Pompeu Fabra on such issues using the Spanish credit register is a testimony to the tremendous value a PCR can bring to clear understanding of the underlying economy. I encourage you to check out his work.

Let me start by explaining the motivation for creating such a database. A vast body of academic literature advocates transparency in credit markets, arguing that it improves the efficiency of the market and helps the creditors as well as the borrowers. One of the reasons the credit information is termed as a 'public good' is its utility to the credit market at large and to the society in general. In the absence of a central database of credit information, the creditors are restricted to the information about their clients based only on their limited transactions or interactions with the clients, and this could lead to suboptimal outcomes.

A central repository, which, for instance, captures and certifies the details of collaterals, can enable the writing of contracts that prevent over-pledging of collateral by a borrower. In absence of the repository, the lender may not trust its first right on the collateral and either charge a high cost on the loan or ask for more collateral than necessary to prevent being diluted by other lenders. This leads to what in economics is termed as pecuniary externality—in this case, a spillover of one loan contract onto outcomes and terms of other loan contracts. Furthermore, in the absence of a PCR, the 'good' borrowers are disadvantaged in not being able to distinguish themselves from the rest in opaque credit markets; they could potentially be subjected to a rent being extracted from their existing lenders who enjoy an information monopoly over them. The lenders may also end up picking up fresh clients who have a history of delinquency that is unknown to all the lenders and this way face greater overall credit risk.

Current Credit Information Systems in India

Let us now have a look at the current credit information systems in our country. The private credit bureaus (CBs) operating in India are regulated by RBI under the Credit Information Companies (Regulation) Act 2005 and include Credit Information Bureau (India) Limited (CIBIL), Equifax, Experian and CRIF Highmark. Each one of these focuses on data analytics to provide credit scores, and allied reports and services. These analytics are useful for the member banks for issuing credit cards as well as for taking decisions (primarily on retail loans) as of now.

The RBI has set up the CRILC in 2014–2015. It is now one of the most important databases for offsite supervision. Here, the Scheduled Commercial Banks (SCBs) in India report credit information of their large borrowers, that is, those having aggregate fund-based and non-fund-based exposure of ₹5 crore and above. It covers around 60 per cent of the loan portfolio and around 80 per cent of the non-performing loans of SCBs. The reporting is done on a quarterly basis, but the slippages are required to be reported in another format on as-and-when basis. The CRILC is designed entirely for supervisory purposes and its focus is on the reporting entities' exposure to the borrower (as individual and/or as a group) under various heads, such as the bank's exposure to a large borrower; a borrower's current account balance; the bank's written-off accounts; and identification of non-cooperative borrowers, among others. However, CRILC captures only limited details about the borrowers such as the industry to which they belong and their external and internal ratings. The pooled information under CRILC is shared with the reporting banks but is not shared with the CBs, the larger lender community, or the researchers.

My colleagues in DSIM are familiar with the Basic Statistical Return (BSR)-1, where account level credit information (an 'account' being a specific loan or a facility between a bank and a borrower) is reported by banks. As the name suggests, it is a statistical return which captures some metadata for the account such as district and the population group of the place of funds utilization; type of account such as cash credit, overdraft, term loan, credit cards, etc.; organization type such as private corporate sector, household sector, microfinance institutions, Non-Profit Institutions Serving Households (NPISH) and non-residents; and occupation type such as agriculture, manufacturing, construction and various financial and non-financial services. The interest rate charged along with the flag for floating vs. fixed is also reported here. These details are not present in CRILC which is a borrower-level dataset rather than an account-level dataset. Though BSR-1 contains a 'health code' for each account, it is not comprehensive enough to cater to the supervisory needs as it is not feasible to aggregate all accounts maintained by a borrower in the absence of a unique identifier across the reporting banks. Due to a number of reasons, even bank-level aggregation of delinquency in BSR-1 will not in general match with that reported through CRILC. Aggregated statistical information with spatial, temporal and sectoral distribution from BSR-1 is shared in the public domain for researchers, analysts and commentators. Account-level data is, however, kept confidential but is shared by the RBI with researchers on a case-to-case basis under appropriate safeguards.

These databases maintained in the RBI are not available to individual banks in real time to take credit decisions at the micro level. They do not capture fully the credit data at origination level. In particular, the 360-degree view is not available to creditors in any of the systems discussed. Individually, some of these systems can be swiftly strengthened with just a few additional fields. For example, capturing in BSR-1 the unique account-holder identifier in the form of Aadhar for individuals and Corporate Identification Number (CIN) for companies may make it possible to view all accounts of each borrower across banks.

Next, I would like to draw your attention to the company finance databases available with the RBI and with the MCA. These contain the audited or unaudited financial results of the corporates submitted by them at various frequencies. Here again the key identifier is the CIN. The power of the information can be substantially enhanced if we can make BSR-1 and CRILC talk to each other and further link them both with the MCA database containing financial results of the corporate sector.

International Experience with PCRs

Let me now turn to the international scenario. A survey conducted by the World Bank reported that as of 2012, out of 195 countries that were surveyed, 87 had PCRs—the numbers must have increased by now. The private CBs are also functioning well in many of the high-income countries and they co-exist with the PCRs. In USA, the Dealscan by Thomson Reuters is a prime example which covers the syndicated loan origination data including information on arrangers; price and maturity terms; credit lines or term loans; and loan characteristics such as covenants. Since banks voluntarily provide credit data at the time of origination itself, it is almost a real-time dataset and one gets to know in a week or two weeks' time whether there is a change in the credit market conditions.

Dun & Bradstreet or DNB in short, is nearly two centuries old and has perhaps the largest commercial database in the world. Their website claims that they track over 265 million company records which they derive from 30,000 data sources and is updated 5 million times per day. DNB's own correspondents gather data on firms by visiting and telephoning the firm's principals. It is interesting to note that in the 19th century, these correspondents, who were often lawyers, included such luminaries as Abraham Lincoln, Woodrow Wilson and Calvin Coolidge (Kallberg and Udell 2003).

Let me give a real-life example to illustrate the utility of such information systems. In the aftermath of the collapse of Lehman Brothers in September 2008, there were economists who asserted that the credit flow in the USA was unaffected by pointing out to the robust credit growth in bank loans. But a deeper analysis of the Thomson Reuters Dealscan data quickly revealed that the credit growth was almost entirely attributable to the corporates drawing down (a form of a 'bank run') on the existing credit lines. The origination of new loans had indeed dried up.

How a PCR Can Help in India

Let us now envisage how exactly a PCR can help in India. First, it is required to improve the credit culture in our country. It has been demonstrated in the 'Doing Business 2017' report that credit information systems impart transparency in the credit market, following which access to credit improves and delinquencies decrease. At present, several Indian banks burdened with mounting NPAs appear less confident in taking credit decisions. A transparent PCR would help the bankers to rely on objective data for making credit decisions and also enable them to defend their actions with market evidence when subjected to scrutiny.

Second, large borrowers get a preference in credit markets due to their existing credentials in the public space. They have established credit history, brand value and supply of collateral. In contrast, small and marginal aspirants, start-ups, new entrepreneurs and small businesses in micro, small and medium enterprises (MSME) sector are disadvantaged as they lack many of those desired qualifications for credit. Transparency of credit information would serve as a 'reputational collateral' for such borrowers. This would not only help promote financial inclusion, but also reward the good borrowers thereby imparting credit discipline. We just have to look at our willingness to transact on eBay to understand how reputation builds up for effectively anonymous sellers from their transaction records captured on a website. Similarly, PCR would help create a level-playing field among different sizes of borrowers.

Third, PCRs in many countries have gone beyond the credit relationship of borrowing entities with financial institutions. They tap other transactional data of borrowers including payments to utilities like power and telecom for retail customers and trade credit data for businesses. Why might such data help? Lenders in the formal sector often hesitate to extend a line of credit to new customers due to the lack of credit scores. Regularity in making payments to utilities and trade creditors provides an indication of the credit quality of such customers. In turn, credit from the formal sector can become accessible to new borrowers, boosting financial inclusion. As a side benefit, the extent of financial inclusion will likely become more precisely measurable for policymakers.

Finally, PCR can have a profound impact for regulatory purposes. In its absence, only fragmented images are available of credit behaviour and indebtedness. PCR will help in getting to a complete picture that is necessary for supervisors and policy makers to assess credit risk of the entire system. To facilitate this, the PCR must cover the following aspects of the credit data: First, the bank-borrower loan-level data detailing loan terms at the time of origination along with data on the borrower's economic and financial health. Second, the internal and external ratings (or credit scores) and their evolution, and where applicable, market-based measures of firm-level and sector-level credit risks. Third, bank-borrower loan-level restructuring data with all details. Fourth, secondary loan sales and price information. Fifth, borrower-debt level default and recovery (loss given default; LGD) data. This would be a good start!

Who Should Operate the PCR?

Large PCRs are operated either by the central banks or by the state authorities in various countries. They are typically not operated by the private sector, though CBs in some jurisdictions capture many of the items discussed above. In some jurisdictions, the raw data collected by the central PCR is shared with the CBs, which in turn make value addition by pooling data from other sources and come up with further analysis such as credit scores/reports to their clients, typically commercial lenders. Since we are talking about a large database containing lots of private information, it also needs to be handled by an authority which is trustworthy in public eye as well as backed by appropriate judicial powers to ensure timely and accurate data gathering. Therefore, it is found internationally that with rare exceptions, the PCRs are managed by central banking or banking supervisory authorities.

In Summary

Let me conclude by restating that a transparent and comprehensive PCR is the need of the hour in India. More and more countries are moving towards this with a view to improving the credit culture in their jurisdictions. Such registers help in enhancing efficiency of the credit market, increase financial inclusion, improve ease of doing business and help control delinquencies. Incorporating unique identifiers for the borrowers (Aadhar for individuals and CIN for companies), RBI's BSR-1 and CRILC datasets can quickly be converted into a useful PCR covering customers of SCBs to start with. It can then be expanded to cover other financial institutions in India. A comprehensive PCR down the road will be even more effective.

Setting up a comprehensive PCR will, however, require much teamwork and vision. It will demand expertise to handle large volumes and varieties of data assembled from diverse sources. It will require working with several stakeholders, other regulators and international agencies with expertise in helping set up such registers. That's a worthy challenge for the pool of statisticians assembled here on the eve of the eleventh Statistics Day. Governor and I hope we can set up, as a matter of priority, a high-level task force that can provide a roadmap for attaining this goal of developing and unleashing a powerful credit information system for our country.

There are several other 'information base' challenges for the long horizon for the team: employment statistics; household inflation expectation survey in rural and informal economy; big-data real-time indicators of prices and consumption; Google images and mobile-phone data for economic activity indicators; just to list a few. Having a go at some of these will be a fitting tribute to Professor Mahalanobis whose contributions were truly long-term and have lived far beyond his immediate lifespan.

Reference

Kallberg, J. G., and G. F. Udell. 2003. 'The Value of Private Sector Business Credit Information Sharing: The US Case.' *Journal of Banking & Finance* 27, no. 3: 449–469.

CHAPTER 6

PUBLIC CREDIT REGISTRY (PCR) AND GOODS AND SERVICES TAX NETWORK (GSTN): GIANT STRIDES TO DEMOCRATIZE AND FORMALIZE CREDIT IN INDIA*

I wish to draw your attention to some major initiatives in gathering and analyzing better credit data that can potentially have a huge impact in creating a financially healthy India.

It is a known fact that a large part of the Indian economy is informal. This year's *Economic Survey* has given us an estimate, sourced in large part from the implementation of the GSTN. About 0.6 per cent of firms—accounting for 38 per cent of total turnover, 87 per cent of exports and 63 per cent of GST (Ministry of Finance 2018) liability—are in what might be called the 'hard core' formal sector in the sense of being both in the tax and social security net. Estimates also suggest that the informal economy employs nearly 50 per cent of the workforce in India (Ministry of Finance 2018). The earnings of some in the informal economy may be at par with their formal economy counterparts, but due to its informal nature, people and businesses in this part of the economy are rendered 'invisible' to the formal banking system. Due to lack of access to formal credit this 'invisibility' adversely affects their ability to increase current income level.

It is no surprise, then, that India's credit-to-GDP ratio stands at a modest 55.7 per cent, compared to China's 208.7 per cent, the United Kingdom's 170.5 per cent and the United States' 152.2 per cent

*The speech was delivered at the Annual Global Banking Conference—FIBAC 2018 organized by the Federation of Indian Chambers of Commerce and Industry (FICCI) and Indian Banks' Association (IBA) on 20 August 2018 at Mumbai. A Theme Talk was also delivered on the subject at the 12th Annual Statistics Day Conference organized by the RBI at Mumbai on 23 July 2018.

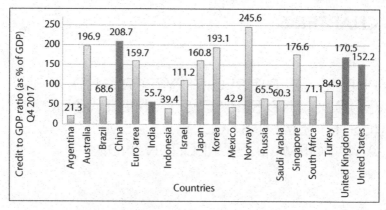

Figure 6.1. Credit-to-GDP Ratio of Select Countries (Q4: 2017)
Source: Bank for International Settlements.

(BIS, Q4 2017 data, see Figure 6.1).[1] In other words, there is financial under-penetration in India.

It is in this context that I will share with you two giant strides being undertaken to help India move towards more equitable and timely access to credit, especially to the underserved. While these strides are being undertaken independently, together they can democratize and formalize credit in India.

PCR for India

The first stride is the creation of a PCR. Last year in my speech[2] at the Annual Statistics Day Conference in RBI, I focused on setting up a PCR in India. Till that time, the concept of PCR was not much discussed in our country, though a large number of countries had already established or were in the process of establishing PCRs. I am happy to quickly recount with you the progress that we have made in this direction thus far. The constitution of a high-level task force (HTF), under the chairmanship of Shri Y. M. Deosthalee and consisting of eminent experts from various stakeholders, was

---

[1] Data from https://stats.bis.org/statx/srs/table/j?m<hig>=</hig>A
[2] A Case for PCR in India: https://rbi.org.in/scripts/BS_SpeechesView.aspx?Id<hig>=</hig>1042

announced by the RBI in Part B of its monetary policy statement dated 4 October 2017.

As enunciated in its terms of reference, the HTF has (a) reviewed the current availability of information on credit and assessed the gaps in India that could be filled by a PCR; (b) studied the best international practices on PCR to determine the scope and target of a PCR for India including the type of information to be covered and (c) deliberated on the structure of the new information system or whether the existing systems could be strengthened and integrated to get a PCR, thereby suggesting a roadmap, including the priority areas, for developing a transparent, comprehensive and near-real-time PCR for India.

The PCR aims to be an extensive database of credit information for 'all' credit products in the country, from point of origination of credit to its termination (repayments, restructuring, default, resolution, etc.), eventually covering all lender-borrower accounts without a size threshold. As of today, information on borrowings from banks, non-banking financial companies (NBFCs), corporate bonds or debentures from the market, external commercial borrowings (ECBs), foreign currency convertible bonds (FCCBs), Masala bonds and inter-corporate borrowings are not available in a single data repository. The main objective of the PCR is to fill this lacuna and capture all the relevant information about a borrower across different borrowing products in one place. Moreover, significant parts of this registry of borrowing contracts and repayment history will be accessible to all stakeholders provided they too share their data with the PCR.

The HTF submitted its report[3] on 4 April 2018 recommending that a PCR should be set up by the RBI in a phased and modular manner. The report of the task force has been placed in the public domain after the top management of the RBI discussed it and had it reviewed by its legal department. An Implementation Task Force has now taken over the job of steering the project.

PCR: What Are the Gains?

Though the HTF report has dwelt in detail on basic questions like: (a) Why is PCR necessary in India? followed by the closely linked

---

[3] https://rbidocs.rbi.org.in/rdocs//PublicationReport/Pdfs/PCRRR09CF7539AC3E48
C9B69112AF2A498EFD.PDF

question (b) What are the functions of the PCR? Let me add my thoughts on the same. The PCR in India has been conceived as a data infrastructure that the financial ecosystem within and outside the RBI would be drawing data from as per the PCR's access policy. The prospective users will include lenders like banks and non-bank lenders including the new 'fintech' lenders; others providing data analytics such as rating agencies and credit information companies; as well as regulators.

Let me mention here the difficulties faced by the RBI in the context of the corporate NPA's problem five to six years ago. Despite the private credit bureaus operating for several years and doing a vital job for retail credit scoring, the central bank could not precisely assemble data on the quality of the credit portfolio of banks' large borrowers at an aggregate level. The data is simply not being reported with integrity and full coverage in case of large corporate borrowers. That is where RBI's CRILC, initiated in 2014, made a huge difference, even if it was somewhat late to be set up. CRILC provides a timely window on any degradation of the credit of a large borrower at a bank to the central bank and to other banks having the same entity as a borrower. The AQR that followed in 2015 relied heavily on CRILC data to cleanse the Augean stables of massive and unrecognized NPAs that have saddled our banks. The credit information system, as a whole, has many such gaps which leave much scope for improvement.

In one of my speeches in July 2017, I had also provided another example of how research based on data from credit registries can inform better policymaking. In the aftermath of the collapse of Lehman Brothers in September 2008, some economists—by pointing to the robust credit growth in bank loans—asserted that the credit flow in the USA was unaffected. But a deeper analysis of the Thomson Reuters Dealscan data quickly revealed that the credit growth was almost entirely attributable to the corporates drawing down on the existing credit lines (a form of a 'bank run'). The origination of new loans had, in fact, dried up.

In another piece of research, Lima and Drumond (2015)[4] discussed the insufficiencies attached to aggregate data when assessing financial stability and showed how micro data available in databases, such as Portugal's Central Credit Register (CCR), enable an assessment of the

---

[4] https://www.bis.org/ifc/publ/ifcb41k.pdf

Table 6.1. Number of Countries with Public Credit Registries (PCRs) and/or Private Credit Bureaus (PCBs)

Neither PCR nor PCBs	Only PCR	Only PCBs	Both PCR and PCBs
24	52	70	44

Source: World Bank's *Doing Business Report: 2018.*

causes of the movements behind the aggregates and thus uncover the potential build-up of imbalances such as the one that eventually led to the European Sovereign debt crisis and engulfed Portugal too. India can bring in a similar level of sophistication to its economic research through careful access to near-real-time and comprehensive credit data that a PCR would capture.

World Bank's Doing Business Report: 2018[5] reports the coverage of the adult population by institutions gathering credit data in select countries, grouped by the existence of only PCR, only Private Credit Bureaus (PCBs) and both PCR and PCBs (Table 6.1). It is to be noted that some countries have opted to have a PCR only for supervisory purposes, where they cover large credits only. It is also documented that the coverage of adult population by PCR and PCBs varies widely depending on the objectives set by the regulators as well as the prevailing socio-economic condition in these countries.

At the broad level, PCR increases the efficiency of lending institutions by reducing information asymmetry; the lender can get a 360° view of the borrower's other outstanding credits and past performance, allowing better screening at the time of credit origination and superior monitoring during the life of the credit. This is a well-studied phenomenon and has been recorded in many research studies. The introduction of public registries and private bureaus has been found to raise the ratio of private credit to GDP in many countries by 7 to 8 per cent over a five-year horizon (Baer et al. 2009). Importantly, credit registries and bureaus do not just increase the 'amount' of borrowing; they are also responsible for improving the 'quality' of borrowing.

India currently has a robust and unique digital identification for every citizen in the form of 'Aadhaar'. Similarly, the CIN as well as

---

[5] http://www.doingbusiness.org/data/exploreeconomies/

GSTN provide identities to businesses. Moreover, India is one of the few countries to provide an authentication service atop these identity services. These identities can be used in a PCR to aggregate data about borrowers from across multiple institutions with a high degree of confidence in the accuracy of merging and referencing of data. Further, the PCR will be a single source of information that has veracity. It will make reporting easier for small financial institutions and also remove the inconsistencies that come from the aggregation across different reporting formats of multiple financial institutions.

With a repository of such trusted data available, banks will be able to take better credit decisions. It can help them recognize early warning signs of asset quality problems by being able to see the performances on other credits. The principle of reciprocity is baked into a PCR. While the lending institutions will be mandated by law to share borrowers' information, most do it willingly, because, in turn, they want to see similar data from other lenders before they make a credit or roll over decision. Further, lenders can compete and offer attractive rates to the borrowers based on their individual risk profiles, instead of relying on an average risk profile for all customers in a sector.

In the Indian context, where many borrowers do not have a credit history to begin with, the PCR will enable good borrowers to distinguish themselves. The envisaged Indian PCR will mandate recording of all material events for all loans on all credit facilities (funded as well as non-funded) extended by all credit institutions—commercial banks, cooperative banks, NBFCs, MFIs, etc.—and also covering borrowings from other sources (Figure 6.2). This will reduce adverse selection, wherein low-risk borrowers are charged higher prices, while high-risk customers pay lower prices on their loans, as lenders cannot adequately distinguish among borrowers.

PCR: Legal Angles

Let me now touch upon briefly on a few key issues around the PCR on the legal front.

1. **Organization:** The PCR is initially being set up within the existing RBI infrastructure. The RBI, being a statutory corporation, can do only those activities which are permitted by

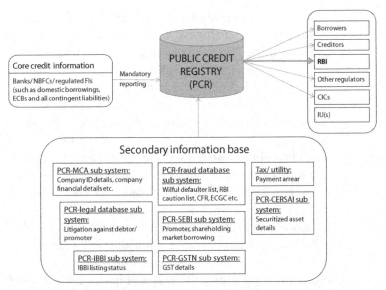

Figure 6.2. Proposed Public Credit Registry (PCR) Information Architecture
Source: Report of the high-level task force (HTF) on PCR for India.

the RBI Act, 1934 or other legislations. In addition to its core central banking functions, the RBI also performs certain promotional functions. However, this promotional activity is limited to 'financial institution' only.[6] Since no financing activity is contemplated for the proposed PCR, it might be difficult to label PCR as a 'financial institution'. This takes it out of the purview of a promotion under the RBI Act, 1934.

Another option is to promote an organization, for that matter incidental to the functions of the RBI[7]—as part of the RBI Act, 1934 or Banking Regulation Act, 1949 or any other enactment. Collection of information, including credit information, from its regulated entities is an important aspect of the regulatory and supervisory functions of the RBI. One can find many provisions in different enactments which enable the RBI to collect such information. If the scope of collection of information for PCR can be deemed to be reasonably

---

[6] See Section 17 (8-AA) of the RBI Act, 1934.
[7] See Section 17 (16) of the RBI Act, 1934.

incidental to the expressly permitted activities of the RBI, a subsidiary or a department for the purpose of setting up and hosting the PCR would be justified. Otherwise, the RBI Act, 1934 can be suitably amended conferring the RBI powers to conduct the business of PCR. Such a specific conferment of power, with clear enumeration of the functions of PCR, would remove the limitations of incidental powers mentioned above.

2. **Confidentiality constraints:** An important issue in connection with the setting up of PCR is the overriding of confidentiality provisions in many enactments, which directly or indirectly bar sharing of information, including credit information, except in manner specifically permitted. As the PCR will have to get information from different sources, the inability of the sources to share such information can be a constraint. To this end, the PCR will have a *consent-based* architecture.

   The notice and choice framework to secure an individual's consent is fundamental to data-processing practices in a digital economy. It is based on the act of an individual providing consent for certain actions pertaining to his/her data. It is essential that users provide consent to an entity sharing data (the 'data provider') before they share data with an entity requesting access (the 'data consumer'). The consent-based architecture of the PCR will strengthen privacy of 'data subjects' by ensuring that the data is accessible only to the 'data consumer', only for stipulated period and only for a stipulated purpose, as consented to by the user.

3. **PCR Act:** Having regard to the complexities discussed above, it is desirable to have a special comprehensive legislation, overriding the prohibitions contained in all other legislations on sharing of information required for the PCR. Otherwise, all such legislations will have to be amended separately, providing an exemption for sharing of information with PCR. It is to be noted that almost everywhere PCRs are backed by a specific enactment of a PCR Act. In India, a PCR Act can enable us transparently and address the entire gamut of governance issues including data acquisition and its dissemination through access rights by various users.

PCR: Linkages to Other Datasets

In my speech in July last year, I talked about how the power of information can be substantially enhanced if we can link CRILC data with the Ministry of Corporate Affairs (MCA) database containing financial results of the corporate sector. PCR should help in connecting to and referencing other databases. A portion of the envisioned PCR's power would derive from these linkages with ancillary information repositories. Figure 6.2 shows the schematics of how PCR proposes to augment the core credit information reported by regulated entities with linkage to other information sources and deliver the full potential of information to the stakeholders. For example, through the CIN it may connect to the company's financial statements. It should make alternate data, like utility bill payments records, available for credit decisions. This can significantly help to foster financial inclusion and democratize credit by allowing lending decisions to be based on 'all' cash-flow activity of a borrower, even when physical asset creation has not yet taken place.

Goods and Services Tax Network (GSTN)

Let me now turn to a seemingly unrelated second stride being undertaken that can help directly address the information asymmetry problem in the credit market. It is one that most of you already know. So I don't want to spend time explaining it, but instead focus on how it can move in lockstep with the PCR in completing a rich journey for formalizing credit in India.

I am talking, of course, about the GSTN. The GSTN, ostensibly, is a way for citizens and businesses to pay their taxes and claim their input tax credit. However, another way to look at the GSTN is as a trusted repository of matched invoices. Sellers upload their invoices to the GSTN; buyers approve the invoices billed to them. Since internal trade amounts to about 60 per cent of GDP, it is a dataset we cannot ignore.

Already, the GSTN has exceeded expectations since its adoption in India. The *Economic Survey* 2018 estimates that GSTN implementation has increased the indirect taxpayer base by more than 50 per cent, with 3.4 million businesses coming into the tax net.[8] It appears

---

[8] Ibid.

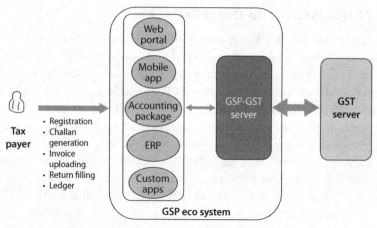

Figure 6.3. Goods and Services Tax (GST) Ecosystem
Source: https://www.gstn.org.in/ecosystem/
Notes: https://www.gst.gov.in/

that the number of GST registrants has risen due to a large increase in voluntary registrations. Small B2C firms want to be part of the GSTN because they buy from large enterprises. In fact, 68 per cent of their purchases are from medium or large registered enterprises, giving them a powerful incentive to register, so they could secure input tax credits on these purchases.

The Input Tax Credit motivation is a strong push towards digitization and formalization of small businesses. Moreover, the acceptance of invoices by the buyers creates a trusted repository of invoices. We know they aren't just cooking their books; they have verified buyers at the other end who vouch for the invoice generated. This gives one a potentially penetrative view into the otherwise invisible 10 million businesses that are now on GSTN, uploading roughly 1 billion plus invoices every month.[9]

The GST ecosystem has a layer between the taxpayer and the GST system (Figure 6.3). The GST Suvidha Providers (GSPs) are envisaged to provide innovative and convenient methods to taxpayers and other stakeholders in interacting with the GST systems. There will

---

[9] Estimates available at: https://economictimes.indiatimes.com/news/economy/policy/ 3–5-billion-invoices-every-month-all-about-the-technology-that-gst-will-bank-on-from-july/articleshow/58907708.cms

be two sets of interactions, one between the app user and GSP and the second between the GSP and the GST system. The GSP can help the taxpayers in GST compliance through their innovative solutions.

By design, invoicing data about their own business is made available to the users of the GSTN. Continuing the theme from the PCR, we already know that trusted, verifiable data from any registry can significantly improve access to credit. Similarly, we expect an explosion in the number of credit products specifically designed for business flow, such as invoice discounting based on GSTN data.

The Interplay of PCR and GSTN

Now, the PCR can aggregate the information of a borrower using the core credit information repository and information lying in a set of sub-systems spread across multiple agencies (e.g. MCA database, GSTN, etc., refer to Figure 6.2), to aggregate information of a borrower. Together, these sub-systems create a universe of verifiable information and allow safe access to the data for all important stakeholders in the financial system. What is noteworthy about these institutions is that they are all digital-native. They have been designed as digital infrastructure, being able to support multiple-use cases atop them, without being partial or overly prescriptive on any one-use case. This is not going to happen in a vacuum. Much of this would not be possible if the other roadblocks to go digital weren't already solved. Other public digital infrastructure such as e-KYC for knowing your customer or unified payments interface (UPI) for digital payments are nudging users towards creating larger data footprints and helping them indirectly improve their creditworthiness.

With this infrastructure in place, we expect the costs for on-boarding those users who are currently excluded by formal credit to nosedive. It will become feasible to serve a large number of customers, operating at a much lower average transaction size. Just like in the fast-moving consumer goods (FMCG) sector, banking and access to credit too will be 'sachetized' to make it more accessible and afford-able for the masses. We want that even a small tea-shop vendor should be able to take a 500-rupee loan at fair rates, say, for only a week, based on such data.

It doesn't stop there. These new institutions can also provide better tools to regulators and researchers to monitor the health of, and provide stability to, the national financial system.

Let me conclude. In a country with a low credit to GDP as ours, efficiently increasing affordability and access to credit are paramount goals. I am excited for what we can achieve when our small entrepreneurs are not capital-constrained, or when health shocks do not send families to usurious loans, and back into poverty. The PCR and the GSTN are two giant strides that utilize modern technological advances for improving information access and quality. Together, they hold the rich promise of enabling us to democratize and formalize credit in India.

References

Ministry of Finance. 2018. *Economic Survey 2017-18, Volume I and Volume II.* Oxford: Oxford University Press.

Baer, Tobiar, Massimo Carassinu, Andre Del Miglio, Claudio Fabiani, and Eduardo Ginevra. 2009. 'The National Credit Bureau: A Key Enabler of Financial Infrastructure and Lending in Developing Economies.' McKinsey Working Papers on Risk No. 14. Available at: https://www.mckinsey.com/~/media/McKinsey/Business%20Functions/Risk/Our%20Insights/The%20national%20credit%20bureau/The%20national%20credit%20bureau.ashx (accessed on 24 April 2020).

CHAPTER 7

SOME REFLECTIONS ON MICROCREDIT AND HOW A PUBLIC CREDIT REGISTRY CAN STRENGTHEN IT*

Sometimes when I sit down to write a new set of remarks, the same old thoughts cross my mind, a bit like one's favourite songs that are so deeply entrenched in the psyche that at the end of a long day when one is reflecting on the subject, they start playing all over again, without any reason and without any conscious decision to rewind to them. In my case, a few striking images flash across my eyes. I have tried in what follows to describe these images and what their collage means for me. They also convey how I try to think about economics and finance more generally—as the media to understand daily situations of households around us and to derive insights on how these situations could be made better, most often in some small ways and occasionally with a big bang.... After all, the origin of the word 'economics' is in the ancient Greek term *oikonomía*, meaning 'management of a household'. Based on careful research, many (notably Professors Abhijit Banerjee and Esther Duflo of Massachusetts Institute of Technology [MIT]) contend, that it is the poor who often practise the best economics as the costs they face from mismanaging their households can be rather high.

* Speech delivered at IIT Bombay Tech Fest, Mumbai on 15 December 2018. I dedicate these remarks to my favourite school teacher, Shailesh Shah Sir, of Fellowship School in Mumbai, who breathed his last on the morning of 5 January 2019; he taught me Indian languages, social sciences and the art of compositional writing; he truly lit the lamp of ambition in all his students and set our imagination on fire.

Parts of these remarks were first prepared in 2017 for a book launch, followed by delivery at several student gatherings and a few convocations. This final version represents the accumulation of my observations at these talks, which culminated at IIT Bombay (IITB) Tech Fest on 15 December 2018. I am grateful to Anujit Mitra, Jose Kattoor and Vineet Srivastava for their valuable inputs.

So let me describe these images that flash across my eyes one by one.

Image 1: Many evenings or nights when I stroll with my brother on our terrace in Mumbai, we are greeted on one side by the Pawan Hans Helipad, the sprawling slums of Nehru Nagar, the deafening din from Swami Vivekananda Road (S. V. Road) and the serene breeze and waves of Juhu beach. I grew up on a crowded street in Girgaum, in South Mumbai. Observing from our first-floor window how people went about their lives on the streets was a favourite pastime in our childhood days. Conditioned by that, while I'm on the terrace, my eyes invariably end up focusing on the slums of Nehru Nagar. Far into the narrow alleys, bustling and jostling in high density are the slum dwellers, appearing as diminutive figurines, with much activity and life all around. A man is fixing a dish antenna on top of his blue roof; an old couple are perched outside a modest hut, savouring what must be some scrumptious desi chat; a woman slamming blow after blow on the clothes she has carefully aligned to wash and almost always a group of children gleefully running around, mostly playing cricket and seasonally flying kites.

Some of the evenings, a plane takes off from the domestic or international airport in the east and heads westward on its way and a chopper swings in and lands at Pawan Hans with much acoustic fanfare. As these sophisticated means of modern transportation make their noisy presence felt, you can see the children bunch together, one of them pointing at the sky, others gallivanting around him to marvel at the spectacle. An instant later of course, the children are nonchalantly back to gully cricket or running after a fallen kite.

One cannot but hope that these children—in that brief moment of marvel—have been imbued with ambition; that their eyes are now set on the sky; that they will have the initiative and will get all opportunity to do what it takes to bridge the gap from their narrow alley to Pawan Hans Helipad next door and to the flight of the giant mechanical birds that fly above.

Will these children take off?
How will their journey be?
Where will they land?

I ponder for a few seconds but then switch attention to the incessant honking of the S. V. Road vehicles.

Image 2: Until about 10 years back, I used to spend a decent chunk of my time as a doctoral student and later as a professor, working with an Indian non-governmental organization (NGO), focused on pre-primary and primary education. This activity had become my umbilical cord to India. On my holiday trips back home from New York or London, I would take out a few days to visit some of their *baalwadis* (daycares) in urban areas, and if travel plans permitted, also the delivery centres for accelerated reading programs in villages. These visits made my interactions with stakeholders more credible, engaging and vivid. But they were also personally rewarding.

There are a few sights, if any, more uplifting than of a child figuring out the alphabet for the first time, reading the first book, flipping pages over and over again in boundless excitement and frenzy or counting and adding up his or her collection of stones, subitizing them soon after—as in figuring out the exact count without counting—by merely glancing at the collection of treasures! It might be the innocent spark on the child's face, or that 'Aha!' or Eureka moment as the child discovers how to read, how to count, how to learn—whatever it is, it works like magic in bowling over the beholder.

One returned from these visits with a shot in the arm to do more; one felt like nurturing the umbilical cord to India further; one realized that joyful learning is an essential groundwork for the journeys, the flights and the ascent that these children will undertake in due course.

Image 3: I am usually en route in car to the office at RBI or Bombay Gymkhana during early mornings. I need to be on S. V. Road before turning for the Milan subway or now the flyover, which connects to the Western Express Highway. Just before the turn, before one reaches the Hanuman temple and Santacruz bus depot, on the left sidewalk, there is—always—a mother toiling away no matter what time of the day. It is clear she is homeless; she has at least two children, both roughly of the same age. Depending on the time of the morning, she has her work cut out. Some days she is waking up the kids with some sternness on her face; on others, she is bathing them with water from an ingeniously figured out water supply; at times she is getting them dressed in school uniforms and then she is often running with the kids, who have their backpacks on, towards the neighbourhood school. From a distance, she seems to be driven with a single-minded focus of ensuring that her kids get their chance to fly and soar. Her role as a mother certainly seems a mighty one, as Yudhisthir answered to the Yaksha's *prashna* (question) in Mahabharata, when asked what is heavier than the Earth.

> *How does the mother make it all work?*
> *Can she afford the books and the supplies?*
> *Is she home when the kids come back?*
> *What job does she do during the day?*
> *Could she be a microentrepreneur?*

The mind is so fickle; however, as soon as the car turns left at the traffic signal and moves onto the flyover, it leaves these questions in the background and embarks on its daily descent.

Image 4: Early on a Saturday morning, already quite bright and sunny, a banker carrying his *thela* (a shoulder bag) steps into the passageway next to a series of *kachcha-pukka* homes. The surrounding is semi-urban. By the time you have blinked an eye, an army of about 20 women, mostly in *saris*, of ages spanning from 20 to 50, and a few even 50+, have gathered around him. They have all borrowed certain sums of money from the banker. They make their repayments one by one; each transaction is logged in a physical register; it is also swiped digitally onto their bank cards with a point-of-sale (POS)-style machine. Some of the women are borrowing again; some taking out monies from their accounts. The registrar of this group of women, appointed for the month, signs off the log after checking the account entries carefully.

Banking is now done. Growth is about to begin.

I am curious to hear more about what these women are doing with the money. All of them, without exception, are entrepreneurs. One has started a *sari* trading business, buying them from the city and selling them in the neighbourhood with a margin; she has built her enterprise over several years and is the recipient of the biggest loan (0.1 million rupees) with the longest maturity (one year) in the group; her friend has acquired a sewing machine with the loan and is stitching blouses to go with the *saris*; another has opened a beauty parlour; yet another has started a soft-drinks stall in her husband's stationery store as there is extra, unused space therein, well utilized especially during the afternoons when customer traffic is thin for stationery but the heat unbearable. There seemed absolutely no shortage of services to be provided in their immediate sphere of influence.

I was especially eager to know what prompted these women to become entrepreneurs in the first place. The answer I got was not entirely expected: in 9 out of 10 cases, women had become entrepreneurs to send their kids to a 'top, English medium school', or to have extra monies for private coaching so the child could excel in the state-level exams or to get the kid to learn some computing and programming as that is where future jobs lie!

Collage of the Images

As these images flashed across my eyes, I realized that rather than being entirely compartmentalized, these images were all linked, that there was a connection between finance—my day job—and these images that my mind had been subconsciously gathering in mornings, evenings and during holidays. An important link was established from financial inclusion to education of children—from microfinance for women entrepreneurs to them sending children to schools, the children in turn having their 'Aha! I did it!!' moments in reading and counting, and to their taking off for the limitless sky and beyond.

Access to finance is the lifeblood of an economy. Its judicious allocation is known to unlock opportunity and growth. It can, in fact, aid even the most fundamental reform for growth by supporting, directly or indirectly, the education of our children, the skilling of our youth and lighting up of their minds with fire and imagination so they can propel themselves, their families and the rest of us, forward. Education is perceived by many families as a ticket to the ride that will catapult them out of economic stress. Leaving aside minor exceptions, as a rule, education is indeed a ticket to such a ride.

A mother taking up an enterprise to shape her child's future has all the 'willingness to pay' her debt. As the child grows, her needs too will rise. She will need a clean credit record to be able to borrow again so as to finance her now bigger liquidity requirements. This way, there is full incentive compatibility between her and the finance provider.

Besides her willingness to pay, the deft handling of her enterprise, induced by the necessity to keep buying the education ticket over time, will strengthen her 'ability to pay'. At any rate, the financier can start with a small loan, use a short tenor to assess repayment ability and open for her a bank account that can help track other payment flows and improve credit assessment. The reputation of the woman entrepreneur as a borrower can build swiftly as she keeps repaying and enable her to secure more credit over longer tenors.

Borrowing as a part of a group reinforces the strong incentives to repay; a default by a borrower when all others are repaying can lead to stigma. Conversely, encouraging of defaults by some can lead to vitiation of the otherwise rich credit culture.

The financier, in turn, can make a healthy spread over their own cost of borrowing funds, even accounting for some losses from early defaults, upon whose realization, the entrepreneur can be rationed from future loans or offered only stricter loan terms and tenor.

This way, the availability of microfinance for microentrepreneurs thrives and benefits the society all around.[1]

So let me turn from these images to my day job at the RBI and what efforts we are undertaking to help ensure that microcredit becomes available to more borrowers; microfinance provides a robust foundation; microenterprise given an additional fillip; and indirectly, in the process, our children offered greater opportunity for schooling and skilling.

PCR—an Important Step to Democratize and Formalize Credit[2]

In an emerging economy like India, it is always felt that the smaller entrepreneurs, mostly operating under the informal economy, do not get enough credit as they are informationally opaque to their

---

[1] At some of the student gatherings and convocations, I ended the remarks here by reciting a poem I received from Yuvaraj Galada on 22 December 2017, called 'The Invitation', written in 1999 by Oriah Mountain Dreamer, that has inspired me immensely (https://www.rbi.org.in/Scripts/BS_SpeechesView.aspx?Id=1069).

[2] For a fuller treatment of this theme, please see my speech 'Public Credit Registry (PCR) and Goods and Services Tax Network (GSTN): Giant Strides to Democratise and Formalise Credit in India', delivered in August 2018 (https://www.rbi.org.in/Scripts/BS_SpeechesView.aspx?Id=1061).

lenders who prefer to provide loans to more transparent larger businesses. Data as of March 2018 of SCBs from RBI's basic statistical returns (BSR) shows that close to half of the outstanding credit is for ticket size above a 100 million rupees and 30 per cent is above 1 billion rupees. Credit penetration is particularly low for the MSME sector where the ticket size is generally believed to be between 1 and 10 million rupees. Even though more than 95 per cent of accounts with SCBs are having sanctioned credit limit less than 1 million each, the amount outstanding on these accounts is only 23 per cent of the total.

Is there a big opportunity for us to rethink and reshape our credit ecosystem for the future so that microcredit can thrive to unlock economic value, as I laid out in my collage of images?

At the RBI, we firmly believe so. We have initiated work on a PCR. We are excited about how we can solve in a fundamental way the information problem affecting access to credit for microentrepreneurs.

Let me elaborate on the information problem and how a PCR can help get around it.

'Information asymmetry' with the borrower is the major difficulty faced by any lender while granting a loan. Put simply, the borrower has more information about her own economic condition and risks than the lender. Credit information systems aim to reduce this asymmetry by enabling the lender to know the credit history with past lenders and the current indebtedness of the borrower. They improve efficiency of credit allocation, as the lender can use credit information systems to properly differentiate and appropriately price (interest rate) as well as alter terms (maturity, collateral, covenants, etc.) of the loan.

What would occur without the credit information systems?

As borrowers build history, lenders would like to protect the information of their profitable customers and may not be ready to share it directly with other lenders. This way, borrowers can get locked to their initial lenders, become vulnerable to gouging in loan terms and, worse, be unable to convey their credit quality to new lenders if existing lenders experience problems of their own (such as due to capital erosion from recognition of losses, as was witnessed in India over the past decade in the form of high retail and MSME cost of borrowing from banks due to spillover from their large corporate borrower loans turning non-performing).

This is where third-party credit information companies come in to play, those that will pool the data from lenders and share the information with 'other' lenders as per the laid-down policy. Globally, PCBs and PCRs both operate in this space. PCBs can be legislatively authorized to receive credit data; however, being for-profit enterprises, they may focus primarily on those data segments around which it is most profitable to build a business model (for example, provision of credit scores based on data gathered). Indeed, it is found internationally that a PCR, being a non-profit enterprise, is able to ensure much better data coverage than PCBs. In turn, the PCBs, when given access to comprehensive data from a PCR can provide better and greater value addition through data analytics and innovations, complementing the PCR.

One can easily surmise that to be useful, it is important for credit information systems to gather complete credit information, possibly even asset-side and cash flow details about the borrower, which is sometimes referred to as the '360-degree view'. Also, the latest information is more important, giving rise to the demand for near-real-time data. That is how the report of the HTF on PCR for India, chaired by Shri Y. M. Deosthalee, has envisaged the PCR to be. The HTF examined the data gaps in the current credit information system in India and recommended that a PCR be set up, backed by an appropriate Act, to improve the information efficiency of the credit market and strengthen the credit culture in India.

How Will the PCR for India Work?

The PCR has been envisaged as a database of core credit information—an infrastructure of sorts on which users of credit data can build further analytics. It will strive to cover all regulated entities (i.e., financiers) in phases and in this way get a 360-degree view of borrowers. It will facilitate linkages with related ancillary information systems outside the banking system including corporate filings, tax systems (including the GSTN) and utility payments. The PCR will have to be backed and governed by a comprehensive PCR Act to be brought in consultation with the government. It will have to follow the latest privacy guidelines based on a laid-down consent framework.

The Proposed PCR Information Architecture

Let me now spend some time on how the PCR will work and help strengthen the credit culture.

1. First, PCR will make borrower information more complete with increasing coverage of lending entities. In particular, it will eventually reach out even to the smallest primary agricultural credit societies. It will also cover entities which may not be regulated by the RBI. This will have to be done in phases and it may take up to three–five years to accomplish, possibly sooner.
2. Second, PCR will vastly simplify and reduce the reporting burdens on the lenders. Other entities, including regulators and supervisors, will be able to access it for core credit information and supplement it with only the incremental part as per their requirement. Many of the statistical returns presently collected by the RBI may also accordingly be substantially rationalized and pruned, freeing up resources in the financial ecosystem for analysis instead of repetitious efforts in data collection, follow-up and cleaning. The same would be the case with other entities that presently collect such data from banks.
3. Third, PCR will have credit data available digitally at a higher frequency than at present. Therefore, it will make credit decision-making faster and efficient.
4. Fourth, refer to Figure 6.2 in Chapter 6, with linkages to other information systems like corporate data from the MCA21 and tax filing or invoicing data or GSTN, it will help the users to access other data on borrowers' assets and evolving cash flows, which are essential for taking efficient credit decisions.
5. Finally, it will be possible within the PCR architecture to address privacy concerns and control access to data with a proper consent-based framework for appropriate usage, better than what is currently feasible. These concerns will have to balance the objective that the PCR is just a step in helping the democratization of credit, whereby credit data is not only used for regulatory/supervisory purposes, but

also leveraged to expand the credit market efficiently. In particular,

a. While an individual will have access to his/her data stored in PCR, he/she should be empowered to share it with other lenders for availing credit.
b. Similarly, lenders need to be given access to their own customers' complete data for monitoring such accounts.
c. Regulators/supervisors will require full access to the data for their work so that they can address systemic risk concerns with the advantage of a holistic view.

To appropriately put in place the required access and control policies, the HTT recommended that a separate PCR Act be brought in. The PCR Act will need to ensure adequate safeguards on data while at the same time address extant restrictions on sharing of credit data that prevent efficient allocation and regulatory supervision of credit. The PCR Act would also have to be comprehensive so as to bring in data from the section of lenders who do not directly fall under the RBI regulations. To this end, the RBI plans to engage with the government and other regulators in the coming months. In the meantime, the RBI has set up an implementation task force that is putting the systems infrastructure in place to kick-start the PCR with data from regulated entities that can be covered either under, or with minor tweaking, of the extant legislative framework.

PCR Can Help 'Sachetize' Microcredit

To build credit models for individuals and small credits, the financier and its modellers are ideally required to know not only outstanding credit for the micro-borrowers, but possibly also their entire repayment history and their cash flow fluctuations, so as to tailor the terms of credit suitably. In the absence of such information, many borrowers may simply get 'rationed' out of the market due to severe information asymmetry faced by financiers.

With a PCR tracking, every credit transaction from its origination to closure (initial terms, repayment, default, restructuring, etc.), and being linked to various digital systems in place (as shown in Figure 6.2), it would be possible to identify and get to know well businesses, even microenterprises and microentrepreneurs. In other words, the PCR could supply the missing link, which is the complete '360-degree view' information of the borrower or prospective borrower. This will allow lenders to assess the borrower's credit risk keeping in view the viability of cash flows, ask the relevant questions (e.g., are there other underlying issues that are affecting the ability to pay the loan in spite of healthy cash flows from the microenterprise?) and price the loan terms without compromising on due diligence.

Based on these, nearly automated-loan sanction and disbursement mechanisms can be devised, as are also being attempted by fintech companies.

In fact, credit products could get transformed with the possibility of sanctioning small ticket loans with short maturity and zero- or low-collateral requirement. Borrowers and entrepreneurs can build their reputation and credit quality by repaying well such initial information-building loans. Gradually, they can borrow more and at longer maturities, potentially making capital investments to enhance productivity. Once their size increases and they register with the GSTN, tax invoices can act as the cash flow verification with PCR. Robust credit history built over a period can work as sturdy collateral, building the trust of the lenders. Such 'sachetization' of credit can rapidly expand access to credit for those MSMEs, hitherto not included in the formal credit market.

As I stressed while describing the 'ability to pay' and 'willingness to pay' of microentrepreneurs, it would remain important not to undermine their inherently strong credit culture by making it easier for borrowers not to repay. That would compromise the essence of how microentrepreneurs build a reputable credit history to differentiate from others and over the time grow in size and economic value creation.

Let me conclude.

There is a deep connection between the images I started with, their collage in my mind and my day job at the RBI. Ultimately, while central banks are not always visible to the common person, their policies have the potential to touch them in a meaningful way. As its etymology suggests, this is what economics must help achieve in the end—better management of the household. It is perhaps a very ambitious vision of our future to believe that a fundamental change in the financial data infrastructure such as a PCR can help improve access to microcredit as well as improve schooling and skilling outcomes for our children and youth, but so be it. My son's poster at his school last year introduced me to a gem from Michelangelo, which underscores why we must keep painting such a vision and persist with efforts to convert it into reality. It says,

> *The greatest danger for most of us lies not in setting*
> *our aim too high and falling short; but in setting*
> *our aim too low and achieving our mark.*

CHAPTER 8

WHAT CAN INDIA'S BANKING SYSTEM LEARN FROM SHAMPOO SACHET REVOLUTION?*

Even seasoned statisticians can be thrown off by India's scale. Its GDP is currently about $2.9 trillion, which makes it the world's fifth-biggest economy in nominal terms and the third in purchasing power parity (PPP), only behind China and the USA. But there is another way to look at these numbers. India has a population of 1.3 billion and the average Indian makes only $2,100 a year in nominal terms and $6,900 in PPP terms. That ranks India 142nd on a GDP per capita basis. So there is a long way to go before everyone shares in the nation's prosperity.

Among the first to realize that India is one of the world's most paradoxical markets, both simultaneously large and small, was the FMCG industry. Up to the late 1970s, most Indians were not even buying shampoo. This was not because they did not want to, but the average bottle of shampoo cost more than most Indians were willing or able to pay. In response, an ingenious entrepreneur put single-use quantities into a sachet that could be sold for 1 rupee each. Sales took off. Customers were offered a first rung on the ladder of consumption and this encouraged them to take the next step.

FMCG companies showed that big problems in India can be addressed by providing small solutions. The act of making affordable, bite-sized packets out of regular products came to be known as 'sachetization'. Sachetization of everything from biscuits to body creams changed the FMCG industry in India. Indians wanted the same things as everyone else, but they could only afford it one sachet at a time.

---

*Reproduced with permission from Acharya (2019).

As a central banker for India, I wondered if we could 'sachetize' finance to lift people out of poverty. India remains one of the most financially under-penetrated large economies in the world. An estimated 50 per cent of the people are employed informally in India. They may earn as much as those in formal employment, but they remain invisible to the banking system. So when they want a loan, the bank denies them credit unless they can offer a hard asset as collateral. The average Indian cannot do this and ends up resorting to informal finance, with usurious rates and onerous terms. These underserved Indians are square pegs; the banking system a round hole. It is no surprise that India's credit-to-GDP ratio stands at just 55.7 per cent, compared to China's 208.7 per cent.

The RBI has taken two important measures to make sachetization in finance happen. The first is initiating steps towards the creation of a PCR. The PCR aims to be a comprehensive database of information for all credit relationships in the country, from the point of origination of credit to its termination (repayments, restructuring, default, resolution and so on).

This eventually covers all lender-borrower accounts without a size threshold. The primary reason for building a PCR is to remove information asymmetry, providing lenders with a 360-degree view of the borrower's liabilities. The secondary reason is to provide bankers with up-to-date information on the quality of their credit portfolio.

The second measure is the creation of the account aggregator—a new financial institution that manages how other financial institutions access your data, based on your consent. It enables users to demand their data from their financial services providers in real time, in a machine-readable format. The account aggregators can gather data from all financial institutions—including banks, NBFCs, mobile money wallets, mutual funds, tax receipts and others who are willing to offer their data over apps. Regulations ensure that the business model of these account aggregators does not encourage reckless collection of data. They have a fiduciary responsibility to you and are not data brokers for the bank. They simply manage the flow of encrypted data and do not actually read it.

Together, the PCR and the account aggregator will allow financial intermediaries to see in near real time the complex patterns of financial cash flows of individuals and businesses. When these systems kick in over the coming months, banks will be able to lend judiciously to India's large underserved population. By employing the power of big data analytics and machine-learning, banks will be able to create individualized financial products for each user.

To get back to shampoo sachets, financial services providers must reduce the size of the packaging and also rethink the formula itself. What is the point of a one-year loan repaid in monthly instalments to a farmer who earns only during harvest? If the formal financing system can understand better the cash flow patterns of individuals, then it can serve the unique needs of Indian customers. This way, with the aid of smarter technology, there is no reason why we can't raise India's credit-to-GDP ratio to bring it in line with those of more high-income nations.

Making cash flow-based credit available to every Indian is our small solution to India's big problem of financial exclusion.

Reference

Acharya, Viral. 2019. 'What Can India's Banking System Learn from the Shampoo Sachet Revolution?' *Special Report India: Banking and Finance. Financial Times*, September 22. Available at: https://www.ft.com/content/e5ff77c6-d3a9-11e9-8d46-8def889b4137 (accessed on 25 April 2020).

PART 3

Incorporating the Financial Cycle in the Monetary Policy Framework

CHAPTER 9

MONETARY POLICY UNDER CHANGING FINANCIAL AND MACROECONOMIC ENVIRONMENT*

Sixth Bi-monthly Policy Statement for the Year 2016–2017: 08 February 2017

This was a tough policy decision to take.

On the one hand, headline inflation has remained low, and there is a good case to be made that there is at least a temporary output gap created due to liquidity shortage induced by the currency replacement. Since our flexible inflation targeting mandate also requires paying attention to growth, it could be natural to lower the policy rate to restore growth levels, especially if the lower policy rate could be passed onto the areas of the economy most affected by the liquidity shortage, in particular, rural households, NBFCs which undertake most of the auto-based lending, and the realty sector.

On the other hand, low-headline inflation has been largely driven by food deflation, and the most recent numbers have been heavily driven by the large dip in vegetable prices. In the past, food deflation has had strong seasonal patterns which have tended to rebound and with vengeance, when rainfall disappoints. While some of the food deflation over the past few months has been steady due to supply-side factors, on balance it is fair to draw the conclusion that statistically, the food component of headline inflation has had less signal to noise quality compared to the core inflation that excludes fuel and food, the latter having been more or less sticky in recent months. Rapid remonetization implies likely swift reversal of the aggregate demand loss and the significant transmission to borrowers of easy funding

---

* Minutes of Bimonthly MPC Decisions from 08 February 2017 to 06 June 2019.

conditions at banks suggests unlikely further transmission of a rate cut by banks.

Given the difficulty in resolving this trade-off between temporary effects on output gap and the persistent nature of core inflation, my attention turned heavily to international factors. Global uncertainty in trade due to protectionist tendencies in major high-income economies, the prospect of a stronger dollar in wake of a probable 'border tax' on imports in the USA, and rising worldwide inflation in food, fuel and metals, have created a significant risk to domestic inflation. Second-round effects on funding costs due to portfolio outflows from debt and equity markets could be substantial if the central bank is not perceived as staying course on credible inflation targeting.

It is important to guard the Indian macroeconomy from global headwinds, and having a reasonably good chance of attaining the 5 per cent target for headline inflation by the end of March 2017, to keep the option open to start getting closer to our long-term target of 4 per cent headline inflation on a durable basis. Overall, this required no rate cut for now and switching to a neutral stance so as to remain fully flexible to raise rates, to stay put or to cut rates, as more data becomes available on both domestic and international fronts.

One final note on the monetary policy decision: the balanced budget, by focusing on fiscal stability and expenditure reorientation to rural and housing, seemed to exonerate the committee from the burden of skewing rates to bridge the output gap and instead allowed the committee to focus squarely on the inflation-targeting mandate.

Such a time, while difficult for interest-rate setting, appears right for pushing forward on structural reforms of the banking sector: its asset quality and resolution and its recapitalization needs both factors that have stunted credit growth at banks; and, the normalization of administered small savings rates that have prevented a seamless transmission of monetary policy to bank funding and lending rates.

First Bi-monthly Monetary Policy Statement for 2017–2018: 06 April 2017

Headline inflation is set to rebound from its recent lows due to the expected (and in the past month, realized) mean-reversion in food inflation, especially in vegetables. Global inflationary trends have remained on the upside too. There is some uncertainty as to when the headline inflation might cross the target inflation rate of 4 per cent and keep inching above, given that inflation without food and fuel is stubbornly above the target rate. We have laid out in the resolution several upside risks, of which geopolitical risks and undoing of the centre's fiscal discipline by the states concern me the most. Commodity prices, especially crude, have been volatile and so has the exchange rate. Hence, risks are evenly balanced around the inflation outlook.

On the growth front, the remonetization is continuing apace and many sectors of the economy are recovering steadily after the transient slowdown. There are signs though that the recovery is somewhat uneven. Private investment, given the high indebtedness of several stressed sectors, remains a particularly weak spot. Household expectations of income, spending and employment appear to have weakened, but may be anchored to the past few months and need to be tracked in the coming months. Other signs of economic activity paint a rosier picture for the growth over the next year, with the external sector having been remarkably resilient.

Should an inflation-targeting central bank react to a narrowing output gap in such a scenario? Given the balanced nature of risks and uncertainty that abounds, I lean towards continuing the neutral stance and pause for now. There are many important issues to attend to, notably (a) resolving bank stressed assets and correcting weak bank balance sheets, (b) mopping up in a more durable manner the surplus liquidity sloshing around post-demonetization and which is keeping short-term money market rates away from the policy rate and (c) unleashing the true potential of our capital markets further, by enhancing liquidity in the corporate bond market and improving the ease and the suite of financial hedging options. It seems an opportune time to focus on these issues.

Second Bi-monthly Monetary Policy Statement for 2017–2018: 07 June 2017

The softness of April inflation prints, in food, and excluding food and fuel, as well as of the Central Statistics Office (CSO)'s revised estimates of growth for 2016–2017, especially Q4, has posed difficult challenges for monetary policy. Our inflation forecasts relied on evidence of gradual reversal after fire sales in several food items, which were partly confirmed by February and March reversion, as well as on the seasonal uptick in food prices during summer. Realized food inflation, however, turned out to be much lower than our forecast. Inflation excluding food and fuel also moderated. The global and goods and services tax (GST) related risks, that we have been concerned about, haven't materialized. One needs to wait for some more time to ascertain whether our capital inflows and exchange rate remain relatively immune to the Federal Reserve's unwinding of its asset purchase program; we might see a pickup in imported inflation otherwise. Similarly, a few more months' data will confirm if the GST rollout is likely to be entirely benign for inflation. It is the collapse of food inflation, however, that remains the primary driver of a steady decline in the headline number. It is clear now that supply factors, in addition to transitory effects, have been playing a significant role for at least three quarters with no sign yet of abating.

The growth slowdown has had two primary components: first, the continuing decline in private investment since the beginning of 2016–2017; and second, the more recent fall in construction activity that is also evidenced in the poor performance of the cement industry and real-estate services.

Have we managed food inflation to a stable level so that the medium-term headline inflation path will remain firmly anchored below 4 per cent? While the continuing food disinflation due to supply-side measures in some high-weight food items would suggest so, the farmer demands one is witnessing with each passing day gives me a pause. I remain concerned though that this may have sown the seeds of a 'tail risk' in the form of fiscally expansive measures that could spark off generalized inflation in due course.

The growth slowdown in Q4 has finally led to the outcome that our estimates of 'output gap', in spite of substantial uncertainty around such estimates, point to the opening up of a negative gap. In the traditional ways of thinking about monetary policy, this would push the interest rate policy towards being more willing to accommodate. I prefer to approach monetary policy through the finance angle where the focus is on effectiveness of the transmission policy: will the interest rate changes have the desired amplifier effects on the economy through the bank and non-bank intermediation sector? On this front, we have a problem. A substantial part of the banking sector balance sheet remains exposed to heavily indebted sectors, a stress that has built up over at least six–seven years. Accommodation in monetary policy during 2015–2016 did not get transmitted to the corporate sector, and private investment remained weak then in spite of the monetary stance. The treasury gains accruing to banks in this time, while not a direct concern for the monetary policy, only masked the true stress of their balance sheets.

In such a scenario, the standard prescription for monetary policy does not necessarily work well. Tolerance for a slightly higher real rate of interest is justified to ensure weak banks do not find the hurdle rate relatively low for evergreening (perennial extension) of bad loans. What is required for monetary policy to do its job better is to address the stress on bank (and highly indebted borrower) balance sheets. The RBI's efforts on this will start in the earnest in a few weeks. Once the transmission mechanism is restored to better health, monetary policy will more pervasively touch different parts of the economy. Targeted interventions to stimulate demand for sectors such as construction, where the supply is likely affected as an intended consequence of recent policies, would be more effective for now; this would not run the risks of evergreening, given the relatively low delinquency rates in bank lending in these segments.

These considerations prevented me from considering a change in stance or recommending a rate cut based on available data, just before the Federal Reserve rate hike and before we had firmly put in place our efforts on resolution of banking sector stress. I will watch the next few months of inflation and real economic activity indicators closely to confirm if lower-than-target headline inflation and negative output gap are persistent.

Finally, I wish to clarify one point. Some suggest that monetary policy should be eased with the explicit objective of recapitalizing the weak bank balance sheets. Nothing could be worse for monetary policy, in my view. This would relax the pressure on good efforts that are underway deploying a slew of measures to improve the banking architecture (through private capital-raising, non-core asset sales, consolidation, divestment and regulatory PCA). In turn, this would trap the monetary policy from changing its direction if data so demands before the resolution of banks is complete. It is best for sake of policy credibility to not mix instruments with objectives they are not meant to target.

Third Bi-monthly Monetary Policy Statement for 2017–2018: 02 August 2017

Inflation prints since the last policy have turned out even lower, though there are emerging signs that certain deflating food items are on a price rebound. Excluding the house rent allowance (HRA) impact, headline inflation is now projected to be lower in Q4 of 2017–2018 as compared with the projection made in the last policy statement. More significantly, inflation excluding food and fuel has eased markedly, falling to around 4 per cent and suggesting a broad-based weakening of underlying demand. Our 12-month ahead headline inflation projection, without the statistical HRA effects, is now just above 4 per cent, even as the inflation path is projected to be on an upward trajectory. Households' inflation expectations have, however, slightly moved up even in the face of recent low inflation prints.

Our output gap estimates turned somewhat negative after the last quarter's growth numbers and associated revisions. Together with easing of underlying inflation and given that our 12-month ahead inflation forecast (excluding the HRA impact) is in line with the mandated target, there seems some room for monetary policy accommodation. Hence, I vote for a policy repo rate cut by 25 basis points (bps) while retaining the neutral stance.

Why the neutral stance? I wish to reiterate that growth slowdown since Q1 2016–2017 is rooted in the stressed balance sheets of our banks and corporates in several sectors. Our output gap estimates that account for financing conditions using recent modelling advances do pick up this protracted slowdown. To address this, our efforts on stressed asset resolution are firmly underway. This very stress has also resulted in poor transmission of monetary policy (except after demonetization, and only for fresh rupee loans, as bank deposits surged).

In my assessment, therefore, our focus at the present juncture should be on improving the conditions for sound transmission such as healthy bank and corporate balance sheets, market-based benchmarking of bank lending rates and a thriving corporate bond market. Higher real rates are justified in the meantime as absent efficient transmission, attempts to address symptoms of balance sheet problems with aggressive monetary easing get wasted and can even backfire by misallocating investments, fuelling asset price inflation, creating false hopes of a growth boost and relaxing the pedal on deeper structural reforms.

I remain concerned about the impact of farm loan waivers on inflation and growth, due to induced departure from fiscal discipline, shift in the nature of state spending and the crowding out of private credit by further state borrowings from the market. Given the additional uncertainty around how much of the real-time economic indicator surprises are due to the likely temporary impact of the GST rollout on business activity, careful scrutiny of upcoming data seems necessary. Hence, I prefer to keep the monetary stance neutral.

Fourth Bi-monthly Monetary Policy Statement for 2017–2018: 04 October 2017

Over the past few years, household inflation expectations have been steadily getting anchored down as they are adapting to the realized inflation outcomes. However, these expectations still remain relatively high, and are likely also manifested in the continuing high level of rural and non-rural wage growth. Recent headline inflation prints have risen significantly in a broad-based manner from its historic low in June; in addition, oil-price risk and global market volatility have risen materially. In such a scenario, it is important in my view for the RBI to persist steadfastly with its objective (and mandate) of keeping medium-term inflation within a striking distance of the target of 4 per cent.

Real-time activity indicators have been volatile over the last two quarters and do not yet paint a clear picture. Hence, it is too early, in my view, to be able to isolate the transient component of the recent one-quarter loss of momentum over and above the gradual decline in overall growth that has taken place since the Q1 of 2016–2017. The gradual decline, which has turned our measures of output gap negative, is best explained by the deleveraging underway in the heavily indebted parts of the corporate sector and in poor credit growth of PSBs given they have inadequate capital relative to impending losses on legacy assets.

Corporate credit risk profile is showing some signs of improving gradually; the large distressed borrowers are being directed to the IBC; and efforts are under way to concretely address PSB's health in near future. These structural changes will revive the affected economic activity, but with a lag. Teething problems, or at least the uncertainty, facing the GST rollout, should also resolve soon. In the meantime, given our inflation outlook has risen quite some distance over the target of 4 per cent, there did not seem much room for monetary policy adjustment.

The RBI remains committed to improving the transmission of monetary policy. I believe there is still some scope left for transmission of past monetary policy accommodation to existing loan portfolio that is tied to the base rate. Our Study Group on the MCLR has proposed what I find a reasonable path going forward in referencing floating rate loans to simple market benchmarks that will improve transparency for borrowers and competitiveness in lending. I am hopeful that switching to one of the recommended benchmarks with more frequent resets will enhance the effectiveness of monetary policy in future.

Fifth Bi-monthly Monetary Policy Statement for 2017–2018: 06 December 2017

The global commodity cycle now seems to have turned with oil prices having also rebounded recently. This has created significant input cost pressures in the economy, which at some stage may get passed on to retail prices. Vegetable prices have also firmed up, creating uncertainty around the extent of seasonal winter moderation in prices. These factors have put headline inflation on a trajectory that will most likely cross the MPC target rate of 4 per cent rather soon and remain above the target in the medium term (even after excluding the HRA impact).

Oil price evolution remains a particular concern. The shale gas response notwithstanding, improving global demand appears to be playing an important role in shaping oil prices along with the extension of Organization of the Petroleum Exporting Countries (OPEC)'s production cuts. This development poses difficult domestic policy challenges—countercyclical adjustment in cess would require fiscal balancing elsewhere, whereas lack of such adjustment would imply pressure on domestic inflation (temporarily latent, since the price pass through at pumps has not been immediate).

The adverse change in overall terms of trade given the commodity cycle upturn has likely also weakened drivers of growth. Nevertheless, there has been some respite in the last quarter's growth prints as well as some of the high frequency indicators of real economic activity in recent months. Our research team's output gap estimates show some closure, attributable in part to improved credit growth and overall flow of financial resources to the commercial sector.

Output gap remains somewhat negative as reflected in present low capacity utilization and high inventory. However, gradually improving credit metrics in several distressed sectors should pave the way for improved investment over the next year. This process is expected to be further supported as cases referenced to IBC resolve, facilitate consolidation and restore pricing power. As PSBs raise capital, receive recapitalization from the government and undertake reforms, credit flows to productive sectors of the economy should improve.

There seems little scope for accommodation or for change of stance at the present juncture. Hence, I vote to keep the repo rate at 6 per cent with neutral stance. Incoming data will be the key to shaping the policy going forward. I remain keen to (a) understand the impact of GST on price levels as its rollout stabilizes, (b) assess in coming months the robustness of growth revival in gross value added (GVA) manufacturing and (c) track the impact of commodity prices on the Indian economy and markets. In parallel, the RBI is examining options to improve the transmission of its policy rate actions from banks to borrowers.

Sixth Bi-monthly Monetary Policy Statement for 2017–2018: 07 February 2018

Headline inflation prints since the last policy have been significantly above the target. While a part of this is statistical due to the centre's HRA implementation, there has also been a rise in inflation sans HRA. A major concern has been the steep rise in oil prices coincidentally with (a) global rates and commodity cycles having turned up and (b) our fiscal deficit having overshot for this year and likely to do so next year too. Hence, even without factoring in the states' staggered HRA implementation and minimum support price (MSP) rises announced in the Union Budget, risks to inflation seem clearly tilted on the upside. Indeed, RBI's projections at 12–14 months in future put headline inflation by more than 50 bps above the target (by then the statistical effect of the centre's HRA implementation would have completely waned).

Such an inflation scenario would imply a raise in policy rates by a pure inflation-targeting central bank, in turn, implying a change in stance from 'neutral' to 'withdrawal of accommodation'. However, two reasons induced me to pause.

First, an important factor determining inflation going forward is likely to be the shale gas production response to rising oil prices; while this response has been somewhat muted, its trigger out of dormancy could dampen oil prices swiftly. I would like to see whether this downside risk plays out in the next few months to have a firmer grip on the medium-term inflation trajectory.

Second, for a flexible inflation targeting framework, the growth trajectory relative to potential output has to be considered too.

On this front, the output gap remains somewhat negative though it has been steadily closing. Structurally, the improving balance sheets of the banking system post the recapitalization package and the ongoing resolution of large stressed accounts have made the recent pick up in credit growth more sustainable. Real economic activity indicators also suggest a broad-based growth revival. While RBI growth projections for next year are in line with this buoyant activity of late, the recovery is nevertheless nascent and worthy of some support in the short run.

Given these trade-offs, I vote for a pause with no change in the neutral stance. The next few months of inflation and growth data will be key to determining the evolution of policy rates. If growth remains robust and inflation prints continue to project headline inflation a year ahead well above the target, then a change in stance from 'neutral' to 'withdrawal of accommodation' might have to be considered.

In the meantime, it would be good to focus on (a) pushing forward the work we have undertaken in improving the transmission of policy rate changes to the real sector and (b) taking the resolution framework for stressed assets to its logical conclusion.

First Bi-monthly Monetary Policy Statement for 2018–2019: 05 April 2018

In my minutes of the February 2018 MPC meeting, I had flagged two reasons that had induced me to pause from voting to begin the process of 'withdrawal of accommodation': first, the possibility of the US shale gas response softening the oil price outlook, and second, growth recovery in the economy still being nascent. Uncertainty on these fronts has now receded.

In spite of the US shale gas response to rising oil prices being robust, inventories have continued to dwindle. The combination of OPEC supply cuts and strengthening global demand appear to be keeping international oil prices at a relatively high level, and the volatility of prices around the high level has been relatively low in the past three–six months. The dwindling stock of inventories implies that a supply side disruption to any one critical source, for instance, due to geopolitical risk, could have a sharp upward impact on prices. On the domestic front, the lack of fiscal space to go easy on fuel cesses implies that prices at the pump will likely mirror movements in international prices. Since global commodity prices as a group are refusing to budge, the overall outlook is not comforting from the standpoint of domestic inflation.

On the growth front, while we have not seen another print from the CSO since the last policy, most real economic activity indicators, including the Purchasing Managers' Index (PMI) data released during the week of MPC meeting, point to growing traction in the drivers underlying growth. In fact, RBI's estimates suggest that the output gap is closing; the finance-adjusted measure, which I personally prefer, shows near complete closure of the output gap due to the resilient credit growth over the past two quarters. This is further confirmed by high frequency data on rural and urban consumption, investment activity revival, and improvement in capacity utilization. In my view, these healthy developments on the economic activity front are likely to remain durable due to steady progress in the time-bound resolution of twin balance sheet problems affecting our banks and corporates.

In view of the above referred developments since the last MPC meeting, I have moved substantially closer to switching from the neutral stance to beginning the process of withdrawal of accommodation. This is in spite of the softening of inflation in recent prints. Let me explain in some detail.

An inflation targeting central bank needs to separate 'signal' from 'noise' in the data:

- Recent prints have softened due primarily to easing of vegetable prices (contributing to over 90 per cent of softening of food inflation in February). Digging into specifics does not suggest that this is due to durable supply management in vegetables. Instead, reasonable conclusion is that vegetable prices continue to show seasonality over years, albeit with some variation in months in which the seasonality kicks in. This volatility is largely 'noise' from an interest-rate setting perspective; this volatility is also not something amenable to monetary policy actions, and certainly not at short horizon of a few months at which it is likely to, and typically does, revert.

- What concerns me is that the more persistent component of headline inflation, which is ex food and fuel, and which one can consider as the 'signal' given its persistence, has strengthened steadily from a trough of 3.8 per cent last June to 4.4 per cent in February (excluding the estimated impact of the centre's HRA increase, i.e., ex-HRA). This rise has been broad-based, consistent with the durability of a growth pickup over this period, and also confirmed by input price pressures and selling price increases reported by firms in the RBI's Industrial Outlook Survey.

- The inflation trajectory over the entire 12-month period is projected, despite the soft print in February, to remain above the MPC target rate of 4 per cent, on a quarter by quarter basis. Note that this is the case even after excluding the HRA impact.

- Professional forecasters surveyed by the RBI also expect the inflation to stay over 4 per cent for much of 2018–2019.

- While there is an inevitable uncertainty around these inflation projections, I view the risks as tilted significantly to the upside given the continuing rise in the ex-food-and-fuel inflation. Besides oil prices, another primary concern is the risk of fiscal slippages, at both the centre and state levels, especially in the form of:

  o A shift away from capital expenditures towards revenue expenditures, as is already being seen in state expenditure to accommodate farm loan waivers.

  o Food price-support measures, on which further clarity is needed, but which clearly induce an upside bias to potential inflation risks (estimates vary widely from 10 bps to close to 100 bps depending on what measures are adopted).

- Finally, as the Indian economy is economically as well as financially integrated with the global economy, a faster normalization of interest rates by systemic central banks can also pose a major challenge to the external sector.

I feel it is important to let some more hard data come in, especially on growth, and allow some more time to let the early skirmishes on the global trade front play out. I am, however, likely to shift decisively to vote for a beginning of 'withdrawal of accommodation' in the next MPC meeting in June. Reinforcement of inflation-targeting credibility that such a shift would signal is crucial in my view for prudent macroeconomic management, on both the domestic and external sector fronts.

Second Bi-monthly Monetary Policy Statement for 2018–2019: 06 June 2018

In the Minutes of the April 2018 MPC meeting, I had indicated my growing concern around underlying inflationary pressures. These pressures have been manifesting as a strengthening of Consumer Price Index (CPI) inflation excluding food and fuel even after adjusting for the impact of Centre's HRA. There has been a rise in input costs due to supply shocks such as the sharp oil price surge witnessed over the past nine months. The strengthening of inflation also reflects aggregate demand pressures, which are confirmed in the now almost-closed output gap, improved capacity utilization figures, and a significant pick up in credit growth. As a result, the projection for medium-term headline CPI inflation has become firmer on the upside; it has moved closer to 5 per cent and away from 4 per cent, the latter being the mandated target of the MPC.

The inflationary pressure also seems to be experienced by the common man. The RBI's Inflation Expectations Survey (IES) of households reveals a uniform picture of hardening of inflation expectations whichever way one looks at the data. Most notably, the 3-month ahead and 12-month ahead inflation expectations have increased sharply by 90 bps and 130 bps, respectively, since the last survey. They are likely explained by the fact that petrol and diesel prices carry salience: fuel prices are in the face and generalize rapidly through transportation costs into prices of general goods and services.

A key uncertainty at present relates to the oil price development over the medium-term horizon that monetary policy operates at. Robust global growth, OPEC and Russian supply cuts, supply shock in Venezuela, and geopolitical uncertainty around the Iranian supply have all pushed international crude prices uncomfortably high in a short span of time. The shape of Brent Futures Curve (now in 'backwardation', i.e., buying oil forward is cheaper than buying it in spot) suggests the markets are pricing in the risk of a 'stock out'—not having access to supply when it is needed. The US shale gas response appears to not have been enough as of yet to dampen this stock-out risk since some of the supply faces pipeline-infrastructure headwinds in reaching the markets.

The one respite for headline inflation prints has been the continuing benign food inflation where seasonal pickup has remained muted due to a collapse in the prices of onions and tomatoes. This has imparted a short-run softening to inflation projections keeping them contained in the first half of 2018–2019 in spite of the rising momentum in CPI ex-food, fuel and HRA. However, if the seasonal pickup does manifest in the first half at some point, then the headline prints will have little abatement from any of its constituents. Under such a scenario, any upward pressure on food prices such as through generous MSPs would exacerbate headline inflation pressures.

Factoring in these considerations, there is no alternative to raising the policy rate by 25 bps so as to signal concern about underlying inflation, manage inflation expectations and guard proactively against a further increase in inflation. However, considerable uncertainties around oil and food prices as well as the playing out of trade wars and global financial market outcomes led me to keep the stance neutral. It will allow the MPC to determine in a flexible manner what further monetary policy response is warranted based on an ongoing assessment of the inflation situation, inflation expectations and growth prints in the coming months.

Third Bi-monthly Monetary Policy Statement for 2018–2019: 01 August 2018

Since the MPC met last in June 2018, inflation prints have been somewhat softer than the RBI's projections. Notably, vegetables and fruits prices have surprised on the downside. However, the underlying inflation as reflected in 'ex-food fuel' segment, especially in petrol and diesel, transportation (including fares), education fees, health services and clothing persists, and does not augur well for headline inflation going forward.

The last three rounds of the RBI's IES of households reflect hardening of the 3-month ahead and 12-month ahead inflation expectations by 110 bps and 150 bps, respectively. The input cost pressures faced by the corporate sector are also reported to be robust. These outcomes are not surprising given that headline inflation— even after adjusting for the statistical effect of the centre's increase in HRA—has remained above 4 per cent, the MPC's mandated target headline inflation rate, for seven out of the past eight months, with a mean as well as median of slightly over 4.5per cent.

Benign food inflation continues to act as a factor pulling forecasts down. It remains to be seen whether the usual summer seasonal pickup in food inflation will simply be delayed by a month or two, or it is a feature of supply-driven soft food inflation prints. However, the major upside risk to food inflation that MPC had highlighted in its past resolutions, namely the award of MSPs, has materialized. There is now a concrete announcement detailing the targeted kharif crops and a much higher than the normal MSP increases. Though significant uncertainty remains regarding the exact rollout of the MSP program, inflation projections by the RBI include the impact of MSP under reasonable procurement assumptions.

Oil prices have moderated somewhat compared with two months back due to an increase in supply from some of the OPEC countries and Russia. Nevertheless, the price of the Indian crude basket remains at elevated levels and is just a throw away from levels that can cause domestic inflation to rise sharply. Hence, while the supply response has had some softening impact on the projections, oil price gyrations remain an important risk going forward.

Factoring these considerations, I am more concerned about upside risks materializing compared to downside risks. This is especially so, as most real-time indicators suggest that growth recovery is likely to be sustainable. As I have mentioned in the past few minutes, estimates suggest that the output gap has more or less closed.

In summary, since past several headline inflation prints have been above the target and projections suggest this will also be the case over the medium term, I vote to raise the policy rate by 25 bps as a step towards fulfilling our inflation targeting mandate while paying attention to growth. The rate hike of June followed by another rate hike will help rein in demand pressures and manage inflation expectations. However, this transmission will occur with a lag. Since that is somewhat far and there is an important interim uncertainty in the form of tariff wars which can rock global growth, financial markets and inflation in abrupt and unexpected ways, I vote to retain the neutral stance of monetary policy.

Fourth Bi-monthly Monetary Policy Statement for 2018–2019: 05 October 2018

Since the August policy, food inflation is surprisingly on the downside. Seasonal pickup in prices of vegetables and fruits in summer months was simply missing due to a combination of increased mandi arrivals, export policies and other supply management measures. This, coupled with a normal monsoon, has shifted RBI's food inflation projections significantly downward.

Elsewhere, fuel inflation continues its rapid upward march. While inflation excluding food and fuel has eased marginally due to lower momentum in certain goods and services, it remains at elevated levels. International crude oil prices keep surging as Iran sanctions approach, creating a difficult choice between pass through to the pump prices and fiscal or quasi-fiscal absorption through excise cuts. The rising oil prices also coincide with the misfortune of weaker current account balance, inducing financial market volatility which raises imported inflation, though the direct impact of oil price on inflation via the consequent fare price impact is much larger. The worry is that this could generalize quickly through transportation and freight costs—input costs—that could get passed on to selling prices as capacity utilization is improving and pricing power is returning to firms.

While there was mild softening in the 12-month ahead inflation expectations of households between June 2018 and September 2018 rounds of RBI's surveys, the 3-month expectations showed a sharp uptick. I am particularly concerned about the near 200 bps increase in the 3-month and 12-month inflation expectations of households, based on the surveys of September 2017 to September 2018. Households are telling us that their inflation outlook has moved palpably upwards. Business expectations of headline inflation as well as input costs are showing similar trends, rising steadily in RBIs and other surveys.

As a result, headline inflation for Q1 of 2019–2020 is projected at 4.8 per cent vis-à-vis the mandated target of 4 per cent, in spite of the benign food inflation outlook. Between the time the projections were finalized for the *Monetary Policy Report*—1 October and 5 October—oil prices have risen steeply, without any signs of durable supply adjustment amidst strong global demand.

Growth has been reasonably buoyant as evidenced by the real economic activity indicators for both the rural economy and the urban counterpart. Our estimates of the output gap suggest that it has virtually closed as per the traditional measures; my preferred finance-neutral output gap (FNOG) measure has in fact turned positive due to asset price growth and especially non-food credit growth that is now in excess of the nominal GDP growth rate.

In such a milieu, the likelihood of oil prices remaining elevated rules out a rate cut anytime soon. Second round effects of the steep oil price rise can be generalized causing inflation expectations to unhinge. Even if pass-through to pump prices is made less than one for one, inflation risk would generalize through fiscal slippage.

Given these factors, and given the flexible inflation-targeting mandate of the MPC, it seems important to signal commitment to keep to the mandate and move forward carefully at an appropriate time, allowing the economy to adjust to the past two back-to-back rate hikes while being vigilant of any emerging inflationary pressures.

Hence, I vote for not to raise the policy rate but change the stance of monetary policy to one of 'calibrated tightening'.

Fifth Bi-monthly Monetary Policy Statement for 2018–2019: 05 December 2018

Since the October 2018 MPC meeting, there have been two downward surprises to realized inflation.

First, food inflation has had an unexpectedly large collapse, again in vegetables and fruits, but somewhat more broad-based than the inflation decline in preceding months; the collapse has been sharper in rural inflation than in urban inflation.

Secondly, international crude oil prices that had been simmering to levels above $85 per barrel also crashed dramatically—by close to

30 per cent. It appears that the 'stock out' supply risk that was priced at the short end of the oil futures curve has subsided as the curve has flattened now compared to its sharp backwardation shape in early October. The oil price crash, in turn, has improved external sector prospects for India and caused the currency to strengthen appreciably, reducing the magnitude of imported inflation.

Together, these factors have resulted in an extraordinary downward revision in the RBI's 12-month ahead inflation outlook. However, the past two months have also been extraordinarily volatile, making it difficult to make a complete sense of recent data. Let me elaborate.

First, it is not easy to ascertain fully at this stage the nature of the collapse of food inflation seen in recent months, particularly in terms of its implications for the food inflation outlook over the medium term. A clearer assessment is particularly clouded by divergence in the direction of price movements in data in key food items provided by the Department of Consumer Affairs (DCA) and realized food inflation for October. Such divergence in the direction is rarely observed. Further examination of data is necessary to understand with greater clarity the drivers of food deflation.

Second, market indicators of uncertainty in international crude oil prices remain high, reflecting the unexpectedly large gyrations in their movement this year and upcoming geopolitical risks such as OPEC supply decision and trade war uncertainty's impact on global demand. The implied volatility in crude oil options markets was around 25 per cent per annum (p.a.) in October, which rose to around 45 per cent p.a. following the oil price crash. This is a rather high level of uncertainty embedded in expectations of market participants.

Third, inflation excluding food and fuel remains persistently high. It is over 6 per cent at present, with only 20–30 bps attributable to the statistical impact of the centre's HRA.

Fourth, the RBI's Industrial Outlook Survey suggests that input cost pressures are still high for firms and expected to remain elevated (consistent with both closing of the output gap and improvement in capacity utilization beyond the long period average). This is expected to result in cost pass through to consumers in the coming months.

Fifth, median household inflation expectations have softened at 3-month horizon by 40 bps but remain unchanged for the 12-month horizon. Over a 12-month period during which the RBI has raised the policy rate by 50 bps, median household expectations of inflation for 3-month horizon have risen by 150 bps and for a 12-month horizon by 120 bps.

Finally, the risk of a fiscal slippage at the centre and/or state levels appears to be considered within the realm of reasonable possibility. As such, the sharp decline in oil prices has provided an opportunity for fiscal consolidation.

In summary, even though the projections have been revised downwards significantly, several upside risks remain. In my view, it is better to understand data somewhat better over the next two months. Counter-factual exercises suggest that with headline inflation at 12-month horizon above the target (at 4.2% in Q2 of 2019–2020), a change in the stance at this stage, especially with heightened oil price volatility, would be premature. In other words, while the recent downward surprises to inflation have significantly reduced the extent of policy tightening required in future, they have not eliminated the requirement altogether.

Turning to growth, the outlook remains overall healthy, though there are some signs of emerging downside risks. On the positive front, investment has picked up and should be buoyed further by improving capacity utilization. Composite PMI stands at its highest level in 24 months. Coincident and leading indicators, such as aggregate bank credit, are increasing above the nominal GDP growth rate. Oil price and external sector pressures have reduced, which should ease financing conditions. On the negative front, there are some segments experiencing slowdown such as auto sales, but at least a part of this appears, in our research, to be linked to fuel price rise of the past six months and regulatory revisions in mandatory third-party insurance requirements. The Q2 print for GDP growth was below the RBI's expectation but the Q1 print was far above. Overall, due to change in macroeconomic conditions, the two-sided growth surprises have not led to revision in our growth forecast for the next 12 months.

On balance, given the relatively short period of time over which inflation has softened, it is important to wait and watch, that is, remain data dependent as well as reliant on clear understanding of the drivers of recent data. I, therefore, vote for keeping the policy repo rate on hold and maintaining the stance of monetary policy as calibrated tightening.

Sixth Bi-monthly Monetary Policy Statement for 2018–2019: 07 February 2019

Since the December monetary policy meeting, food inflation prints have continued to be soft, mainly due to vegetables and fruits witnessing healthy domestic production combined with imports (in some cases). In fact, several food groups are now in deflation, continuing with the momentum of recent food inflation prints that were available at the time of the December policy. Fuel inflation has eased due to a drop in international liquefied petroleum gas (LPG) prices. Headline inflation excluding food and fuel has moderated somewhat due to a fall in crude oil prices and complete waning of the central government employees' HRA effects; nevertheless, it remains at a highly elevated level, ranging between 5.6–6.2 per cent over the past three prints, with inflation in health and education components showing a spike in December due to unexpected rise in prices of medicines and private tuition costs.

The RBI headline inflation projections were already revised substantially downward from October to December by 40–80 bps for different quarters over a 12-month projection horizon. The additional downside surprise relative to December projections has been small, around 10 bps on a quarterly basis. Inflation expectations of households as measured by RBI's IES reveal a softening by 80 bps at 3-month horizon and 130 bps at 12-month horizon, possibly reflecting the adaptive nature of household expectations in response to the softness of recent inflation prints; importantly, they too indirectly confirm the ground reality and revision in inflation perceptions, especially in food and fuel categories.

Based on these data and other considerations, the RBI's quarterly inflation projections over the next 12-month horizon have been further revised downwards and imply headline inflation steadily rising but remaining below the target rate of 4 per cent.

My understanding of composition effects and risks around these projections is as follows:

One, inflation excluding food and fuel remains elevated and persistent, so it seems crucial to understand if the sharp increase in momentum observed in health and education components is one-off or not. While it seems reasonable to treat it as one-off for now, if it does sustain, then, it could push inflation excluding food and fuel into uncomfortable territory. Unfortunately, there is no decisive way to resolve this issue other than to wait for and analyze a few more prints.

Second, international Brent Crude prices have stabilized in the short run. Nevertheless, it is too early to forget or rule out the wild gyrations from geopolitical risks as were observed over the past six months. Given our oil imports and the implied current account deficit effects, headline inflation responds particularly adversely to upside risk from crude oil prices.

Third, the recent low momentum in food prices is assumed to have a structural component over the next 12-month horizon as there appears to be a supply glut in several food items at both domestic and international levels. Vegetable prices, however, are vulnerable to sudden reversal from their deflationary momentum.

More importantly, the assumption of sustained low momentum in food prices leads to a consideration of the risk of agrarian distress. Such distress will necessitate a political-economy response in the form of fiscal support to the agrarian economy in the short run; effects of such fiscal support may play out partly over the next 12 months and partly beyond. Besides stimulating rural demand and restoring rural wages, such a response could get generalized into headline inflation; this could arise, for example, by aggravating the input cost push arising in the financing of the real economy from fiscal and quasi-fiscal financing, especially from National Small Savings Fund (NSSF) into bank deposit rates and from fiscal/quasi-fiscal market borrowings into corporate bond yields. Our counterfactual exercises suggest that such upward pressure on headline inflation would require commensurate policy rate action over the next 12 months.

In other words, the assumption of particularly benign food inflation in the short run imparts significant upside risk to the inflation trajectory, at the short- and/or medium-term horizons, from the fiscal adjustments that would be necessary to address resulting agrarian distress and to boost rural demand.

Fourth, while inflation expectations have moved downwards in the most recent survey, when compared to the December 2017 survey, they remain higher at the 3-month horizon. In other words, anchoring of inflation expectations of households is still an ongoing process and it is somewhat early to assume its sustenance going forward based on the most recent adjustment.

On balance, I remain concerned about (a) the elevated level of inflation excluding food and fuel, (b) upward risks that could emanate from oil prices and fiscal implications of sustained food deflation and (c) lack of adequate and sustained downward adjustment in household inflation expectations over the past 12 months.

Turning to growth, concerns around global growth, especially in major advanced economies and emerging markets embroiled in tariff wars, have gathered momentum. In response, several central banks have decided to be patient with their rate hike plans and/or have revised growth projections downwards. My assessment is that unless these concerns turn into recessionary risks, they could in fact be positive for the Indian economy as a reduction in aggregate global demand keeps Brent Crude oil prices under check.

Domestic indicators for economic activity are overall mixed. Overall corporate performance in Q3 of 2018–2019 was stable; capacity utilization—absolute or seasonally-adjusted—has remained robust and close to or above 75 for the past two quarters; PMI manufacturing and services continue to remain in expansion mode at healthy levels and consumer sentiment surveyed by the RBI has improved. The primary weak coincident economic indicators have been auto sales and production. Our internal research suggests that this weakness reflects in part the lagged impact of high fuel prices during Q2 and part of Q3 of 2018–2019, an effect that should gradually reverse, as well as due to one-off policy changes such as in emission standards and third-party insurance requirement.

Traditional measures of the output gap suggest some opening up, that is, realized output below the potential output; however, my preferred measure, the FNOG, remains positive, that is, realized output is slightly above the potential output, as it captures the healthy aggregate credit growth and stable stock market performance. This is also consistent with the elevated level of inflation excluding food and fuel.

Combining my inflation and growth assessments and given the MPC's mandate to target headline inflation at 4 per cent on a durable basis while paying attention to growth, I prefer to 'take off the helmet' but 'stay within the crease'. That is, I vote for a change in the stance from 'calibrated tightening' to 'neutral' to retain policy flexibility at future dates based on incoming data, but to hold the policy rate at 6.5 per cent. Given the elevated level of inflation excluding food and fuel, our counterfactual exercises do not suggest any room for accommodation; keeping the policy rate at 6.5 per cent under these exercises turns out to be 'just right' over the medium term.

In my view, a rate cut decision now would be heavily dependent on the assumption of sustained weak momentum of food prices all through the next 12 months, which, as I explained, must be viewed as coincident with significant upside risk from fiscal measures needed to address agrarian distress. It seems better to me, in times of presently healthy levels of growth, to wait till the next policy by when uncertainties I have highlighted, especially around one-off surprises in health and education inflation, oil prices and global recessionary risks, could resolve. The growth print for Q3 would also be available by then for understanding any soft spots in the domestic real economy and their drivers.

Finally, recall that I did vote for a rate cut in August 2017; at that point of time, all components of inflation had experienced downward trends, upside risks to inflation had reduced and growth was weaker. That constellation of parameters gave me greater comfort to cut the policy rate than at the present juncture. Should a similar situation evolve in the next two months, I would have greater clarity for future policy action.

First Bi-monthly Monetary Policy Statement for 2019–2020: 04 April 2019

In the minutes of the February 2019 MPC meeting, I had provided several reasons for why I had voted to keep the policy rate at 6.5 per cent and the stance at neutral.

Since then, the headline inflation prints have revealed further softening of inflation in January, followed by a pickup in February. Notably, inflation excluding food and fuel softened unexpectedly in January, while reverting somewhat in February; nevertheless, it remains uncomfortably close to 5.5 per cent. Food inflation, in contrast, has behaved more in line with the expectations; fuel inflation has remained unusually weak.

As per my assessment, these outcomes combined with a further softening of household inflation expectations and a marginal opening up of the output gap (traditional measure), would have justified a rate cut of 25 bps from 6.5 per cent to 6.25 per cent at the April meeting.

In particular, the softening of inflation excluding food and fuel gives greater durability to the inflation path remaining around the target rate of 4 per cent in the medium term even if the policy rate were to be reduced from 6.5 per cent to 6.25 per cent. However, given that the MPC had already cut the policy rate to 6.25 per cent at its February meeting, the relevant decision now for me was whether to reduce the policy rate further from 6.25 per cent.

I vote for keeping the policy rate unchanged at 6.25 per cent for similar reasons as echoed in my February meeting statement, with some additional uncertainties that I flag below.

First, oil prices have marched upwards by an additional 10 per cent since the February policy. This rise has taken the Brent Crude price closer to $70 per barrel. Its momentum cannot be taken lightly given the uncertainty witnessed last year on oil prices and the pressure it puts on inflation, the external sector and financial markets. While the pass through to consumers remains somewhat incomplete at present, it will eventually hit the pump prices and generalize through transportation fares into non-fuel components of headline inflation.

Second, food deflation has attendant fiscal risks, as I explained in detail in my February meeting statement. Fiscal responses to deal with agrarian distress resulting from low food prices can impart a significant upside risk to the inflation trajectory, an uncertainty that may get partly resolved in the coming months.

Third, let me reiterate that inflation excluding food and fuel remains uncomfortably close to 5.5 per cent, that is, at elevated levels as through most of the past 12 months. This is confirmed also in rising staff costs in the formal sector. Conversely, it is only the benign food inflation that is allowing the monetary policy to not respond to the discomforting elevated levels of inflation excluding food and fuel. An important observation on food inflation is in order; in all of recent years, even as the level of food inflation has trended downward, it has remained highly volatile within each year; peak-to-trough cycle in food inflation typically tends to be of around eight months duration, and the month of February has already shown some seasonal uptick in prices of several food items. Hence, soft food inflation may not persist for long, a scenario in which the elevated level of inflation excluding food and fuel would steer the headline inflation away from the target rate of 4 per cent. This can risk hardening of inflation expectations of households.

Fourth, professional forecasters are pegging inflation trajectory somewhat higher than that of the RBI; this is due to their factoring in some fiscal slippage for this year as well as post-election as gathered from their qualitative responses. Dissaving induced by such fiscal slippage also creates a rather weak transmission of monetary policy to the private and household sectors of the economy as bank deposits compete with small savings and corporate bonds with government securities.

These factors combined with mixed news regarding the prospects of a normal monsoon suggest to me that this is a particularly inopportune time to reduce the interest rate. In two to four months, several uncertainties as posed above are likely to be resolved, helping steer interest rates in a clear direction, upwards or downwards or simply staying put, depending on how the risks play out. In the meantime, efforts could be made to improve the financial system structurally for better transmission of monetary policy to the real economy, especially as there are headwinds to such transmission from the rise in overall public sector borrowing requirement.

On the growth front, signals from the domestic economy are mixed. Capacity utilization continues to improve which augurs well for future investment, and services growth remains robust; however, consumption demand shows signs of weakness. Global growth is exhibiting a synchronized slowdown; as I have contended in my past statements, mild moderation of global growth benefits India through a downward pressure on oil prices; it is extreme moderation that hurts India and more so through the financial flows channel rather than the trade channel, the latter having been largely insensitive to external prospects in recent years.

Aggregate flow of financial resources to the commercial sector remains robust with banks substituting for the weak credit growth of non-banks; bank credit growth continues to be above nominal GDP growth; equity markets have been buoyant; foreign portfolio flows have reversed into India following the dovish stance of advanced country central banks; together, these imply that the FNOG, my preferred measure of output gap which accounts for financial cycles, continues to remain closed.

On balance, therefore, notwithstanding signs of weakness in growth evinced in high frequency economic indicators, I am inclined to wait for some more time for incoming data to resolve several important uncertainties that will shape the Indian economy in the coming one or two years. The counterfactual exercises suggest that 6.25 per cent policy repo rate is just 'right' for achieving the headline inflation target of 4 per cent on a durable basis in the medium term; continuing oil price rise or fiscal impulses or seasonal uptick in volatile vegetable prices would likely require some tightening down the road; only a substantial collapse in global growth, which seems unlikely at present given proactive responses of central banks in advanced economies and China, would justify a rate cut at this point. Hence, I am erring on the side of caution, choosing to be patient, rather than supporting another rate cut on the back of MPC's February decision to cut the rate.

Second Bi-monthly Monetary Policy Statement for 2018–2019: 06 June 2019

'Why do old men wake so early? Is it to have one longer day?' wonders Santiago, the old fisherman, in *Old Man and the Sea* by Ernest Hemingway. I found myself preparing and writing these minutes early too, perhaps so I could have one longer drafting day!

Since the April 2019 meeting of the MPC, inflation prints have been more or less consistent with RBI's projections. Food inflation has risen more than expected, driven significantly by a seasonal summer uptick in vegetable prices. In contrast, inflation excluding food and fuel (ex-food-fuel) has registered a significant broad-based decline of 90 bps; this was both unexpected and unusually large in magnitude over a short period of two months. I have always put significant weight on ex-food-fuel inflation in my assessment of future inflation trajectory as it tends to be the more persistent component of headline inflation and it contains better signals about the underlying aggregate demand pressures. The signal conveyed by substantial softening of ex-food-fuel inflation has only been corroborated by the large negative surprise of the Q4 of 2018–2019 GDP print, pulled down by a sharp deceleration in gross fixed capital formation (GFCF) growth to 3.6 per cent, a 14-quarter low, explained possibly at least in part by a hysteresis effect induced by the pre-election uncertainty.

Altogether, this led to the following considerations at my end regarding the inflation outlook:

1. The broad-based decline in ex-food-fuel inflation is the primary contributor to softening of the inflation trajectory at the horizon of 12 months. While the level of ex-food-fuel inflation is presently at 4.5 per cent, the fact that the level of food inflation is relatively low ensures that the headline trajectory over the next 12 months projected by the RBI staff remains below the MPC target of 4 per cent, reaching 3.7 per cent in Q4 of 2019–2020.

2. Food momentum has picked up significantly; late monsoon and prevailing drought conditions in many states suggest this momentum may sustain beyond just vegetable prices. While vegetable prices show seasonality during April–August that tends to reverse partly during September–March, the reversal pattern is less clear for the food basket as a whole. Nowcast data suggest that momentum in food prices is broad-based in May too, though it has softened from the first fortnight to the second fortnight. Overall, this has imparted an upward push to the food inflation trajectory, more so in the short term.

3. Fuel prices had been rising internationally until the third week of May but have since corrected by over 10 per cent due to the evolving trade war uncertainty and its implications for global demand in a scenario of more than expected supply response. The pass through to domestic prices has, however, been incomplete. Hence, there is a latent inflation of around 15 bps that will enter headline inflation if and when passed through; else, if it is absorbed by the government (through lower profits of public sector undertakings) then it will likely get generalized into headline inflation in due course through a higher fiscal deficit. Thus, even as the correction in fuel prices pulls the inflation trajectory down, the incomplete pass through over the past few months negates some of the decline.

In summary, compared to the April 2019 policy, short-term headline inflation trajectory has risen but the 6–12-month trajectory has somewhat softened. For a change, I am not comparing this pattern to that observed in the revision of inflation expectations of households or in the survey of professional forecasters as these were received before the release of the Q4 of 2018–2019 GDP print.

There is, however, an important upside risk to RBI's projected inflation trajectory that I wish to highlight in particular—that of fiscal slippage.

Estimates of overall public sector borrowing requirement (PSBR)—which appropriately accounts for extra-budgetary resources and other off-balance sheet borrowings of central and state governments—have now reached between 8 per cent and 9 per cent of GDP.[1] This is at a level similar to that in 2013 at the time of the 'taper tantrum' crisis. Following are some salient implications:

1. While the consolidated fiscal deficit of the centre and states might have improved since 2013, the PSBR suggests otherwise.
2. PSBR has risen since 2014 even during high GDP growth years. The rise in PSBR in fact reflects a structural pattern of greater government expenditures and not just cyclical (such as due to weak tax collections from low growth). In other words, there is a significant aggregate demand push linked to government expenditure that needs to be recognized as a source of inflation; in particular, correct economic measurement of the fiscal slippage should factor in the implications of a rising PSBR rather than rely solely on the consolidated fiscal deficit figures.
3. Even the cyclical component of PSBR, such as that in the last year due to lower tax collections, raises the inflation trajectory through an increase in issuance of public debt and country risk premium that feed into imported inflation.
4. Further, PSBR impairs monetary policy transmission due to crowding out effects on market financing through public bonds and on bank deposits through small savings which continue to offer rates that are significantly higher than market yields. This channel bites particularly when the domestic savings rate is on a decline and increases economy's reliance on external sources of funding.

The upcoming Union Budget is, therefore, key to understanding the inflation outlook, especially the response to ongoing distress in the agrarian economy, caused in part by low food prices and reflected in

---

[1] https://www.rbi.org.in/Scripts/BS_PressReleaseDisplay.aspx?prid=47359#F1

low rural inflation of less than 2 per cent compared to urban inflation that remains above 4 per cent. Would the response worsen the fiscal outlook for the next year and beyond, or keep it contained through pursuit of much-needed reforms for the agricultural sector and reduction/rationalization of other revenue expenditures? Equally importantly, the pattern of PSBR evolution during the rest of 2019–2020 would also be critical for assessing the inflation outlook. Hence, the MPC needs to carefully watch out for these fiscal developments.

Turning to growth, the Q4 of 2018–2019 GDP print has widened the traditional measure of the output gap to be more negative. Several coincident economic indicators for Q1 of 2019–2020, such as consumer durables and non-durables consumption as well as investment activity continue to remain weak. It is to be noted though that my preferred measure of the output gap—the FNOG—remains closed as (a) aggregate credit growth remains above nominal GDP growth rate, (b) the impact of the past two policy rate cuts will provide fuller transmission to the real sector over the next year and (c) the post-election reduction of financial market uncertainty has led to a softening of the bond yields and a rebound in equity markets in May. In other words, growth has slowed down, but financial conditions have eased which should provide a tailwind to growth and help investment activity revive on the back of steadily improving capacity utilization.

Nevertheless, on balance, I concluded that the mixed picture on economic growth has morphed into one where at least some aspects have weakened considerably over the past two quarters.

In the April 2019 policy, I had voted to keep the policy rate at 6.25 per cent, whereas the MPC had cut the policy rate to 6 per cent. Counterfactual exercises suggest that under the baseline projections of the RBI, the policy repo rate at 6 per cent is just 'right' in the short term to achieve MPC's mandated target of 4 per cent headline inflation in the medium term. However, the large decline in ex-food-fuel inflation since the April policy implies some space in these counterfactual exercises to accommodate growth weakness with a policy rate cut of around 20 bps sometime in the middle of 2019–2020.

I do remain concerned about the following upside risks to inflation:

1. The monsoon uncertainty imparting further spike in food prices and the possibility of vegetable price reversal in winter

months turning out to be lower than expected. Not only would this worsen the inflation outlook directly, but potentially also indirectly via the fiscal channel as it would aggravate the agrarian distress.

2. The rise in implied volatility of international crude oil prices from 30 per cent to 50 per cent over the past month even as oil prices have corrected downwards.

3. The possibility of an upward level-shift in the price of the Indian crude basket due to a shift in its composition from Iran and Venezuela to other oil suppliers.

4. The fiscal undercurrents impacting the generalized inflation outlook. As also conveyed earlier, I worry especially about a worsening of the PSBR in conjunction with rising oil prices, say due to geopolitical tensions; such a coincidence creates a 'twin deficit'—fiscal and current account deficits—scenario for imported inflation, a glimpse of which we have had only recently during H1 of 2018–2019.

Let me elaborate on the last of these upside risks. The Indian economy appears to experience 'twin deficit' related vulnerability on a regular basis when external shocks amplify domestic weaknesses. The key to dealing with such a scenario is the ability and the willingness of the central bank to maintain credibility of inflation targeting when imported inflation tends to rise steeply (for example, due to rising oil prices, widening fiscal and current account deficits, and, in turn, depreciating currency). Since monetary policy response will cool down inflation only with substantive lags, some headroom needs to be maintained in the inflation trajectory below the mandated target so as to absorb the steep rise in imported inflation without the headline moving far away from the target. Similarly, headroom needs to be retained in the policy rate space so as to help revive growth with monetary accommodation once the economy has cooled off and twin deficits reined in. In my assessment, this is exactly the 'robust' approach that the MPC had adopted during the last year.[2]

Finally, a few words on the trade war uncertainty and India are in order. By not being a significant part of global supply chains in manufacturing, India's direct exposure to the present correction

[2] https://www.rbi.org.in/Scripts/BS_PressReleaseDisplay.aspx?prid=47359#F2

in global growth is likely to be somewhat muted. Indeed, this consideration has led to India being perceived by investors as somewhat of a 'safe haven' economy. Hence, it is my view that growth concerns for India based on moderate trade war concerns are somewhat overstated. A full-scale trade war blowout may, however, result in an emerging markets sell-off by foreign portfolio investors, engulfing India's external sector and raising prospects of imported inflation, especially if it coincides with a worsening PSBR, and even more perversely, if instead of easing due to weak global growth, oil prices were instead to rise from geopolitical tensions.

Counterfactual exercises suggest that a fiscal slippage of 50 bps (a conservative assessment based on the PSBR estimates) or an oil price increase of 10 per cent leave no space to cut the policy rate below 6 per cent.

How should I vote? I found that I was speaking to myself as Santiago, the old fisherman, in *Old Man and the Sea* by Ernest Hemingway:

> It is better to be lucky. But I would rather be exact.
> Then when luck comes, you are ready.

In spite of my dilemma, I vote—albeit with some hesitation—to frontload the policy rate cut from 6 per cent to 5.75 per cent (a 50 bps rate cut from my April vote to keep the policy rate at 6.25%). This would provide an insurance to help prevent the output gap from widening further or the FNOG from turning negative. The MPC will need to remain on guard and be prepared to provide such insurance in a symmetric manner if upside risks to inflation were to materialize.

I also vote to change the monetary policy stance from neutral to accommodative. This is because the uncertainty around the upside risks to inflation I have highlighted will resolve only gradually over the next few months and can be factored into future MPC decisions in a data-dependent manner, but seem highly unlikely to lead to a rate hike at the next policy.

CHAPTER 10

MANAGING THE FINANCIAL CYCLES IN EMES: A CENTRAL BANKER'S PERSPECTIVE*

Emerging markets are characterized by several features that make them vulnerable to external sector stress. Two most important characteristics are a fiscal deficit and a current account deficit. These are often referred to in economic literature as the 'twin deficits' that make emerging markets vulnerable to the risk of a 'sudden stop': Adverse global financial conditions interact with domestic stresses of the emerging markets, resulting in an outflow of foreign capital or, at a minimum, ebbing of inflows into the emerging markets.

What are the implications of these characteristics of emerging markets? One important consequence of a sizeable fiscal deficit is the crowding-out[1] of investments of the economy's private sector. Typically, in emerging markets, saving rates are not high relative to the investment needs. In fact, savings may not even be financialized. All and this make it hard for the private sector to borrow because most of the domestic savings are consumed by borrowings of the

---

* Based on the discussion of 'The global financial cycle' (Author: Claudio Borio, Head of Monetary and Economics Department, Bank for International Settlements) by Dr Viral V. Acharya, Deputy Governor, RBI in the Conference on 'The Current Global and European Financial Cycle: Where do we stand and how to we move forward?'— Jointly organized by the Bulgarian National Bank and the Bank for International Settlements on 08 July 2019 at Sofia, Bulgaria.

[1] For more details, please refer to the speech on 'Why Less Can be More: On the Crowding-out Effects of Government Financing', delivered at the 16th K. P. Hormis Commemorative Lecture organized by the Federal Bank Hormis Memorial Foundation on 17 November 2018 at Kochi (https://www.federalbank.co.in/documents/10180/21836713/Hormis+Memorial+Lecture+2019/935fbdcc-36a2-49ed-877d-3f2c1ebd67ba).

public sector. Those corporations in the private sector that have adequately high credit ratings (or credit quality, in general) tap into foreign markets by borrowing abroad. Thus, one characteristic of the emerging markets—the fiscal deficit—results in borrowing abroad by the private sector, which increases the vulnerability of the country to the global financial cycle.

The 'global financial cycle' means different things to different people. In my own research, I have found that some combination of the Federal Reserve's interest rate stance, measures of global stock market volatility (notably the VIX in the USA), measures of the commodity price cycle, perhaps some indicators of flows into emerging markets—or a principal component or a common factor of all these variables—is what one can consider operationally as reflecting the state of the global financial cycle. If you are a market practitioner, this is essentially something like a 'risk-on' or a 'risk-off' sentiment indicator.

The global financial cycle is important because it interacts with the crowding-out risks and other characteristics of the emerging markets. This interaction can, however, be tricky to fathom.

To see this, consider an emerging market where the fiscal deficit is high and there is crowding-out of the private sector at work. Suppose the easing of the global financial cycle primarily allows the sovereign to borrow more from abroad, possibly in foreign-currency denominated debt. If that happens, then the global financial cycle makes the country more vulnerable in a 'sudden stop' sense, in case the sovereign bonds run into a rollover problem. This does not then bring any beneficial outcome for the crowded-out private sector; if anything, because the sudden stop risks will become amplified when the global financial cycle turns adverse, the sovereign borrowing abroad can add to the country's risk-premium and crowding-out risk, in turn, forcing the private sector to invest even less.

There is another possibility though—in case of some emerging markets, sovereigns do not borrow abroad or allow foreign investors to invest in domestically issued government bonds (more generally, impose some macroprudential caps on foreign ownership of government debt). If the private sector can borrow abroad, then this at least has the good fortune of relaxing the crowding-out problem of these corporates to the extent that they had been unable to tap adequately into domestic savings; in other words, the easing of the global financial cycle enables the private sector to get its hands on to foreign savings for making its investments. Nevertheless, there could be adverse consequences if the economy gets overheated during the global financial cycle and imports expand faster than exports, widening the economy's current account deficit (the second characteristic I highlighted about the emerging markets). So, on the one hand, the crowding-out restrictions get relaxed when the global financial cycle eases, but on the other hand, the external sector vulnerability indicators can get worse and amplify sudden stop risks when the global financial cycle turns adverse.

What causes the global financial cycle to turn adverse? There could be an increase in interest rates globally, a rise in uncertainty or VIX, a surge in commodity prices like in oil, a default on a sovereign bond or a revision of emerging markets' growth prospects. Such shocks can lead to a generalized pull back of foreign capital flows from emerging markets. Somewhat perversely, countries vulnerable to the twin deficits are likely to be the most affected as they are also the most likely to have increased their vulnerability during the benign phase of the global financial crisis. In turn, these are also the countries to experience a larger correction when the global financial cycle turns adverse.

The correction manifests itself most notably in terms of depreciation of the exchange rate. To borrow an analogy from Hyun Shin of the Bank for International Settlements regarding the behaviour of the exchange rate of an emerging market during the global financial cycle—in good times, the currency appreciates 'up the stairs' and in bad times, it comes 'down the escalator'. In other words, the exchange rate of an emerging market could experience a seemingly calm episode of steady appreciation, but when the global financial cycle turns, it depreciates sharply, resulting in greater imported inflation as well as higher rollover costs for corporations and sovereigns that have issued bonds to foreign capital providers. The resulting spillovers accentuate the sudden stop risks substantially.

Now, let us switch attention to the 'domestic financial cycle' of the emerging markets. I will focus on how the domestic financial cycle could be modulated through policy interventions of regulators like the central bank in order to dampen the impact of the global financial cycle. This is indeed one of the core themes of Claudio Borio's work.

1. First, I will discuss the 'monetary policy' decisions of the domestic emerging market economy. Whether monetary policy is countercyclical or procyclical to the global financial cycle depends strongly on whether the monetary authority, typically the central bank, adopts a financial stability perspective against the global financial cycle, or it views the global financial cycle as a form of relaxation of the emerging market's crowding-out problems.

   Let me elaborate. Suppose the domestic monetary policy leans against the wind of the global financial cycle. That is, during the benign phase of the global financial cycle when foreign capital chases emerging markets, domestic interest rates are either raised or maintained steady. In this case, foreign flows into sovereign or corporate borrowings could amplify some domestic growth, but not overly so as the domestic financial cycle is acting in a manner countercyclical to the global financial cycle. When the reversal of the global financial cycle occurs, the domestic monetary policy would benefit from having preserved policy buffer space to accommodate and deal with the risks that the economy may have a hard landing from the withdrawal of foreign flows.

   However, the converse is possible if crowding-out effects in the emerging market are strong, the global financial cycle substantially relaxes the private sector's financial constraints, and the domestic monetary authorities emphasize growth instead of financial stability, accommodating at a time when the global financial cycle is in the benign phase. This can potentially cause the economy to overheat and widen the current account deficit. This procyclical strategy may work out okay if inflationary pressures in the economy are not too strong; nevertheless, it renders the economy more vulnerable to a reversal of the global financial cycle and could end up being a myopic strategy if no policy buffer has been left to accommodate in such a reversal scenario.

   There is an important message herein regarding how the domestic and the global financial cycles interact in emerging markets. My view is that the emerging markets with large twin deficits should factor in financial stability considerations and adopt a counter-cyclical approach in their domestic cycle relative to the global financial cycle.

2. The second important part of the domestic financial cycle is what I am going to call 'external sector management', typically undertaken by the central bank. This includes building up of the foreign exchange reserves to stem sharp currency depreciation and the use of macroprudential restrictions on the extent of foreign capital flows into sovereign and corporate debt markets. In joint work[2] with Arvind Krishnamurthy of the Graduate School of Business at Stanford University, Arvind and I argue that while a number of central banks in emerging markets accumulate reserves when the global financial cycle is benign, hoping to deploy these reserves to stabilize the currency when the global financial cycle reverses, this strategy doesn't quite work well unless there are macroprudential quantity restrictions on the inflows of the foreign capital. Put simply, reserves and macroprudential restrictions on foreign capital flows act as complementary tools for external sector management.

Our simple idea is that the reserves accumulated by the central bank by being deployed to stem sharp currency depreciation, are essentially an insurance for all those who would have been hit adversely by the depreciation of the exchange rate (for example, the importers or corporates and the sovereign that have borrowed abroad). Knowing that the central bank has provided an implicit put option to stabilize the currency, they will rationally anticipate that the currency won't depreciate as much as it would have if the reserves were lower. Therefore, the reserves engender a moral hazard in the form of a build-up of large unhedged positions by importers or excessive foreign borrowing by corporates and the sovereign in terms of the resulting exposure to the risk of sudden stop or currency depreciation.

In turn, unless the central bank employs macroprudential limits on the extent of capital inflows via foreign borrowings or requires hedging by the importers (or imposes restrictions

[2] https://rbidocs.rbi.org.in/rdocs/Speeches/PDFs/GSNSENYU240C656D860B464 E9F41B7C4E53D707B.PDF

on the size of unhedged positions of the importers), all benefits of the reserves can get completely 'undone'. When the global financial cycle turns adverse, the central bank will have more reserves but also a greater demand for the reserves relative to the domestic currency. Recognizing this, optimal external sector management by the central bank requires 'both' reserves accumulation and macroprudential constraints on sudden stop vulnerability that builds up during the benign phase of the global financial cycle.

Conversely, if the central bank engages in reserves accumulation 'without' macroprudential controls on foreign capital flows, then the outcomes can be destabilizing, especially if it is not recognized that the vulnerabilities are increasing precisely because the reserves are being accumulated.

To summarize, both countercyclical monetary policy—which Claudio Borio stresses as being quite crucial—and management of reserves along with macroprudential controls on capital flows could be effective in leaning against the wind of the global financial cycle.[3]

---

[3] Other researchers such as Hyun Shin and Helene Rey (of London Business School) have taken some of these insights to make sense of asset prices, volatility in financial markets, and 'risk-on/off' effects of dollar appreciation, all stemming from the movement in the global financial cycle.

PART 4

Improving Monetary Policy Transmission

Part 4

Improving
Monetary Policy
Transmission

CHAPTER 11

MONETARY TRANSMISSION IN INDIA: WHY IS IT IMPORTANT AND WHY HASN'T IT WORKED WELL?*

When I travel from my residence in Vile Parle (West) to the RBI Central Office in Fort, I pass Kenilworth—the birthplace of late Homi Jehangir Bhabha. It is a good way to start and end the day, being reminded not only of his immense intellect but also of his deep sense of service to India.

Let me start with some technical jargon and then explain from the first principle, the part of it I wish to focus on. With the amendment of the RBI Act in 2016, the 'primary objective of the monetary policy is to maintain price stability while keeping in mind the objective of growth'. The MPC constituted under the amended RBI Act is mandated to determine the policy repo rate to achieve the specified medium-term inflation target of 4 per cent, within a band of +/–2 per cent.

For the RBI to achieve its mandate effectively, it is extremely important that an economic process referred to as 'monetary

---

* Speech delivered at the Inaugural Aveek Guha Memorial Lecture, Homi Bhabha Auditorium, Tata Institute of Fundamental Research (TIFR) on 16 November 2017. I am thus grateful to Professor Dipan Ghosh, who was the Dean of students during my time at IIT Bombay, for inviting me to speak today in the Homi Bhabha Auditorium, and to Dr Subhendu Guha, for having endowed this lecture series at the TIFR in memory of his dear son, Aveek Guha. 'Aveek', a beautiful Bengali name meaning 'fearless', is exactly how all research needs to be, taking on seemingly insurmountable challenges, fighting it out with grit, and along the way, dissecting, reflecting and distilling truth to its essence until it is unearthed in some recognizable form from beneath its scratchy exterior. The TIFR is a daunting proposition for any researcher to speak at. I hope that I can progress some way towards meeting its highest standards in the form of this talk, by raising an issue that is germane to all of us in today's forum and that is worthy of being tackled in due course—that of, monetary transmission in India: why is it important and why hasn't it worked well?

transmission' works seamlessly. Any impediment to this process of monetary transmission hampers the achievement of our mandate. We, therefore, monitor and analyze monetary transmission on a regular basis, and undertake corrective steps to enhance its efficacy, if it seems broken or critically imperfect.

What is monetary transmission? It is essentially the process through which the policy action of the central bank is transmitted to the ultimate objective of stable inflation and growth. The policy action consists typically of changing the interest rate at which it borrows or lends 'reserves' (in our case, rupees) on an overnight basis with commercial banks. In other words, monetary transmission is the entire process starting from the change in the policy rate by the central bank to various money market rates such as interbank lending rates, to bank deposit rates, bank lending rates, households and firms, government and corporate bond yields and to asset prices such as stock prices and house prices, culminating in its impact on inflation and growth. The transmission mechanism hinges crucially on how monetary policy changes influence households' and firms' behaviour. This change can take place through several channels. Studying these channels is a vast subject in finance and economics literature. Therefore, given the time constraint, I will only cover a few key aspects. I will then explain how and why monetary transmission has, and more importantly, has 'not', worked in India, and also touch briefly upon how we could improve it.

Channels of Monetary Transmission

Changes in the central bank's policy rate impact the economy with lags through a variety of channels, the primary ones being (a) 'interest rate channel', (b) 'credit channel', (c) 'exchange rate channel' and (d) 'asset price channel'.

Let us start with how the 'interest rate channel' works. The immediate impact of a change in the monetary policy rate is on the short-term money market rates (such as call money rate, certificates of deposits, commercial papers and T-bills), key financial markets (exchange rate, equity prices) and also on medium- and long-term instruments (yields on dated government securities and corporate bonds). The impact is typically quick and broadly one-to-one from the policy rate to short-term money markets rates such as the call-money rate which is the unsecured or uncollateralized interbank lending rate: a bank will be willing to part with its reserves overnight to another bank only if it earns at least the rate that it could earn by parking these funds with the central bank; and, if banks compete adequately for such lending, then the rate will in fact track closely the central bank's policy rate. The impact of the policy rate on other market rates varies across tenors and instruments depending upon the liquidity conditions and other factors such as how interest rates vary at different maturities.

In turn, the central bank's changes in its policy rate are expected to impact the banks' cost of funds, both the rates they would pay to depositors and the rates they would demand for making loans. For example, when a central bank reduces the policy repo rate with the intention to support aggregate demand in the economy, the expectation is that there would be a reduction in the banks' cost of funds and lending rates, and in the spectrum of market interest rates (and vice versa when the policy rate is increased). Lower lending interest rates of banks provide a boost to demand for bank credit from various segments of the society, for instance, from individuals and households for loans for consumer durables (such as automobiles) and for housing and from entrepreneurs for new or increased investment in plant and machinery. An increased demand for automobiles, housing and machinery generates increased demand for the inputs including labour in these industries, and hence, an increase in overall demand, incomes and output in the economy. As this process continues, it eventually puts upward pressure on wages of labour and prices of inputs, and this way, raises inflation. A central bank mandated to maintain stable prices while taking account of growth, thus faces a trade-off while lowering or raising its policy rate.

The implicit assumption here is that bank balance sheets are strong and in a position to step up quickly the supply of credit in response to lower funding cost and higher demand for credit—the bank lending or the 'credit channel' of transmission. Cross-country evidence indicates that monetary transmission is greatly hindered if bank balance sheets are weak in that they do not have much loss-absorption capacity to deal squarely with their problem loans—indeed, the evidence suggests that there might be evergreening of bad loans and increased 'zombie' lending, lending to distressed firms at subsidized rates to kick the can of loan defaults down the road—resulting in misallocation of resources, productivity losses and weak growth. This way, attempts to stimulate growth with aggressive policy rate cuts when there are bank balance sheet problems get wasted and can even backfire in the form of malinvestments, creating false hopes of a growth boost and relaxing the pedal on deeper balance sheet and structural reforms of the banking sector (Acharya et al. 2016). The effectiveness of this bank credit channel is a critical issue in the current juncture in India to which I will come back later.

Lower interest rates also boost asset prices such as housing and equity prices as these can now be purchased at cheaper borrowing costs. The resulting boost to household/corporate wealth and improved cash flows on the back of lower interest rates also add to the demand impulses. This is the 'asset price channel' of monetary transmission. Higher asset prices can enhance the value of the collateral or net worth of the borrowers, interacting with the bank lending or credit channel, enhancing the capacity to borrow more and at competitive rates, reinforcing the impulses to aggregate demand.

Finally, lower domestic interest rates could lead to a depreciation of the domestic currency, on the one hand making exports more competitive in the global market and adding to domestic demand and economic activity, but on the other, could also have a direct upward impact on the domestic currency prices of imported inputs, making imports (for example, crude oil) costlier. This is the 'exchange rate channel' of transmission.

All the channels that I have described earlier—the interest rate channel, the bank lending or credit channel, the asset price channel and the exchange rate channel—are not stand-alone channels; rather, these work at the same time, and may reinforce or interact with each other, so that their individual impact is difficult to disentangle. It also needs to be recognized that the transmission mechanism is complex. The speed and strength at which the central bank's policy rate changes travel to the rest of the economy and could vary widely from country to country depending on the structure of the economy and the state of its financial system.

Monetary Policy Lags

The available empirical evidence for India suggests that monetary policy actions are felt with a lag of 2–3 quarters on output and with a lag of 3–4 quarters on inflation, and the impact persists for 8–12 quarters. Among the channels of transmission, the 'interest rate channel' has been found to be the strongest.[1] Given that monetary policy impacts output and inflation with long (and often variable) lags, it is critical for monetary policy actions to be forward-looking, that is, monetary policy needs to respond to 'expected' output and inflation developments. Of course, the expected evolution of output and inflation is uncertain, thereby rendering the transmission analysis even more challenging, adding to the complexity of the central bank's decision-making (and creating exciting opportunities for its critiques!). The key point is that if parts of the transmission machinery are broken, then monetary policy would be less effective.

Transmission from Policy Rate to Bank Lending Rates in India: Performance

The Indian financial system remains bank-dominated, though the share of NBFCs and markets (corporate bonds, commercial paper, equity, etc.) in overall financing of the economy is steadily rising. Hence, the overall efficacy of monetary transmission in India hinges critically on the extent and the pace with which banks, taking a cue from—and induced by—the changes in the policy repo rate, adjust their deposit and lending rates and meet adequately the economy's demand for credit. Overall, data suggests that the pass-through from policy rate changes to bank lending rates has been slow and muted. This lack of adequate monetary transmission remains a key policy concern for the RBI as it blunts the impact of its policy changes on economic activity and inflation.

Since the deregulation of interest rates in the early 1990s, the RBI has made several attempts to improve the speed and extent of the monetary pass-through by refining the process of setting lending interest rates by banks, while at the same time imparting transparency

---

[1] *Report of the Expert Committee to Revise and Strengthen the Monetary Policy Framework* (Chairman: Urjit R. Patel), 2014, Reserve Bank of India. The lags of 2–4 quarters that I just noted are the average lags over the sample periods of various studies, and the actual lags at any given point of time could be vastly different from these average lags, depending upon factors such as the stage of the domestic and the global business cycle, the domestic liquidity and financial conditions, the fiscal stance, the health of the domestic banking sector and the non-banking sector.

to borrowers and flexibility to banks in the process of interest rate setting. We have transited from the 'prime lending rate (PLR)' system 1994 to the 'benchmark prime lending rate (BPLR)' system 2003, the 'base rate' system (2010), and the present 'marginal cost of funds-based lending rate (MCLR)' system 2016. Let me explain these interest rate setting regimes briefly, before I turn to an assessment of the performance of the (legacy) base rate and (prevalent) MCLR systems.

In India, as in a number of other countries, a large proportion of loans is at floating rates, that is, the interest rate charged to the borrower keeps changing depending on the reset periodicity. The floating rate is linked to some 'benchmark rate' (which ideally varies over time in consonance with the changing macroeconomic and financial conditions and, in particular, the central bank's policy rate). Banks also charge a spread over the benchmark to factor in terms of premia and credit risk, among other factors. The actual lending rate is the benchmark plus the spread. The benchmark could be 'internal or external'; an internal benchmark will be based on elements which are in part under the control of the bank such as cost of funds, while an external benchmark is outside the control of the bank (for example, it could be market-determined rate such as certificate of deposit [CD] rate or treasury bill rate or interbank offer rate or it could simply be the central bank's policy rate). The virtue of an external benchmark is that it is transparent, common across banks and borrowers can compare various loan offers by simply comparing spreads over the benchmark (all else, such as maturity of the loan, being equal). As market rates normally move in line with the central bank's policy rate, an external benchmark is globally considered and adopted as more appropriate than an internal benchmark for transmitting monetary policy signals. In India, the RBI has provided the banks flexibility to use both the internal and external benchmarks, but the banks seem to have preferred internal benchmarks over external benchmarks on two key grounds: first, the internal benchmark reflects their cost of funds; and second, it has been perceived that there have not been until recently any robust and vibrant external benchmarks.

In October 1994, when the RBI deregulated lending rates for credit limits over ₹0.2 million, banks were required to declare their PLR—the interest rate charged for the most creditworthy borrowers—taking into account factors such as cost of funds and transaction costs. The PLR was, thus, expected to act as a floor for lending above

₹0.2 million. However, the experience with its working was not satisfactory mainly for two reasons: (a) both the PLR and the spread charged over the PLR varied widely, and inexplicably so, across banks; and perhaps more importantly, (b) the PLRs of banks were rigid and inflexible in relation to the overall direction of interest rates in the economy.

In view of these concerns, the RBI advised banks in April 2003 to announce BPLRs, taking into account the cost of funds, operational costs, minimum margin to cover regulatory requirements (provisioning and capital charge) and profit margin. The BPLR system also fell short of its desired objective of enhancing transparency and serving as the reference rate for pricing of loan products, with a large part of the lending taking place at interest rates below the announced BPLRs. The share of sub-BPLR lending was as high as 77 per cent in September 2008, rendering it difficult to assess the transmission of policy rate changes of the RBI to lending rates of banks. The residential housing loans and the consumer durable loans were outside the purview of the BPLR. As such, sub-BPLR lending became a major distortion in terms of cross-subsidization across borrower categories.

Next, the drawbacks of the BPLR system led to the introduction of the base rate system in July 2010. The base rate was also based, inter alia, on the costs of borrowed funds; an indicative formula for arriving at the base rate was also provided. The base rate was to be the minimum rate for all loans (except for some specified categories) with the actual lending rate charged to the borrowers being the base rate plus borrower-specific charge or spread. In practice, the flexibility accorded to banks in the determination of cost of funds—average, marginal or blended cost—caused opacity in the determination of lending rates by banks and clouded an accurate assessment of the speed and strength of the transmission. Moreover, banks often adjusted the spread over the base rate to benefit the new borrowers while leaving the transmission through the base rate weak for existing borrowers.

The weaknesses and rigidities observed with the transmission under the base rate system led to the present system, that is, the MCLR system effective from 1 April 2016. With banks required to determine their benchmark lending rates taking into account the 'marginal' cost of funds (unlike the base rate system where banks had the discretion to choose between the 'average' cost or the marginal cost [or blended cost] of funds), lending rates were expected to be more sensitive to the changes in the policy rate under the MCLR system vis-à-vis its predecessor (the base rate). The actual lending rate is based on MCLR plus a spread (business strategy and credit risk premium). The base rate system was allowed to be in operation concomitantly for the loans already contracted, pending their maturity or a shift to the MCLR system at mutually agreeable terms between the bank and the borrower.

The expected benefits of the MCLR system—better transparency, more flexibility and faster transmission—have, however, continued to elude as documented in the RBI's recent study, 'Report of the Internal Study Group to Review the Working of the Marginal Cost of Funds Based Lending Rate System' (Chairman: Dr Janak Raj), the analysis wherein indicates that the transmission

- has been 'slow and incomplete' under both the base rate and the MCLR systems, although it has improved since November 2016 under the pressure of large surplus liquidity in the system post demonetization (Table 11.1).
- was 'significant on fresh loans but muted for outstanding loans' (base rate and MCLR).
- was 'uneven across borrowing categories'.
- was 'asymmetric over monetary policy cycles—higher during the tightening phase and lower during the easing phase'— irrespective of the interest rate system.[2]

Transmission from Policy Rate to Bank Lending Rates: Some Issues

What explains the slow and incomplete pass-through from the policy rate changes to the lending rates? Two broad factors have dampened transmission to the lending rates.

First, a sizeable legacy loan portfolio of banks is still linked to the base rate (about 30 per cent of the outstanding bank loans). Lending rates under the base rate system are relatively stickier than the loans linked to MCLR. During the current easing cycle of monetary policy,

---

[2] For instance, the pass-through to outstanding loans from the repo rate was around 60 per cent during the tightening phase (July 2010 to March 2012), while it was less than 40 per cent during the subsequent easing phase (April 2012 to June 2013)

Table 11.1. **Transmission from the Policy Repo Rate to Banks' Deposit and Lending Rates**

(Variation in Percentage Points)

Period	Repo Rate	Term Deposit Rates		Lending Rates			
		Median Term Deposit Rate	WADTDR[a]	Median Base Rate	Median MCLR[b] (1-year)	WALR[c]: Outstanding Rupee Loans	WALR: Fresh Rupee Loans
October 2017 over end-December 2014	−2.00	−1.66	−1.99	−0.75	[d]	−1.39	−1.92
October 2017 over 01 April 2016	−0.75	−0.94	−1.08	−0.15	−1.15	−0.75	−0.94
Memo:							
			Pre-demonetization				
January 2015 to October 2016	−1.75	−0.99	−1.26	−0.61	[d]	−0.75	−0.97
01 April 2016 to October 2016	−0.50	−0.27	−0.35	−0.01	−0.15	−0.11	0.01
			Post-demonetization				
November 2016 to October 2017	−0.25	−0.67	−0.73	−0.14	−1.00	−0.64	−0.95

Source: RBI.
Notes: Latest data for WALRs and WADTDR pertain to September 2017.
[a] WADTDR: Weighted Average Domestic Term Deposit Rate.
[b] MCLR: Marginal Cost of Funds Based Lending Rate.
[c] WALR: Weighted Average Lending Rate.
[d] MCLR system was put in place in April 2016.

as against 200 bps cumulative cut in the repo rate, the base rate has declined by about 80 bps. Since the introduction of the MCLR in April 2016, as against the cumulative cut in repo rate by 50 bps, the base rate has declined by just about 20 bps (Figure 11.1). The RBI Study Group's analysis suggested that banks deviated in an ad hoc manner from the specified methodologies for calculating the base rate and the MCLR to either inflate the base rate and MCLR or prevent the base rate and MCLR from falling in line with the cost of funds.[3]

Second, spreads charged by banks over MCLR were adjusted to offset the changes in MCLR, thereby impacting the overall reduction in lending rates. The spread over the MCLR could vary from bank to bank due to idiosyncratic factors. However, as the Study Group observed, banks adjusted the spread over the MCLR arbitrarily in several ways and the variations in the spreads across banks appeared too large to be explained based on bank-level business strategy and borrower-level credit risk.[4] The Study Group also observed that while the spread over the MCLR was expected to play only a small role in determining the lending rates by banks, it has turned out to be the key element in deciding the overall lending rates.

What explains the muted pass-through from policy rate to bank lending rates, either by banks not changing the benchmark rate or by adjusting the spread?

---

[3] The ad hoc adjustments included, inter alia, (a) inappropriate calculation of the cost of funds, (b) no change in the base rate even as the cost of deposits declined significantly, (c) sharp increase in the return on net worth out of tune with past track record or future prospects to offset the impact of reduction in the cost of deposits on the lending rate and (d) inclusion of new components in the base rate formula to adjust the rate to a desired level. The slow transmission to the base rate loan portfolio was further accentuated by the long (annual) reset periods.

[4] For example, the Study Group found that: (a) large reduction in MCLR was partly offset by some banks by a simultaneous increase in the spread in the form of business strategy premium ostensibly to reduce the pass-through to lending rates; (b) there was no documentation of the rationale for fixing business strategy premium for various sectors; (c) many banks did not have a board approved policy for working out the components of spread charged to a customer; (d) some banks did not have any methodology for computing the spread, which was merely treated as a residual arrived at by deducting the MCLR from the actual prevailing lending rate and (e) the credit risk element was not applied based on the credit rating of the borrower concerned, but on the historically observed probability of default (PD) and loss given default (LGD) of the credit portfolio/sector concerned.

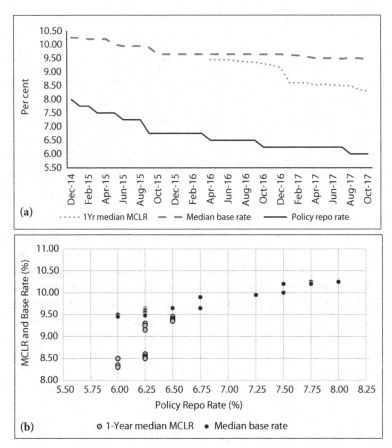

(a)

······ 1Yr median MCLR ── ── Median base rate ─── Policy repo rate

(b) ○ 1-Year median MCLR ● Median base rate

Figure 11.1. Transmission from Policy Rate to Bank Lending Rates: Some Issues

One plausible underlying reason is the rate rigidity on the liability side of banks caused by several factors. In India, about 90 per cent of total liabilities of banks are in the form of deposits. Bank deposits are predominantly at fixed interest rates, thereby imparting rigidity to the transmission process. Further, over 36 per cent of the term deposits of banks have maturity of three years and above (Table 11.2), implying their rates get reset infrequently and with significant lags to policy rate changes. While the banks' marginal cost of funds may drop quickly with a cut in fresh deposit rates, the average cost of deposits comes down rather slowly, which weakens the transmission, especially in the case of the base rate system.

Table 11.2. Maturity Profile of Term Deposits of Scheduled Commercial Banks (SCBs)

(% Share in Total Term Deposits)

End-March	Up to 90 days	91 Days–6 Month	6 Month–1 Year	1–2 Years	2–3 Years	3–5 Years	5 Years and above
2005	13.9	10.5	15.0	23.4	10.7	18.1	8.4
2010	6.9	8.4	13.7	37.9	12.3	12.4	8.3
2015	7.5	4.1	12.6	40.4	10.1	11.4	13.9
2016	7.2	4.0	9.2	43.3	10.6	11.8	14.0

Source: Handbook of Statistics on the Indian Economy, RBI.

What is often not recognized is the large access our banks have to low cost CASA funds. CASA funds constitute about 40 per cent of aggregate bank deposits with the share of saving deposits at around 31 per cent. Importantly, banks are free to decide saving deposit interest rates since October 2011, but until recently, most of the banks chose to leave the saving deposit rate unchanged, ignoring completely monetary policy signals. For instance, the major banks kept their saving deposit rate unchanged at 4 per cent between October 2011 and July 2017, even as the RBI's policy rate moved significantly over this period from 8.5 per cent in October 2011 to 7.25 per cent in August 2013. It increased again to 8.0 per cent by January 2014, before declining to 6.0 per cent by August 2017.

Furthermore, the deterioration in banking sector health due to worsening of asset quality over the past 2–3 years and the expected loan losses in credit portfolios also seem to have induced large variability in spreads in the pricing of assets. With undercapitalized banks aiming to protect their net interest margins (NIMs)[5]—indeed, weak banks' NIMs have remained broadly unchanged in the face of large stressed assets—so as to maintain profitability in the short term even at the expense of long-term profits as well as deposits and lending shares, the transmission to lending rates has been severely impacted. In effect, there has been a cross-subsidization of corporate loan losses by lending rates in healthier sectors such as in retail.

Finally, the competition that banks face from alternative instruments of financial savings—such as mutual funds and small saving

---

[5] NIM is defined as the difference between a bank's interest income (on its loans and assets) less its interest expenditure (on its deposits and other borrowings).

schemes—also seems to have made banks hesitant in varying the interest rates on term deposits in consonance with policy rate signals. Although bank deposits have some distinct advantages in the form of stable returns (vis-à-vis mutual fund schemes) and liquidity (vis-à-vis small saving schemes), bank deposits are in a disadvantageous position in terms of tax-adjusted returns in comparison with these schemes.

All of these factors have imparted rigidity to the liability side of banks' balance sheet with respect to policy rate changes, in turn inducing behaviour to make the rates on the asset side of banks' balance sheet rigid too.

Improving Transmission: The Way Forward

Drawing from its comprehensive analysis, the RBI's Study Group has suggested a number of steps to enhance transparency and transmission from monetary policy signals to the actual lending rates. Their recommendations pertain to improving transmission based on the existing lending rate system as well as a fundamental reform of the interest rate setting process. Let me touch upon the four major recommendation by the Study Group.

In view of the less than desired transmission and transparency under the 'internal' benchmark-based lending rate systems—PLR, BPLR, base rate and MCLR—so far, the Study Group has recommended that there is need to shift to an 'external' benchmark-based lending rate system. The internal benchmark-based pricing regimes are not in sync with global practices on pricing of bank loans. Given the scope of arbitrariness under the MCLR system, the Study Group has recommended that the switchover to an external benchmark needs to be pursued in a time-bound manner. While recognizing that no external instrument in India meets all the requirements of an ideal benchmark, and after analyzing the pros and cons of 13 possible candidates, the Study Group has recommended that the treasury bill rate, the CD rate, and the RBI's policy repo rate are better suited than other interest rates to serve the role of an external benchmark. The Study Group has recommended that all floating rate loans beginning 1 April 2018 could be referenced to one of the three external benchmarks selected by the RBI after receiving and evaluating the feedback from stakeholders.

Second, the Study Group has recommended that the decision on the spread over the external benchmark could be left to the commercial judgment of banks, with the spread remaining fixed all through the term of the loan, unless there is a credit event (as per standardized or ex ante mutually agreed definition of 'credit event').

Third, the periodicity of resetting the interest rates by banks on all floating rate loans, retail as well as corporate, be reduced from once in a year to once in a quarter to expedite the pass-through from the monetary policy signal to the actual lending rates.

Fourth, to reduce rigidity on the liabilities side, banks be encouraged to accept deposits, especially bulk deposits, at floating rates linked directly to the selected external benchmark.

The common theme underlying these recommendations is to improve monetary transmission by ensuring that changes in the policy rate transmit quickly and adequately to banks' lending rates in a transparent manner without any cross-subsidization and discrimination between existing and new borrowers. The idea is also to make the banks' liability side more flexible so that the objectives of improving monetary transmission by the RBI and maintaining healthy net interest rate margins by banks are aligned.

The report of the Study Group, which was put in the public domain on 4 October 2017 has generated much interest and extensive feedback to the RBI from all stakeholders, not only banks but also general public and media. We have received a number of useful suggestions and comments on the recommendations of the Study Group. These are being examined carefully and would help us to take a considered view, factoring in transition costs and providing a calibrated path to the desired benchmarking system.

Improving Monetary Transmission: Shoring up Bank Balance Sheets

As explained earlier, even as the RBI has reduced its policy repo rate by 50 bps since October 2016 and by a cumulative 200 bps since December 2014, the banking sector's credit growth has remained much muted. While weak demand for bank credit could be one of the factors leading to the observed slowdown in credit growth, a primary cause of the slowdown had also been the weak balance sheets of public sector banks (PSBs) in view of large non-performing assets (NPAs), which seem to have made banks averse to risk and induced them to reduce the supply of credit: undercapitalized banks have capital only to survive, not to grow (Acharya 2017). The dominance of the supply side factor has also been borne out by the fact that the credit growth of PvtSBs (better asset quality and well-capitalized on average) remains robust, whereas there has been a sharp deceleration in the credit growth of PSBs (especially the ones with high-stressed assets).

Against this backdrop, the enactment of the IBC in December 2016, the promulgation of the Banking Regulation (Amendment) Ordinance 2017 (since notified as an Act), and the subsequent actions taken thereunder in the form of the RBI requiring banks refer the largest, material and aged NPAs to the IBC, have made the IBC a lynchpin of the new time-bound resolution framework for bank NPAs.

These initiatives will now be supported by the government's decision to recapitalize PSBs in a front-loaded manner, with a total allocation of ₹2.1 trillion, comprising budgetary provisions (₹181 billion), recapitalization bonds (₹1.35 trillion) and raising of capital by banks from the market while diluting government equity share (around ₹580 billion).

The two steps together—asset resolution and bank recapitalization— are expected to strengthen bank balance sheets significantly and improve the banks' ability and willingness to lend at rates in consonance with policy rates and result in an improved monetary transmission.

Concluding Observations

In summary, efficient monetary transmission is a sine qua non for the successful pursuit of its objectives by any central bank. Over the past two decades, it has been the endeavour of the RBI to strengthen the monetary transmission process, but these efforts have yet not yielded the desired results. The transmission from the policy repo rate to bank lending rates, which is the dominant transmission channel in India, has remained a matter of concern. With the recent explicit objective of price stability mandated by the legislature, the issue of smooth monetary transmission has assumed an added significance. Against this backdrop, we have recently put out a report by the Internal Study Group to address the weaknesses of the existing monetary transmission system. A key suggestion before us is to whether to shift the loan pricing system from an internal benchmark to an external benchmark. The RBI will take a considered view in the matter at an appropriate time.

In my view, there is a deeper economic issue at hand in the recommendation to move towards an external benchmark. The issue is: who should bear the interest rate risk in the economy—the borrower, the depositor, or the bank? Who is likely to be better at managing the interest rate risk? Retail depositors and borrowers are unlikely to have efficient tools to manage the interest rate risk. Banks, however, should have the wherewithal to manage interest rate risk. Similarly, bulk depositors and large corporate borrowers can also be expected to be in a position to manage the interest rate risk. Non-bank financial institutions with less exposure to interest rate risk, such as insurance and pension funds, could also be good repositories of this risk. Foreign banks may be able to offset interest rate risk globally. A combination of interest-rate risk transfer mechanisms through market products such as interest-rate derivatives (swaps, in particular) and securitized products such as collateralized loan obligations (CLOs) will spring about, provided banks indeed have to manage the interest rate risk rather than have it as a matter of convenience to pass it onto borrowers.

Hopefully, I will focus sometime soon on these issues in a companion piece—'Monetary transmission in India: how can it be improved'?

References

Acharya, V. V., T. Eisert, C. Eufinger, and C. W. Hirsch. 2016. 'Whatever It Takes: The Real Effects of Unconventional Monetary Policy.' NBER Working Paper, New York University Stern School of Business. Available at: https://ssrn.com/abstract=2740338 (accessed on 25 March 2020).

Acharya, Viral V. 2017. 'The Unfinished Agenda: Restoring Public Sector Bank Health in India.' 8th R. K. Talwar Memorial Lecture. Available at: https://rbidocs.rbi.org.in/rdocs/Speeches/PDFs/IIBFVA09072017437215FBE69A442CB8E227778F5A2B23.PDF (accessed on 25 April 2020).

CHAPTER 12

IMPROVING MONETARY TRANSMISSION THROUGH THE BANKING CHANNEL: THE CASE FOR EXTERNAL BENCHMARKS IN BANK LOANS*

I'm often asked a question by my friends, 'How is it that a central bank can change just the policy rate and expect it to affect macroeconomic outcomes?' It is a deep question that is worth thinking about from first principles. In central banking parlance, the policy rate 'dial' turned by a central bank causes the economy to 'traverse' along its contours of growth and inflation via a mechanism called 'monetary transmission'. In other words, monetary transmission is the process through which changes in the policy rate by the central bank, in pursuit of the ultimate objectives of price stability and growth, are transmitted to the real economy. This transmission involves changes in the policy rate being reflected contemporaneously, or possibly over time, in the entire spectrum of interest rates relating to the interbank market, commercial paper, certificates of deposits, government securities and corporate bonds, and the banks' deposits and loans. Ordinarily central banks do not directly control long-term rates. They do, however, control short-term rates by being monopoly suppliers of currency and reserves (bank deposits with the central bank). A smooth transmission from short-term rates to long-term rates is critical as changes in long-term interest rates subsequently influence spending decisions of businesses and households, and hence output and prices.

Efficient monetary transmission requires many pre-conditions to be satisfied. These include: (a) availability of an efficient payment and settlement system for monetary transactions; (b) active liquidity

---

* Speech delivered at the Delhi School of Economics on 14 January 2019 (Acharya 2020).

management by the central bank so that the supply of liquidity matches its demand and thus interbank rates remain close to the policy rate; (c) well-integrated financial markets for facilitating interest rate arbitrage across financial market segments; (d) a healthy and well-capitalized banking system so that banks are not constrained in their lending operations; (e) liability and asset structures of the banks responsive to interest rate changes by the central bank and (f) the absence of distortions such as interest subvention and administered rates of interest that are out of sync with market rates.

Unsurprisingly therefore, the issue of monetary transmission has all along been important for the RBI. However, it has assumed a special significance in the context of the amendment to the RBI Act in 2016, which mandates the RBI to conduct monetary policy for achieving price stability as its primary objective while being mindful of growth. This mandate is difficult to achieve unless supported by a robust transmission mechanism. The policy rate adjustments by the MPC are intended to percolate down to the entire spectrum of interest rates, especially bank lending rates, so that the economy stays close to its 'steady state', that is, inflation close to the mandated target and growth close to its potential path; and in case there is any shock, the endeavour of the MPC is that the economy be brought back to the steady state by adjusting the policy repo rate. If the economy is overheated but lending rates of the banks do not rise in response to the raising of policy rate by the MPC, then credit demand of firms and households would continue to remain robust; consumption and investment by households and firms will continue to rise; and, as a result, the corresponding aggregate demand conditions in the economy would not allow inflation to drop. Conversely, in an easing cycle of monetary policy, if a decline in the policy rate is not followed by a reduction in bank lending rates, consumption and investment demand will not increase to help bring inflation and growth back to the steady state levels.

RBI's Proposal for Market Benchmarking of Floating Rate Loans

To enable monetary transmission, RBI designed bank lending rate systems during the era of liberalized interest rates. These systems required that banks link the rates on their floating rate loans to a 'benchmark' rate determined by each bank. The benchmark rates were expected to respond to policy rates. Monetary transmission in India has, however, been considered so far to have been less than satisfactory.[1] In particular, neither the prime lending rate (PLR) system introduced in 1994 nor the benchmark PLR (BPLR) system in 2003 succeeded in providing effective monetary transmission. The base rate system introduced in July 2010, followed by the MCLR system in April 2016, also continue to suffer from the same rigid response of bank lending rates to policy rate changes as did the previous systems.

The Expert Committee to Revise and Strengthen the Monetary Policy Framework[2] (Chairman: Dr Urjit R. Patel) in its report released on 21 January 2014 observed that unless the cost of banks' liabilities moves in line with the policy rates as do interest rates in money market and debt market segments, it will be difficult to persuade banks to price their loans in response to policy rate changes. Hence, it was necessary to develop a culture of establishing external benchmarks for setting interest rates on bank loans as well as deposits. The committee felt that while these benchmarks should emerge from market practices, the RBI could explore playing a proactive and supportive role in their emergence.

The *Report of the Household Finance*[3] (Chairman: Tarun Ramadorai), which was submitted in August 2017, also observed the deficiencies in the interest rate setting system in banks, especially the factors that delay transmission or complicate comparison across banks. It recommended that banks should quote loan rates not based on bank specific MCLR rates, but on the policy repo rate or some other standard market rate. The report argued that this would not only bring about transparency, as borrowers can easily compare across banks, but also improve customer protection.

Keeping in mind the observation made by the Patel Committee and the Report on the Household Finance, the RBI constituted an

---

[1] For a fuller treatment of why monetary transmission has not worked well in India, please see my earlier speech 'Monetary transmission in India–Why is it important and why hasn't it worked well?' (November 2017). Available at: https://www.rbi.org.in/Scripts/BS_SpeechesView.aspx?Id=1049 (accessed on 25 March 2020).
[2] https://www.rbi.org.in/Scripts/PublicationReportDetails.aspx?UrlPage=&ID=743
[3] https://rbidocs.rbi.org.in/rdocs/PublicationReport/Pdfs/HFCRA28D0415E2144A009112DD314ECF5C07.PDF

Internal Study Group to *Review the Working of the Marginal Cost of Funds based Lending Rate (MCLR) System*[4] (Chairman: Dr Janak Raj). The report of the Study Group, released on 4 October 2017, identified the factors that have impeded monetary transmission in India. The group also recommended that banks use market rates or the policy repo rate as benchmark for pricing floating rate loans. The RBI's response to the feedback received from the banks and other constituencies was released in February 2018 as an addendum to the report.[5]

Finally, on 5 December 2018, the RBI proposed that the floating rate loans (personal or retail loans, loans to micro and small enterprises and any other category of loans at the bank's discretion) extended by banks from 1 April 2019 shall be linked to either the policy repo rate or a market benchmark rate (three-month or six-month T-Bills or any other rate produced by the Financial Benchmark India Private Limited [FBIL]). The spread over the benchmark rate would remain unchanged unless the borrower's credit assessment undergoes a substantial change and as agreed upon in the loan contract.

Let me elaborate on the important details around this sequence of events.

Evolution of Lending Rate Systems in India

The first regime of PLR was introduced in 1994. However, both PLR and spread over PLR were seen to vary widely across banks/bank groups. Moreover, the prime lending rates continued to be rigid and inflexible in relation to the overall direction of interest rates in the economy. With the aim of introducing transparency and ensuring appropriate pricing of loans—wherein the PLRs truly reflected the actual costs—the PLR was converted into a reference benchmark rate and banks were advised in 2003 to introduce the BPLR system, which gave them freedom to lend below the BPLR. While lending below the BPLR was expected only to be at the margin, in practice about 77 per cent of the banks' loan portfolio was at sub-BPLR. This clouded the true assessment of monetary transmission.

In a nutshell, both the PLR and BPLR systems did not produce adequate or uniform monetary transmission to the real economy.

---

[4] https://www.rbi.org.in/Scripts/PublicationReportDetails.aspx?UrlPage=&ID=878
[5] https://www.rbi.org.in/Scripts/PublicationReportDetails.aspx?UrlPage=&ID=893

In July 2010, the RBI replaced the BPLR system with the 'base rate' system. The actual lending rate was the bank-specific base rate (for which an indicative formula was also prescribed) and the spread. However, the flexibility accorded to banks in the determination of cost of funds (average, marginal or blended cost), which was a key component of base rate calculation, resulted in opacity in the computation of base rate. In particular, the average cost of funds did not move much in line with monetary policy changes due to the nature of the term of fixed-rate deposits. Moreover, banks often over time changed the spread over the base rate for some borrowers, while leaving the base rate unchanged.

Given these deficiencies, the RBI introduced a new lending rate system for banks in the form of the Marginal Cost of Funds Based Lending Rate (MCLR), tied to the marginal funding cost of each bank, in April 2016. However, unlike the BPLR and the base rate, the formula for computing the MCLR was fully prescribed, though some discretion remained with banks. The MCLR has, however, continued to suffer from the same flaw as the earlier lending rate systems in that transmission to the existing borrowers has remained muted since banks adjust—in many cases in an arbitrary manner—the MCLR and/or spread over MCLR, which has kept overall lending rates high despite the monetary policy being accommodative from January 2015 to May 2018.[6]

Monetary Transmission: Recent Evidence

Evidence that monetary transmission in India has not been satisfactory in the recent period is presented in Table 12.1 and Figure 12.1. As against the policy rate cut of 200 basis points during January 2015 to May 2018, the weighted average term deposit rate (WATDR) declined by 193 basis points. However, the weighted average lending rate (WALR) on outstanding rupee loans declined only by 154 basis

---

[6] In his speech, in June 2016, 'The fight against inflation: a measure of our institutional development' (https://rbidocs.rbi.org.in/rdocs/Speeches/PDFs/PR29533A11C 296335D44BDBB14DB24A696042B.PDF), the then RBI Governor Dr Raghuram G. Rajan noted that 'All in all, bank lending rates have moved down, but not commensurate with policy rate cuts'. For a fuller treatment of why monetary transmission has not worked well in India, please see my earlier speech 'Monetary transmission in India– Why is it important and why hasn't it worked well?' (November 2017).

Table 12.1. Transmission from the Policy Repo Rate to Banks' Deposit and Lending Rates

(Variation in Percentage Points)

Period	Repo Rate	Term Deposit Rates		Lending Rates				
		Median Term Deposit Rate	WADTDR[a]	Median Base Rate	Median MCLR (1 year)	WALR – Outstanding Rupee Loans[a]	WALR – Fresh Rupee Loans[a]
January 2015 to May 2018	−2.00	−1.58	−1.93	−0.80	[b]	−1.54	−2.05
Memo:							
			Pre-demonetization				
January 2015 to October 2016	−1.75	−0.99	−1.26	−0.61	[b]	−0.69	−0.97
			Post-demonetization				
November 2016 to May 2018	−0.25	−0.59	−0.67	−0.19	−0.79	−0.85	−1.08
June 2018 to December 2018	0.50	0.16	0.14	0.00	0.27	0.06	0.48

Source: RBI.
Notes: WADTDR: Weighted average domestic term deposit rate
WALR: Weighted Average Lending Rate
MCLR: Marginal Cost of Funds Based Lending Rate
[a]Latest data for WALRs and WADTDR pertaining to November 2018.
[b]MCLR system was put in place in April 2016.

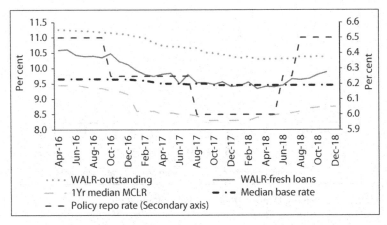

Figure 12.1. Lending Rates of Scheduled Commercial Banks
Source: RBI.

points. Reduction in the WALR on fresh rupee loans was higher at 205 basis points as the banks passed on the benefits in the reduction of MCLRs more to the new borrowers than to the existing borrowers. However, significant transmission occurred 'only' post demonetization following the increase in low-cost current account and savings account (CASA) deposits due to surplus liquidity with the banking system. In the more recent period, in response to the increase in the policy rate by 50 basis points (from June to December 2018), WALR on fresh rupee loans increased by 48 basis points, but only six basis points on outstanding rupee loans. Also, the median base rate hardly moved (Figure 12.1). Since about 24 per cent of the banks' loan portfolio is still at the base rate/BPLR, this impaired the overall monetary transmission to outstanding rupee loans.

Equally importantly, banks also did not change saving deposits interest rate for six long years from October 2011 to July 2017, though monetary policy was changed in both the directions during this period (Figure 12.2). Saving deposits constitute about 28 per cent of bank deposits. If banks do not change interest rates on saving deposits in tune with the policy rates, then transmission to lending rates will naturally remain muted as seen in Table 12.1 and Figure 12.1.

Let us now turn to the fundamental question of why monetary transmission through these benchmark rate systems employed to date has remained weak.

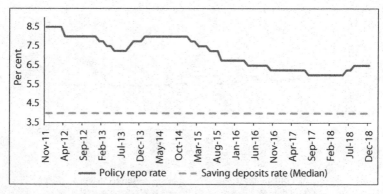

Figure 12.2. Saving Deposits Rate and Policy Repo Rate
Source: RBI.

An Internal 'versus' External Benchmark

Each of the above-mentioned four lending benchmarks prescribed so far in India can be considered as 'internal' in that banks can set the benchmark rate themselves or choose at their discretion many of the elements that go into the prescribed formulae. Thus, being under the control of a bank, an internal benchmark is prone to be adjusted in a discretionary manner that suits the interests of the bank, possibly at the expense of the borrowers and the economy. In fact, the report of the study group pointed out several instances where banks arbitrarily adjusted the MCLR/base rate, which impeded transmission of policy rate cuts to borrowers.

In contrast, the RBI policy rate and 91-day/182-day T-bill rate are 'external' benchmarks, which are exogenous to each bank and adjust automatically and likely contemporaneously to both expected and unexpected policy rate changes.[7]

There is another distinct advantage of external benchmarks vis-à-vis internal benchmarks. An external benchmark is transparent and known to borrowers and lenders alike. An internal benchmark is bank-specific and renders a product comparison of different banks difficult, whereas an external benchmark will be uniform across banks and facilitate product comparison. Given these advantages

---

[7] In rare cases, the possibility of collusion in the case of market-based benchmarks such as T-bill rate (but not the policy repo rate) cannot be ruled out.

Table 12.2. Proportion of Loans Linked to Internal and External Benchmarks: A Cross-country Comparison

Country	Internal	External	Total
Thailand	95	5	100
Indonesia	90	10	100
Switzerland	80	20	100
Turkey	55	45	100
Malaysia	45	55	100
United Kingdom	45	55	100
Taiwan	40	60	100
Singapore	30	70	100
South Korea	10	90	100
China	0	100	100

Source: Credit Suisse Research, HDFC Bank.

over internal benchmarks, external benchmarks are now used extensively in most countries in the world, especially the high-income ones (Table 12.2).

An external benchmark alone, however, will not be sufficient to achieve the desired objective of effective monetary transmission and transparency, as long as banks continue to have an absolute discretion to change the spread over the benchmark. The report of the MCLR study group pointed out several cases where banks changed the spread over the MCLR to offset fully or partly the changes in MCLRs. It was observed that while banks were keen to attract new customers by offering them competitive pricing, they often denied the benefits of changes in the MCLR to existing borrowers by changing the spread. This impeded monetary transmission of policy rate cuts as shown in Table 12.1. Indeed, such practices by banks also raised the issue of consumer protection. It is for this reason that the RBI has also proposed that the spread over the benchmark rate should remain unchanged through the life of a loan, unless there is a change in the credit assessment of the borrower—an arrangement that can be contractually agreed upon between the bank and the borrower.

Thus, the proposals to introduce an external benchmark *and* keep the spread unchanged need to be seen jointly. The underlying philosophy is to make the entire process of setting lending rates by banks transparent and improve monetary transmission. Banks would have the complete freedom to fix the spread over the external benchmark for new borrowers at the time of the origination of the loan; the fixed spread over the benchmark through the tenure of the loan for given credit quality would, however, limit the scope for arbitrary spread adjustments after the loans have been sanctioned and thereby preclude the undoing of changes in the benchmark rate.

Issues Raised by Banks

The Indian Banks' Association (IBA) and some banks individually provided feedback to the RBI on the recommendations of the Study Group, essentially making three points:

1. 'External benchmarks recommended do not reflect cost of funds of banks'

   First, the bank funding cost is not related directly to any of the external benchmarks. Most banks in India are funded primarily by retail deposits and not from the wholesale market as is the practice abroad. Therefore, if interest rates on deposits remain sticky, banks will not find it an attractive proposition to lend at rates linked to an external benchmark which may change every day, unless they manage the resulting interest rate risk well.

2. 'Markets to hedge interest rate risk in India are illiquid'

   The second issue raised was that banks in India are currently not in a position to hedge an interest rate risk given the absence of a developed interest rate swap (IRS) market. In the absence of such a market, either bank profitability could come under pressure, or loan spreads could become higher as a compensation for interest rate risk. Banks also highlighted that in the absence of a reliable term money market, use of any benchmark will leave the discretion on pricing of term premium with the banks. Banks argued that the more ideal benchmark—from the perspective of banks— should be based on the deposit rates of the banking system as a whole. Banks also pointed out that they have experimented with floating rate deposits in the past, but the response had not been encouraging. Retail depositors are particularly averse to such products. Even institutional/wholesale depositors prefer fixed rates when they perceive that interest rates have peaked and an easy cycle of monetary policy is about to begin, banks argued.

3. 'Banks need flexibility to change spread'.

The third point made by banks was that in a deregulated interest rate environment, spread over the benchmark—be it internal or external—must be the exclusive domain of the commercial banks. Also, for a variety of pure commercial reasons, spread cannot be fixed forever. Credit risk premium is time-varying and expected credit losses do change over time. For example, the spread itself could become a function of the interest rate cycle. At times, banks may have to reduce spreads just to retain customers; some customers may back their loans with more collateral at a later stage of the loan, requiring a downward adjustment of the spread; for many project loans, as risks decline after the gestation lag and based on repayment track record, the spread may have to be lowered and so on. Therefore, according to banks, market competition alone should lead to convergence of spreads, and regulatory prescriptions on whether the spread should change or remain fixed would not be in sync with the spirit behind the deregulation of interest rates.

Let me briefly respond to these issues raised by banks.

Addressing the Concerns Raised by Banks

1. 'External benchmarks recommended do not reflect cost of funds'

First, the argument that banks' funding cost is not related to the external benchmark as loans are funded mainly through deposits and not through market borrowings is not entirely persuasive. In a competitive market, loans should, like products in any industry, be priced at the level at which the market clears them, not at cost. The only way cost-linked pricing can sustain is either through regulatory mandate or through cartelization. In either case, this is not in the interest of bank borrowers.

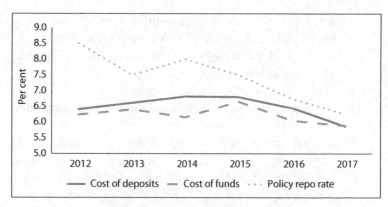

Figure 12.3. Cost of Deposits/Funds and Policy Repo Rate
Source: RBI.

Furthermore, the argument that market benchmarks are not linked to the cost of funds is easily addressed by linking liabilities to market benchmarks as well. Fixed rate loans can be funded using fixed rate deposits. The gaps/mismatches can be managed through interest rate derivatives, a point to which I will turn later.

Moreover, the cost of deposits or funds of scheduled commercial banks is, in fact, getting closely aligned with the policy repo rate over the past few years (Figure 12.3). At any rate, banks would have the freedom to set the spread to factor in the extra cost of funding (the difference between the external benchmark and the average cost of funds), term premium, credit risk or any other costs (such as operating costs).

2. 'Markets to hedge interest rate risk in India are illiquid'

Let me now turn to the second issue that banks do not have adequate hedging facility for interest rate risk. Banks have rightly observed that in India, the IRS market is not yet fully developed. Apart from the Mumbai Interbank Offer Rate (MIBOR) based overnight index swaps (OIS), liquidity in the other instruments is rather thin (Table 12.3).[8]

---

[8] The OIS refers to the exchange of overnight floating interest rate with fixed interest rate. The OIS market in India has a term structure up to 10 years, but most segments are not liquid. The market participation is highly concentrated with only a section of

Table 12.3. Distribution of Outstanding Interest Rate Swap Products across Tenors (End-November 2018)

(₹ Billion)

Benchmark	Less than 1 Year	1 Year- 5 Years	Above 5 Years	Total Outstanding
MIBOR–Gross notional	20,556	17,500	134	38,190
MIBOR–Net notional	4,449	1,120	40	5,609
MIFOR–Gross Notional	782	2,969	258	4,008
MIFOR–Net notional	171	549	81	801
INBMK–Gross notional	11	40	–	50
INBMK–Net notional	9	25	–	34

Source: Clearing Corporation of India Limited (CCIL).

However, it needs to be recognized that the development of any market is demand driven. Hence, once the need for hedging interest rate risk increases after the adoption of an external benchmark in floating rate loans, the IRS market could also develop. Creating demand first could help generate a supply response from those willing to bear interest rate risk in the IRS market.

Banks, being the major intermediaries in the financial sector, have collective responsibility to contribute to market development, at least by active participation. Citing under-developed derivatives markets amounts to an admission of their joint failure to perform this role. Table 12.4 shows that not only is the participation of banks in the OIS markets not commensurate with the size of their interest rate risk exposure, some banks, at present, do not participate at all in this market.

Indeed, a more market-linked balance sheet would encourage and incentivize banks to participate in the interest rate derivatives markets. The RBI, on its part, has taken

---

the banks active in the OIS market. The daily volume in the OIS market is only around ₹150 billion as against an average daily bond market volume of ₹400–500 billion. Wider participation by banks in the OIS market is necessary for improving liquidity in these markets, which is necessary for banks to off-load their significant duration risk onto others.

Table 12.4. Category-Wise Participation in Mumbai Inter-Bank Offer Rate (MIBOR) Overnight Indexed Swaps (End-November 2018)

(Amount in ₹ Billion)

Participants	Gross Notional Amount	Per cent of Aggregate	Number of Participants
Foreign banks	40,375	52.9	19
Private banks	16,379	21.4	11
Public sector banks	4,167	5.5	10
Primary dealers	15,459	20.2	6
Grand total	**76,379**	**100.0**	**46**

Source: Clearing Corporation of India Limited (CCIL).

several initiatives to give a fillip to interest rate derivatives markets which include:

- Allowing introduction of money market futures and interest rate options;
- Easing constraints in the short-selling market to encourage larger participation and
- Broadening the participation base by proposing free non-resident access for hedging in the domestic market.

In particular, the proposal to extend non-residents access to the OIS market for purposes other than hedging could potentially address most of the concerns expressed by banks about lack of depth in the IRS market.

3. 'Banks need flexibility to change spread'

Let me now come to the issue about the flexibility in fixing/re-fixing the spread any time during the term of floating rate loans. Such flexibility goes against the essence of floating rate loans. The only adjustable element in the floating rate loans linked to a benchmark should be the benchmark itself and not the spread, unless there is a large material change, for example, a mutually agreed credit event and attendant outcomes such as change in collateralization of the loan. It is important that these conditions that lead to a reset of the spread are part of the contractual loan conditions and are mutually acceptable. The responsibility of demonstrating that these conditions have not been used exploitatively should rest on the bank. The risk faced by the banks from time-varying credit risk premium can be built into the spread at the time of loan origination, at the complete discretion of banks, as is done in externally benchmarked floating rate contracts in other parts of the world.

Alignment of Interest Rate Setting Practices of NBFCs with Those of Banks

NBFCs have been growing rapidly in the recent period. The share of NBFCs in total credit extended by the banks and the NBFCs together increased from 9.5 per cent in March 2008 to 16.8 per cent in March 2018. As a result, the relative significance of NBFCs in the financial system has been growing and they are becoming increasingly important in monetary transmission. However, interest rate setting processes vary markedly across NBFCs. While some NBFCs link their lending rates to banks' base rates/MCLRs, others use their own PLRs to set interest rates. Some other NBFCs do not appear to have any interest rate benchmark—internal or external—for pricing their loans. The periodicity of reset of interest rates on floating rate loans also differs from one customer to another and is set arbitrarily by the loan sanctioning authority.

For effective monetary transmission to the financial intermediaries and ultimately to the real economy, it is necessary that the interest rate setting processes of NBFCs are aligned with those of banks—in terms of interest rate benchmarks, the spread remaining fixed over the benchmark during the life of the loan, the circumstances that could result in a change in the spread over the tenor of the loan and the periodicity of interest rate reset. Such harmonization would provide banks and NBFCs a level playing field to operate in, while at the same time facilitate effective monetary transmission across the entire range of financial intermediaries.

Keeping in view the proposed changes for banks, the RBI has constituted another internal study group to (a) examine the current interest rate setting practices by the NBFCs; (b) suggest measures to harmonize the interest rate setting processes of the NBFCs with those of the banks; and (c) suggest an appropriate roadmap for such harmonization.

Conclusion

Past loan-pricing arrangements in India that provided banks a one-sided facility to fix rates periodically have been inimical to monetary transmission. Such arrangements are increasingly discouraged in modern financial economies. The reaction to the policy announcement by the RBI on 5 December 2018 to link all floating rate loans (personal or retail loans and loans to micro and small enterprises or any other category of loans at the bank's discretion) extended by the banks to either the policy repo rate or a market benchmark rate from 1 April 2019 has generally been positive. Theoretically, a borrower deprived of monetary transmission by a bank could refinance the floating rate loan by going to another bank, but in practice, this competitive argument does not work well. The borrower is often left with little choice because of the cost and efforts involved in shifting from one bank to another, especially because loans of different banks with internal benchmarks are not comparable. The RBI's proposed system of external benchmarking will increase transparency of bank loan products. The proposed external benchmark system is not prescriptive unlike the previous regulatory dispensations. In particular, banks will have greater flexibility (in choosing the external benchmark and credit spread) and the borrower will enjoy greater transparency compared to the current opacity in lending rates that are linked to an internal benchmark.

It is interesting to note that in March 2018, a foreign bank launched a mortgage product linked to an external benchmark, namely the three-month Treasury Bill Benchmark linked Lending Rate (TBLR), which is the transparent reference rate published by FBIL. The interest rate on the loan benchmarked to TBLR is reset on a quarterly basis. While the bank has continued to offer one-year MCLR linked home loan, 95 per cent of the new loans are now linked to TBLR, indicative of the widespread acceptance of an external benchmark by the home loan customers.

Ultimately, if banks do not pass on the monetary policy impulses to bank-dependent borrowers such as households and MSMEs, then monetary policy would have to adjust more dramatically to move the economy towards the steady state. In the past, this has meant that to bring the costs of bank loans down, interest rate cuts have had to be significantly large. However, this lowered market interest rates—that move in tandem with policy rates unlike internal benchmark rates—to levels that implied negative real rates of market borrowings for government and large corporates that can access financial markets. The resulting fiscal and corporate debt excess not only raised inflation to uncomfortable levels but also left the banking sector laden with massive losses, imposing significant 'tax' on the poor and bank-dependent borrowers. Thus, external benchmarking of floating rate loans proposed by the RBI will not only improve monetary policy transmission, but indirectly, also help maintain macroeconomic and financial stability.

Reference

Acharya, Viral V. 2020. 'Improving Monetary Transmission through the Banking Channel—The Case for External Benchmarks in Bank Loans.' *Vikalp, The Journal for Decision Makers* 45, no. 1.

PART 5

Developing Viable Capital Markets and Ensuring External Sector Resilience

CHAPTER 13

UNDERSTANDING AND MANAGING INTEREST RATE RISK AT BANKS*

In the period after the global financial crisis, bank exposures to sovereign debt have increased significantly in many economies, including advanced ones, deepening the linkage of bank balance sheets with sovereign debt. Several important drivers are deemed to be at work behind this phenomenon:

1. Exceptionally accommodative monetary policy in advanced economies, coupled with a general post-crisis fall in the risk appetite of global investors, created a natural demand to hold sovereign debt of safe-haven economies.

2. Under Basel capital regulations for banks, sovereign bond exposures continue to attract zero per cent risk weight in home countries and some currency unions, besides not being subject to concentration limits. This makes sovereign bonds a more attractive investment for banks vis-à-vis other assets of similar riskiness. Liquidity of sovereign bonds as well as such securities being eligible collateral for refinance by central banks only further adds to their attractiveness.

3. Liquidity coverage ratio (LCR) regulation (under Basel III) also requires banks to hold high-quality liquid assets (HQLA). Though there are other securities eligible as HQLA, the cost and ease of holding are the most attractive for sovereign bonds.

---

*Speech delivered at the FIMMDA Annual Dinner, 2018 organized by the Fixed Income Money Market and Derivatives Association of India (FIMMDA) on 15 January 2018 at Hotel Taj Mahal Palace, Mumbai. Thanks to FIIMDA and its organizing team for inviting me to deliver this keynote address at its Annual Meet. This speech was about understanding and managing better the interest rate risk at Indian banks.

While sovereign bonds may be safer and more liquid than other instruments at a given point of time, there is no guarantee that they will remain so as both credit risk and liquidity risk of sovereign debt are dynamic in nature, and in fact, can shift deceptively so as these risks materialize from seemingly calm initial states.

Sovereign Debt-Bank Nexus and Eurozone Sovereign Debt Crisis

The potential negative impact of sovereign debt-bank nexus and the need for addressing it has attracted much international attention, particularly in Europe. Exposures of resident banks to domestic sovereign debts in countries that faced debt crisis (Greece, Italy, Ireland, Portugal and Spain [GIIPS]) increased significantly during and after the crisis. Moreover, the increased exposure of banks to sovereign debts exhibited a domestic bias in case of the riskier sovereigns, that is, the GIIPS, with share of resident banks increasing while that of non-residents declining; the holdings of resident banks continue to be at a high level (Figure 13.1).

The large holdings of domestic sovereign debt by banks played a key role in exacerbating the sovereign debt crisis in peripheral European countries. From January 2007 to the first bank bailout announcement in late September 2008, there was a sustained rise in bank credit spreads while sovereign credit spreads remained low. During September–October 2008, bank bailouts became a pervasive feature across high-income economies and there was a significant decline in bank credit spreads with a corresponding increase in sovereign credit spreads. In effect, bank bailouts transferred credit risk from the financial sector to the sovereigns (Acharya, Drechsler and Schnabl 2012; 2015). However, and especially post the Greek default in 2010, sovereign spreads in the GIIPS widened too over the German Bunds due to macroeconomic concerns in the European periphery, causing significant valuation losses for banks and casting doubt on their solvency.

Concomitantly, rising yields on sovereign bonds enticed banks to stock up on their domestic sovereign exposures. With continuing access to short-term funding, notably in deposit and money markets, banks in GIIPS and even some non-GIIPS countries increased investments in GIIPS sovereign bonds so as to purchase 'carry' over

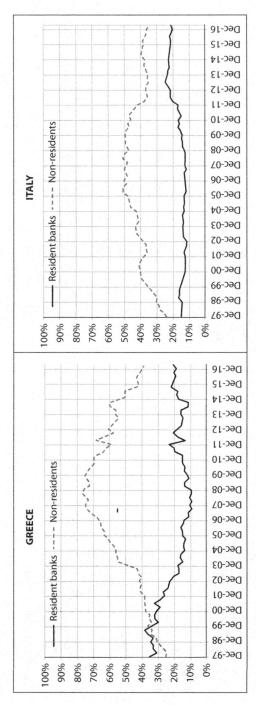

Figure 13.1. *(continued)*

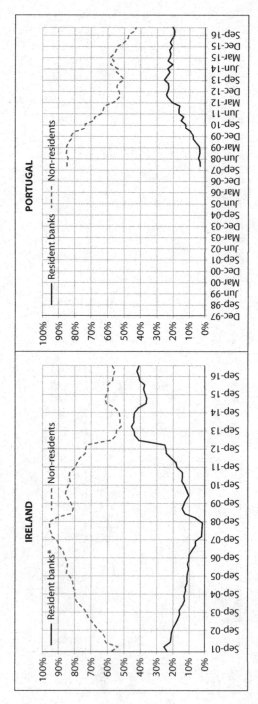

Figure 13.1. (*continued*)

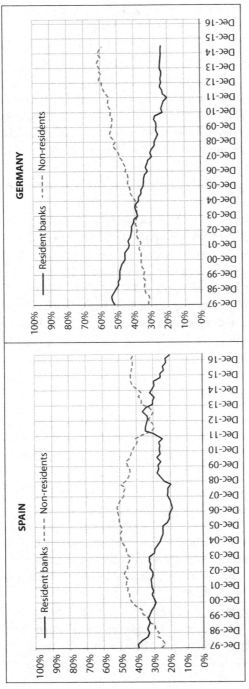

Figure 13.1. Holding of Sovereign Bonds by Resident Banks and Non-residents for GIIPS and Germany

Source: Bruegel database of sovereign bond holdings developed in Merler and Pisani-Ferry (2012) updated as of March 2017.

Notes: Data for Germany is based on 'General Government Debt' and includes both sovereign bonds as well as loans.

*'Resident banks' in Ireland do not exclude holdings by the Bank of Ireland.

the German Bunds, hoping for future convergence of yield (Acharya and Steffen 2015). This 'carry trade' was particularly attractive for undercapitalized banks as a way to gamble for resurrection, effectively chasing quick treasury gains with no additional capital requirement, but doubling up on economic risks if the carry were to widen even further ... and it did. The Greek default and ensuing sovereign debt crises in the GIIPS countries showed that banks having significant exposures to sovereign debt were the most susceptible to fluctuations in sovereign borrowing costs and faced attendant market plus funding consequences.

Such sovereign debt-bank nexus creates a two-way feedback loop. As banks are highly exposed to the domestic sovereign, any adverse movement in yields or materialization of a sovereign event could trigger bank undercapitalization and bailouts, which imply further sovereign borrowing and rising sovereign yields, leading to further erosion of bank capital and need for further bailouts and so on (Acharya, Drechsler and Schnabl 2012; 2015).

Understanding and managing well the banking sector's exposure to risks embedded in domestic sovereign debt is thus not just a matter of the banking sector's profits and capital, but in fact it is one of overall macroeconomic stability.

The Indian Context

In India, the linkage between sovereign debt and bank balance sheets has always been strong given the SLR prescriptions for banks and the historical role that banks have played in supporting public debt. Banks, under section 42 of the RBI Act, 1934, are required to maintain minimum liquid assets (basically government securities—both central government securities [G-Secs] and sub-sovereign securities called state development loans [SDLs]) as a percentage of Demand and Time Liabilities (DTL). This ratio has historically been as high as 38.5 per cent, but has gradually come down to 19.5 per cent now (Figure 13.2), being brought steadily in line with international levels of the LCR under Basel III.

The resulting large holding of G-Secs and SDLs by banks exposes them to re-pricing of the governments' borrowing costs which could rise due to inflationary, fiscal or other domestic as well as global macroeconomic developments. I propose to (a) draw attention

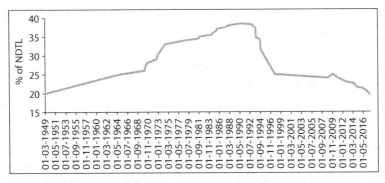

Figure 13.2. Statutory Liquidity Ratio
Source: Database on Indian Economy, RBI.

to the significance of this interest rate risk exposure of Indian banks, (b) urge banks to pay greater attention and devote more resources to their treasury operations and (c) lay out some options available to banks for managing the risk efficiently.

Understanding Interest Rate Risk at Banks

Let us start by first principles. Interest rate risk is most simply understood by looking at the (approximate) price equation for a bond portfolio when there is a (small) change in the underlying interest rates, such as the level of the government's borrowing cost:

$$\Delta P = - P \times D \times \Delta Y,$$

Where Δ denotes change, P denotes the portfolio's market value, D denotes the 'duration', a measure of the interest rate sensitivity of the portfolio, and Y denotes an underlying interest rate (or portfolio yield.)

In other words, the value of the investment portfolio is a function of three factors:

1. The size of the portfolio denoted by P.
2. The duration denoted by D, which roughly captures the weighted average maturity of cash flows of bonds in the portfolio.
3. The increase in yields denoted by ΔY.

For example, a portfolio of size 1 trillion with 10 years of duration, falls in value by 10 billion upon a 0.1 per cent or 10 basis points (bps) rise in the 10-year G-Sec benchmark yield.

Let us consider each of these factors, in turn, in the present and historical Indian context.

Size of the Portfolio[1]

The share of commercial banks in outstanding G-Secs is around 40 per cent (June 2017). Investment of scheduled commercial banks (SCBs) in G-Secs as a percentage of their total investment was around 82 per cent for FY 2016–2017. The corresponding figure for PSBs for FY 2016–2017 is slightly higher at 84 per cent. This exposure has noticeably increased since 2014 (Figure 13.3a).

In spite of the relative stability of the consolidated Debt/GDP ratio of the government, the investor base for G-Secs in India is primarily limited to domestic institutions. As a result, there are often situations of oversupply of government bonds relative to demand. This appears to be the case especially for Indian banks going by their high excess SLR holdings. One of the reasons for banks to end up holding high levels of government debt is because in the Indian

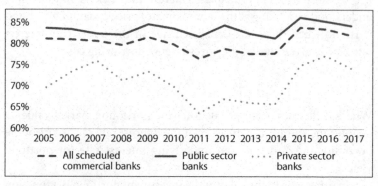

Figure 13.3a. Investment in Central Government Securities as Percentage of Total Investment

---

[1] Government securities are defined under law as both central government securities (G-Secs) and state development loans (SDLs). In terms of management of interest rate risk in the investment book, both are equally important. In this speech, however, data and figures pertain to only G-Secs for simplicity. Inclusion of SDLs would not change the broad conclusions, and as they contribute to interest-rate risk, would only strengthen them.

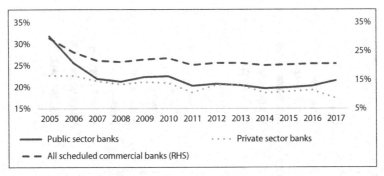

Figure 13.3b. Investment in Central Government Securities as Percentage of Total Assets

Source: Database on Indian Economy, RBI.

milieu, they end up as residual holders in case of relative oversupply, as the appetite of other major institutional investor categories such as insurance and pension funds is limited by their investment mandates. Another important reason in recent times has been the excess liquidity in the banking system that did not end up being parked at the RBI's liquidity mop-up operations which would have kept duration risk minimal. Instead, the surplus liquidity found its way into G-Secs as domestic sovereign debt is the most attractive investment for capital-starved banks looking for short-term gains even if at the expense of greater duration (as I explained earlier, this was the case also in the European context).

As a result, the 'size' of the banking sector's balance sheet exposure to G-Secs, and hence, its interest rate risk, is high in an absolute sense, and is relatively elevated, when measured in proportion to total assets, for PSBs relative to private banks (Figure 13.3b).

Duration of Investment Book and the Maturity Structure of G-Secs

The high interest rate exposure of banks from their G-Sec portfolios is attributable to not only the size of their holdings, but also to the increasing maturity of primary issuance. The weighted average maturity of the stock of G-Secs has increased steadily from 9.66 years in 2012–2013 to 10.67 years in 2017–2018 (Figure 13.4). The average tenor of annual issuance during the last five years has been high at around 15 years.

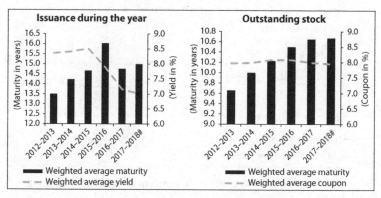

Figure 13.4. Weighted Average Maturity/Yield of Central G-Secs
Source: RBI Annual Report.

What are implications of this changing maturity structure of G-Secs for the duration of bank investment portfolios?

The investment portfolio of banks is classified under three categories, namely 'held to maturity (HTM)', 'available for sale (AFS)' and 'held for trading (HFT)'. Banks normally hold securities acquired by them with the intention to hold them up to maturity under HTM category. Only debt securities are permitted to be held under HTM with a few exceptions, for example, equity held in subsidiaries. Holding securities under HTM provides cushion for banks from valuation changes. However, holding in HTM book is subjected to a ceiling.

AFS and HFT categories together form the trading book of banks. Banks are permitted to decide on the extent of holdings under AFS and HFT based on their trading strategy, risk appetite, capital position, etc. Securities held under both of these books are required to be marked to market. The HFT book is required to be marked to market on a more frequent basis than AFS. The valuation frequency of investment is typically a determinant in the composition of the investment book of banks. Correspondingly, shares of HTM, AFS and HFT are 55.4 per cent, 42.5 per cent and 2.1 per cent, respectively, as on September 2017 (*Financial Stability Report*, RBI, December 2017).[2] The average modified duration of the AFS book of banks is currently

---

[2] https://www.rbi.org.in/Scripts/BS_PressReleaseDisplay.aspx?prid=42642

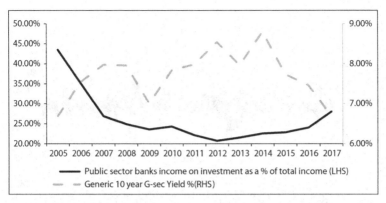

Figure 13.5. Public Sector Banks' (PSBs) Income on Investment as a Percentage of Total Income versus Generic Yield Movement

Source: Database on Indian Economy, RBI and Bloomberg.
Notes: Income on investments includes interest and dividend flows, plus profit/loss from sale of investments.
Movement in yields–Phases of sustained yield rise.

around 2.9 years. The comparable figure for PSBs is higher at 3.5 years and for PvtSBs is at 2.0 years.

With relatively high duration and concentration of G-Secs in investment portfolio, bank earnings and capital remain exposed to adverse yield moves, especially as the share of investment income has been on the rise in the last five years. Figure 13.5 captures this fact succinctly that investment income of banks is highly sensitive to G-Sec yields—yields had by and large fallen in recent years, and consequently, investment income went up. In turn, and given the muted credit growth over this period, especially at PSBs, investment income has again started playing a rather important role in determining bank earnings.

Phases of Sustained Rise in G-Sec Yields

G-Sec yields in India have undergone episodic phases of sustained rise of close to 200 bps at regular intervals. Figure 13.6 identifies three major phases for the 10-year benchmark yield over the past 15 years:

1. Phase I: Second half of 2004 when the interest rate cycle turned up from 5 per cent to over 7 per cent, following a prolonged rally.

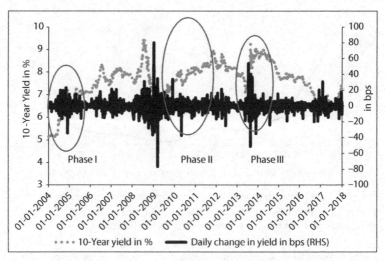

Figure 13.6. 10-Year Generic G-Sec Yield and Daily Change in Yield
Source: Bloomberg.

2. Phase II: Post the global financial crisis when yields rose from around 5.25 per cent in December 2008 to around 8.80 per cent by November 2011.

3. Phase III: During the taper tantrum episode when yields rose from around 7.25 per cent at end-May 2013 to just below 9 per cent by end-December 2013.

My point in showing this time-series and episodic phases of G-Sec yield movements is that banks should not be surprised repeatedly when government bond yields rise sharply, and their investment profits drop. RBI's Financial Stability Reports (FSR) have regularly pointed out the impact of such large interest rate moves on capital and profitability of banks. Banks should know and understand this risk rather well. Perhaps they do, and the issue is really one of incentives that lead to their ignoring this risk, which I will turn to next.

Heads I Win, Tails the Regulator Dispenses

How have these episodic phases of sustained rise in G-Sec yield played out?

During Phase I, responding to the clamour for regulatory for-bearance, banks were permitted to hold G-Secs up to the mandated

SLR of 25 per cent of DTL under the HTM accounting category. Regulations also enabled banks to shift securities from other accounting categories into the HTM category, as a one-time measure, a feature that has now acquired an annual dimension.

A similar one-time transfer was extended during Phase III, in addition to deferment in recognition of valuation losses by six months, from September 2013 to March 2014.

The impact of the persistent rise in yields during Phase II was eased to a great degree by regular open market purchases by RBI, which are typically employed for durable liquidity management and to ensure the proximity of money market rates to the overnight policy rate, rather than for management of long-term G-Sec yields.

These are also the sort of measures some banks have again requested RBI to adopt in the current phase of rising yields, wherein yields have moved up from around 6.50 per cent at end-August 2017 to around 7.45 per cent now.

Interest rate risk of banks cannot be managed over and over again by their regulator. The regulator, in interest of financial stability, is caught in such situations between a rock and a hard place, and often obliges. However, the trend of regular use of 'ex-post' regulatory dispensation to ease the interest rate risk of banks is not desirable from the point of view of efficient price discovery in the G-Sec market and effective market discipline on the G-Sec issue. Nor does it augur well for developing a sound risk management culture at banks. Recourse to such asymmetric options—'heads I win, tails the regulator dispenses'— is akin to the use of steroids. They get addictive and have long-term adverse effects in the form of frequent relapse even though their use may be justified to relieve occasional intense pain. Hence, it would be better for the banking system to build its own immunity and strength, that is, emphasize internally—and put in place processes for—efficient management of interest-rate risk.[3]

Let me then discuss what could be done by banks to achieve this.

---

[3] There are other reasons for banks to focus more closely on interest rate risk that I haven't touched upon in interest of simplicity and brevity. For instance, banks face not just the interest rate risk of the investment portfolio but also to the risk in the banking book. The present guidelines require banks in India to compute change in economic value of equity (ΔEVE) and net interest income (ΔNII) for the entire balance sheet and not just for the banking book positions. However, in order to promote global

Managing Interest Rate Risk at Banks

Management of the increasing interest rate exposure of the banking system needs to address both sides of the sovereign-bank nexus. While the long-term investor participation in government bond market needs to be deepened—both domestically and internationally—and the maturity structure of government debt kept sensitive to implications for bank balance sheets, banks also need to manage the interest rate risk on the balance sheet by dynamically managing its size and duration as well as accessing markets for risk transfer.

The desirable options follow from the bond price equation I presented earlier:

$$\Delta P = - P \times D \times \Delta Y.$$

Interest rate risk management options can thus be categorized as follows:

1. Measures that address P, namely the G-Sec portfolio size of banks:

   The size of the G-Sec portfolio of banks is mainly a function of balance sheet choices made by banks among competing assets. Recognizing at the outset that G-Sec portfolio is subject to interest rate risk, a risk-management strategy can be put in place along the following lines:

   a. The bank's board in discussions with the treasury head and chief risk officer (CRO) can approve the risk limit for the portfolio in terms of the capital that can be 'put at risk'. This assigned-risk capital, much like a corporate budget, should transform into a risk strategy and be guarded in a manner that adjusts for changing risks rather than merely serving as an easy-to-game compliance limit.

---

consistency, transparency and comparability of interest rate risk in the banking book (IRRBB) with that of global banks, banks would be required going forward to compute IRRBB separately and disclose it based on revised BCBS standards. Similarly, the *Report of RBI's Internal Study Group to Review the Working of the Marginal Cost of Funds based Lending Rate (MCLR) System* (available at: https://www.rbi.org.in/scripts/PublicationReportDetails.aspx?ID=878) has recommended that floating rate loans be referenced to an external benchmark. Once introduced, this would expose banks to higher market risk, necessitating more active management of interest rate risks.

b. The assigned-risk capital should not get wiped out under reasonable stress scenarios, which can be modelled as high-confidence-level tail events for bond yields under 'value at risk or expected loss' approach. In other words, banks should not lose capital allocated to the treasury function other than with an extremely small likelihood.

c. Given the non-linearity in yield movements ('the risk that risk will change', or in other words, yield volatility being stochastic), as manifested in the episodic volatility phases I showed, banks should also factor in historical stress scenarios. Under these historical 'stress tests' as well, capital allocated to the treasury function should not get wiped out.

d. In addition, banks should conduct 'reverse stress tests', that is, ask the question as to what kind of G-Sec yield movements, parallel shift at a minimum but ideally also yield-curve steepening, would wipe out the allocated capital? Indeed, such reverse stress tests[4] have been recommended by the RBI and could become part of board-level risk discussions.

e. However, no stress test is perfect; and, no risk measure such as value at risk or expected losses which use historical distributions can anticipate fully the nature of future yield movements. Hence, banks also need to adopt 'robust' risk controls for resilience. This can involve 'concentration limits', so banks do not exceed their exposure to G-Secs beyond an internally agreed total proportion of assets; or the excess SLR should be commensurate in risk terms with the bank's capital allocation for investments.

f. In order to further address treasury-level incentive issues, banks may consider imposing dynamic 'stop loss limits'. In order to avoid further losses once they exceed a particular percentage of assigned risk capital, any risk addition must slow down, potentially even stop (depending on the extent of realized capital loss), and

---

[4] https://www.rbi.org.in/scripts/NotificationUser.aspx?Id=8605&Mode=0

not be gerrymandered through security rotation or by senior management turning a blind eye. Instead, the realized losses and residual risks should escalate through CRO to the bank board and the risk in the investment portfolio gradually scaled down in a time-bound manner depending on its size.

g.   In addition, there should be 'ex-post settling up' as a career incentive for the treasury head and all significant risk takers: those who swing bank investment portfolio for the fences and put bank capital at excessive limits relative to the approved levels should be held accountable when their bets go bad due to poor or no risk management. Not all volatility is due to 'black swan' events that deserve risk-takers being carried through.

h.   Finally, there is usually an uninspiring chatter every time G-Sec yields show a sustained rise that the market is irrational in its movements. Not only is it not difficult to separate rational market movements from irrational ones at high frequency, such proclamations are a sign that those betting on government bonds while chatting such are clueless about the drivers of market movements. Isn't that a good time for the bank senior management to rein in their treasury portfolio risks?

None of this is rocket science but does require at the highest level of bank governance mechanisms a recognition of interest rate risk, an incentive to manage it, and a top-down organizational strategy to implement it.

2.   Measures that address *D*, namely the duration risk of banks: How can banks better manage their duration risk?

The efficiency with which this risk is currently managed leaves a lot to be desired. While duration risk management is constrained by the G-Secs issuer's choice of maturity structure and liquidity in the secondary bond market, the risk can be managed more nimbly by also availing of hedging markets. PSBs account for about 70.6 per cent of the banking sector assets. However, their participation in such hedging markets is limited or negligible. While their share in secondary market trading of G-Secs is about 33 per cent, their share in hedging activity in the IRS and interest rate future (IRF) segments is only 4.61 per cent and 13.40 per cent, respectively.

Let me elaborate. RBI introduced rupee interest rate derivatives in the OTC market, viz., IRS and forward rate agreement (FRA), in 1999. IRFs were first introduced in the Indian markets in 2003 but only the current bond future contract, introduced in 2014, has seen reasonable activity. Liquidity in the interest rate products has generally been low. The open interest and daily volume in the interest rate futures market are usually between ₹20 and 30 billion while the daily volume in the overnight indexed swap (OIS) interest rate swap market is around ₹150 billion. Besides, only a section of the banks is active in the OIS market. Compared to an average daily bond market volume of ₹400–500 billion, interest rate derivative markets are thus rather thin.

Wider participation by banks in interest rate derivative markets—both futures and swaps—is necessary for improving liquidity in these markets, which is necessary for banks to off-load their significant duration risk onto others. As more hedgers access these markets, there would be incentives for market makers to allocate more capital to these activities, kicking off a virtuous cycle of interest rate risk-sharing and leading over time to a more vibrant derivative market.

In other words, the treasury functions at banks need to be modernized with urgency, subjected to careful scrutiny by boards, overlaid with prudent risk management practices, and trained to employ hedging instruments specifically targeted at managing interest rate risk.

This takes me to the important issue of how banks should manage 'large' changes in yields.

3. Measures that address the valuation impact in scenarios with potentially large changes in yield:

Given the nascent stage of our interest rate derivative markets, banks need to manage exposures to large changes in yield with a multitude of instruments and trading platforms. All options should be on the table. An often-cited reason for the lack of such comprehensive risk management by banks is that hedging markets that can enable neutralization of large changes in yield lack the size or depth or liquidity to meet the needs of large banks. True as this argument is at some level, it is the very lack of participation by large banks that makes these markets illiquid and small. RBI systematically engages with the market to take necessary steps to create an enabling environment for markets to develop—creating trading, settlement and reporting infrastructure, introducing products, easing processes, etc.

India's G-Sec market infrastructure is arguably the best in the world. We have enabled guaranteed settlement in G-Secs, forex and IRSs. Despite the existence of the facility to short sell and availability of futures and swap markets, it appears that for most banks, investment activity essentially consists of two steps—buying and hoping for the best. But hope should not be a treasury desk's primary trading strategy.

RBI has also permitted money market futures about a year back. Those directions were a significant deviation from the earlier prescriptive approach. Exchanges were given complete freedom to design and introduce products. We are yet to receive any proposal for approval.

Similarly, interest rate options were also permitted sometime back, but the market has still not kicked off. Years back, RBI introduced the 'when issued' market and 'STRIPS', but neither has gained traction.

Does all this imply that these interest rate products have no use for any participant? Or is it just that the market, dominated by banks, is not used to availing of risk management options, hoping instead for regulatory forbearance when episodic yield increase rears its ugly head?

Conclusion

Let me summarize. Market liberalization does not just involve the regulator easing business processes, introducing new products and creating new markets; it also requires participants to take the initiative to reskill themselves for constantly evolving market conditions and products. Market development is a two-way interactive process between market participants and regulators. We are hoping that Fixed Income Money Market and Derivatives Association of India (FIMMDA) can rally banks and play its part going forward.

Finally, it is encouraging that FIMMDA is developing the code of conduct covering its members' activities in the interest rate markets. Along with Foreign Exchange Dealers' Association of India (FEDAI)'s recent adoption of the Global Foreign Exchange Code, the entire range of bond, currency and related derivative markets would be subject to professional conduct in line with best international practice, once FIMMDA adopts the code. I hope that this process can be hastened and FIMMDA members adopt the code signing it on a public website by the end of the current quarter.

References

Acharya, Viral V., Itamar Drechsler, and Philipp Schnabl. 2012. 'A Tale of Two Overhangs: The Nexus of Financial Sector and Sovereign Credit Risks.' *Financial Stability Review*, no. 16. Available at: http://pages.stern.nyu.edu/~sternfin/vacharya/public_html/FSR16_ACHARYA_28-03_annotable.pdf (accessed on 25 April 2020).

Acharya, Viral V., Itamar Drechsler, and Philipp Schnabl. 2015. 'A Pyrrhic Victory? Bank Bailouts and Sovereign Credit Risk.' *Journal of Finance* 69, no. 6: 2689–2739. Available at: http://pages.stern.nyu.edu/~sternfin/vacharya/public_html/pdfs/ADS_final.pdf (accessed on 25 April 2020).

Acharya, Viral V., and Sascha Steffen. 2015. 'The "Greatest" Carry Trade Ever? Understanding Eurozone Bank Risks.' *Journal of Financial Economics* 115, no. 2 (February): 215–236. Available at: http://pages.stern.nyu.edu/~sternfin/vacharya/public_html/pdfs/carrytrade_jfe_v10June2014.pdf (accessed on 25 April 2020).

Merler, Silvia, and Pisani-Ferry, Jean. 2012. 'Who's Afraid of Sovereign Bonds.' *Bruegel Policy Contribution*, no. 2 (February). Available at: http://bruegel.org/publications/datasets/sovereign-bond-holdings/ (accessed on 31 March 2020).

CHAPTER 14

GLOBAL SPILLOVERS: MANAGING CAPITAL FLOWS AND FOREX RESERVES*

Emerging markets (EMs) are affected by a global financial cycle originating in high-income economies (Rey 2013). An increase in risk appetite of high-income economies, perhaps spurred by easy monetary policy, leads to a surge in capital flows to EMs. These foreign capital flows, especially foreign portfolio investments (FPI) in debt and equity markets (as against foreign direct equity investments or FDI), can reverse quickly, leading to a sudden stop and a sharp macroeconomic slowdown. Managing this capital flow cycle is a central concern for EM governments (De Gregorio 2010; Ostry et al. 2010).

These points are evident in events of the last 10 years. Figure 14.1 plots, as an example, FDI and FPI flows into India over the period 2004 to 2017. FPI flows drop sharply in the global financial crisis before rising in the post-crisis period, when high-income economy interest rates are low. They reversed again in the taper tantrum of 2013, when investors feared that the Federal Reserve may tighten monetary policy (Krishnamurthy and Vissing-Jorgensen 2013). When these fears eased in 2014, capital flows resumed before falling

---

*Speech was delivered at the Conference of the National Stock Exchange (NSE)—New York University (NYU) Initiative on the Study of Indian Capital Markets on 14 December 2017 (Acharya and Krishnamurthy 2019).

We are grateful to Saswat Mahapatra, Jack Shim and Jonathan Wallen for their excellent research assistance. Authors are grateful for feedback from Governor Urjit Patel and participants at the Reserve Bank of India Financial Market Operations, Regulation and International Departments' 2017 Retreat in Bekal (Kerala, India) and NYU-Stern/IIM-Calcutta 2017 Conference on India. We also thank Markus Brunnermeier, Guillaume Plantin, Ricardo Reis and participants at the XXI Annual Conference of the Central Bank of Chile for their comments. The views expressed are entirely those of the authors and do not in any way reflect the views of the Reserve Bank of India.

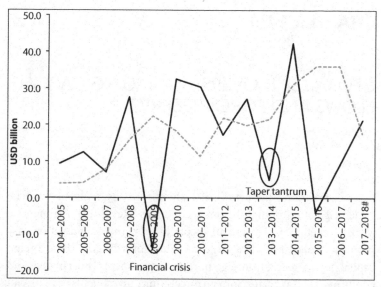

Figure 14.1. Volatility of Foreign Portfolio Investment (FPI) and Foreign Direct Investment (FDI) Flows

Source: RBI.
Notes: Net foreign direct investment (FDI) in dotted line and net portfolio investment (FPI) in plain. Data for 2017–2018 updated until October 2017.

again in late 2015 as the Federal Reserve indeed raised the rates. The figure also plots FDI flows, which are far more stable.

The capital flow reversal in the taper tantrum episode led to a sharp depreciation of the Indian rupee (INR). Figure 14.2 plots the exchange rate (dotted line) from 2004 to 2017, with the shaded region indicating the taper tantrum period. The rupee depreciated by over 30 per cent against the US dollar in the summer of 2013, more so than other EMs on average (plain line in graph).

In response to such capital flow volatility and attendant consequences on exchange rates, EMs have adopted two main strategies: hoard foreign reserves and impose capital controls. Reserves can act as a buffer against a sudden stop. See Obstfeld, Shambaugh and Taylor's (2010) discussion of the intellectual history and underpinnings of the role of foreign reserves as a buffer against sudden stops. Capital controls that reduce external debt limit the vulnerability of an EM to sudden stops. The IMF study by Ostry et al. (2010) provides a comprehensive examination of the motivation behind capital controls as well as the effectiveness of such controls in practice.

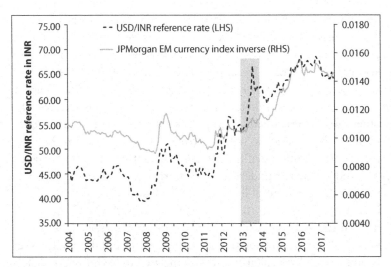

Figure 14.2. Exchange Rate and 2013 Taper Tantrum
Source: Bloomberg, DBIE, RBI.

This chapter revisits the topic of capital flow management, and particularly the interaction between two commonly deployed instruments to achieve it, namely foreign reserves policies and capital controls. In practice as well as in much of the literature on capital flow management, capital controls and reserves management are cast as *alternative* instruments which can both reduce sudden stop vulnerability. Our principal theoretical result is that these policies interact and should be seen by central banks as *complementary* instruments. Better capital controls enable more effective reserve management. Likewise, a higher level of foreign reserves dictates stronger capital controls.

Jeanne (2016) is another study that examines the complementarity between these instruments in a somewhat different setting than ours.

The intuition for our key result is simply stated. One way of interpreting the sudden stop is as a state of the world in which foreign creditors refuse to roll over both external (foreign currency) short-term debt and domestic (local currency) short-term debt. This can trigger both a currency crisis and a roll over/banking crisis. Borrowers with external debt will fire sale domestic assets to convert to foreign currency to repay foreign creditors. Foreign holders of domestic debt will convert repayments from this debt into foreign currency.

The liquidation of domestic assets for foreign currency triggers a currency crisis. The roll over problem triggers defaults and a banking crisis. Consequently, our model embeds the twin-crisis nature of sudden stops in EMs (Kaminsky and Reinhart 1999). The crisis is worsened if the aggregate amount of the external and the domestic short-term debt is higher, as this results in more fire sales. On the other side, in the *extremis*, central bank reserves can be used to reduce currency depreciation as well as borrower defaults. Therefore, reserves reduce the magnitude of the fire sale discount in prices. But ex ante, they induce greater undertaking of short-term liabilities by the borrowers, a form of moral hazard from the insurance effect of reserves in case of sudden stops: the greater the reserves, the lower the anticipated fire sale discount in prices and, in turn, the greater the undertaking of short-term liabilities. Hence, unless the build-up of reserves is coincident with capital controls on the growth of short-term liabilities, the insurance effect of reserves is undone by the private choice of short-term liabilities. In other words, reserves and capital controls are complementary measures in the regulatory toolkit.

With capital flows into both foreign-currency- and domestic-currency-denominated assets, there arises a further complementarity result. If capital controls can only be introduced on one margin, say foreign-currency debt, then they cannot be too tight. Otherwise, there is the prospect of arbitrage of capital controls between the two markets: borrowing short-term will switch to domestic-currency assets, even if domestic borrowing is costlier in a spread sense as it enjoys weaker capital controls. We show that with an additional instrument, say capital controls on domestic-currency debt, capital controls as a whole can be more effective, which then makes reserve polices also more effective. We show that the design of capital controls in such a setting where the emerging-market currency is internationalized to some extent requires careful weighing of the gains from attracting capital flows, typically in the form of lower cost of borrowing abroad relative to domestically, against the cost of sudden stops and the cross-market regulatory arbitrage of capital controls. Though the main thrust of our analysis prevails that central banks should not design reserves management and capital control policies as substitutes; they are in fact complements enhancing each other's effectiveness.

Our paper contributes to the large literature on the role of reserves and capital controls in managing sudden stops. Ostry et al. (2010)

provide a comprehensive examination of the motivation behind capital controls, as well as the effectiveness of such controls in practice. Obstfeld et al. (2010) discuss the intellectual history and underpinnings of the role of foreign reserves as a buffer against sudden stops. Aizenman and Marion (2003) rationalize the build-up of reserves in Asia as a response to precautionary motives. Jeanne and Rancière (2011) provide a quantitative analysis regarding how much reserves a central bank should hold, shedding light on the well-known Greenspan-Guidotti rule (Greenspan 1999). In this literature, typically both reserves and capital controls are viewed as precautionary tools to buffer against sudden stops (see, e.g., Aizenman 2011). Thus, the literature typically takes the perspective that these tools are substitutes, whereas our main result is that they are complements. Our paper is also related to the classic analysis of Poole (1970) studying the optimal choice of instruments. The principal difference between our analysis and Poole's is that in his model the instruments are substitutes, while in our case they are complements. We discuss this further in the conclusion.

Section 1 presents empirical evidence suggestive of the complementarity perspective. Section 2 builds a model to analyze reserves and capital controls jointly. Finally, as a case study for the analysis, in Section 3 we discuss how capital controls have been used in India and how they map into the model's economic forces and implications.

Section 1

EM Liquidity: Empirical Evidence

The left panel of Figure 14.3 plots the total foreign reserves held by central banks in a sample of EMs over the period 1999 to 2015.[1] There is a dramatic increase in foreign reserves after the global financial crisis. From 2006 to 2015, reserves increased from $0.78 trillion to just over $1.7 trillion. Indeed, many policymakers and academics have described the reserves accumulation as a proactive capital flow management strategy. Carstens (2016) documents the dramatic increase in the volatility of capital flows after 2006 (see Chart 3 of his paper). He notes that the accumulation of international reserves is

_____

[1]

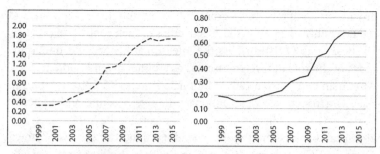

Figure 14.3. Aggregate Foreign Reserves and External Short-Term Debt for Emerging Markets

Source: International Monetary Fund.
Notes: The left-panel graphs the aggregate foreign reserves, in trillions of USD, across a sample of emerging markets, from 1999 to 2015. The right-panel graphs the aggregate external short-term debt (<1 year) of these countries.

the primary policy tool EMs have used to manage this capital flow volatility.

The right panel of Figure 14.3 graphs the aggregate external short-term debt of these EMs. As is well understood in the literature, reserves can act as a buffer against withdrawals of these flows in the event of a sudden stop. External creditors may choose not to roll over their short-term debt, which indicates a liquidity need for the country that is partially covered with foreign reserves. The Greenspan-Guidotti rule, already mentioned earlier, is a prescription that EMs hold reserves equal to external debt less than one year in maturity. It is apparent that as foreign reserves have grown, short-term debt has also grown.

Figure 14.4 below graphs India's forex reserves, showing that they rose steadily after the global financial crisis and until 2011, dipping slightly by 2012 and then remaining relatively flat until the taper tantrum. In an absolute sense, India's reserves had accumulated by the 2013 taper tantrum to exceed the level in the crisis of 2008 levels, thus suggesting greater external sector resilience. However, the net capital outflow after the Federal Reserve's taper announcement led to a sharp depreciation in the exchange rate, as evident from Figure 14.2. The culprit is short-term debt: the diagnosis of resilience is reversed if one accounts for the build-up of external debt in India.

Figure 14.5, Panel A, plots the time series of India's external debt, which rose steadily and was at close to 25 per cent relative to GDP around the taper tantrum. Equally important, the short-term component of this debt (with residual maturity less than one year) is

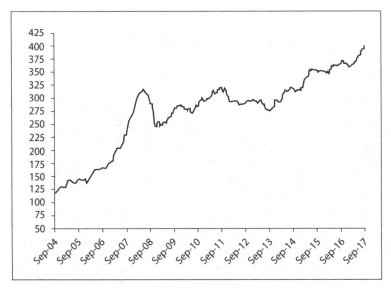

Figure 14.4. Foreign Exchange Reserves for India (USD Billion)
Source: RBI.

seen in Figure 14.5, Panel B, to have also risen steadily (to around 20% short-term debt) by the 2013 taper tantrum.

Let us define liquidity (or external-sector resilience) metric at the country level:

$$\text{Liquidity}_{i,t} = \frac{\text{Reserves}_{i,t} - \text{ST Debt}_{i,t}}{\text{GDP}_{i,t}}. \tag{1}$$

Figure 14.6 shows that the liquidity measure had been steadily declining for India from a peak of above 20 per cent prior to the global financial crisis to a low of below 10 per cent by the taper tantrum, thus more accurately capturing the loss of resilience as witnessed during the period from May to August of 2013.

To summarize, the case of India in the build-up to the taper tantrum suggests that forex reserves, per se, were not adequate in measuring external sector resilience against sudden stops. The model we develop in this chapter studies the linkage between reserves and short-term debt. We will argue theoretically that reserve adequacy is contingent upon the quantity and quality of debt and, in particular, the extent of short-term external debt. Our theoretical analysis also points to the mechanism whereby the

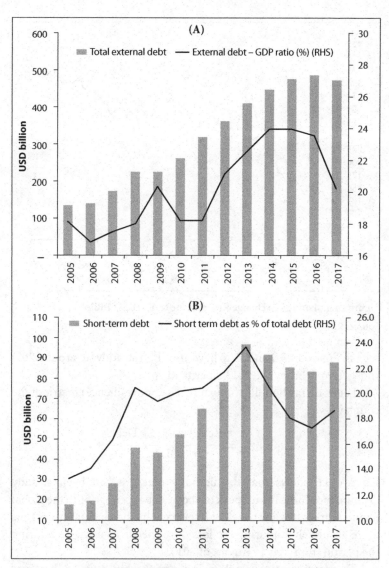

Figure 14.5. **(A) India Total External Debt (B) Short-Term External Debt**
Source: *India's External Debt*, a status report, 2016–2017 by GoI.

increase in reserves in part likely drove the rise in short-term external debt although it is difficult to causally identify this economic force from the data we have presented.

We next investigate the linkage between reserves and short-term debt more broadly across EMs, asking how well the liquidity metric

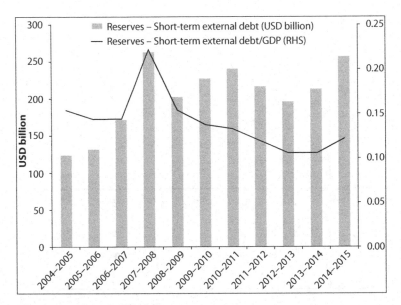

Figure 14.6. Country Liquidity

Source: World Bank, RBI, Ministry of Statistics and Programme implementation.
Note: Country liquidity = **Reserves – Short-term external debt/GDP**

in equation (1) discriminates among countries in their exposure to the global financial cycle.

Figure 14.7 plots country liquidity as of 2013, as in equation (1) with $t = 2013$, against asset price changes, for a group of EMs. We consider asset price changes from June 2013 to October 2017. We begin in June 2013 to include the start of the taper tantrum. Over this period, the global financial cycle turns back towards high-income economies, so that, on average, EM currencies depreciate (see Panel C). The figure reveals that the liquidity metric discriminates between the EMs that are more and less sensitive to the financial cycle. From Panel C, we see that countries that are more liquid experience less depreciation in their currencies. Likewise, more liquid countries see sovereign-bond yield spreads rise less (Panel A) and experience higher domestic stock market returns (Panel B).

That is, in all cases, higher liquidity is associated with a more favourable EM asset price outcome.

We next turn to high frequency data. The relation in Figure 14.7 reflects a correlation over a long-time window, where the global shock is negative for EMs. At a high frequency, we can hope to uncover

(A) Change in Sovereign-Bond Spread

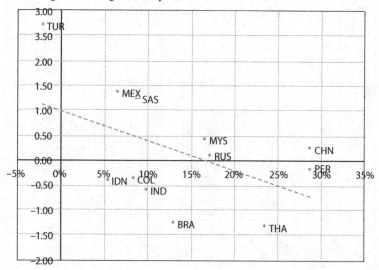

(B) Stock Market Return

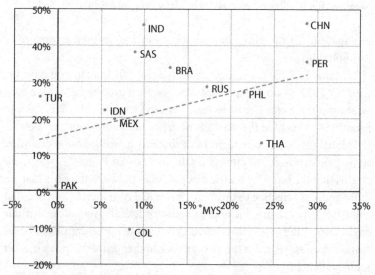

Figure 14.7. (*continued*)

(C) Currency Appreciation

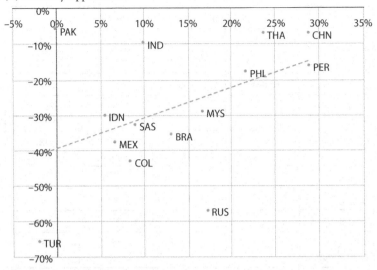

Figure 14.7. Sovereign Bond Yield, Stock Market Return and Currency Appreciation for Emerging Markets versus Liquidity

Source: International Monetary Fund.
Notes: The graphs plot country liquidity as of 2013 (see equation [1]) against asset price changes, for a group of emerging markets. (A) Plots liquidity on the x-axis against the change in sovereign-bond yield spreads from June 2013 to October 2017 on the y-axis. (B) Plots a similar relation for the country stockmarket return. (C) Plots the EM currency appreciation against the USD. In all cases, higher liquidity is associated with a more favourable EM asset price outcome.

more shifts in the global cycle and hence better document a relation between liquidity and EMs performances. Our approach builds on the literature and particularly Rey (2013), who notes the importance of the VIX for the global cycle. We proxy for the global factor using the VIX multiplied by –1 (i.e., the negative of the VIX). Our normalization is that when the global factor is high, we say that capital flows are favourable to EMs. Using the AR(1) innovations to the global factor, we estimate the heterogeneous effect of the global financial cycle on countries with different degrees of liquidity.

Table 14.1 reports the results of panel data regressions. In Panel A, the dependent variable is the daily change in the sovereign-bond spread of a given country. The independent variables are the global factor innovations in Columns (1) and (2), and the global factor innovations interacted with liquidity, as well as liquidity by itself, in

Table 14.1. Liquidity and Shocks to Global Factor

(A) Change in Sovereign-Bond Spread

	(1)	(2)	(3)	(4)
Global factor	−0.0788	−0.0620	−0.1326	−0.1163
	(3.88)***	(3.47)***	(4.14)***	(4.28)***
Global factor × Liquidity			0.0812	0.0770
			(7.91)***	(8.05)***
Liquidity			0.0057	−0.0277
			(0.13)	(0.37)
Country FE	Y	Y	Y	Y
Year FE	Y	Y	Y	Y
Restrict to large shock	N	Y	N	Y
R^2	0.01	0.04	0.01	0.05
N	21,340	2,047	13,741	1,419

(B) Stock Market Return

	(1)	(2)	(3)	(4)
Global factor	0.2878	0.2669	0.2775	0.2788
	(6.87)***	(7.07)***	(4.14)***	(4.63)***
Global factor × Liquidity			−0.0026	−0.0350
			(0.03)	(0.47)
Liquidity			−0.0029	0.0514
			(0.12)	(0.72)
Country FE	Y	Y	Y	Y
Year FE	Y	Y	Y	Y
Restrict to large shock	N	Y	N	Y
R^2	0.07	0.23	0.07	0.22
N	25,545	2,535	17,549	1,892

(continued)

(C) Currency Appreciation				
Global factor	0.1496	0.1314	0.2101	0.1860
	(5.08)***	(5.15)***	(3.87)***	(3.91)***
Global factor × Liquidity			−0.0937	−0.0860
			(2.27)**	(2.43)**
Liquidity			−0.0020	0.0364
			(0.09)	(0.97)
Country FE	Y	Y	Y	Y
Year FE	Y	Y	Y	Y
Restrict to large shock	N	Y	N	Y
R^2	0.07	0.21	0.08	0.24
N	27,631	2,756	17,837	1,935

Notes: This table reports regressions of daily asset price changes against a global factor, constructed as described in the text, and the global factor interact with the liquidity measure (see equation [1]). Data is from January 2011 to October 2017. Panel A reports results for sovereign-bond spreads, Panel B for the domestic stock-market return, and Panel C is for EM currency appreciation against the USD. In columns (2) and (4), we restrict the observations to large shocks, defined as those in the 5 per cent tails of the distribution of daily changes in the global factor. $**p < 0.05$; $***p < 0.01$.

columns (3) and (4). We include country and year fixed effects in all regressions. Columns (2) and (4) restrict the data to observations with large global shocks, defined as those in the 5 per cent tails of the distribution of daily global innovations to check for non-linearities. The independent variables have been normalized by dividing by their standard deviation, so that the coefficients can be interpreted as the effect of a one-sigma change.

We see that the global factor innovation comes in with a negative coefficient in all four columns. There is no discernible difference between the cases where we restrict the observations to large shocks, indicating no evidence of non-linearities. The negative coefficients are to be expected as the global factor is defined in terms of good news for EMs (hence, for instance, sovereign-bond spreads fall). The more relevant covariate for our analysis is the second row, which is the global factor innovation interacted with liquidity. Higher liquidity dampens the impact of innovations in the global factor on changes in sovereign-bond spreads. The regression results are consistent with the pattern evident in Figure 14.7.

Panel B reports results for the domestic stock market returns. Stock returns load positively on the global factor. The interaction term has a negative sign, indicating dampening, but the coefficient is not statistically different from zero.

Panel C is for the currency appreciation of the EMs. As expected, the coefficient on the global factor innovation is positive. Again, we see evidence of the dampening effect as the coefficient on the interaction is negative and significant.[2]

These results from our data analysis indicate that asset price changes in EMs depend on the global shocks, consistent with a number of papers in the literature (see Calvo, Leiderman, and Reinhart 1996; Rey 2013). We also see that the impact of the global factor depends on the liquidity of the EM, which in turn depends on the foreign reserves of the central bank and the external short-term debt of the EM, as we may expect from the literature on international reserves as a buffer against sudden stops. The next section builds on these observations to construct a model to study the management of capital flows when there are multiple policy instruments, namely reserves management and capital controls.

Section 2

Model of Macroprudential Management of Capital Flows

This section lays out a model of firms of EMs, more generally, banks or governments, which borrow from foreign investors to fund high return investments. The model is closest to Caballero and Krishnamurthy (2001), and Caballero and Simsek (2016). Foreign

---

[2] We have experimented with specifications where we include reserves and short-term debt separately in these regressions for Panels A–C. We would expect that the coefficients on these measures will have opposite signs, when interacted with the global factor. However, there is not enough variation in the data to detect this pattern.

investors are 'fickle' in the sense of Caballero and Simsek (2016): They may receive a shock that requires them to withdraw funding from the EM. The loss of funding leads to a fire sale, which depreciates the exchange rate and creates an external effect for all the borrowers as in Caballero and Krishnamurthy (2001). The central bank has foreign reserves that it can use to reduce the fire sale and stabilize the exchange rate. We study the connections between the central bank's actions and private sector's borrowing decisions. We first lay out a model where all borrowings is via an external debt market, that is, dollar debt. We then introduce foreign lending in domestic-currency debt.

Model with External Debt Market

The model has three classes of agents: domestic borrowers (B), foreign lenders (FL), and a central bank (CB). There are three dates: $t = 0$, 1, 2. Date 0 is a borrowing and investment date, at date 1 there are shocks and at date 2 there are final payoffs.

There is a continuum of borrowers with unit mass. Each B has a project that requires capital and own labour. B's utility is:

$$U^B = E\{c_2 - l_0 - l_1\} \ c_2, l_0, \ l_1 \geq 0, \tag{2}$$

where c_2 is date 2 investment and l_0 and l_1 are disutility from labour at date 0 and date 1.

The borrower has an investment project at date 0. B can create K units of capital by borrowing,

$$L^F = K \tag{3}$$

goods from foreign lenders and providing labour of $l_0(K)$, with $l_0(\cdot)$ increasing and convex. The project pays $(1 + 2R)K$ at date 2 and cannot be liquidated early.

FL are the only lenders at date 0. They have a large endowment of goods and are risk neutral. FL's required return in lending to the EM is $1 + r$. A period in which developed market interest rates are low corresponds to a period when r is low. Additionally, if risk appetite for EM bonds is high, we can think of r as being low.

Our key assumption is that lenders are fickle. With probability φ they may receive a retrenchment shock at date 1, in which case they need to withdraw their funding. We assume that it is not possible to write contracts contingent on this shock. Consequently, the FL lend via one-period loans that may or may not be rolled over. It is clearest to think of these loans as in units of 'dollars'.

If a loan is not rolled over, borrowers owe foreign lenders $L^F(1 + r)$ dollars. Loans must be repaid; bankruptcy costs are infinite. To repay a loan, the borrower turns to domestic lenders to borrow funds against collateral of K units of the project. We assume these lenders are present at date 1 and are willing to lend against collateral of K at interest rate of r. The borrower raises $(1 + r)K$ domestic currency (rupees), with promised repayment of $(1 + 2r)K$, converts this to $e(1 + r)K$ dollars, so that the borrower raises a total of $e(1 + r)K$. Here, e is the exchange rate in units of dollars per rupee. A depreciated rupee corresponds to a low value of e. The shortfall to the borrower, that is, owed dollar debt minus funds raised from the domestic loan, is $K(1 + r)(1 - e)$. The borrower makes up this shortfall by working hard and suffering disutility,

$$l_1 = \beta(K(1 + r)(1 - e)), \tag{4}$$

with $\beta(\cdot)$ increasing and convex. By doing so, and with funds from the domestic loan, the borrower repays $(1 + r)K$ in full. $\beta(\cdot)$ is modeled as disutility of labour to keep the model concise rather than to reflect realism. We think of $\beta(\cdot)$ as the deadweight cost of bankruptcy. More generally, it can reflect costly adjustments that must be made in order to meet debt payments.

The central bank has total foreign exchange reserves of X^F which it can use to stabilize the exchange rate. We assume that the exchange rate at all dates other than the retrenchment state is one, and can fall to $e < 1$ in the retrenchment state. Henceforth, when discussing the exchange rate e, this e refers to the exchange rate in the retrenchment state at date 1.

Given e we can write the borrower's problem. The utility from choosing $K = L^F$ is,

$$U^B = 2(R - r)L^F - l_0(L^F) - \phi \times \beta(L^F(1 + r)(1 - e)). \tag{5}$$

Define $\Delta \equiv R - r$. The first order condition (FOC) is:

$$l_0'(L^F) = 2\Delta - \phi \times (1 - e)(1 - r)\beta'(L^F(1 + r)(1 - e)). \tag{6}$$

Note that Δ matters in the model, more so than the level of R or r. We henceforth set $r = 0$ (7)

to simplify some expressions. The term Δ can be thought of as the carry offered by the EM.

In equilibrium in the retrenchment state, borrowers pledge K units of collateral to raise L^F rupees and exchanges these domestic funds for X^F units of dollar. The exchange rate is then,

$$e = \frac{X^F}{L^F} \qquad (8)$$

Throughout our analysis, we will assume that parameters are such that $e < 1$. The exchange rate expression reflects the fire sale externality in our model. When a borrower increases date 0 borrowing and investment, he pushes up K, which then implies that the date 1 retrenchment exchange rate is more depreciated, thus increasing the debt burden ($L^F[1 - e]$) to all borrowers. Substituting from (8) into (5) above, we can write the aggregate borrower utility as

$$2\Delta L^F - l_0(L^F) - \phi \times \beta(L^F - X^F).$$

This aggregate corresponds to a welfare function for borrowers who account for the effect of their borrowings (L^F) on the exchange rate and hence the repayment ability of the other borrowers. The FOC for the aggregate is,

$$l'_0(K) = 2\Delta - \phi \times \beta'(L^F - X^F) \qquad (9)$$

We compare (6) to (9) and see that,

Proposition 1. *(Overborrowing)*

1. Let $L^{F,\mathrm{priv}}$ be the solution to the first order condition in (6), and $L^{F,\mathrm{agg}}$ be the solution to (9). Since $1 > 1 - e$, the private solution features overborrowing:

$$L^{F,priv} > L^{F,agg}$$

The private choices of K and L^F are larger than the coordinated choices.

2. Take the case where β is linear, or not too convex.[3] Then, since e is increasing in X^F, the private sector overborrowings (gap between private and coordinated solution) increase in X^F. Central bank reserves are a form of bailout fund. The larger the bailout fund, the greater the private sector borrowings.[4]

How can borrowers implement the coordinated optimum? In our model, there are at least two solutions. A planner can set a borrowing limit on L^F which directly implements the optimum. Or, the planner can set a tax rate on external borrowing, τ^F, so that a borrower who raises L^F pays $\tau^F L^F$ to the planner, who then rebates the funds to the borrowers. With this tax, the borrower would maximize:

$$2\Delta L^F - l_0(L^F) - \phi \times \beta(L^F(1-e)) - \tau^F L^F + T. \qquad (10)$$

where $\tau^F L^F$ is the borrowing tax and T is the lump sum rebated to the borrower. The optimal tax is set so that the private FOC is equal to the social FOC. It is straightforward to see that,

$$\tau^F = \phi \times e\beta'(L^F(1-e)). \qquad (11)$$

The tax is increasing in the probability of the foreign run state, ϕ. It is also increasing in the expected marginal deadweight cost of the retrenchment state, $e \times \beta'(L^F(1-e))$, which we note is itself increasing in L^F. Our result that capital flow taxes on EM borrowers can beneficially correct an overborrowing problem is similar to Caballero and Krishnamurthy (2004) and Jeanne and Korinek (2010).

---

[3] The caveat is necessary because if reserves are large enough that e approaches one, then the cost of bankruptcy goes to zero.

[4] If we do not assume r <hig>=</hig> 0, which we have for simplicity, then it can be shown that as r falls and hence Δ rises, K and L^F rise. Since $\beta(\cdot)$ is convex, the term $\beta'(L^F - X^F)$ is increasing in K (and L^F). Thus, a lower world interest rate, or increase in foreign investors' risk appetite, exacerbates the overborrowing problem. If bankruptcies create spillovers to un-modelled sectors, via bank losses for example, that are increasing in the amount of bankruptcy, then β is increasing in K and the problem is reinforced.

Optimal Reserve Holdings and Taxes

We next study the central bank's holdings of reserves and consider how reserve holdings affect welfare. Suppose that holding reserves for the central bank comes at a cost $\kappa(X^F)$, where κ is an increasing and convex function of X^F. We take this cost in reduced form. We can think there are other forms of capital flows, say FDI or equity, which the central bank uses to accumulate foreign reserves. In this case, κ is the opportunity cost of the alternative activity. Then, consider the following welfare function:

$$W(L^F, X^F) \equiv 2\Delta L^F - l_0(L^F) - \phi \times \beta(L^F - X^F) - \kappa(X^F) \quad (12)$$

How much X^F would a central bank choose knowing that the choice of X^F affects L^F? We optimize over X^F given that $L^F(X^F)$. The FOC is,

$$L^{F'}(X^F) \{2\Delta - l_0'(L^F) - \phi \times \beta'(L^F - X^F)\}$$
$$+ \phi\beta'(L^F - X^F) - \kappa'(X^F) = 0$$

The term in brackets $\{\cdot\}$ can be simplified using the private FOC, (6). We find:

$$-L^{F'}(X^F) \times \phi \times e\beta'(L^F - X^F) + \phi \times \beta'(L^F - X^F) - \kappa'(X^F) = 0$$

so that,

$$\phi\beta'(L^F - X^F) = \frac{\kappa'(X^F)}{(1 - eL^{F'}(X^F))} \quad (13)$$

It is instructive to compare this expression to the case where the central bank can directly choose L^F. In that case, the term in the brackets $\{\}$ goes to zero so that the FOC is

$$\phi\beta'(L^F - X^F) = \kappa'(X^F) \quad (14)$$

In this latter case, the intuition for the choice of X^F is clear. The marginal cost of reserves is increasing in κ' and the marginal benefit of holding reserves is the reduction in expected default cost $\phi\beta'(L^F - X^F)$. The optimal holding of reserves equates these two margins.

In the former case, when the private sector chooses L^F, the cost of reserves is higher. Algebraically we can see it is higher since

$1 - eL^{F\,\prime}(X^F) < 1$ as $e > 0$ and $L^{F\prime}(X^F) > 0$. Intuitively, the private sector chooses a higher L^F in response to a higher X^F. Therefore, the effective cost of reserves is increased from κ' to $\dfrac{\kappa'}{1 - eL^{F\prime}(X^F)}$. The central bank recognizes that increasing X^F provides beneficial insurance, but that the private sector will undo some of this beneficial insurance by overborrowing and increasing L^F. The central bank cuts back on its optimal reserve holdings as a result.

To summarize:

Proposition 2. (Complementarity between policy instruments I)

- If the central bank can directly choose L^F via a borrowing limit or an external-borrowing tax, then it chooses X^F to solve (14). Call this maximized value X_{**}^F.

- If the central bank does not have instruments to directly affect L^F, then it chooses X^F to solve (13). Call this maximized value X_*^F. We then have that,

$$X_{**}^F > X_*^F$$

- With two instruments, taxes and reserves, the central bank can do strictly better than with only one instrument. The two instruments are complements in the sense that taxing ability allows for more reserve holdings; likewise, more reserve holdings dictate higher taxes.[5]

Heterogeneity among Borrowers

We extend the model to allow for heterogeneity. Suppose that in a retrenchment shock some firms are more exposed than others. In particular, suppose that the probability a given firm will suffer loss of funding in the retrenchment shock is p_i where i indexes borrowers. We can think of p_i as capturing the relative safety of a firm. We may expect that larger, more stable or more export-oriented firms will be less exposed to the retrenchment shock.

Borrower i's problem is to maximize,

$$U^{B,i} = 2\Delta L^{F,i} - l_0(L^{F,i}) - \phi p_i \times \beta(L^{F,i}(1 - e)) - \tau^{F,i}L^{F,i} + T \quad (15)$$

---

[5] This complementarity result is derived in a somewhat different setting by Jeanne (2016).

where we have allowed the tax rate to be borrower-specific, $\tau^{F,i}$. The FOC is,

$$l_0'(L^{F,i}) = 2\Delta - \phi p_i \times (1-e)\,\beta'\,(L^{F,i}(1-e)) - \tau^{F,i}$$

Aggregating across all the borrowers, accounting for the likelihood of retrenchment for borrower i given loan amount $L^{F,i}$, the equilibrium exchange rate is,

$$e = \frac{X^F}{L^F} \text{ where } \overline{L}^F = \int_i p_i L^{F,i}\,di \tag{16}$$

Next, consider the coordinated solution where we use an equal-weighting welfare function:

$$\overline{U}^B = \int_i U^{B,i}\,di \tag{17}$$

By differentiating with respect to an increase in borrower-i's loan amount, accounting for the effect on all other j through the exchange rate, we have that:

$$
\begin{aligned}
\frac{\partial \overline{U}^B}{\partial L^{F,i}} = &\left(2\Delta - l_0'(L^{F,i})\right) - \phi p_i \times (1-e)\beta'\,(L^{F,i}(1-e))) \\
&- \phi p_i \int_j \left(p_j e\beta'\,(L^{F,j}(1-e))\frac{L^{F,j}}{L^F}\right)dj
\end{aligned}
\tag{18}
$$

The second term on the right-hand side is the externality term. Increased borrowing by i puts pressure on the exchange rate in proportion to the borrower's retrenchment exposure p_i.

The optimal tax rate is chosen to equate the social and private margins. It is straightforward to derive that:

Proposition 3. (Borrowing taxes)

The optimal tax on borrower-i is,

$$\tau^{F,i} = \phi p^i \int_j \left(p_j e\beta'\,(L^{F,j}(1-e))\frac{L^{F,j}}{L^F}\right)dj \tag{19}$$

Note that the term in the integral in (19) is common across all borrowers. So, if we compare the optimal tax rate for two borrowers, i and i', we find

$$\frac{\tau^{F,i}}{\tau^{F,i'}} = \frac{p^i}{p^{i'}}$$

Finally, the tax rate expression (19) simplifies substantially for the special case of the model where the bankruptcy cost is linear, $\beta(z) = B \times z$. In this case,

$$\int_j \left(p_j e \beta' (L^{F,j}(1-e)) \frac{L^{F,j}}{L^F} \right) dj = \bar{p} e B$$

so that,

$$\tau^{F,i} = \phi p^i \times \bar{p} e B$$

which can be readily compared to (11) for the homogeneous borrower case. The optimal tax is proportional to the pressure caused by borrower-i times the increase in expected bankruptcy cost caused by the additional borrowing.

The central implication of this analysis is that, in general, capital flow taxes should be borrower-specific and depend on the fire sale externality imposed by a given borrower. In many cases, such contingency is hard to implement. But it is nevertheless the implication of the theory. Indeed, our analysis implies that, if taxes are set positive but uncontingent on borrower type, an across-firm distortion rises. High p^i borrowers will over-borrow, while low p^i borrowers will underborrow, all relative to the social optimum.

Domestic Loan Market

We return to the homogeneous borrower case but extend the model to introduce a domestic (rupee) loan/bond market at date 0. The market is for borrowing in local currency from either domestic or foreign lenders. Given our focus on foreign lending, we suppress domestic lenders, or alternatively can think of our modelling as net of the loans from domestic lenders. The date 0 cost of borrowing on domestic loans is $r^D > r$. The higher rate stems from the possibility of a currency depreciation, weaker legal protection in the domestic market, higher information requirements to ensure sound collateral and so on. As noted earlier, we fix the currency to be worth one at date 0 and in the non-retrenchment state. It may depreciate to $e < 1$ in the retrenchment state. Additionally, the cost for a foreign lender to participate in the local market is s, covering the collateral issues mentioned. Thus, the return to an external lender in the domestic bond market is,

$$(1 - \phi)(1 + r^D) + \phi(1 + r^D)e - s.$$

Since foreign lenders can either buy domestic bonds or foreign bonds by paying r, the domestic interest rate must satisfy:

$$r^D - r \approx s + \phi(1 - e) \tag{20}$$

The domestic spread reflects the cost of lending in the local market, s and the loss to foreign lenders due to the exchange rate depreciation in the sudden stop state. As noted, we set $r = 0$ so that the required return on domestic borrowing simplifies to $r^D = s + \phi(1 - e)$. A borrower who agrees to repay L^D at date 1 raises $\dfrac{L^D}{1 + s + \phi(1 - e)}$ at date 0.

We have described the rate r^D on borrowing at date 0. Next, consider date 1. We assume that in the roll over market at date 1, the cost of domestic borrowing is r rather than r^D. Although asymmetric, this latter assumption serves to simplify some algebraic expressions.

Foreign lenders can lend domestically or externally, and run at date 1 against either type of debt with probability φ. Define total borrowings as

$$K = L^F + \frac{L^D}{1 + s + \phi(1 - e)} \tag{21}$$

where L^F is external loans from foreign lenders and L^D is domestic loans from foreign lenders.

At date 1, if there is retrenchment shock, borrowers have to come up with L^F dollars to repay external debt. They raise $L^F(1-e)$ via domestic loans, and pay for the shortfall via the bankruptcy/adjustment costs of $\beta(\cdot)$.

In the domestic loan market, the retrenchment shock also leads to a need for funding. We assume (symmetrically with the case of external debt) that other domestic lenders are able to step in and roll over the borrower's debts. However, the foreign lenders receive their local funds of L^D and convert them into dollars since they need to retrench into dollars. This potentially depreciates the exchange rate:

$$e = \frac{X^F}{L^F + L^F} \text{ for } e < 1 \tag{22}$$

A larger outflow triggers a greater depreciation; and the central bank can intervene to reduce the depreciation by using foreign reserves of X^F. Note our symmetric treatment of foreign and domestic loans. Our model captures a sudden stop as a 'twin crisis' in the sense of Kaminsky and Reinhart (1999) and Chang and Velasco (2001). A domestic debt crisis triggers an outflow of capital which adds to a currency crisis.

Given e, the borrowers choose their investment and funding at date 0. They maximize,

$$U^B = 2\Delta L^F + (2\Delta - r^D)\frac{L^D}{1 + r^D} - l_0(K) - \phi \times \beta(L^F(1 - e))$$

The second term here reflects that when $r^D > 0$ domestic borrowing results in less profits than foreign borrowings.

For the analysis of this section we assume that that the bankruptcy cost is linear in its argument, that is, $\beta(x) = Bx$. Then,

$$U^B(L^F, L^D, e) = 2\Delta \left(L^F + \frac{L^D}{1 + r^D}\right) - l_0\left(L^F + \frac{L^D}{1 + r^D}\right)$$
$$- \phi \times B \times L^F - (1 - e) - (s + \phi(1 - e))\frac{L^D}{1 + r^D}$$

This expression highlights the key difference between domestic and foreign borrowings. External borrowing brings a potential bankruptcy cost of $B \times L^F(1-e)$. The *borrower* bears the retrenchment cost expost and accounts for it when making the ex-ante borrowing decision. Domestic borrowing avoids this cost but requires the higher *ex-ante* spread of $r^D = s + \phi(1-e)$. The *lender* bears the retrenchment cost ex-post, and charges for it ex ante by increasing the domestic spread. Next consider the central bank's objective.

$$W(L^F, L^D, X^F) = 2\Delta \left(L^F + \frac{L^D}{1 + r^D}\right) - l_0\left(L^F + \frac{L^D}{1 + r^D}\right)$$
$$- \phi \times B \times L^F(1 - e) - (s + \phi(1 - e))\frac{L^D}{1 + r^D} - \kappa(X^F) \tag{23}$$

We simplify this expression and the following algebra by assuming that r^D is relatively small so that we can take $\frac{1}{1 + r^D} \approx 1$. In this case, we rewrite the objective as

$$W(L^F, L^D, X^F) \approx 2\Delta(L^F + L^D) - l_0(L^F + L^D)$$
$$- \phi \times B \times L^F(1 - e) - (s + \phi(1 - e))L^D - \kappa(X^F) \tag{24}$$

The central bank chooses (L^F, L^D, X^F) to maximize $W(\cdot)$. Differentiating, we have that,

$$\frac{\partial w}{\partial L^F} = 2\Delta - l'_0(K) - \phi(1-e)B + \phi(L^D + BL^F)\frac{\partial e}{\partial L^F}$$

and,

$$\frac{\partial w}{\partial L^D} = 2\Delta - l'_0(K) - (s + \phi(1-e)) + \phi(L^D + BL^F)\frac{\partial e}{\partial L^D}$$

These two expressions give the marginal value of more domestic loans and foreign loans. Notice from (22) that $\frac{\partial e}{\partial L^D} = \frac{\partial e}{\partial L^F}$. That is, an extra unit of either domestic or foreign loans results in the same pressure on the exchange rate and hence has the same fire sale externality. This is because in the case of an extra unit of foreign loans, the borrower worsens the fire sale with the extra unit of loans. In the case of domestic loans, the lender worsens the fire sale with the extra unit of domestic loans. But the marginal fire sale impact does not depend on the denomination of the loan.[6] Then, the difference in these marginal values is,

$$\frac{\partial w}{\partial L^F} - \frac{\partial w}{\partial L^D} = s + \phi(1-e) - \phi(1-e)B.$$

Foreign borrowing is socially preferable if the domestic spread s is high and the bankruptcy costs B are low, otherwise domestic borrowing is preferred.

Next, consider implementation of the optimum. Suppose that the spread s is high so that foreign borrowing is preferred to domestic borrowing. How can the central bank implement the optimum via taxes? This case superficially appears similar to our early analysis. However, there is a key difference. Increasing taxes on foreign borrowing decreases aggregate borrowing, but also *shifts borrowing*

---

[6] In our formulation L^F and L^D appear symmetrically in equation (22). But it is also plausible that a unit of external borrowing applies more pressure on the exchange rate in the sudden-stop state. In this case, the external borrowing carries a higher externality than the domestic borrowing, analogous to our study of heterogeneity among borrowers. We set this effect aside because it is not central to our conclusions. For an analysis of the issue, see Caballero and Krishnamurthy (2003).

to domestic markets. To see this, let us write the borrower's objective with the foreign debt tax:

$$U^B(L^F, L^D, e) = 2\Delta(L^F + L^D) - l_0(L^F + L^D) - \phi \times B \times L^F(1-e)$$
$$- (s + \phi(1-e))L^D - \tau^F L^F \tag{25}$$

The derivative of U^B with respect to the two forms of borrowing are:

$$\frac{\partial U^B}{\partial L^F} = 2\Delta - l_0'(K) - \phi(1-e)B - \tau^F$$

and,

$$\frac{\partial U^B}{\partial L^D} = 2\Delta - l_0'(K) - (s + \phi(1-e))$$

As taxes, τ^F, increase, the borrower optimally chooses lower foreign borrowings L^F. However, if

$$\phi(1-e)B + \tau^F > s + \phi(1-e)$$

the borrower takes no external loans and shifts fully to domestic borrowing. At this point, the tax policy is completely ineffective.

We account for this substitution effect by placing an additional constraint on the central bank. The central bank maximizes (24) subject to a constraint on taxes:

$$\tau^F \leq s + \phi(1-e) - \phi(1-e)B \tag{26}$$

The final result of the analysis is that the tax constraint can be relaxed. Suppose that the central bank can also tax domestic borrowing. Then, the tax constraint becomes

$$\tau^F \leq \tau^D + s + \phi(1-e) - \phi(1-e)B \tag{27}$$

We highlight this result as:

Proposition 4. (Complementarity between policy instruments II)

Domestic-borrowing taxes, external-borrowing taxes and holdings of foreign reserves are complimentary policy tools. With the ability to level a tax on domestic borrowing, the central bank can decrease aggregate borrowing without distorting the balance between foreign and domestic borrowing, which results in a higher welfare for the economy.

Section 3

Macroprudential Measures Deployed in India

India has deployed a range of macroprudential measures to contain the impact of sudden stops and reversals of foreign capital flows, and the concomitant shocks to the financial and real sector. Many of these measures had been in place prior to the taper tantrum; however, the taper tantrum led to a further revision of their nature, as explained below. In this section, we discuss these measures through the lens of our theoretical model of optimal capital controls.

India has three principal kinds of external debt once various forms of government debt from multilateral agencies, as well as non-resident Indian deposits, are excluded (the latter have usually been a source of stability for India during stress episodes): FPI in domestic debt (in both G-Secs at the central and state level, as well as corporate bonds); ECB, which are typically loans to Indian corporations, quasi-government entities or private firms, denominated in foreign currency; and, introduced most recently, the rupee-denominated bonds (RDB) or 'Masala bonds' issued overseas, again by quasi-government entities or private firms, typically listed on the London Stock Exchange.

Net investments (stock in Panel A, flow in Panel B) in these various segments of external debt are plotted over time in Figure 14.8. The ECB contributed to the bulk of such external debt flows until the taper tantrum, after which time the FPI debt flows have overtaken as the most significant component. It is also worth pointing out the growth in Masala bonds in 2017 as ECB borrowings fall. This switch in the nature of external debt is also reflected in Table 14.2 which shows that the foreign-currency-denominated external debt has steadily declined since 2014 while the INR-denominated component has grown. We will discuss this substitution pattern in terms of Proposition 4.

Macroprudential capital controls with regard to these different forms of external debt are briefly explained below, placing the various controls into broad categories so as to interpret them in terms of our model's normative implications:

(A) Debt Stock

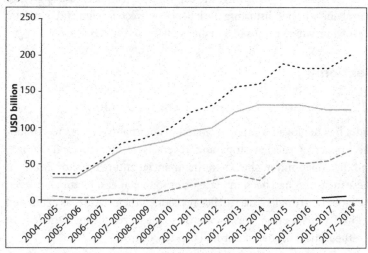

(B) Debt Flows

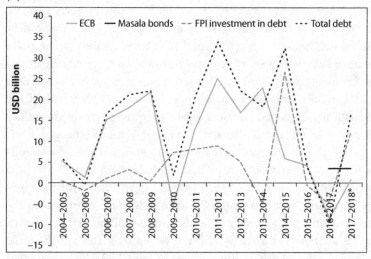

Figure 14.8. Debt Stock and Flows

Source: RBI, NSDL and SEBI.
Note: * Updated until October 2017.

Caps on Exposure to Global Shocks

These are presently in the form of absolute size limits on (a) total FPI in domestic securities by asset class, with separate limits for G-Secs,

Table 14.2. Currency Composition of External Debt (%), End of March

Currency	Year						
	2011	2012	2013	2014	2015	2016 (PR)	2017 (QE)
1 US Dollar	55.3%	56.9	59.1	61.1	58.3	57.1	52.1
2 Indian Rupee	18.8	20.5	22.9	21.8	27.8	28.9	33.6
3 SDR	9.4	8.3	7.2	6.8	5.8	5.8	5.8
4 Japanese Yen	10.9	8.7	6.1	5.0	4.0	4.4	4.6
5 Euro	3.6	3.7	3.4	3.3	2.3	2.5	2.9
6 Pound Sterling	1.6	0.9	0.7	1.1	0.9	0.8	0.6
7 Others	0.4	1.0	0.6	0.9	0.9	0.5	0.4
Total (1 to 7)	100.0%	100.0	100.0	100.0	100.0	100.0	100.0

Source: Based on data from RBI, CAAA, SEBI and Ministry of Defence.
Notes: PR—partially revised; QE—quick estimate.

SDLs and corporate bonds, amounting to around $39 billion, $6 billion and $36 billion, respectively, or a total of about $80 billion across the three asset categories; and on (b) ECBs and Masala bonds together, amounting to a total of about $130 billion.

From the standpoint of our model, the aggregate short-term external liability that cannot be rolled over relative to the forex reserves of the country is what matters for macroeconomic outcomes in the sudden stop state. Moreover, the complementarity perspective of our model indicates that borrowing limits should be closely tied to the central bank's holdings of foreign reserves.

In practice, the limits discussed have either been set as a percentage of the underlying market size (as in the case of the G-sec and SDL limits), or set as an absolute number (as in the case of corporate debt limits). In both cases, roll-out of the limits has been calibrated over quarters, that is, gradually, presumably based on considerations outside of our model such as implications of capital inflows on the exchange rate. Our analysis suggests that optimal limits should depend on 'stocks' of debt rather than 'flows'. They should also be contingent on central bank reserve holdings.

That being said, there are several aspects to these limits which conform to the model's implications. In particular, there are limits by investor and by borrower-or issuer-type, as well as restrictions on the nature of the debt. These aspects have evolved over time given

India's experience with external sector vulnerability. We discuss these aspects next.

Restrictions on Investors by Heir Horizon of Investment

Within FPI limits for G-sec, SDLs and corporate bonds, there are sub-limits by investor type as shown in Table 14.3, in particular, for 'long term' versus 'general' investors, where long-term category includes insurance firms, endowments and pension funds, sovereign wealth funds, central banks and multilateral agencies; whereas general category covers all other qualified institutional investors. The long-term category has been added to the corporate bonds limit only since October 2017. Prior to July 2017, the unutilized portion of the long-term category was transferred to the general category, a feature that has since been removed.

These investor-specific investment restrictions can be understood in terms of Proposition 3. We showed that limits should be type-dependent, where type referred to the borrower. By extension, it follows that limits should optimally depend on investor horizon to the extent that the immediacy demanded by short-term investors (typically carry traders) creates a fire sale externality in the sudden stop state. There is no obvious rationale within our model, however, for the transfer of unutilized long-term limits to short-term investors, as this would over time increase the short-term investor limit towards the overall limit, as indeed has been the case for India.

Table 14.3. Foreign Portfolio Investment (FPI) Limits (USD Billion)

Central Government Securities				State Development Loans		
Effective for Quarter	General	Long Term	Total	General	Long Term	Total
2017–2018 Q3	29.29	9.31	38.60	4.63	1.44	6.07
Corporate Bonds						
Effective for Quarter	Long-Term FPIs Infrastructure	General	Total			
2017–2018 Q3	1.47	33.64	35.10			

Source: RBI, DBIE.

Interestingly, FPI restrictions in the past also included sub-limits for 100 per cent debt funds as against minimum 70:30 equity-debt investment ratio funds. In addition, there were minimum lock-in periods of up to three years on investors once they purchased Indian debt securities. While such restrictions would also find support under our model as ways to limit the type of short-term external debt, these have over time been replaced entirely by investor categories based on horizon (long-term vs general) and minimum maturity restrictions (which we explain below).

Counter to our theoretical analysis, long-term investors such as pension funds, insurance companies and sovereign wealth funds were not allowed by India to be eligible lenders in external commercial borrowings (ECBs) until 2015. There is, however, an indirect policy attempt to ensure that the sudden stop risk does not directly affect the domestic banks (who have significant deposit liabilities), a feature that our model would support. This is achieved by disallowing the refinancing of ECBs by Indian banks as well as preventing the underlying ECB exposure to be guaranteed by Indian banks, financial institutions or NBFCs.[7]

Restrictions on Maturity of the Underlying Investment

Presently, FPIs are disallowed altogether from investing in liquid short-term money-market debt instruments such as T-bills or commercial paper (CP). Prior to the taper tantrum however (November 2013 to be precise), there was a carve-out for FPI investments in T-bills and CP, as shown in Table 14.4. Since the taper tantrum, India has introduced even tighter restrictions in the form of residual maturity restrictions of investments by FPIs in debt holdings to be of minimum three years of maturity at origination or purchase. If one assumes that the arrival of the sudden stop state is exogenous, as in our model, then these restrictions are potentially effective ways of limiting short-term external debt in case such a state materializes.[8]

---

[7] These restrictions on domestic financial institutions were in part also to avoid the ever-greening of non-performing loans.

[8] Another possible rationale for requiring FPIs to hold longer-dated instruments is that it exposes them to greater interest-rate risk, which could deter excessive presence of short-term investors looking for 'carry' by arbitraging interest-rate differentials with an early exit.

Table 14.4. Debt Investment Restrictions

Type of Securities	April 2013 $ bn	Jun 2013 $ bn	Nov 2013 $ bn
1. Government debt	25	30	30
a. T-bills within overall limit	5.5	5.5	5.5
b. Carved out limit for SWFs & other LT FIIs	–	5	5
2. Corporate bond	51	51	51
a. CPs within overall limit	3.5	3.5	3.5
b. Credit enhancement bonds within overall limit	–	–	5
3. Total limit (1+2)	76	81	81

Source: DBIE, RBI.

A similar rationale for limiting the maturity of underlying external debt also exists for ECBs. Following the taper tantrum, policies were revised in November 2015 to require that a borrower could undertake an ECB of up to $50 million (foreign-currency-denominated under the so-called Track-I of ECB, or INR-denominated under Track-III of ECB) with minimum average maturity of three years; or up to $50 million if the maturity is five years. In contrast, no borrowing limit within the overall ECB limit is imposed for borrowings meeting a minimum average maturity of 10 years (for foreign-currency-denominated borrowing under Track-II of ECB). These maturity restrictions were not as onerous prior to the taper tantrum.

Restricting High-Liquidity Demanders

Our model suggests a Pigouvian form of taxation, wherein borrowers who contribute more to the fire sale externality in the sudden stop state are charged a greater tax for taking on short-term external debt (see Proposition 3). Indian capital controls ensure that only relatively high credit quality borrowers tap into ECBs by (a) imposing coupon ceilings by debt issue, (b) carving out sub-limits on investments in risky instruments such as unlisted corporate bonds and security receipts (a form of distressed asset resolution instrument) and (c) ruling out excessive correlated liquidations by having investment sub-limits by sector. These restrictions limit ECBs to high-rated borrowers as suggested by our model. However, this form of differential taxation

Table 14.5. Evolution of All-in-Cost (AIC) Spread (in bps) over Libor-6 Month/Swap

Minimum Average Maturity	3–5 Year (bps)	More than 5 Year
2004–2005	200	350
2007–2008	150	250
2008–2009	200	350
2009–2010	300	500
2011–2012	350	500
2015–2016	300	450

Source: DBIE, RBI.

does not exist for domestic debt issuances purchased by the FPIs, except to the extent that the current market-practice in the domestic corporate debt market is to fund only relatively high-rated investment-grade borrowers.

Closest to the model are the all-in-cost (AIC) issuance cost ceilings for ECBs, which prescribe that borrowers in three-to five-year range cannot issue ECBs at a coupon of six-month LIBOR+ ceiling as indicated in Table 14.5. A higher ceiling applies for issuances greater than five-year maturity. These ceilings have evolved over time in a somewhat counter-cyclical manner relative to the evolution of six-month LIBOR (Figure 14.9): as global interest rates eased post the global financial crisis, the coupon ceilings were raised, and with global rates tightening since 2015, the ceilings were lowered.

Regulatory Arbitrage between Domestic and Overseas External Debt

India permitted ECB borrowings denominated in rupees (Track III) in September 2014. For macroprudential reasons and as ECBs were envisioned as bilateral loan arrangements, they faced various tenor and AIC constraints, end-use requirements, eligibility requirements on borrowers and lenders, and the like, as explained earlier. Borrowings under Track III were, however, not subject to cost caps that applied to other ECBs, as the borrowing was considered as not subject to exchange rate risk. It is unclear as per our model if this is necessarily the correct distinction since there is still the sudden stop risk on roll over of rupee-denominated ECBs. Nevertheless, the scope of eligible borrowers and lenders remained similarly restrictive as for dollar ECBs.

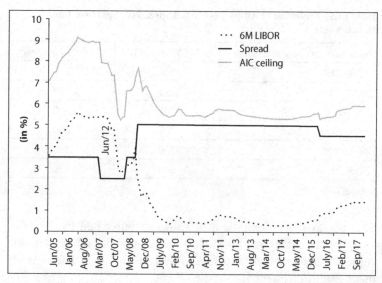

Figure 14.9. All-in-Cost for External Commercial Borrowings (ECBs) with 5-Year Minimum Maturity

Source: RBI.

To widen the international investor base for corporates, an additional route of RDB or Masala bonds, was introduced in September 2015. Since these were intended to be bonds issued under market discipline, they were subjected to a more relaxed regulatory regime. Most important of these is the much wider scope of eligible borrowers (any corporate or body corporate including real estate investment trusts or REITs and infrastructure investment trusts or InvITs), eligible investors (any investor from FATF-compliant jurisdictions), and end-use (no restrictions except for a small negative list). Masala bonds also had an advantage vis-à-vis the FPI route in domestic bonds insofar as investors in Masala bonds did not have to register in India and the bonds were issued in international finance centres such as London with well-established financial and legal infrastructure. Further, there was no listing requirement for Masala bonds. FPI investments were subsequently allowed in unlisted instruments, but were subjected to a cap.

As noted, at the inception of this market, Masala bonds were viewed by regulators as bond-market borrowings similar to other FPI investments. They received a liberal regulatory treatment under the presumption that these bonds would have transparent pricing and other forms of market discipline. In actual practice, many Masala bonds issuances were essentially bilateral loans issued as bonds, often to related entities. Coupon rates in many instances had no linkage with market-borrowing rates and varied from extremely low rates (related party transactions to circumvent ECB and FDI restrictions) to high rates (to circumvent the AIC ceilings under the ECB route). Complicated structures using Masala bonds were also used to bypass ECB cost caps. The overall evidence from issuances suggested that many entities were exploiting the relaxed regulatory treatment of Masala bonds to bypass ECB norms on bilateral funding arrangements.

Recognizing this regulatory arbitrage between ECB and Masala bonds and recognizing that both were vulnerable to sudden stops because the source of capital was foreign creditors, India chose to harmonize their regulations. In June 2017, the RBI prescribed cost caps (treasury yield + 300 bps) as well as minimum maturity period for Masala bonds (3 or 5 years, depending on the issue size). The minimum maturity period also harmonized the Masala bond investments by foreign creditors to the restrictions on FPI in domestically issued debt. Masala bonds were also not allowed to be issued to related entities. Such harmonization, and the observed regulatory arbitrage by issuers and investors in the pre-harmonization period, reinforces the importance of setting capital flow management policy based on the entirety of an EM's tools.

Conclusion

We have analyzed the macroprudential use of reserves and capital controls to manage sudden stops in EMs. Our principal conclusion is that these tools are complements. Hoarding reserves is beneficial against sudden stops but creates incentives for the private sector to undo the insurance offered by reserve holdings. In this context, limits on borrowing increase the efficacy of reserve holdings. Our complementarity perspective also implies that the optimal holding of reserves depends on the set of policy instruments available to affect private borrowings. Optimal reserve holdings are increasing in the efficacy of such instruments.

In his classic analysis of policy instruments, Poole (1970) studies the use of the money supply and interest rate as instruments to stabilize output. In his baseline, both money supply and interest rate are equally effective instruments: they are substitutes. This leads to the result that either can be used as instrument. He then considers the case where there is some slippage in the transmission mechanism that varies across the instruments. In this case, he shows that the low-slippage instrument should be used more, while the high-slippage instrument should be used less, to stabilize output.

The complementarity logic for managing capital flows turns this result around. We show that the efficacy of one instrument (reserves) depends on the use of the other (capital flow taxes). Then, as the slippage in one instrument falls, both instruments should be used more, rather than just the low-slippage instrument.

Where does this end? We have studied three instruments, but what if there were 50 instruments available to the central bank, some of which were more effective than others? Should the central bank use all 50 of these instruments? Should it use some more than others? Suppose that the central bank is only able to use three out of the 50 instruments; either implementation challenges or slippage issues in the other instruments render them unusable. Our perspective implies that it should use less of the three instruments than in the case where all instruments are used. Complementarity implies that the marginal effectiveness of an instrument is increasing in the use of others. This is the main lesson from our analysis.

References

Acharya, Viral V., and Krishnamurthy A. 2019. 'Capital Flow Management with Multiple Instruments.' In *Monetary Policy and Financial Stability: Transmission Mechanisms and Policy Implications, Edition 1*, edited by Álvaro Aguirre and Markus Brunnermeier and Diego Saravia, 169–203. Santiago: Central Bank of Chile.

Aizenman, J. 2011. 'Hoarding International Reserves versus a Pigovian Tax-cum-subsidy Scheme: Reflections on the Deleveraging Crisis of 2008–2009, and a Cost Benefit Analysis'. *Journal of Economic Dynamics and Control* 35, no. 9: 1502–1513.

Aizenman, J., and N. Marion. 2003. 'The High Demand for International Reserves in the Far East: What Is Going On?' *Journal of the Japanese and International Economies*, 17, no. 3: 370–400.

Caballero, R. J., and A. Krishnamurthy. 2001. 'International and Domestic Collateral Constraints in a Model of Emerging Market Crises'. *Journal of Monetary Economics* 48, no. 3: 513–548.

———. 2003. 'Excessive Dollar Debt: Financial Development and Underinsurance'. *Journal of Finance* 58, no. 2: 867–893.

Caballero, R. J., and A. Krishnamurthy. 2004. 'Smoothing Sudden Stops'. *Journal of Economic Theory* 119, no. 1: 104–127.

Caballero, R. J., and A. Simsek. 2016. 'A Model of Fickle Capital Flows and Retrenchment'. Technical Report, National Bureau of Economic Research.

Calvo, G. A., L. Leiderman, and C. M. Reinhart. 1996. 'Inflows of Capital to Developing Countries in the 1990s'. *Journal of Economic Perspectives* 10, no. 2: 123–139.

Carstens, A. 2016. 'Overview Panel: The Case for Emerging Market Economies'. *Proceedings, Economic Policy Symposium, Jackson Hole* 1–65.

Chang, R., and A. Velasco. 2001. 'A Model of Financial Crises in Emerging Markets'. *Quarterly Journal of Economics* 116, no. 2: 489–517.

De Gregorio, J. 2010. 'Tackling the Capital Inflow Challenge'. Economic Policy Papers. Central Bank of Chile.

Greenspan, A. 1999. 'Currency Reserves and Debt'. Speech, World Bank Conference on Recent Trends in Reserves Management, Washington, DC, April 29, 1999.

Jeanne, J., and A. Korinek. 2010. 'Excessive Volatility in Capital Flows: A Pigouvian Taxation Approach'. *American Economic Review* 100, no. 2: 403–407.

Jeanne, O., and R. Rancière. 2011. 'The Optimal Level of International Reserves for Emerging Market Countries: A New Formula and Some Applications'. *Economic Journal* 121, no.555: 905–930.

Jeanne, O. 2016. 'The Macroprudential Role of International Reserves'. *American Economic Review* 106, no. 5: 570–573.

Kaminsky, G. L., and C. M. Reinhart. 1999. 'The Twin Crises: The Causes of Banking and Balance-of-Payments Problems'. *American Economic Review*, 473–500.

Krishnamurthy, A., and A. Vissing-Jorgensen. 2013. 'The Ins and Outs of LSAPs'. *Proceedings, Economic Policy Symposium, Jackson Hole.*

Obstfeld, M., J. C. Shambaugh, and A. M. Taylor. 2010. 'Financial Stability, the Trilemma, and International Reserves'. *American Economic Journal: Macroeconomics* 2, no. 2: 57–94.

Ostry, J. D., A. R. Ghosh, K. F. Habermeier, M. Chamon, M. S. Qureshi, and D. B. S. Reinhardt. 2010. 'Capital Inflows; the Role of Controls'. IMF Staff Position Notes 2010/04. International Monetary Fund.

Poole, W. 1970. 'Optimal Choice of Monetary Policy Instruments in a Simple Stochastic Macro Model'. *Quarterly Journal of Economics* 84, no. 2: 197–216.

Rey, H. 2013. 'Dilemma Not Trilemma: The Global Cycle and Monetary Policy Independence'. *Proceedings, Economic Policy Symposium, Jackson Hole*, 1–2.

CHAPTER 15

DEVELOPMENT OF VIABLE CAPITAL MARKETS: THE INDIAN EXPERIENCE*

Capital markets play a crucial role in the economic development of a country. They provide financial resources required for the long-term sustainable development of the economy. Development of viable capital markets is, therefore, considered an important element in the macro-financial policy toolkit, including for objectives such as financial stability and the transmission of monetary policy.

The Committee on Global Financial System (CGFS), which meets at the Bank for International Settlements (BIS), constituted a working group to examine global trends in capital market development, identify various factors (legal, institutional, structural and conjunctural) that foster the development of robust capital markets and consider the role of policy including prudential measures. The working group, co-chaired by the People's Bank of China (PBOC; Dr Li Bo) and the RBI (Dr Viral V. Acharya), focused on issues primarily related to the development of markets in bond and equity securities.[1] While these issues are arguably of greater relevance to emerging market economies, they were found to be of significant interest even for advanced economies.

---

*Speech delivered at a conference at the Indian School of Business, Hyderabad on 29 June 2019.These remarks collectively summarize the presentations made earlier at the RBI symposium on Establishing Viable Capital Markets, 29 May 2019; the Institute for Indian Economic Studies (IIES), Tokyo, Japan, 10 June 2019; the meeting with FPIs, Tokyo, Japan, 11 June 2019; the National University of Singapore (NUS) Asian Leaders in Financial Institutions (ALFI) Programme, Bengaluru, 20 June 2019, and Fireside Chat at the Indian School of Business, Hyderabad, 29 June 2019.
[1] The Report was delivered to the CGFS at the BIS meeting on 23 January 2019 and is available at https://www.bis.org/publ/cgfs62.pdf

The *CGFS Report* identified the 'drivers' of capital market development and categorized them into two types:

1. Drivers which create an 'enabling environment' for financial development include:
    *   Macroeconomic stability
    *   Broad respect for market autonomy
    *   Fair and efficient legal and judicial systems
    *   An efficient regulatory regime that creates conditions favourable for financial contracts.

2. Drivers which are 'capital market specific' include:
    *   Easy access to high-quality material information
    *   Diversity in the investor base
    *   Efficient market ecosystem for trading and robust market infrastructures
    *   Openness towards international investors while maintaining macroeconomic stability
    *   Markets for hedging and funding securities.

The *CGFS Report* made six broad 'policy recommendations':

1. Promoting greater market autonomy
2. Strengthening legal and judicial systems for investor protection
3. Enhancing regulatory independence and effectiveness
4. Increasing the depth and diversity of the domestic institutional investor base
5. Opening up capital markets internationally in a bidirectional manner
6. Developing complementary markets for derivatives, repo transactions and securities lending.

Policy initiatives in India have been largely in sync with the findings and recommendations of the *CGFS Report*. I shall discuss these and future policy directions after providing a brief overview of the Indian capital markets. While the scope of the *CGFS Report* is the entire capital market, I will largely confine this speech to the markets regulated by the RBI, namely interest rate markets and (to a lesser extent) foreign exchange markets.

Overview of the Indian Capital Markets

Indian capital markets have a history of more than a century. However, they remained largely inactive till the 1970s. Partial liberalization of the economy and pro-capital market policies during the 1980s infused some life into the markets, but it was only the economic liberalization of the 1990s that provided a lasting impetus. Today, segments of India's capital markets are comparable with counterparts in many of the advanced economies in terms of efficiency (price discovery), tradability (low impact cost), resilience (co-movement of rates across product classes and yield curves) and stability. In particular, their ability to withstand several periods of stress, notably the Asian financial crisis in 1997–1998, the global financial crisis in 2007–2009 and the 'taper tantrum' episode in 2013, is a sign of their increasing maturity.

In terms of 'size', all the major segments of the capital market, namely the Central Government securities (G-Sec) market, market for State Development Loans (SDL), corporate bond market and equity market—the so-called 'cash markets'—have experienced consistent growth during the past few decades in terms of primary issuance, market capitalization (for equity market) and trading volumes in the secondary market. Equity market remains the largest segment, even as G-Sec, SDL and corporate bond markets have grown steadily (Figure 15.1).

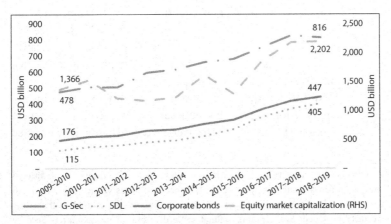

Figure 15.1. Growth in Outstanding Stock of the Indian Capital Markets
Source: RBI and SEBI.

1. **Growth of the G-Sec market:** A streamlined, transparent and market-based primary issuance process has underpinned the development of the G-Secs markets, both central G-Secs and SDLs. In the primary G-Sec markets, issuances are made as per a half-yearly pre-announced calendar. The calendar specifies the amount, tenor and issuance dates. The tenor of the G-Secs goes up to 40 years. G-Secs are mostly fixed-coupon bonds, although instruments such as inflation-linked bonds, capital-indexed bonds, floating-rate bonds and bonds with embedded options are also issued. Currently, all issuances are done through weekly auctions. Issuances are supported by primary dealers (PDs) who fully underwrite the issue. Auctions are conducted through both competitive bidding (for all residents, FPIs and non-resident Indians [NRIs]) and non-competitive bidding (for retail investors, largely). More than 90 per cent of the issuances are done through reopening of existing securities which has contributed significantly to market liquidity by spreading out ownership across a large number of investors. The RBI has also introduced 'when issued' segment for the G-Sec market since 2006.[2]

   The profile of both G-Secs and SDLs in terms of stock and flow characteristics is shown in Tables 15.1 and 15.2. The weighted average coupon on G-Secs has remained stable across interest-rate cycles imparting stability to the debt profile as the average maturity of issuance (more than 10 years) is one of the longest, globally, helping limit, the rollover risk, for the central government. SDL issuance has increasingly formed a much greater share of issuance relative to the G-Secs, increasing from around 25 per cent of issuance in 2013–2014 to around 45 per cent in 2017–2018.

2. **Liquidity of the G-Sec market:** Liquidity in the secondary market for G-Secs has noticeably improved over the past decade (Figure 15.2). The average daily volume in the G-Sec

---

[2] 'When issued', a short form of 'when, as and if issued', indicates a conditional transaction in a security authorized for issuance but not as yet actually issued. All 'when issued' transactions are on an 'if' basis, to be settled if and when the actual security is issued. Such trading facilitates the distribution process for G-Secs by stretching the actual distribution period for each issue and allowing the market more time to absorb large issues without disruption.

Table 15.1. Characteristics of Central G-Secs

Year	Issued during the Year		Outstanding Stock	
	Weighted Average Yield (%)	Weighted Average Maturity (Years)	Weighted Average Coupon (%)	Weighted Average Maturity (Years)
2013–2014	8.4	14.2	8.0	10.0
2014–2015	8.5	14.7	8.1	10.2
2015–2016	7.9	16.0	8.1	10.5
2016–2017	7.2	14.8	8.0	10.7
2017–2018	7.0	15.0	8.0	10.7
2018–2019	7.8	14.7	7.8	10.4

Source: Annual Report of RBI (2017–2018) and DBIE, RBI.

Table 15.2. Issuance Profile of Government Borrowings (in US $ Billion)

Year	Central G-Secs		State Governments SDLs	
	Gross Issuance	Outstanding Stock at (End-March)	Gross Issuance	Outstanding Stock at (End-March)
2013–2014	90	609	31	174
2014–2015	91	648	36	199
2015–2016	85	674	41	243
2016–2017	80	754	56	321
2017–2018	91	795	63	346
2018–2019	83	837	70	404

Source: DBIE, RBI.

and SDL markets has remained higher than that of corporate bond and equity cash markets. The liquidity in G-Secs is, however, mainly concentrated in a few benchmark securities, particularly the 10-year benchmark, and SDLs are relatively less liquid than the G-Secs, yielding typically 50–75 bps more than the G-Secs in terms of yield at the 10-year tenor. The average bid-ask spread for liquid securities in the G-Sec market has remained less than a basis point during the last few years (Figure 15.3). Strikingly, bid-ask spread as well as

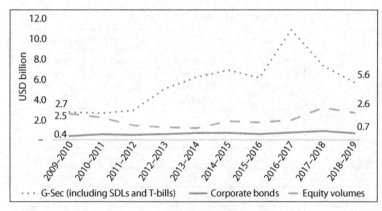

Figure 15.2. Secondary Market Liquidity in Terms of Average Daily Volume
Source: Clearing Corporation of India Limited (CCIL) and SEBI.

the price impact of trade for the 10-year Indian G-Sec benchmark are comparable to or lower than those for most of the advanced economies of the world including the USA, the United Kingdom, France and Germany (Figure 15.4).

There are several proximate drivers for this liquidity in the Indian G-Sec market:

a. Regular issuance of the 10-year benchmark has concentrated trading interest in this segment of the yield curve. Efforts are now being made to regularize issuance of benchmark securities at shorter maturities (2 and 5 years).

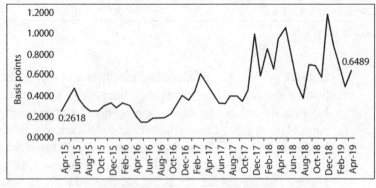

Figure 15.3. Average Bid-Ask Spread for Liquid Government Securities
Source: CCIL.

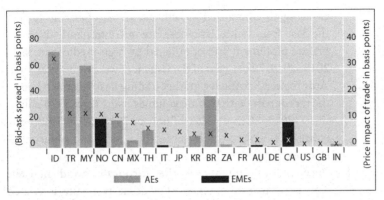

Figure 15.4. Ten-Year Benchmark G-Sec Liquidity in Different Countries

Source: Establishing Viable Capital Markets, CGFS Papers No 62.
Notes:
[1] Average of daily bid-ask spreads in May 2018, defined as: (ask price − bid price)/bid price × 100, i.e., the return cost of executing a round-trip transaction in the bond.
[2] Based on $10 million transaction amount using estimates from the Bloomberg Liquidity Assessment (LQA) function, June 2018.

b. Secondary market transactions are predominantly (around 80%) conducted in an anonymous electronic negotiated dealing system-order matching (NDS-OM) system which is unique in the world for debt trading. While the remaining transactions happen over the counter (OTC) outside the NDS-OM, they are nevertheless reported to the NDS-OM platform.

c. Near real-time dissemination of trade information publicly accessible on the website of the CCIL ensures price transparency.

d. Settlement is guaranteed by the CCIL and takes place through delivery versus payment (DvP) mechanism on T + 1 basis. Guaranteed settlement implies that there is no risk of delivery failures to investors from each other.

e. Finally, enabling of short selling facilitates a two-way interest adding to activity and price discovery in the market.

3. **Growth and liquidity in the corporate bond market:** The corporate bond market has grown over the years to a size of $447 billion of outstanding stock as at the end of March 2019,

clocking an annualized growth rate of 13.5 per cent during the last four years. Issuances are predominantly through private placement and dominated by high-credit issuers. In 2018–2019, 79 per cent of the issuances were by entities rated 'A' or higher. Secondary market trading has also picked up in the recent past, with trading volumes rising from $170 billion in FY 2014–2015 to $267 billion in 2018–2019. Trading is entirely OTC with trades settled bilaterally and reported to stock exchanges.

4. **Recent developments in the corporate bond market:** Consistent investment interest by domestic institutions such as mutual funds, pension funds and insurance funds as well as FPIs has helped in developing the corporate bond market. Tri-party repo ('sale and repurchase') in corporate bonds has been introduced by the exchanges recently with a view to encourage trading interest. Implementation of the IBC starting December 2016 is expected to go a long way in improving participation in the corporate bond market by strengthening the protection of creditor rights, in a market presently characterized by one of the lowest recovery rates (25%) in the world (Figure 15.5). With greater confidence in

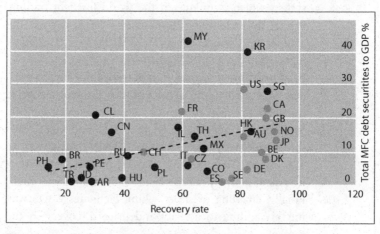

Figure 15.5. Corporate Bond Market Size and Recovery Rate

Source: Establishing Viable Capital Markets, CGFS Papers No 62.
Notes: Recovery rate in cents on the dollar from the World Bank Doing Business database.
NFC = Non-financial corporate.

time-bound and efficient resolutions under the IBC, foreign investors are likely to explore investment in sub-investment grade and distressed corporate assets.

a. **Investor base:** There has been a conscious and continuous effort by the RBI to expand the investor base and thereby liquidity of the markets it regulates, while preserving financial stability. The investor base for G-Secs, for instance, has expanded over the past decade in terms of an increase in the share of holdings by insurance companies and corporates and a corresponding decrease in the share of holding by commercial banks (Figure 15.6). In parallel, calibrated access for global investors through the FPI route is helping broaden the investor base, while also bringing in diversity of trading views and strategies.

b. **Funding and derivatives markets:** A necessary condition for the development of capital markets is the existence of funding and securities lending markets as well as derivative markets for risk transfer. Repo funding in Indian G-Secs is fairly deep with average daily volume of about $20 billion (Figure 15.7). In case of interest rate derivatives, there is reasonable liquidity in IRF and OIS markets.[3] Much of the recent increase in activity can be attributed to the RBI allowing non-residents to participate in interest rate derivatives markets for both hedging and trading purposes.

Policy Initiatives in India

I will now discuss the policy measures taken in India vis-à-vis the findings and recommendations of the *CGFS Report*.

1. **Enabling environment**

a. **Macroeconomic stability:** India's GDP growth has been one of the highest among large economies during the last decade and half (Figure 15.8). Double digit inflation of few years prior to the 'taper tantrum' episode has been

---

[3] An OIS is an IRS agreement where a fixed rate is swapped against a pre-determined published index of a daily overnight reference rate for an agreed period.

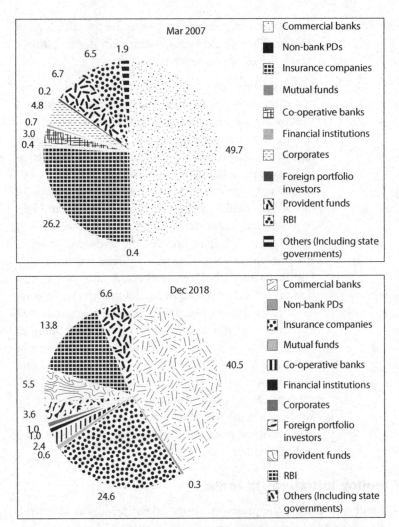

Figure 15.6. Holding Pattern for G-Secs (% Held by Each Investor Group)
Source: DBIE, RBI.

tamed, facilitated by a shift by the RBI in 2016 to flexible inflation targeting with a headline target of 4 per cent (+/– 2%) for the MPC. High levels of inflation make holdings of financial assets economically unattractive relative to non-financial assets such as housing and gold. The important reform of flexible inflation targeting, helped by low oil prices and food-supply management,

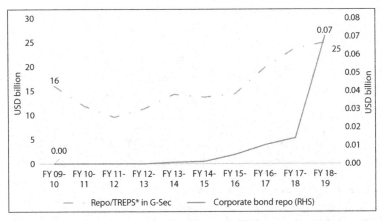

Figure 15.7. Average Daily Volume in G-Sec and Corporate Bond Repo

Source: CCIL.
Notes: * Tri-party Repo System (TREPS). Tri-party repo in G-Secs went live on 05 November 2018. Currently, the CCIL acts as the 'tri-party agent' for the G-Secs, while the Bombay Stock Exchange (BSE) and the National Stock Exchange (NSE) operate as tri-party agents for corporate bonds.

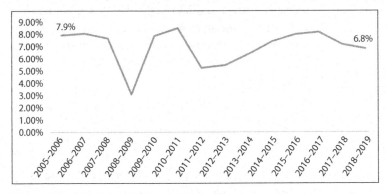

Figure 15.8. Trends in GDP Growth in India

Source: DBIE, RBI.
Note: GDP at constant prices with base year 2011–2012.

has kept the headline inflation under control during the last five years, relative to the MPC's mandated target (Figure 15.9). This way, two preconditions of macro-economic stability—stable growth and low inflation—necessary for financialization of savings and capital market development are now in place in India.

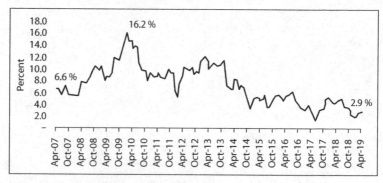

Figure 15.9. Trends in Inflation in India

Source: DBIE, RBI.
Notes: Data till April 2014 is based on industrial worker, general index with base year 2001 and thereafter new CPI, combined with 2012 as the base year.

2. Promoting market autonomy

    a. **Rationalizing regulatory guidelines and procedures**: In active coordination with the government and other financial market regulators, the RBI has undertaken a series of reforms and rationalization of existing policies. These measures also seek to ensure financial stability and instil confidence among stakeholders. Some important examples include:

        i. Liberalizing the process for innovation of new products.

        ii. Moving away from a prescriptive approach to a principle-based regulatory approach.

        iii. Minimizing interference in the market process by eschewing ad-hoc 'approvals'.

        iv. Attempting to achieve comprehensive market regulations by addressing gaps, in particular, by issuing market abuse regulations and benchmark regulations, as well as regulating trading platforms.

    b. **Development of financial market institutions and infrastructure**: A well-developed and reliable infrastructure is a prerequisite for safe and efficient functioning of financial markets. Acknowledging this principle, the RBI has taken several steps to put in place an effective infrastructure in the markets it regulates, the salient steps being:

i. Introduction of an anonymous trading platform for G-Sec called the NDS-OM.

ii. Introduction of Legal Entity Identifier (LEI) code for OTC derivatives markets as well as non-derivatives markets.

iii. Development of a foreign exchange trading platform ('FX-Retail') aimed at bringing down transactions costs for retail users (August 2019).

iv. Constituting an independent financial benchmark administrator, namely, the Financial Benchmarks of India Ltd. (FBIL).

c. **Macroprudential management of investment restrictions for domestic and foreign investors:** It has been a constant endeavour of the RBI to rationalize, and wherever consistent with macroprudential objectives, to relax restrictions in the form of investment limits imposed on the market participants:

i. The RBI has reduced the SLR stipulation on the minimum percentage of net demand and time liabilities (NDTL) to be held in G-Secs and SDLs by banks in a calibrated way (Figure 15.10) from close to 40 per cent in 1990 to below 20 per cent at present. This important relaxation has resulted in a greater flexibility for banks in their investment decisions and added to the diversity of investor base in G-Secs and SDLs (Figure 15.6)—which, in turn, have aided efficient pricing of these bonds.

ii. The RBI has been calibrating access for FPIs in debt markets to provide them greater latitude in managing their portfolios in terms of increased FPI investment limits (Figures 15.11 and 15.12) as well as expanded eligibility of instruments and tenor for FPI investments.

iii. Recently, the RBI has introduced the voluntary retention route (VRR) scheme to relax the macroprudential restrictions for FPIs that are willing to

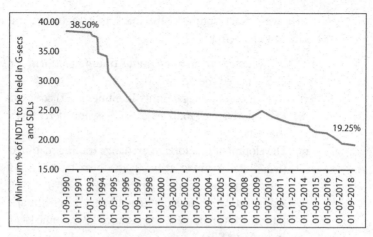

Figure 15.10. Reduction in the Statutory Liquidity Ratio (SLR) for Banks
Source: DBIE, RBI.

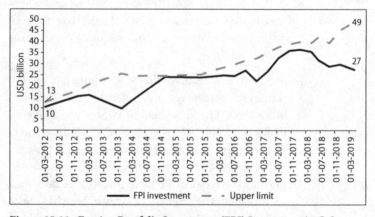

Figure 15.11. Foreign Portfolio Investment (FPI) Investment in G-Secs vis-à-vis Limit
Source: National Securities Depository Limited (NSDL), CCIL.

retain a significant portion of their investments in the country for a minimum retention period (presently three years).

3. **Strengthening the legal and regulatory framework for investor protection:** One of the most critical building blocks of market infrastructure is a proper legal framework which

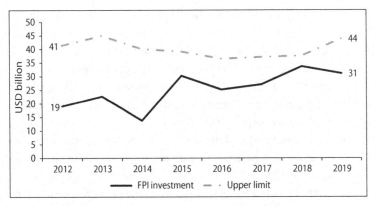

Figure 15.12. Foreign Portfolio Investment (FPI) Investment in Corporate Debt vis-à-vis Limit

Source: National Securities Depository Limited (NSDL).

ensures investor protection by acting as a deterrent to market abuse and malpractices. In India, the Public Debt Act (1944), the Securities Contract Regulation Act (1956) and the Government Securities Act (2006) govern the formalization of issuance and transfer of securities. In parallel, the RBI Act (1934) confers powers on the RBI to regulate money, derivatives, repo and government securities markets. With the IBC (December 2016), the legal framework for financial regulation is also moving closer to being comprehensive and effective in the context of non-financial corporate borrowers. However, the lack of resolution framework for non-bank financial entities remains a crucial gap that deserves prompt attention of the authorities.

Let me now turn to some of the other important drivers of market development.

4. **Capital market specific drivers: Disclosure regime**: As per the cross-country survey findings of the *CGFS Report*, proper and timely disclosure by the issuers in corporate bond market is a prerequisite for gaining investors' confidence in this market. Conversely, lack of adequate disclosures raises the financing costs of corporates, especially sub-investment grade ones, and keeps the capital markets small. Recognizing this, regulators in India have emphasized and mandated high-quality and timely disclosures by issuers. However,

a few instances of recent defaults in commercial paper and corporate bond markets have raised concerns about the quality of disclosures, even for investment-grade firms. These concerns are worthy of careful scrutiny and assessment relative to the best international practices to help fine-tune standards for the timely disclosure of default-relevant information by corporates.

5. **Deepening the domestic institutional base**: Expanding the investor base leads to increasing diversity in the market (see Section 2.7). Efforts in this direction need to be sustained, with a particular focus on the domestic institutional investor base. Improving pension and insurance coverage for households can be a priority as it not only leads to social welfare outcomes, but also leads to a stronger and more stable investor base for capital markets. Better financialization of household savings could be a catalyst for retail participation in markets, in turn providing a boost to collective investment vehicles such as mutual funds.

6. **Bidirectional opening of markets to international participation**: One of the key drivers of market development recognized in the *CGFS Report* is opening up of the market to foreign participants although it entails managing global spillover risks. The RBI has taken calibrated steps in opening up its regulated markets to foreign participants as discussed earlier and also allowed domestic players to participate in overseas markets:

   a. Both G-Sec and corporate bond markets have experienced growing investment by FPIs in response to the relaxation of FPI participation limits (as shown in Figures 15.11 and 15.12).

   b. In consultation with the government, the RBI has decided to permit offshore trading and settlement of G-Secs through International Central Securities Depositories (ICSD) for non-residents who do not want to undergo the domestic FPI registration procedure.

   c. Similarly, in March 2018, the RBI freed up overseas hedging by residents of commodity price risk and freight risk overseas. Residents were permitted to hedge both direct and indirect commodity risk through specified instruments. For direct exposure, all price risk on all commodities is now permitted to be hedged overseas, while for indirect exposure, residents can hedge overseas the price risk on industrial metals only. Further, revised directions treat risks acquired from domestic and cross-border transactions at par.

To manage the global spillover risks arising from such reforms, prudential limits have been in place alongside most of these reforms to ensure consistency with the overall state of capital account liberalization for India.

7. **Developing complementary markets:** Deep and liquid complementary markets such as repo and derivatives play a crucial role in the growth of the cash markets as they help investors in funding and hedging. Over the past few years, the RBI has taken measures to help develop repo markets for both G-Secs and corporate bonds. Introduction of tri-party repo (August 2017) has been a success for the G-Sec market; however, tri-party repo is yet to pick up in the corporate bond market. Similarly, securities lending works well for G-Secs although wider participation (especially by large holders of G-Secs such as mutual funds, insurance companies and pension funds) is required to avoid occasional episodes of excessive volatility in borrowing costs. To boost derivatives markets, efforts are required in encouraging better risk management by domestic institutions, especially banks.

   All these regulatory measures have resulted in a consistent growth in liquidity in the repo markets. With the untapped interest rate derivatives market set for a pickup in the risk management activity of banks and non-banks, the role of these complementary markets will strengthen in the years to follow.

8. **Other recent initiatives**

   a. **Task force on offshore rupee markets:** The RBI constituted a task force in February 2019 to examine in-depth issues relating to the offshore rupee markets and recommend appropriate policy measures to align incentives for non-residents to gradually move to the domestic market for their hedging requirements and also to ensure the stability of the external value of the rupee. The *Report of the Task Force* is due by mid-July 2019.

b. **Internal working group on market timings:** The RBI has set up an internal working group on market timings which will comprehensively review the timings of various markets that are under the purview of the RBI, and will assess the necessary payment and settlement infrastructure that can support coordinated timings across these markets. The *Working Group's Report*, after submission, will be released for public feedback.

c. **Task force on the development of secondary market for corporate loans:** The RBI has constituted a task force on the development of secondary market for corporate loans. It will suggest required policies for facilitating the development of a secondary market in corporate loans, including loan transaction platform for stressed assets, creation of a loan contract registry, its ownership structure and related protocols such as the standardization of loan information, independent validation and data access. The *Report of the Task Force* is due by the end of August 2019.

d. **Committee on the development of housing finance securitization market:** The RBI constituted this committee to assess the state of housing finance securitization markets in India, study the best international practices as well as lessons learnt from the global financial crisis and propose measures to further develop these markets in India by identifying critical steps required such as, inter alia, definition of conforming mortgages, mortgage documentation standards, digital registry for ease of due diligence and verification by investors, avenues for trading in securitized assets, etc. The *Report of the Committee* is due by the end of August 2019.

In summary, it should be clear that while Indian capital markets have evolved steadily to a stage of long-run viability, the potential for developing and strengthening them further is limitless....

'Let us, then, be up and doing,
With a heart for any fate;
Still achieving, still pursuing,
Learn to labour and to wait.'

—*A Psalm of Life* by
Henry Wadsworth Longfellow (1807–1882)

PART 6

Striking the Right Balance
Enhancing the Autonomy of the Central Bank, the Markets and the Real Economy

CHAPTER 16

ON THE IMPORTANCE OF INDEPENDENT REGULATORY INSTITUTIONS: THE CASE OF THE CENTRAL BANK*

No analogy is perfect; yet, analogies help convey things better. At times, a straw man has to be set up to make succinctly a practical or even an academic point. Occasionally, however, real-life examples come along beautifully to make a communicator's work easier. Let me start with an antecedent from 2010:

'My time at the central bank is up and that is why I have decided to leave my post definitively with the satisfaction of my duty fulfilled', Mr Martin Redrado, Argentina's central bank chief, told a news conference late on Friday, 29 January 2010.

'We have arrived at this situation because of the national government's permanent trampling of institutions', he said. 'Basically, I am defending two main concepts: the independence of the central bank in our decision-making process and that the reserves should be used for monetary and financial stability'.

The roots of this dramatic exit lay in an emergency decree passed by the Argentine government led by Cristina Fernandéz on 14 December 2009 that would set up a Bicentennial Stability and

---

* Speech Delivered at the A. D. Shroff Memorial Lecture in Mumbai on 26 October 2018. I am grateful to Governor Dr Urjit R. Patel, RBI for his suggestion to explore this theme for a speech, for referring me to the work of the Late Deena Khatkhate (2005), and for his constant encouragement, feedback and guidance. I am also indebted to insightful exchanges with Professor Rakesh Mohan of Yale University and former Deputy Governor of the RBI; Dr Nachiket Mor of Bill and Melinda Gates Foundation, during his term as a Central Board Member of the RBI; my fellow Deputy Governor, N. S. Vishwanathan; my colleague, Dr Michael D. Patra, Executive Director and Monetary Policy Committee member; as well as Jose Kattoor, Mridul Saggar and Vineet Srivastava of the RBI. All errors that remain are my own.

Reduced Indebtedness Fund to finance public debt maturing that year. This involved the transfer of $6.6 billion of the central bank reserves to the national treasury. The claim was that the central bank had $18 billion in 'excess reserves'. (In fact, Mr Redrado had refused to transfer the funds; so the government attempted to fire him, by another emergency decree on 7 January 2010 for misconduct and dereliction of duty; this attempt, however, failed, as it was unconstitutional.)

Besides sparking off one of the worst constitutional crises in Argentina since its economic meltdown in 2001, the chain of events led to a grave reassessment of its sovereign risk.

Within a month of Mr Redrado's resignation, Argentine sovereign bond yields and the annual premium cost for buying insurance against loss from default on Argentine government bonds (measured as the sovereign credit default swap spread) shot up by about 2.5 per cent or 250 bps, by more than a fourth of their prior levels.

Alberto Ramos, Argentinian analyst at Goldman Sachs, noted on 7 February 2010:

Using central bank reserves to pay government obligations is not a positive development and the concept of excess reserves is certainly open to debate. It weakens the balance sheet of the central bank and provides the wrong incentive to the government, as it weakens the incentive to control the rapid expansion of spending and to promote some consolidation of fiscal accounts in 2010.

Even more damagingly, a risk that Governor Redrado had warned about came to the fore. By beginning of January 2010, Thomas Griesa, a New York judge, had frozen the Argentine central bank's account held at the Federal Reserve Bank of New York, following claims of investors that the central bank was no longer an autonomous agency but under the thumb of the country's executive branch.

(The above summary is based in part on *Argentina's central bank chief resigns*, Jude Webber, Financial Times, 30 January 2010; and *Argentina: Bank independence at stake as Redrado exits*, Jason Mitchell, Euromoney, 7 February 2010)

This complex interplay of the sovereign's exercise of its powers, the central banker's exit and the market's revolt, will be at the centre of my remarks on why it is important for a well-functioning economy to have an independent central bank, that is, a central bank that is independent from the executive branch of the government. I will also try to lay out why the risks of undermining the central bank's independence are potentially catastrophic, a 'self-goal' of sorts, as it can trigger a crisis of confidence in the capital markets that are tapped by the governments (and others in the economy) to run their finances.

Why Nations Succeed (or Fail)

Before I delve into this complex interplay, I wish to place the independence of the central bank in a more general context.

Academic discourse by political economists recognizes the key role played by the rule of law and accountability of governments in enabling countries to flourish. Francis Fukuyama (2011) considers these two elements, along with adequate state-and institution-building, as 'all' being critical for 'getting to Denmark', or in other words, creating stable, peaceful, prosperous, inclusive and honest societies.

Acemoglu and Robinson (2012) summarize their body of work on the primacy of the quality of institutions in explaining the political and economic success or failure of states. Taking examples of 'twin' country case studies (such as S. Korea and N. Korea), the book elaborates the following important distinctions:

- 'Inclusive' economic and political institutions involve plurality in decision-making which help guarantee the rule of law and foster talent and creativity; in the presence of such institutions, economics and politics do not become hostage to a set of incumbents likely to be hurt by change.
- In contrast, 'extractive' institutions limit access to a country's economic and financial resources to the ruling elites, hinder change and innovation and over time, lead to stagnation and atrophy of the country's potential.

In conversations with former colleagues at New York University's Stern School of Business (NYU Stern), it was routine to categorize economies as encouraging and supporting either 'value creation', whereby entrepreneurs believed their 'mantra' of success lay in challenging orthodoxy, or 'rent extraction', wherein businesses found value primarily from joining hands with regressive state policies and crowding out others who had no such access.

Regardless of the preferred theory and terminology for the importance of institutions, it is well accepted that they include, inter alia, property rights and their enforcement, the judiciary, and the election office in a democracy, instituted not just de jure but allowed to operate independently and function effectively de facto.

Somewhat less celebrated is the institution of an independent central bank, perhaps not just because the central bank is a relatively new kid on the block (in most cases less than a century old), but also because it interacts less directly with the public though its true influence is far-reaching.

Government and the Central Bank: A Tale of Two Horizons

A central bank performs several important functions for the economy: it controls the money supply; sets the rate of interest on borrowing and lending money; manages the external sector including the exchange rate; supervises and regulates the financial sector, notably banks; it often regulates credit and foreign exchange markets; and seeks to ensure financial stability, domestic as well as on the external front.

The world over, the central bank is set up as an institution 'separate' from the government; put another way, it is not a department of the executive function of the government; its powers are enshrined as being separate through relevant legislation. Its tasks being somewhat complex and technical, central banks are ideally headed and manned by technocrats or field experts—typically economists, academics, commercial bankers and, occasionally, private sector representatives, appointed by the government but not elected to the office. This architecture reflects the acceptance of the thesis that central banks should be allowed to exercise their powers independently.

Why is the central bank 'separate' from the government? I will offer what I find to be a particularly intuitive explanation:

1. The first part of the explanation relates to the horizon of decision-making of a government vis-à-vis that of the central bank.

A government's horizon of decision-making is rendered short, like the duration of a T20 match (to use a cricketing analogy), by several considerations. There are always upcoming elections of some sort—national, state, mid-term, etc. As elections approach, delivering on proclaimed manifestos of the past acquires urgency; where manifestos cannot be delivered upon, populist alternatives need to be arranged with immediacy. Less important in the present scenario, but only recently so, wars had to be waged, financed and won at all costs. This myopia or short-termism of governments is best summarized in history by Louis XV when he proclaimed, 'Apres moi, le deluge!' (After me, the flood!)[1]

In contrast, a central bank plays a test match, trying to win each session but importantly also survive it so as to have a chance to win the next session and so on. In particular, the central bank is not directly subjected to political time pressures and the induced neglect of the future; by virtue of being nominated rather than elected, central bankers have horizons of decision-making that tend to be longer than that of governments, spanning election cycles or war periods. While they clearly have to factor in the immediate consequences of their policy decisions, central bankers can afford to take a pause, reflect and ask the question as to what would be the long-term consequences of their, as well as the government's, policies. Indeed, by their mandate, central banks are committed to stabilize the economy over business and financial cycles and hence, have to peer into the medium to long term. Unsurprisingly, central banks strive to build 'credibility' through a series of difficult choices that reflect sacrificing short-term gains for long-term outcomes such as price or financial stability.

2. The second part of the explanation as to why the central bank is separate from the government relates to the observation

---

[1] See Acharya and Rajan (2013) for a complete theoretical analysis modelling government myopia and populism (maximizing simply the cash-flow and spending each period) in the presence of a sovereign debt market; implications for the policies governing the financial sector; and attendant risks in the form of economic repression and financial crises.

that much of what the central bank manages or influences—money creation, credit creation, external sector management and financial stability—involves potential front-loaded benefits to the economy but with the possibility of attendant 'tail risk' in the form of back-loaded costs from financial excess or instability. For example,

a. Greater supply of money can facilitate ease of financial transactions, including the financing of government deficits, but this can cause economy to over-heat in due course and trigger (hyper-) inflationary pressures or even a full-blown crisis that eventually require sharper monetary contractions.

b. Excessive lowering of interest rates and/or relaxation in bank capital and liquidity requirements can lead to greater credit creation, asset-price inflation and semblance of strong economic growth in the short term, but excessive credit growth is usually accompanied by lending down the quality curve which triggers mal-investment, asset-price crashes and financial crises in the long term.

c. Allowing foreign capital flows to flood into the economy can temporarily ease the financing pressures for an expanding government balance sheet and the crowded-out private sector, but a 'sudden stop' or exodus of these flows in future can trigger a collapse of the exchange rate with adverse economy-wide spillovers.

d. Sweeping bank loan losses under the rug by compromising supervisory and regulatory standards can create a façade of financial stability in the short run, but inevitably cause the fragile deck of cards to fall in a heap at some point in future, likely with a greater taxpayer bill and loss of potential output.

While not always the case, often the required interventions for stable growth are structural reforms by the government with upfront fiscal outlay; however, these may compromise populist expenditures or require displeasing incumbents. As a result, it might seem as an expedient solution to the government to ask/task/mandate/direct the central bank to pursue strategies that generate short-term gains but effectively create tail risks for the economy. To protect the economy from such short-termism, the central bank is designed to be at a safe distance from the executive branch of the government.

Undermining the Independence of the Central Bank

Now, although the central bank is formally organized to be separate from the government, its effective horizon of decision-making can be reduced for short-term gains by the government, if it so desires, through a variety of mechanisms, inter alia,

    a. Appointing government (or government-affiliated) officials rather than technocrats to key central bank positions, such as Governor and, more generally, senior management.

    b. Pursuing steady attrition and erosion of statutory powers of the central bank through piecemeal legislative amendments that directly or indirectly eat at separation of the central bank from the government.

    c. Blocking or opposing rule-based central banking policies and favouring instead discretionary or joint decision-making with direct government interventions.

    d. Setting up parallel regulatory agencies with weaker statutory powers and/or encouraging development of unregulated (or lightly regulated) entities that perform financial intermediation functions outside the purview of the central bank.[2,3]

---

[2] The most striking example is the presence of government-sponsored enterprises (GSEs) to support mortgages and home ownership in the United States. The GSEs are outside of any regulatory purview of the Federal Reserve, but have been deployed by successive governments to pursue populist housing policies, contributing significantly to the imbalances that led to the Global Financial Crisis of 2007–2008 and the ensuing Great Recession (see, Acharya et al. 2011, for details).

[3] See Acharya (2015) for discussion on the resulting need to ensure that the central bank has regulatory scope over parts of 'shadow banking' that are likely to be systemically important.

If such efforts are successful, they induce policy myopia in the economy that substitutes macroeconomic stability with punctuated arrival of financial crises.

Therefore, there are several reasons why enshrining and maintaining central bank independence ends up being an *inclusive* reform for the economy, and conversely, undermining such independence a regressive, *extractive* one:

i. When the government is seen often making efforts to dilute the central bank's policies and effectively coercing the central bank into such dilutions, banks and private sector spend more time lobbying for policies that suit them individually, at the cost of collective good, rather than investing in value creation and growth.

ii. When governance of the central bank is undermined, it is unlikely to attract or be able to retain the brightest minds that thrive on the ability to debate freely, think independently and effect change; attrition of central bank powers results in attrition of its human capital and deterioration of its efficiency and expertise over time.

iii. When important parts of financial intermediation are kept outside the purview of the central bank, systemic risks can build up in "shadow banking" with private gains in good times to a small set of players but at substantive costs to future generations in the form of unchecked financial fragility.

As such, the divergence in the horizon of decision-making between government and the central bank that I have highlighted need not lead to any operational incompatibility as long as it is well-understood and well-accepted by both parties that it is precisely given this divergence that the central bank is formally separated from the executive office and meant to conduct its functions in an independent manner. The central bank can of course make mistakes and is generally held publicly accountable through parliamentary scrutiny and transparency norms. This way, the institutional arrangement of independence, transparency and accountability to the public not only balance but also strengthen the central bank's autonomy. However, direct intervention and interference by the government in operational mandate of the central bank negate its functional autonomy.

'Kiss of Death': Incurring the Wrath of Markets

Far-sighted government leaders may be able to reap benefits of convincing voters about the importance of investing in macroeconomic stability; for instance, by claiming credit for the long-term nature of financial sector outcomes attained by allowing the central bank autonomy in decision-making and delivery of its core functions. When such a measured perspective of an independent central bank as a key element of durable economic prosperity is missing and/or government myopia so rife as to lead to regular inroads into central banking apparatus and decisions, unfortunate accidents can arise. Macroeconomic management can become a tug of war between securing stability and inflicting misdirection; daily operational decisions lead to power struggles; and, as the central bank is forced to bend over backwards to retain credibility in the face of imminent pressures that would erode its independence, counter efforts to reduce its independence escalate.

As this dynamic plays out, markets watch keenly, and if uncertainty grows and confidence in central bank independence and credibility erode, then markets rap bond yields and exchange rate on the knuckles!

Let me elaborate.

Modern economies are, by and large, not autarkies; they rely on capital markets to finance their investments. This is especially true of governments as reflected in the relatively large size of sovereign (and quasi-sovereign) debt markets, denominated in domestic currency as well as foreign currency. As long-term risks such as inflation or financial instability rise, markets reprice sovereign debt and may potentially shun its financing altogether. This could have immediate spillovers to other markets such as for foreign exchange and foreign investments, potentially putting at risk also the external sector stability of the economy.

Therefore, the presence of this third player—the market—in the back and forth between a government and the central bank (more generally, regulatory institutions) is an important feedback mechanism. The market can discipline the government not to erode central bank independence, and it can also make the government pay for its transgressions. Interestingly, the market also forces central banks to remain accountable and independent when it is under government pressure.[4]

Besides the market revolt and strictures during the Argentine episode of 2010 that I recounted in my introductory remarks, it is to be noted that both of this year's EM sovereign bonds and currency meltdowns got catalyzed through a perception of government influence on central bank's monetary policy, including through sporadic communication by government with public on its desire to control the central bank's decision-making. In one case, a rate cut in the wake of rising inflation and mounting fiscal deficit did the damage; and in the other, it was a public pronouncement by the premier of the state about the 'evils' of interest rate hikes even when inflation was in double digit terrain.

Indeed, the market censure need not be limited to EMs. The public expression of government's bewilderment and disappointment at monetary tightening in the world's largest safe-haven economy, again at a time of rising inflation and fiscal deficit, has raised in minds of investors scenarios under which its reserve currency status cannot anymore be taken for granted (The Economist 2018).

Barry Eichengreen, Professor of Economics and Political Science at the University of California, Berkeley, covers superbly, in his recent piece (2018), this critical feedback role of the market:

There are good reasons why countries ... delegate monetary policy decisions to technocrats appointed for their expertise. They can take the long view. They can resist the temptation to manipulate monetary conditions for short-term gain. Privileging long-term stability, as history has shown, is positive for economic performance. And it is on this performance that elected leaders, rightly or wrongly, are judged.

Thoughtful politicians understand this. Hence their support for central bank independence and their respect for the convention that

---

[4] An interesting suggestion from Michael Patra is that perhaps economies should not only have rules that delineate clearly the roles of the government and the central bank, but also a dispute resolution mechanism *a la* the World Trade Organisation (WTO). The very presence of a referee would recognize that differences in objectives and horizons of decision-making arise; central bank and government can (to borrow his exact words) 'go in there, slug it out, come out battered, but in understanding, since there has to be a clear winner whose hand will be upheld by the jury'.

they should refrain from seeking to influence central bank decisions. Unfortunately, not all politicians are thoughtful. Not all have the patience to wait for long-term gains. Not all are pleased when appointees refuse to bow to their wishes. And not all are respectful of inherited institutions and conventions, be they central bank independence or, more broadly, the division of powers.
The question is whether they pay attention to markets.

What Barry Eichengreen is perceptively observing is that if a government were to pay attention to markets, it would realize that central bank independence is in fact its strength and the central bank a sort of a true friend, someone who will tell the government unpleasant but brutally honest truths and correct to the extent it can any adverse long-term consequences of government policies.

Let me now turn to how all this relates to the RBI.

The Late Deena Khatkhate provides a masterful and scholarly assessment in *Reserve Bank of India: A Study in the Separation and Attrition of Powers* (2005). Some of the discussion below draws heavily from his assessment and is updated for developments since then. Other excellent discussions of the central bank's autonomy and independence in the Indian context are contained in lectures by the RBI's former Governors, Dr C. Rangarajan (1993) and Dr Y. V. Reddy (2001; 2007). As we will see below, other Governors and Deputy Governors have also carried this abiding theme through their tenures. For some of them, even when the RBI's independence has been unclear de jure, governments have in the end have had the wisdom to support it de facto; for others, however, the RBI's independence has remained a work in progress, an enduring challenge that the nation has been grappling with on an ongoing basis.

Progressive Evolution in Restoring Independence of the RBI

While the RBI has always derived several important powers from the RBI Act, 1935 and the Banking Regulation Act, 1949, what matters is the effective independence with which these powers can be exercised in practice. Over time, great strides have been undertaken by successive governments at the behest of the central bank, several economists and umpteen committee reports, to restore the operational independence of the RBI. I will touch upon three such areas of healthy progress.

1. **Monetary policy:** The RBI, like many central banks of the time, got quickly trapped into the socialist planning policies of post-independence government, setting not just the rate of interest on money but practically all rates of credit at different maturities, as well as doing sectoral credit allocation to the real economy.

   Post the deregulation of interest rates in the 1990s, monetary policy achieved a more modern dimension. To start with, there was a 'multiple indicators' approach to setting interest rates. Having too many objectives for monetary policy violates the Tinbergen principle of 'one objective, one instrument'; it also renders it difficult to understand or communicate what the interest-rate setting is attempting to achieve at any point of time. Importantly, this approach entertained much regulatory discretion, often at the level of an individual, namely the RBI Governor. This made independence of monetary policy individual-specific; in other words, it allowed for government pressure to creep in easily for keeping rates low at times of fiscal expansion under one guise or the other.

   This is exactly a setting where rules would be better than discretion, in particular to avoid the time-inconsistency problem, highlighted in the work of Nobel laureates Finn Kydland and Edward Prescott in 1970s and early 1980s. Kydland and Prescott (1977) consider the implication that people, including investors, could look into the future and anticipate the behaviour of self-interested governments, so that a discretionary monetary policy could end up being compromised by government pressures, leaving inflationary expectations unanchored, whereas a monetary policy committed to a rule would be harder to bend and keep inflationary expectations at bay.[5]

---

[5] See also Buiter and Sibert (2000), who lay out the theoretical basis for the required legal and institutional arrangements, primarily operational independence of the central bank, for an effective monetary policy.

Following several episodic bouts of double-digit inflation, a war on inflation and inflationary expectations, was finally launched in September 2013 by the then Governor Raghuram G. Rajan; the Urjit Patel Committee Report to revise and strengthen the Monetary Policy Framework was released in 2014; and, finally, the RBI Act was modified in August 2016 to constitute the MPC.

The MPC consists of three RBI members, including the Governor who reserves a casting vote and three external members appointed by the government. The MPC has been legislatively awarded a flexible inflation-targeting mandate of achieving 4 per cent CPI inflation in the medium term while paying attention to growth with operational independence to achieve it, and with accountability in terms of transparency around the MPC's resolution, minutes summarizing each individual committee member's decision, bi-annual monetary policy reports and a written report to the government in case a +/– 2 per cent band around the target inflation level is violated for three quarters in a row.

The MPC, two years old since, has attempted steadfastly through its rate-setting decisions to build credibility of the inflation target, a process that is generally believed and empirically documented, to help lower the long-term bond yields as well as stabilize the exchange rate. While the jury will remain out for some time on the economic impact of the flexible inflation-targeting framework, it is incontrovertible that the MPC has given monetary policy an independent institutional foundation. The government deserves much credit for its far-sightedness in legislating the required changes to strengthen this aspect of the central bank's independence and distancing itself in the process from monetary decision-making (other than through the appointment of external members on the MPC).

2. **Debt management:** For several decades post-independence, the RBI participated in short-term Treasury Bill issuances of the Government of India (bearing extraordinarily low interest rates) to fund its fiscal deficits. The RBI also publicly acknowledged that its open market operations (OMOs) were primarily geared to manage the government bond yields.

This implied that the central bank balance-sheet was always available as a resource—just like tax receipts—ready to monetize excessive government spending. Unsurprisingly, high inflation in India was engineered to please both Milton Friedman and Thomas Sargent, that is, it was always both a monetary and a fiscal phenomenon, as these two Nobel laureates in economics had respectively argued (Friedman 1970; Sargent 1982).

Eventually, recognizing the fiscal imprudence and inflationary risks engendered by such automatic monetization of government deficits, joint efforts between the RBI and the government during 1994–1997 limited deficit financing from the RBI to the capped Ways and Means Advances (WMA). The Fiscal Responsibility and Budget Management (FRBM) Act of 2003 explicitly prohibited the RBI from participating in primary issuances of the government securities. Open market operations came to be designed to sterilize the impact on domestic money supply of foreign exchange interventions and/or to meet durable liquidity needs of the economy, rather than to fund deficits. While there have been relapses to old habits, overall these changes have left the task of government debt management with the RBI as primarily being one of auctioning government debt and helping it switch between securities or conduct buybacks, rather than of intricate involvement in fiscal planning, and more importantly, in its funding.

Furthermore, the repressive levels of SLR and Cash Reserve Ratio (CRR), which ensured substantial portions of bank deposits were channelled to the government or were readily available to debase in value through monetary expansion, have now been rationalized to be more or less in line with international prudential standards. For instance, in case of SLR, the level has been steadily reduced and the plan is to harmonize it with the Basel III LCR.

3. **Exchange rate management:** In the Five Year Plans post-independence, prices including the exchange rate were assumed to be constant; however, since the true value of the Indian rupee fluctuated with market prices and macroeconomic conditions, the Sterling holdings had no choice but

to take an undue hit. The underlying true value of the rupee was also affected heavily—but not reflected in reality—by monetary policy and debt management operations that were implicitly supporting the ballooning of government deficits. The result of the fixed exchange rate regime in the midst of 'fiscal dominance' was that the RBI was essentially a silent spectator in the build-up to the inevitable exchange rate disequilibrium (though arguably this was true of much of the world at that time).

Since 1976, when the level of the rupee moved to being a 'managed float' against a basket of currencies, and especially since 1993, the exchange rate has gradually evolved from being entirely a fixed rate to being market-determined for all practical purposes. The RBI deploys reserves management and macroprudential controls on foreign capital flows to manage excessively large movements. With a flexible inflation-targeting mandate for interest-rate policy and funding of fiscal deficit no longer the objective of monetary operations, the desired exchange rate management rests with the RBI.

Ongoing Challenges in Maintaining Independence of the RBI

Few important pockets of persistent weakness, however, remain in maintaining independence of the RBI. Some of these areas were also identified in the 2017 Financial Sector Assessment Programme (FSAP) of India by the IMF and the World Bank (WB) as ways to strengthen the independence of the RBI, an area in which the FSAP rates India as 'materially non-compliant'.

1. **Regulation of PSBs:** One important limitation is that the RBI is statutorily limited in undertaking the full scope of actions against PSBs—such as asset divestiture, replacement of management and board, license revocation and resolution actions such as mergers or sales—all of which it can and does deploy effectively in case of private banks. The significant implications of this limitation were highlighted in detail in Governor Urjit Patel's speech (Patel 2018). To reiterate

from the FSAP (Para 39 in Summing up Responsibilities, Objectives, Powers, Independence, and Accountabilities, the Basel Core Principles Detailed Assessment Report):

Legislation should be amended to enable the RBI to extend all the powers currently exercised over PvtSBs to PSBs; in particular, regarding Board member dismissals, mergers and license revocation ... It should also remove the option of an appeal to the government when the RBI revokes a license. If statutory changes are difficult, the RBI and the government should consider adopting a framework agreement whereby the government would acknowledge the RBI's full operational authority and independence in supervision and regulation, as they did recently for monetary policy.

---

2. **The RBI's balance sheet strength:** Having adequate reserves to bear any losses that arise from central bank operations and having appropriate rules to allocate profits (including rules that govern the accumulation of the capital and reserves) is considered an important part of central bank's independence from the government (see, for example, Moser-Boehm 2006). A thorny ongoing issue on this front has been that of the rules for surplus transfer from the RBI to the government (Cogencis 2018), an issue that relates closely to the leading Argentine example in my introductory remarks. It has been covered deftly by Rakesh Mohan (2018) in the last of his three-part series of recent articles on the RBI, titled *Protect the RBI's Balance-Sheet*;[6] therein, he elucidates why a central bank needs a strong balance sheet to perform its full range of critical functions for the economy. I quote his main points below:

First, ... The longer-term fiscal consequences would be the same if the government issued new securities to fund the expenditure. {R}aiding the RBI's capital creates no new government revenue

---

[6] https://www.business-standard.com/article/opinion/protect-the-rbi-s-balance-sheet-118100401270_1.html

on a net basis over time, and only provides an illusion of free money in the short term.

Second, ... The use of such a transfer would erode whatever confidence that exists in the government's intention to practice fiscal prudence.

Third, ... In theory, a central bank can implement monetary policy appropriately with a wide range of capital levels, including levels below zero. In practice, the danger is that it may lose credibility with the financial markets and public at large and may then be unable to attain its objective if it has substantial losses and is seen as having insufficient capital.

Are fears with regard to possible central bank losses illusory? According to the BIS, 43 out of 108 central banks reported losses for at least one year between 1984 and 2005.

It is also argued by some that the government can always recapitalise a central bank when necessary. This is certainly true in principle but is practically difficult when the government itself suffers from fiscal pressures and maintains a relatively high debt-GDP ratio, as is the case in India. What is also important is the erosion of central bank independence both in reality and perhaps, even more importantly, in optics. ...

Once again, better sense has prevailed, and the government has not raided the RBI's balance sheet.

---

3. **Regulatory scope:** A final issue is one of regulatory scope, the most recent case in point being the recommendation to bypass the central bank's powers over payment and settlement systems by appointing a separate payments regulator (also covered by Rakesh Mohan in his series, Ibid). The RBI has published its dissent note[7] against this recommendation on 19 October 2018.

Conclusion

Let me conclude with some notes of gratitude and dedication as well as some for further reflection.

---

[7] https://www.rbi.org.in/Scripts/BS_PressReleaseDisplay.aspx?prid=45287

Mr Y. H. Malegam has been a former Board Member, long-time adviser, friend and well-wisher of the RBI. He is someone I personally admire for his intellect, clarity of thinking and sagacity.

The Late Ardashir Darabshaw Shroff served as India's non-official delegate in 1944 at the United Nations 'Bretton Woods Conference' on post-war financial and monetary arrangements. One of his primary concerns was to seek a permanent seat on the executive board of the IMF and the World Bank, which unfortunately did not materialize. To me, his most important contribution was the co-founding in 1954 of the Free Forum Enterprise think tank which through open dialogue presented a counterpoint to the socialist tendencies that were taking roots in the country in the post-independence government era. Sucheta Dalal's biography, *A. D. Shroff-Titan of Finance and Free Enterprise* (2000), notes that George Woods, one of the most popular presidents of the World Bank, said of him:

Nobody could accuse A. D. Shroff of hiding his opinions and in the later years of his life, very rarely were those opinions fashionable in India. Yet few patriots did more than he {did} to make friends for the Indian nation and to build confidence in that nation among those throughout the world whose business it is to provide capital for sound investment opportunities.

In all humility, to emulate A. D. Shroff's freedom to criticize policy 'actuated by the single motive of trying to promote the good of my country' (from his letter to Sir Osborne Smith, the first Governor of the RBI), I chose the theme of the importance of independent regulatory institutions, and in particular, that of a central bank that is independent from an over-arching reach of the state. This theme is certainly one of great sensitivity, but I contend it is of even greater importance to our economic prospects. I earnestly hope that I have done some justice to his immortal legacy to independent economic discourse and policymaking.

In the process, I have attempted to convince you that we have made good progress in earning the RBI's independence, most notably in the monetary policy framework (changes wherein, along with the Insolvency and Bankruptcy Code and the Goods and Services Tax, were considered as crucial structural reforms by Moody's in upgrading India's sovereign rating 11 months ago). To secure greater financial and macroeconomic stability, these efforts need to be extended to effective independence for the RBI in its regulatory and supervisory powers over PSBs, its balance sheet strength and its regulatory scope. Such endeavour would be a true 'inclusive' reform for the Indian economy's future. Thankfully, it is 'only' a matter of making the right choices, which I believe as a society we can with adequately thoughtful 'what-if' analysis; I have sketched a scenario, which several parts of the world are currently witnessing, of great risks to nations from undermining the independence of their central banks.

In his excellent biography, *Volcker: The Triumph of Persistence* (2012), my former NYU Stern colleague, Bill Silber, describes in vivid detail how in the 1980s, the then Federal Reserve Governor Paul Volcker adopted a curmudgeonly approach to setting interest rates to target inflation. Besides resisting any and all pressure to keep rates low, which would have effectively allowed cheap funding—in the short term—of President Reagan's expansionary deficit-based manifesto, Volcker engaged personally with the President to convey the perils of running high fiscal deficits right after double-digit inflation had just been tamed. In the end, Volcker won the day as wise counsel prevailed, deficits were reined in and inflation tamed even further. I would argue that through Volcker's tough stance on inflation and candour on risks from government's fiscal plans, the institution of the Federal Reserve had in fact been President Reagan's true friend.

As many parts of the world today await greater government respect for central bank independence, independent central bankers will remain undeterred. Governments that do not respect a central bank's independence will sooner or later incur the wrath of financial markets, ignite economic fire and come to rue the day they undermined an important regulatory institution; their wiser counterparts who invest in the independence of a central bank will enjoy lower costs of borrowing, the love of international investors and longer life spans.

References

Acemoglu, Daron, and James Robinson. 2012. *Why Nations Fail: The Origins of Power, Prosperity and Poverty.* New York, NY: Crown Business.

Acharya, Viral V. 2015. 'Financial Stability in the Broader Mandate for Central Banks: A Political Economy Perspective.' Working Paper #11, Hutchins Center on Fiscal & Monetary Policy at Brookings. Available at: https://www.brookings.

edu/research/financial-stability-in-the-broader-mandate-for-central-banks-a-political-economy-perspective/ (accessed on 25 April 2020).

Acharya, Viral V., Stijn van Nieuwerburgh, Matthew Richardson, and Lawrence White. 2011. *Guaranteed to Fail: Fannie Mae, Freddie Mac and the Debacle of Mortgage Finance*. Princeton, NJ: Princeton University Press.

Acharya, Viral V., and Raghuram G. Rajan. 2013. 'Sovereign Debt, Government Myopia and the Financial Sector'. *Review of Financial Studies* 26, no. 6 (June): 1526–1560. Available at: http://pages.stern.nyu.edu/~sternfin/vacharya/public_html/Sov_debt_Jan_11_2013_RFS_standard.pdf (accessed on 25 April 2020).

Buiter, Willem, and Anne C. Sibert. 2000, 16 October. 'Targets, Instruments and Institutional Arrangements for an Effective Monetary Policy', Seventh L. K. Jha Memorial Lecture, delivered by Willem Buiter at the Reserve Bank of India, Mumbai.

Cogencis. 2018. 'Govt Pegs RBI Excess Capital at 3.6 Trln Rupees, Seeks It as Surplus'. 03 August. Available at: http://www.cogencis.com/newssection/govt-pegs-rbi-excess-capital-at-3-6-trln-rupees-seeks-it-as-surplus/ (accessed on 01 April 2020).

Dalal, Sucheta. 2000. *A. D. Shroff-Titan of Finance and Free Enterprise*. New Delhi: Penguin Books.

Eichengreen, Barry. 2018. 'Investors Have the Power to Tame Erdogan and Trump: Politicians Should Think Carefully before Seeking to Influence Central Banks'. *Financial Times*, August 19.

Friedman, Milton. 1970. 'The Counter-revolution in Monetary Theory', First Wincott Memorial Lecture, Transatlantic Arts.

Fukuyama, Francis. 2011. *The Origins of Political Order: From Pre-human Times to the French Revolution*. New York, NY: Farrar, Straus and Giroux.

Khatkhate, Deena. 2005. 'Reserve Bank of India: A Study in the Separation and Attrition of Powers'. In *Public Institutions in India: Performance and Design*, edited by Devesh Kapur and Pratap Bhanu Mehta. Oxford: Oxford University Press.

Kydland, Finn E., and Edward C. Prescott. 1977. 'Rules Rather than Discretion: The Inconsistency of Optimal Plans'. *Journal of Political Economy* 85, no. 3 (June): 473–492.

Mohan, Rakesh. 2018. 'Preserving the Independence of the RBI' (3 October 2018); 'Responsibility Fulfilled' (4 October 2018); 'Protect the RBI's Balance-sheet' (5 October 2018; *Business Standard*. Available at: https://www.business-standard.com/article/opinion/protect-the-rbi-s-balance-sheet-118100401270_1.html (accessed on 30 March 2020).

Moser-Boehm, Paul. 2006. 'The Relationship between the Central Bank and the Government'. In *Central Banks and the Challenge of Development*. Basle: Bank for International Settlements.

Patel, Urjit R. 2018. 'Banking Regulatory Powers Should be Ownership Neutral.' Inaugural Lecture–Center for Law & Economics; Center for Banking & Financial Laws, Gujarat National Law University, Gandhinagar. Available at: https://www.rbi.org.in/Scripts/BS_SpeechesView.aspx?Id=1054 (accessed on 30 March 2020)

Rangarajan, C. 1993. 'Autonomy of Central Banks.' 10th M. G. Kutty Memorial Lecture at Calcutta, 17 September 1993.

Reddy, Y. V. 2001. 'Autonomy of the Central Bank: Changing Contours in India.' Speech Delivered at Indian Institute of Management, Indore.

Reddy, Y. V. 2007. 'Evolving Role of the Reserve Bank of India: Recent Developments.' Speech Delivered on the Foundation Day of the Institute of Development Studies, Jaipur, 30 June 2007.

Sargent, Thomas J. 1982. 'The Ends of Four Big Inflations.' In *Inflation: Causes and Effects,* edited by Robert E. Hall. Chicago, IL: University of Chicago Press.

Silber, William. 2012. *Volcker: The Triumph of Persistence.* New York, NY: Bloomsbury.

The Economist. 2018. 'A Debate about Central-bank Independence Is Overdue.' Finance and Economics. October 20. Available at: https://www.economist.com/finance-and-economics/2018/10/20/a-debate-about-central-bank-independence-is-overdue (accessed on 25 April 2020).

CHAPTER 17

WHY LESS CAN BE MORE: ON THE CROWDING OUT EFFECTS OF GOVERNMENT FINANCING*

I had the pleasure of reading the biography of Shri K. P. Hormis, founder of the Federal Bank, *Hormis—Legend of a Great Banker with Passion for Development,* written by Shri K. P. Joseph.

Shri Hormis, as the biography vividly recounts, was not just an institution-builder, whose legacy in setting up the Federal Bank in 1931 survives today and well, but also someone who epitomized a passion for excellence, morality and development. In particular, his interest in setting up the Federal Bank was to help build a modern Kerala and India. To this end, he laid great emphasis on the role of funding entrepreneurship at grassroots level for long-term stability of the economy, while never compromising on financial stability: 'The purpose must be to develop the small man and his profession by providing him with the necessary funds. But by no means should this be done at the risk of the bank's profit or the nation's economy'.

This simple principle in itself, if implemented well throughout the financial system, would address many of the country's development challenges.

What do I mean when I say, 'less can be more'? What I have in mind is that sometimes less for the government can be more for the economy.

---

* This speech was delivered at the 16th K. P. Hormis Commemorative Lecture organized by the Federal Bank Hormis Memorial Foundation on 17 November 2018 at Kochi. I thank the Federal Bank Managing Director and Chief Executive Officer, Mr Shyam Srinivasan, and the dignitaries from the Federal Bank's top management and the Board, that deemed me suitable for this honour. I thank Nirupama Kulkarni and Bhavika Nanawati of Centre for Advanced Financial Research and Learning (CAFRAL), and Seema Saggar of the RBI from whom I have developed the body of results in this speech. I am grateful to Sitikanta Pattanaik and Vineet Srivastava for useful inputs. The views expressed herein do not necessarily reflect the views of the RBI.

When governments undertake a lot of expenditure, they may spend beyond immediate revenues and raise financing but may be constrained by the limited pool of savings in the economy. In turn, when a government dissaves and takes away a large portion of these savings, there is less left for the private sector, eventually 'crowding out' investments by the private sector. Crowding out can imply that (a) the private sector is unable to generate adequate financing; (b) the private sector has to pay higher costs to raise its financing and (c) the private sector needs to rely on external financing, that is, dip into savings abroad.

The question I will raise and try to answer is: Does government borrowing crowd out the private sector in India and what are its ramifications? I will first set up the global context and then move on to why this is an important question to ask in the Indian context. After characterizing and quantifying the crowding out channels for India, I will explain how crowding out can interact with external sector fragility, lead to financial sector fragility and weaken the transmission of monetary policy. I will conclude with some possible remedies.

The Global Context

Many countries in the world today have a 'fiscal deficit'—defined as fiscal spending that is not met by revenues collected by the government. Governments are able to spend beyond their immediate tax collection because they can collect taxes in future and can borrow from markets against the expected future stream of tax collections. In essence, they can float government bonds or employ financial repression of banks so as to channel domestic savings to finance fiscal deficits. Barring Germany, Russia and South Korea, all G20 countries were running a fiscal deficit as of 2018. While India is not an exception in terms of 'having' a fiscal deficit, it stands out in terms of the 'size' of its fiscal deficit which was recorded at 6.68 per cent of GDP in 2018,[1] surpassed only by Brazil at 6.84 per cent (Figure 17.1a).

---

[1] A more precise indicator of the financing gap of the domestic economy, that is, Public Sector Borrowing Requirements (PSBR), which includes borrowings by general government (central, state and local government), public non-financial corporations (central and state public sector undertakings [PSUs]) and public financial corporations (banks and financial institutions), is estimated for India to be between 8 per cent and 9 per cent in 2017–2018 and 2018–2019 (please see 'India's interim budget tries to strike a balance, but the real story is off-balance

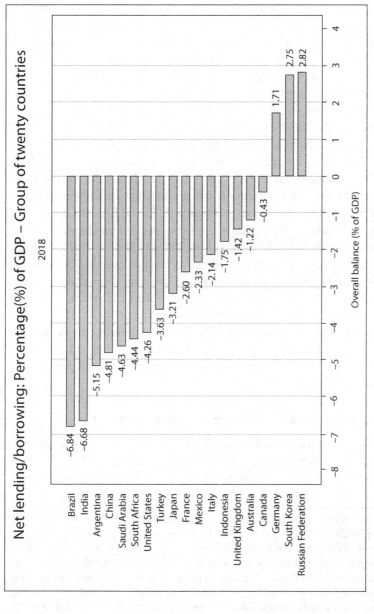

Figure 17.1a. Fiscal Deficit of G20 Countries in 2018

Source: IMF Fiscal Monitor

Fiscal deficits need not always be harmful. At many stages of the development of a country, the government needs to play a coordinating role in providing public goods such as education, health, infrastructure, etc. Usually, in economics, 'capital' expenditure undertaken by the government is thought of as 'good' spending if it is to create public goods, since these can be used over a period of time by private individuals and enterprises to invest more and thereby potentially contribute to higher growth. Viewed this way, certain types of government investments 'crowd in' private investments and increase the size of the overall pie.

In contrast, if most of the government spending is *revenue* expenditure—for example, subsidies or various kinds of social welfare programmes—then it may improve economic stability in the short term by giving a temporary boost to consumption and demand, but usually will not lead to long-term growth. By and large, such spending does not catalyze the private sector to invest more, and hence, does not have growth multiplier effects as from the investment in public goods. Furthermore, when most of the government's fiscal deficit is due to revenue expenditures, the overall pie does not expand because the private sector possibly shrinks. This is because the private sector too may need to borrow in order to invest but can get 'crowded out' if the government is using up most of the savings in the economy for revenue expenditures. Hence, the simplest test of the crowding out phenomenon is often to look for an inverse relationship between private debt and government debt.

International Evidence of Crowding out

Consider two advanced economies which have extremely large government borrowing programmes: The USA and Japan. The USA (left panel, Figure 17.1b) has more than 100 per cent of GDP in borrowings,

---

sheet [https://www.jpmm.com/research/open/url/t59R6MoBP2TDuvd0dwmJQX eqNrH5bbaYaWAjzhcpqL-HdLFEIO-J_2rPFgYlUTC0TNfVjjWzXCeFeFDf_Esd 5uH6j913pZ8NjGs5iFNY4GxZ4Oocxdi8eON9bvLao4aKGr6dxROBdTIfqQV zxQ0uRNoShAChXFU-hZryq7svj4LqlymuKM6qVt4cOET878hU?];RBIisaclose-call next week' and 'India in 2019: still waters run deep' [https://www.jpmm.com/research/ open/url/t59R6MoBP2TDuvd0dwmJQXeqNrH5bbaY9SVKShg8aAIse-Pld Y6PSDbDdytnYdRhtwduldt628ot-2XSlL4MJ4ZE5IUExTm849Zw0iHYNpDF HtS_EC8Zl1GzXmxFgOLGh4kTlydV4G8C3exHtSuP4gUC7qowtsQUjHU0fv-vNfunV40c7gGiPy6RQpOvvMO0?]).

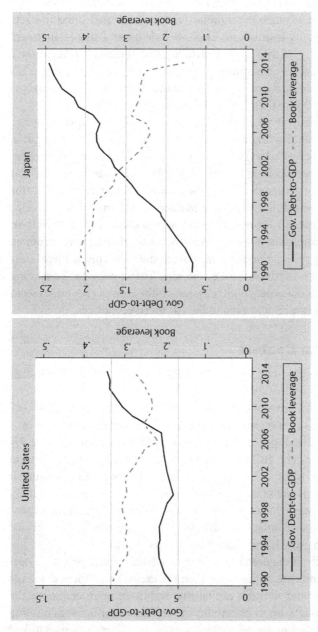

Figure 17.1b. Government Debt to GDP and Corporate Leverage: USA and Japan

Source: Demirci, Huang and Sialm (2019).

Notes: The left-hand panel shows the time-series data for government debt to GDP and corporate leverage (book) for the USA. The right-hand panel shows the corresponding data for Japan.

while Japan (right panel, Figure 17.1b) has even higher borrowings. Of course, these advanced economies have sophisticated bond markets and high-quality institutions. They are 'safe havens', that is, investors perceive that it is with almost certainty that these governments will repay their debt. Furthermore, global trading is predominantly in US dollars, so investors are especially keen to buy and hold US government bonds due to their unique safety and liquidity features.

Importantly, if we examine the leverage of the corporate sector in these economies (Figure 17.1b), we see that there has been a fall in corporate leverage over time while government borrowings have risen. Economists are reaching the conclusion through a variety of tests that in times when governments increase their borrowing, corporate sector leverage comes down (Graham, Mark and Roberts 2014). Broadly, time-series data in Figure 17.1b do seem to confirm that there is an 'inverse' relationship between government borrowing and corporate leverage, suggesting that when the government does more, there is less for the private sector of these economies. Therefore, what I am going to show for India is not country-specific—the laws of economics seem to work in a similar way even in the advanced economies.

The Indian Context

Why is crowding out potentially an important issue in the Indian context?

First, India's mix of expenditure at the government level is heavily skewed towards revenue expenditure. Capital expenditure as a proportion of total government expenditure has been consistently below 15 per cent. In fact, if we examine the budgets of the central government over a period of time, almost 90 per cent of the budget composition is the same, year after year; hence, there is only a small proportion over which some leeway is left to undertake capital expenditure. In other words, fiscal deficits in India are less likely to 'crowd in' long-run growth and more likely to 'crowd out'.

Secondly, if the domestic savings available to fund private investment demands are not enough, then the excess investment demands can only be met through capital inflows. In an open economy, the financing constraint to growth for the private sector is not as binding as in a closed economy; nevertheless, external sector challenges linked to the risk of a 'sudden stop' of capital flows—as witnessed during the 'taper tantrum' episode of 2013—set the limit on the extent to which

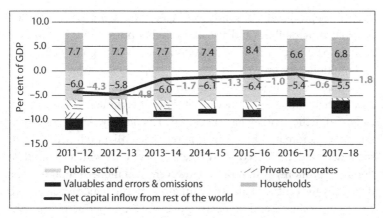

Figure 17.2. Sectoral Resource Gaps (Net Financial Saving-Investment Balance) for India

Source: Central Statistics Office.

saving-investment imbalances can be funded by foreign capital on a sustained basis without amplifying vulnerabilities. As per the national accounts data, in India, the magnitude of the challenge is too obvious from the saving-investment imbalance positions of key sectors in the economy (Figure 17.2 and Annex 17A.1). The household sector is the only sector which generates net financial savings (i.e., net of financial liabilities); the public sector and the private corporate sector are both deficit sectors. The general government sector (adjusted for valuables and errors and omissions) exhausts the entire financial savings of households, leaving no domestic financial savings for the private corporate sector (in the sense of national accounts identity).

The net capital flow line in Figure 17.2 moves with the magnitude of the savings-investment imbalance of the private corporate sector. This clearly shows how foreign capital inflows absorbed in the economy, that is, the current account deficit, often exceed what are considered sustainable levels and approach 5 per cent of GDP, when the saving-investment imbalance in the private corporate sector widens (as in 2011–2012 and 2012–2013 before the taper tantrum). Figure 17.2 also shows how subdued private investment activity and associated lower saving-investment imbalance in the private corporate sector help keep the external imbalance or the current account deficit within sustainable levels (as in the post taper tantrum period). Lower net resource gaps from the public sector—which is possible only through fiscal consolidation—can thus significantly contain external vulnerabilities and also allow higher proportions of domestic savings to be used by the private sector, possibly with greater efficiency and multiplier for growth.

Finally, a coincident phenomenon with India's sustained high fiscal deficit is that over a period of time, government borrowings in India from the market has increased. Historically, the government relied on 'automatic financing' wherein the RBI purchased government debt and monetized government expenditure which would then flood the economy with money. However, such monetization of fiscal deficits by the central bank can be inflationary and hence is considered a poor mix of fiscal and monetary policies. Over a period of time, the RBI, following the Fiscal Responsibility and Budget Management (FRBM) Act, 2003 has gradually distanced itself from automatic funding of government deficits.[2] Consequently, the government has increased its market-based borrowings.

As Figure 17.3 shows, government borrowing relative to GDP for India has ranged from 67 per cent to 85 per cent of GDP since 2000. This ratio has outpaced the ten emerging markets shown and only since 2015 has Brazil overtaken India. The high government borrowing to GDP numbers point to the large dissaving by the Indian government. Figure 17.4 shows that the Indian government's absolute borrowing level has increased exponentially since 1997, particularly so since the global financial crisis. Indeed, this phenomenon is observed for many economies, including high-income ones, being driven in part by increasing populist pressures to spend on welfare programs in the wake of weak economic growth.

These three phenomena, namely the government focus on revenue expenditure as opposed to capital expenditure, external financing of fiscal deficit and private investment net of domestic savings, and the fiscal deficit being increasingly funded through

---

[2] For historical developments regarding gradual transition towards market-based government financing, please refer to my speech 'On the Importance of Independent Regulatory Institutions–The Case of the Central Bank' delivered as the A. D. Shroff Memorial Lecture in Mumbai on Friday, 26 October 2018 (https://www.rbi.org.in/Scripts/BS_SpeechesView.aspx?Id<hig>=</hig>1066) and the Kale Memorial Lecture on 'Central Banking in India: Retrospect and Prospects' delivered by Dr Y. V. Reddy, on 8 February 2019 (http://www.yvreddy.com/kale-memorial-lecture-8th-february-2019/).

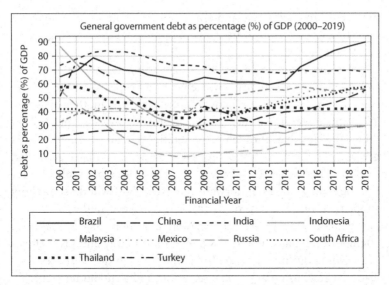

Figure 17.3. General Government Gross Debt (Percent of GDP) for Select EMEs

Source: IMF World Economic Outlook, April 2019 (data for 2019 are projections).

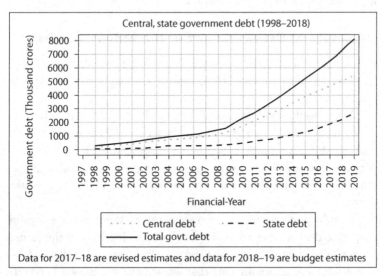

Figure 17.4. Central and State Government Borrowing (India)

Source: RBI.

market borrowing, make India a good candidate for the study of crowding-out effects and their manifestations in the banking sector and financial markets.

Has the exponential growth of government and state debt in India led to a reduction in the debt-raising capacity of the private sector in the economy? We could in principle ask another question: When the government increases its borrowing by say, 1 per cent of the GDP, does that, through some multiplier, lead to growth that is greater than the growth that the private sector could have generated by borrowing 1 per cent of the GDP? These 'fiscal multiplier' questions are not that straightforward to answer. So I will do something simpler. A recent body of research that I have undertaken with Nirupama Kulkarni, Bhavika Nanawati and Seema Saggar makes an attempt to estimate how large some of the quantity and price effects of crowding out might be for India; the research doesn't necessarily lead to a conclusion as to whether or not India should be incurring the presently high levels of fiscal deficit or government borrowings. Nevertheless, I hope to convince you of the important potential costs to bear in mind, if the governments keep doing more and more rather than enabling more and more of the private sector.

Channels of Crowding out in the Indian Context

Before proceeding to the evidence on crowding out effects for India, let us understand the most basic channels through which crowding out can occur.

Why should good companies not be able to offer higher returns to convince investors and savers if they are indeed the better growth engines of the economy compared to the government? In that case, perhaps there wouldn't be much crowding out in the first place. However, there are three channels through which this logic breaks down.

First, if government borrowing increases, then the investors in corporate debt may expect corporate taxes to increase in the future because the government will need to repay higher levels of debt. Corporates will also anticipate that investment will not be as profitable if taxes increase in the future and hence they may dial back on investment today. These channels may lead to a fall in private sector borrowing and investment when government borrowing rises.

Besides this 'real' channel of crowding out, there are two other important 'financial' channels of crowding out: (a) the 'bank lending' channel and (b) the 'corporate bond market' channel. Let me explain each one of these in detail.[3]

Bank Lending Channel of Crowding out

When government debt to GDP ratio increases, banks end up buying a huge chunk of the incremental issuance of government bonds. Historically, India has had extremely repressive levels of SLR, which is the proportion of deposits (formally, net deposit and time liabilities or NDTL) that a bank must hold in the form of government bonds. At its peak, the SLR was close to 40 per cent, that is, of ₹100 deposited in a bank, ₹40 would automatically be used to fund government deficits. The SLR, in effect, became a coercive tool to facilitate excessive government borrowing. Over a period of time, the SLR levels have been brought down by the RBI to presently below 20 per cent.[4] When SLR is at a high level of 40 per cent of ₹100 deposited in a bank, only ₹60 is available to the bank for credit creation to the private sector. If, instead, the SLR goes down to 20 per cent, then an additional ₹20 is freed up for potential deployment by banks towards private sector credit creation. If a private company's bonds provide a more desirable risk-return profile for the bank, then the bank would lend to the private company rather than to the government.

This is considered as the 'bank lending channel'—if banks end up with balance sheets that are stuffed with government bonds, they engage in less credit creation for the private sector of the economy. This is a simple but important point. Every time the government does

---

[3] For a theoretical treatment of how government myopia and populism affect sovereign debt dynamics, entangle sovereign debt with the financial sector (banks) and induce economic repression (crowding out; see Acharya and Rajan 2014; Acharya, Drechsler, and Schnabl 2015). For an earlier treatment with context that is specific to India, also see Buiter and Patel (2012). There are other channels of crowding out specific to India such as the impact on deposit rates and deposit base of banks due to competition from above-market rates on National Small Savings Fund (NSSF); see *Urjit Patel Committee Report*, 2014 (https://rbidocs.rbi.org.in/rdocs/Publication Report/Pdfs/ECOMRF210114_F.pdf).
[4] A significant carve-out from the SLR is also permitted for being reckoned as high-quality liquid assets (HQLA) for the purpose of LCR.

more, the banking sector is generally less able to lend to others in the economy. This channel likely affects most adversely those private borrowers in the economy that are most reliant on bank financing such as the MSMEs.

Corporate Bond Market Channel of Crowding out

A second financial channel through which crowding out occurs is the 'corporate bond market channel'. As I previously mentioned, government debt tends to be safer than non-government debt as governments have taxation power that private enterprises do not. Given their safety, investors (and central banks) are more readily prepared to lend against government debt as collateral than with non-government debt as collateral. In other words, government debt provides a 'convenience yield' to investors in the form of safety and liquidity relative to corporate bonds. In turn, when the supply of government bonds increases, investors such as banks, mutual funds, pension funds, insurance companies, etc., argue that on the margin, they would prefer to hold government bonds as opposed to even the highest-rated corporate bonds or securitized paper against housing and MSME loans. This relative preference creates another potential channel for crowding out.

Quantity Effects of Crowding out

I now turn to the evidence on crowding out in India.[5] Figure 17.5 shows a simple illustration of this phenomenon. The y-axis measures total debt of the corporate sector—including bank credit, corporate bonds and some other forms of financing such as ECBs that corporations rely on for borrowing from the international markets. The x-axis measures the level of government debt (includes both central and state government debt) in the economy. The graph shows that the

---

[5] While the time-series patterns to follow clearly capture some years of 'shocks' to private debt that were unrelated to government borrowing, such as due to the twin balance sheet deleveraging of corporates and banks post 2014, the body of evidence presented reflects a robust set of patterns over two decades from 1997 to 2016 and needs to be seen in its totality and consistency across various tests. Several graphs to follow employ variables on the natural logarithmic (Ln) scale in order to reduce the impact of outliers on the observed patterns.

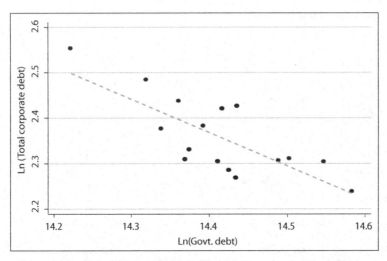

Figure 17.5. Government Borrowing and Total Corporate Debt (India)

Source: Center for Monitoring Indian Economy (CMIE) and RBI (1997–2016).
Notes: 'Ln'—natural logarithm.

relationship between government and corporate borrowing is strongly negative. That is, in times when Indian government's debt is high, corporations in the economy are borrowing less.

Now, let us break up this effect into the two channels that I have described above: the effects of bank lending and bond market borrowing. Figure 17.6 summarizes the results. The left panel shows the impact on bank credit. When Indian government's debt increases, there is less bank credit to private enterprises (MSME loans, large corporate loans, etc.). The right panel shows that corporate bonds also fall when government borrowing increases, though the impact is smaller compared to the left panel. As you can imagine, a typical MSME is not able to issue bonds in the market and needs access to bank loans for funding. Only the large companies can access the bond markets to fulfil their funding needs. This possibly explains the stronger crowding out effect of government borrowing on bank credit (for a relatively bank-dominated economy such as India) than on bond market financing.

The effects are in fact rather large. When government debt increases by 10 per cent of the GDP, corporate debt issuances fall by 7.3 per cent. In 2015–2016, when total government debt increased

Bank Credit Bonds

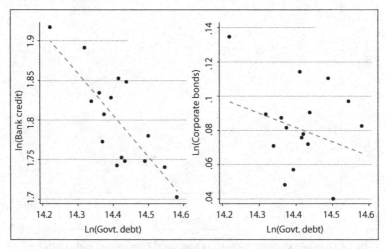

Figure 17.6. Government Debt Bank Credit and Corporate Bond Debt (India)

Source: CMIE and RBI.
Notes: The left-hand panel shows the impact of government borrowing on bank credit. The right-hand panel shows the impact of government borrowing on corporate bonds (1997–2016).

by 12.6 per cent, corporate debt declined by 9.1 per cent. The bulk of this effect operated through the bank credit channel which accounted for 6.7 per cent of the decline in corporate borrowing.

Next, I show some direct evidence for the bank lending channel of crowding out. The y-axis in Figure 17.7 shows how much of government bonds banks hold out of total assets on their balance sheets, and the x-axis shows the total government debt to GDP. The slope of the relationship is positive. When Indian government debt to GDP increases by 10 per cent, the bank holdings of government bonds as a percentage of their assets increase by 1.4 per cent. In unreported results, the relationship is found to hold for both public sector and private banks.

Now, what happens to bank credit when banks hold more of government bonds? To answer this, I explicitly link bank holdings of government debt to the amount of bank credit to the private sector. The y-axis in Figure 17.8 shows bank loans to the private sector as a percentage of bank assets and the x-axis shows the holdings of government bonds on bank balance sheets as a percentage of bank assets. Figure 17.8 reveals that the more banks lend to the government,

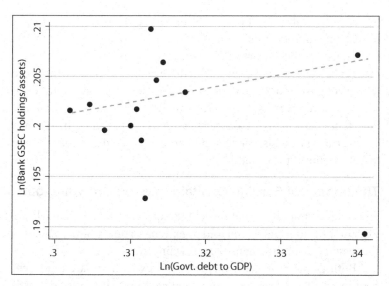

Figure 17.7. Government Debt and Bank Holdings of Government Debt (India)

Source: CMIE and RBI (1997–2016).

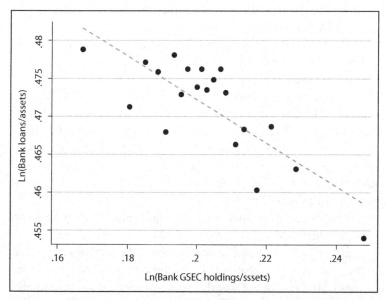

Figure 17.8. Bank holdings of Government Debt and Bank Loan Advances (India)

Source: CMIE and RBI (1997–2016).

less is the availability of loans to the private sector in the economy. In terms of magnitude, this is indeed the primary crowding out channel that appears to be at work in the Indian economy.

Let us remind ourselves of the three results so far: (a) the more there is of government debt, the less there is of corporate sector debt; (b) the more there is of government debt, the more government debt there is on banks' balance sheets and (c) the more banks own of government bonds, the less they provide as credit or loans to the private sector of the economy.

The Impact of Foreign Capital Flows on Crowding out

I will next limit the attention to the corporate bond channel and explain the important role played by external capital flows in affecting the magnitude of this channel of crowding out.

Both government and corporate bonds in India are at present held in part by foreign investors. There are mutual funds and institutional investors from, among other places, New York, London, Singapore and Hong Kong, who increasingly fund India's investments. Overall, this is a healthy development. India is a high growth economy compared to the rest of the world, but as shown in Figure 17.2 and Annex 17A.1, savings in the domestic economy are not adequate to fund all of its consumption expenditure and investment. Conversely, advanced economies in the rest of the world whose savings exceed their investment needs find it attractive to invest in India.

For sake of illustration, consider years such as 2016–2017, or most of 2017–2018, when there was much foreign money chasing India. In 2017–2018, for example, about $20.8 billion of FPI came into the country. In striking contrast in 2018–2019, about $12.5 billion (up to 1 March 2019) of the FPI money had left the country. About two-thirds of the FPI outflows had, in fact, been in government debt and corporate debt.

What does this fluctuation in foreign capital flows have to do with crowding out?

In a globally integrated Indian economy, the pool of savings that is available for investment is not just domestic savings, but also the savings of the rest of the world that are earmarked for investments in India. If investors start pulling out money from India, for example, to invest in the USA instead, then the global pool of savings for investment in the Indian economy shrinks and the crowding out effects of high government borrowing will be particularly severe on the private sector.

Let me elaborate.

When the government increases its borrowings, large and well-rated private companies which are internationally visible and have transparent balance sheets can borrow from foreign investors that are willing to invest in these companies. Then, domestic dissaving by the government does not bite as much because there are global savings that can fund the private sector. The empirical evidence in Figure 17.9 confirms this intuition. The left panel shows that in times of high foreign portfolio (FPI) investments in the economy (i.e., annual FPI flow is above the median level during 1997 to 2016), there is no crowding out as there appears to be little impact of increased government borrowing on the level of corporate debt. Governments can borrow more and yet the level of corporate debt remains virtually unaffected because whatever is the crowding out impact on the private sector from the government dissaving, foreign investors substitute for it by financing the private sector. In fact, there could be an indirect

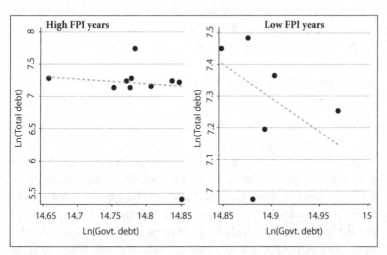

Figure 17.9. Government Debt and Corporate Borrowing for Firms with Access to the Bond Markets (India)

Source: CMIE and RBI.
Notes: The left-hand panel shows the impact of government borrowing on total debt when FPI is high. The right-hand panel shows the impact of government borrowing on corporate bonds when FPI is low. High FPI refers to periods where the annual FPI is above median during 1997–2016.

benefit even to the MSMEs. If the large corporations can borrow directly from foreign investors, then the greater proportion of the bank credit is available for the MSMEs.

In contrast, consider a year like 2018–2019, when FPI in debt of the economy was not that large (in fact, it was negative). Foreign investors were unwilling to invest even in government bonds. If government increases borrowing in such a year, then more government bonds will have to be held by banks, mutual funds, pension funds, insurance companies, etc., in the domestic economy. Foreign investors are unwilling to invest in corporate bonds, so corporations will 'also' be vying for the domestic pool of savings. As the right-hand panel of Figure 17.9 shows, crowding out begins to rear its ugly head in such a scenario. The figure shows that when FPI flows are low (i.e., annual FPI flow is below the median level during 1997 to 2016), a 10 per cent increase in government borrowing results in a 6.9 per cent decline in total corporate borrowing. Put simply, if the government chooses to expand borrowing in a year when foreign investors are unwilling to invest in the country, the pie of savings available to the private sector doesn't have any room to expand globally. Ideally, in such a year, it might be desirable that the government borrowing contracts in order to sustain the availability of bank loans and bonds for the private sector of the economy.

Crowding out Effects on the Corporate Cost of Borrowing

To further examine the mechanism driving the crowding out of corporate debt by government borrowing, let us study the impact of government borrowing on the price of debt or bond yields. When government debt to GDP increases by 1 percentage point, Figure 17.10(a) implies that the yields of the highest-rated (AAA) bonds increase by 2.3 percentage points. Interestingly, there is only a limited impact on the yields of lower-rated (AA) bonds. In a relative sense, the AA–AAA yield spread in fact declines when government debt increases. Figure 17.10(b) illustrates this graphically: a 1 percentage point increase in government debt to GDP results in a 1.7 percentage point decrease in the AA–AAA yield spread.

One concern in analyzing the crowding out effects of government debt is that governments may increase borrowing particularly

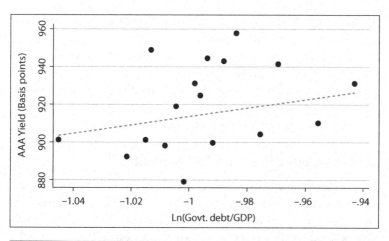

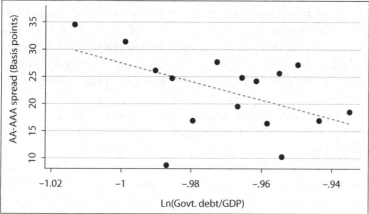

Figure 17.10. Corporate and Sovereign Spreads and Government Debt to GDP (India): Impact of Government Borrowing (2006–2016) on (a) AAA Corporate Yields (b) the Spread of Corporate AA Bonds over AAA Bonds

Source: Bloomberg and RBI.

in periods when the economy as a whole is doing poorly (see also Footnote 5). Thus, the decline in corporate borrowing may be due to an increase in credit risk and/or a decline in the demand for corporate debt issuance. The fact that the AA–AAA spread 'declines' when government debt increases gives assurance that this is not what is driving the evidence. Since a market-or economy-wide decline should affect the lower rated firms more severely, such a competing hypothesis would predict an 'increase' in the AA–AAA spread. Contrary to this hypothesis, we find increases in government debt are accompanied by decreases in the AA–AAA spread.

This evidence points to a crowding out channel at work, especially for the cost of AAA-rated corporate debt, which has safety and liquidity features closer to those of the government debt; with large issuances of government debt, AAA-rated bonds are not valued as much for these features by corporate bond investors.

Crowding out Effects on Financial Stability

Interestingly, the crowding out effect of government borrowing can have significant implications also for financial stability. If the cost of credit for corporations rises because the supply glut of government debt is flooding the savers (as shown in previous section, especially for the highest-rated borrowers), then corporations are induced to borrow at shorter maturities. This is because usually it costs less to borrow at the short-term, say up to one year, rather than to borrow at the long-term, say for five to ten years (where governments typically tend to borrow). Over five to ten years, economic outcomes are typically more uncertain; hence, if corporations want to borrow at these maturities rather than three or six months, banks and corporate bond markets will be willing to fund them only at a higher cost or risk premium.

It turns out that not only does the corporate sector borrow less when the government borrowings increase, but also it borrows more short-term. In Figure 17.11, the y-axis shows the proportion of corporate borrowing in the form of long-term borrowings (i.e., of maturity greater than one year) and the x-axis shows the amount of government debt. The left panel shows that the relationship between government borrowing and the share of corporate debt that is long-term is negative for non-financial firms. In terms of economic magnitude, when government debt increases by 10 per cent, the share of long-term debt in corporate borrowings falls by 2.3 per cent.

To understand the significance of this result, let us ask: Why is it important for a corporation to borrow long-term? Suppose the enterprise has a business of auto ancillary parts. In order to produce the right ancillary parts for the new brand of cars (say, electric vehicles) that are coming to the market, it needs to undertake capital expenditure so as to change the kind of axels and shafts it is producing. In particular, it should ideally invest in state-of-the-art machines and

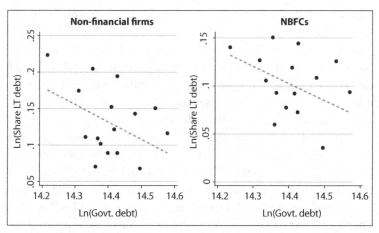

Figure 17.11. Government Debt and the Share of Long-Term Borrowing by Corporates (India)

Source: CMIE and RBI (1997–2016).

plants that will produce the right calibrations for the new vehicles. By its very nature, such capital expenditure implies that there will be an upfront investment and it will be some time before there is a payback on investment. The enterprise may have to wait for sales to pick up before the revenues increase. If the enterprise borrows short-term, then it can become difficult to undertake and sustain large capital expenditure because within a quarter or two, the bank or the market may not roll over the debt and instead ask the enterprise to pay back the borrowed money giving rise to funding stress or rollover risk. Hence, ordinarily it is desirable for an enterprise to borrow at a maturity that is long enough to match the average duration of cash flows from its underlying projects. However, the enterprise may be tempted to borrow short-term and willingly court the rollover risk if the cost of borrowing long-term becomes unduly high due to crowding out from increased government borrowing at long maturities.

What is particularly striking is that this is true even for the financial sector. The NBFCs are increasingly playing a greater role in credit creation in the Indian economy. The ability and willingness of NBFCs to borrow long-term comes down when government borrowing increases; not only does their total debt comes down in response, but they rely more and more on short-term paper. The right panel in

Figure 17.10 shows that when government debt increases by 10 per cent, the share of long-term debt for NBFCs comes down by 1.7 per cent. If NBFCs rely on short-term debt and are hit by a shock, such as loan defaults or an inability to roll over the financing against illiquid assets, then they can experience the unfortunate confluence of asset-quality and funding pressures with adverse impact on their balance sheets and future intermediation activity.

Thus, not only does government borrowing crowd out the private sector, but it can also induce the private sector to borrow more short-term, which can increase financial fragility. Might such forces have partly contributed to the surge in asset-liability mismatch of the NBFC sector for 12 months starting in the second half of 2017 when there was an upward revision in the quantum of government borrowings? I find this an intriguing possibility that is worthy of further inquiry.

Crowding out Effects on Monetary Policy Transmission

Let us now situate the issue of government borrowing in matters of importance to policymakers who set interest rates such as the RBI's MPC. When the central bank cuts the policy rate with a view to reducing economy-wide cost of funds, the ultimate objective is to make more and cheaper credit available to the economy, in part also by getting corporate bond market participants to accept lower yields. Such pass-through of the RBI's interest rate decisions (monetary policy transmission) is generally seen to be much weaker than one-for-one; a standard quarter-point (25 bps) cut in the repo rate translates during the quarter into a 7.5 bps fall in yields for AAA-rated bonds and a mere 4.25 bps for BBB-rated ones. However, these averages mask differences that arise as a result of the crowding out effects arising from debt issuance by the government.

Concretely, transmission of a rate cut in India is found to be about twice as strong when the government debt is below the median level: a 25 bps cut in the repo rate results in a 15 bps fall in the yields of the AAA-rated bonds and a 7.5 bps fall in the yields of the BBB-rated bonds. In contrast, if we focus only on episodes when government debt is above the median level, a repo rate cut decreases yields by only 7.5 bps and 3.25 bps for AAA-and BBB-rated borrowers, respectively. Figure 17.12 graphically illustrates that the

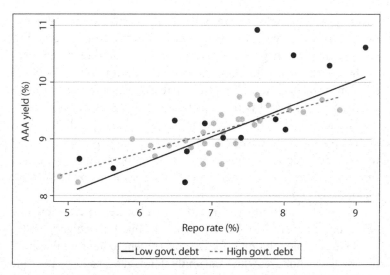

Figure 17.12. Monetary Policy Transmission during Period of High and Low Government Borrowing (India)

Source: Bloomberg and RBI.
Notes: Figure shows the transmission of monetary policy during above-median and below-median periods of government borrowing during FY 2006–2016. The dotted line captures the transmission of policy rate when government borrowing is above its median level, and the plain line captures the transmission of policy rate when government borrowing is below its median level.

sensitivity of the yields of the AAA-rated bonds to the repo rate is lower during periods of high government debt.

This evidence suggests that high levels of issuance of public debt can render monetary policy actions ineffective by interfering with the sound transmission of monetary policy. The rationale is possibly linked to the pricing effects documented previously under the heading 'Crowding out Effects on the Corporate Cost of Borrowing'. As more government debt floods markets, the relative safety and liquidity premium attached by investors to high-rated corporate bonds diminishes, raising the cost of borrowing especially for AAA-rated borrowers and making it relatively less sensitive to policy rate cuts.

Concluding Observations

Let me summarize. There is a growing trend in the global economy to ask for more to be undertaken by governments. This is justified when the government is providing goods that the private sector cannot provide an adequate measure—such as education, health and infrastructure. However, if we examine government budgets and observe how much gets spent on capital expenditures to provide public goods,; it is often abysmally small. Of course, the political economy explanation would be that there is a demand for the revenue expenditures in that it is the constituencies and stakeholders themselves that want governments to undertake these expenditures. The kind of phenomena I have enumerated should help us all understand that the revenue expenditures or welfare programmes demanded from the governments come at a cost to investments by the private sector in the economy.

What are some possible remedies to alleviate the crowding out effects of the government financing in India that I have highlighted?

One possible solution is for the government to improve the share of capital expenditures which currently stands at a meagre 14 per cent for India. Serious rationalization could be undertaken in the form of cutting back on subsidies and programmes that are not delivering long-run growth, and instead, focusing on the provision of public goods such as education, health and infrastructure.

Another way is for the government to reduce its borrowings in the market by divesting more of its public sector enterprise shares. There could be efficiency gains if there are more private investors playing an effective role in the governance of public sector enterprises. This would reduce the need for the market borrowings by the government and that way reduce the crowding out; it would enhance productivity, raise net government dividends and facilitate a greater balanced budget compared to outcomes under high government borrowings.

Yet another way would be for the government to improve adherence to the FRBM targets (and reduce the ease with which goalposts are shifted to future) by adopting recommendation of the Fourteenth Finance Commission and the FRBM Review Committee (2016–2017) to establish an independent 'fiscal council'. Such a council could monitor the government's performance on sticking to the fiscal targets and roadmap by assessing regularly the progress in fiscal consolidation or lack thereof, and providing standardized reports on the displacement of fiscal deficits into off-balance sheet borrowings (as noted by the Comptroller and Auditor General [CAG] 2019; also see Footnote 1).

Finally, there could be continued emphasis on efficient rollouts of important structural reforms such as the time-bound resolution of non-performing assets under the IBC and the creation of national markets via the GST. The much-needed land, labour and agricultural reforms could be undertaken, all of which can help crowd in private sector growth.

To conclude with a recollection of my favourite composer ... when it comes to borrowings and fiscal deficit, governments should take inspiration from Sachin Dev Burman's sublime but masterfully minimalistic music for the songs of *Pyaasa*; Burman *da* proved that less can indeed be more by crowding in everyone else, so can the government!

References

Demirci, Irem, Jennifer Huang, and Clemens Sialm. 2019. 'Government Debt and Corporate Leverage: International Evidence'. *Journal of Financial Economics* 133, (April): 337–356.

Graham, John, Mark T. Leary, and Michael R. Roberts. 2014. 'How Does Government Borrowing Affect Corporate Financing and Investment?' NBER Working Paper No. w20581 (October). Available at: https://ssrn.com/abstract= 2510589 (accessed on 31 March 2020).

Acharya, Viral V., and Raghuram G. Rajan. 2014. 'Sovereign Debt, Government Myopia and the Financial Sector'. *Review of Financial Studies* 26, (June): 1526–1560. Available at: http://pages.stern.nyu.edu/~sternfin/vacharya/public_html/ Sov_debt_Jan_11_2013_RFS_standard.pdf (accessed on 20 April 2020).

Acharya, Viral V., Itamar Drechsler, and Philipp Schnabl. 2015. 'A Pyrrhic Victory? Bank Bailouts and Sovereign Credit Risk'. *Journal of Finance* 69, (June): 2689–2739. Available at: http://pages.stern.nyu.edu/~sternfin/vacharya/public_ html/pdfs/ADS_final.pdf (accessed on 20 April 2020).

Buiter, Willem H., and Urjit R. Patel. 2012. 'Fiscal Rules in India: Are they Effective?' *The Oxford Handbook of the Indian Economy*. Oxford: Oxford University Press.

Annex 17A.1. Financial Resource Gaps of the Private Corporate Sector and the Public Sector Relative to Available Household Financial Savings (India)

(as Percentage of GDP)

	2011–2012	2012–2013	2013–2014	2014–2015	2015–2016	2016–2017	2017–2018
I. Available financial savings of households for use by the public sector and the private corporate sector							
a. Households' financial savings	7.7	7.7	7.7	7.4	8.4	6.6	6.8
II. Net HH financial savings available for the private corporate sector after use by the Public sector (including valuables and E&Os)							
b. Public sector resource gap	−6.0	−5.8	−6.0	−6.1	−6.4	−5.4	−5.5
c. Valuables and E&O	−2.3	−3.1	−1.2	−0.9	−1.5	−1.7	−2.7
d. (= a − b − c). Net resource gap of the public sector (net of valuations and E&O) after fully absorbing household financial savings	−0.5	−1.2	0.5	0.4	0.6	−0.5	−1.3
III. Corporate sector financing savings, financial investment and net resource gap							
e. Savings	8.3	8.7	9.6	10.3	11.1	10.7	10.8
f. Investment	12.9	13.4	12.7	12.9	13.1	11.5	11.5
g. (= e − f). Private corporate sector resource gap	−4.6	−4.7	−3.1	−2.6	−2.0	−0.8	−0.7

IV. Private financial corporate sector							
h. Savings	1.2	1.3	1.2	1.4	0.8	0.9	0.9
i. Investment	0.4	0.3	0.2	0.4	0.4	0.1	0.6
j. (= h − i). Net	0.8	1.0	1.0	1.0	0.4	0.8	0.3
Both public sector (net of valuables) and private corporate sector depend on private capital flows to meet their net resource gaps							
h (= d + g + j). Net capital inflows from ROW (CAD)	−4.3	−4.9	−1.6	−1.2	−1.0	−0.5	−1.7

Source: Central Statistics Office.

EPILOGUE

No country can take growth for granted.

This applies even more so if a country is not consciously and constantly engaged in securing financial stability to its macroeconomic shores with hoops of steel and is in fact prone to jettisoning financial stability for myopic fiscal adjustments or political gains.

Financial stability is not just a lofty term to be used to justify any and all extraordinary central banking or regulatory measures, typically quick-fix bandages that are patched on to the surface of wounds, when underlying imbalances materialize and begin to stifle growth. Such remedial measures are designed with much speed and often without careful deliberation, leaving behind an inevitable trail of unintended outcomes that sow the seeds of future instability. At best, extraordinary measures should be deployed to buy some time to undertake deeper structural reforms. When the extraordinary measures themselves become the primary tool for providing financial stability, the economy simply ends up fighting one war after the other, each one set up by an incomplete victory over the past one.

Financial stability is in fact about taking 'the right stance' for the economy ahead of time–maintaining its financial sector in robust health and with ample immunity so that the economy can grow well in a sustainable manner. This can be achieved by positioning the financial sector structurally in such a way that even the ordinary toolkit of central banking and regulatory actions has the desired impact on households, corporations, and micro-, small- and medium-sized enterprises. This reduces the reliance on extraordinary measures on a frequent basis. Reaching such a stable state requires, as I have argued throughout the book, the following:

- The financial sector remains mostly well-capitalized and the undercapitalized entities are promptly corrected to healthier state or quarantined to avoid further haemorrhaging.
- Defaults and losses are recognized, resolved and disclosed publicly in a timely manner.
- The transmission of monetary policy to the real economy is strengthened via the development of efficient viable markets and without undue regulatory interference in price setting by markets.
- The external sector is safeguarded at all times.
- The right balance is struck between the government, the private sector, the markets and the regulators, especially the central bank, so they work in sync with each other without being under the dominance of, or being crowded out, by the government.

Yes, maintaining financial stability necessitates that regulators such as the central bank lean against the winds of fiscal dominance by sticking to well-designed rules for decision-making (such as inflation-targeting mandate for monetary policy, prompt corrective action for dealing with undercapitalized banks, Basel standards for bank capital and liquidity requirements, etc.). Exercise of excessive discretion only opens up the door to an excessive accommodation of short-term political pressures.

As financial stability often requires enduring short-term pain for long-run growth, it is not easy to be its gatekeeper anywhere in the world, and certainly not so in India. To the extent I had some influence as a deputy governor of the RBI, I did not strike compromises on what really mattered for restoring financial stability, neither with the Governors nor with the Government of India. At times it wasn't easy, but I continue to believe that it was worth fighting for. It was the right stance.

Let me end with the hope that more and better gatekeepers of financial stability will spring up tomorrow at the RBI, the Government of India and other parts of the financial system, helping to complete this unfinished agenda.

My optimism that over time, free-spirited, hard-working and inspired minds will make India and the world a stronger economy and a better place to live in knows no bounds.